D1175350

THE FACES OF JUSTICE AND STATE AUTHORITY

THE FACES OF JUSTICE AND STATE AUTHORITY

A Comparative Approach to the Legal Process

Mirjan R. Damaška

Yale University Press
New Haven and London

Designed by James J. Johnson
and set in Aldus and Palatino
Printed in the United States of America.

Library of Congress Cataloging-in-Publication Data

Damaška, Mirjan R., 1931–
    The faces of justice and state authority.

    Includes index.
    1. Justice, Administration of.   2. Courts.
3. Law and politics.   I. Title.
K2100.D36   1986   347   86–7729
ISBN 0–300–03567–5 (alk. paper)   342.7

---

*The paper in this book meets the guidelines for
permanence and durability of the Committee on
Production Guidelines for Book Longevity of the
Council on Library Resources.*

---

10   9   8   7   6   5   4   3   2   1

To My Parents
toplini starog doma

Contents

Acknowledgments

The idea for this book stemmed from a felt need to reconcile my native and my adopted legal cultures. To bring this idea to fruition might have been too lonely an endeavor without my friend Bruce A. Ackerman: he constantly encouraged me to continue the project, prodded me to refine its basic organization, and unstintingly shared his ideas about how to integrate insights from my past and present professional lives. But since our frequent exchanges were also animated by a spirit of amicable disagreement, he is happily absolved of any complicity in specific lines of argument I follow.

During the early stages of my research, a fellowship from the National Endowment for the Humanities in the academic year 1978–79 enabled me to take time off from teaching and to roam freely among some of the great libraries of Europe. Intellectual debts acquired there are acknowledged in the footnotes.

While I have benefited from comments by many people on various drafts of the present study, the contributions of three colleagues proved especially valuable. Abraham Goldstein, Martin Shapiro, and Stephen Schulhofer were generous in expressing their disagreements with many aspects of the work in progress, making acute observations, and offering helpful suggestions. Their criticism and their insistence on further elaboration induced me to make numerous changes in the manuscript. Harry Wellington and Guido Calabresi, my deans at the Yale Law School, provided material help and buoyed my spirits. Alice Miskimin, Esq., proved to be the most sensitive of editors: her labors have been as skillful as they are unobtrusive.

If the title of this book seems consciously to echo Sybille Bedford's *Faces of Justice*, it reflects my admiration for her vivid and colorful reportage from the courtrooms of Europe.

Last but not least, I owe special thanks to Maria, with whom I share *gaudiarum periculorumque*, for her gracious sacrifice of so many evenings and weekends during the gestation of this book.

Introduction

An immense and bewildering subject opens up before one who contemplates the diversity of arrangements and institutions through which justice is variously administered in modern states. The range of diversity is such that it eludes expression in terms of a common vocabulary and makes us uncertain about the adequacy of our basic points of reference. Does the legal process require, as is sometimes believed, an interaction of three independent sides—a claimant, a respondent, and a decision maker—or can it also take the form of an *affaire à deux* between an individual and a state official? For the process to retain its legal nature, is it necessary that it be controlled, directly or indirectly, by a state "judge"? What are the essential attributes and functions of this official? Is he primarily a conflict resolver, or an enforcer of state policy, an educator, and a *therapeuta*? Do individuals implicated in proceedings remain "parties" if they are turned into evidentiary sources, suppliers of information needed by the state to pursue its policies and programs? What are the minimal requirements of due process in modern states? These and many other questions cry out for explication because of the variety of answers given them in modern legal systems.

Not all differences in the institutional setting and in the forms of justice are visible at first sight. Some lurk behind superficial similarities and can be discerned only on close inspection. No wonder, then, that a consensus is sometimes proclaimed on points where agreement is mainly a rhetorical achievement. Virtually all states subscribe to the view that judges should be independent and that the accused should be presumed innocent until proven otherwise, but the unanimity begins to break down as soon as one considers the implications of these views and their operational meaning in the administration of justice of various countries.

It cannot be denied that on many such issues divergent arrangements and clashes of opinion about existing arrangements can be found within a single country. This is clearly illustrated by the crazy quilt of variant procedural and institutional patterns in American jurisdictions, and by the persistent debate over reform of the American administration of justice. Yet no matter how wide the range of differences appears domestically, to an external vision such internal disunity often seems but a variation within a larger identity: notions of what is "fair" and "orderly," of how judicial institutions should be structured, and similar parameters for the choice of alternatives are frequently shared. Modes of categorizing issues are generally and unreflectively accepted: the idiom in which the debate proceeds is distinctively the same.

To get a sense of the much wider range of actual differences and of the limits on the community of discourse, one need not go outside the Western world. It suffices to consider some well-known—albeit ill-defined—contrasts between Anglo-American (common-law) and Continental (civil-law) systems of procedure. Proper ways of developing proof and argument are notoriously different in the two settings: direct and cross-examination by lawyers on one side, judicial interrogation on the other. That the criminal defendant can waive the right to trial by pleading guilty appears normal to Anglo-American lawyers, but strangely inappropriate to Continental lawyers in whose systems all cases— regardless of whether the accused confesses—must go to trial. That the civil party has the right not to testify is widely accepted in Europe, but almost shocking to Anglo-Americans. That most common-law systems place more severe restrictions on evidence gathering in criminal than in civil cases is almost beyond comprehension on the Continent. Less familiar, because more difficult to identify, are discrepant ideas on some basic issues such as the place of the trial in relation to the preliminary and the appellate process, or the precise nature of the judicial office. If unobserved, these subtle differences can cause serious misunderstandings between Anglo-American and Continental lawyers. Each group then suddenly discovers illusory bonds of commonality and a family resemblance on its side of the divide that separates the administration of justice in civil- and common-law countries.

Moving east, as our vision should at this late stage of Western affairs, the provincialism of our discourse surfaces in different ways. The administration of justice in the Soviet Union and its European followers exhibits many aspects that must strain conventional categories and offend legal sensibilities of Western lawyers, be they of common- or of civil-law variety. Common lawyers may find the role of the judiciary and of the bar too narrow in Western Europe, but this reduction seems only one of nuance when set against the diminished role of judges and lawyers in the Soviet Union. Traditional Western concepts are also offended by the relative ease with which judgments can be altered in communist systems. On the other hand, while there is increasing talk in the West about "symbolic functions" of the legal process, even relatively radical proposals for reform seem timid and modest compared with the strongly "edifying" overtones of Soviet procedural style. Farther east, in China one encounters systems of justice so different from ours that a discourse inscribed with the particularities of Western development fails us almost completely. Observed through conventional Western lenses, processes through which Chinese justice is administered hardly qualify as "legal": trials, lawyers—even courts or law as a semi-autonomous discipline—appear extrinsic and dispensable.

Can this stupendous diversity be made intelligible, or reduced to a manageable set of patterns? At a minimum, can a conceptual framework be developed to assist us in tracing similarities and differences in component parts? Such a framework is the principal theme of this book. Reflection on this topic has been quite extensive: diverse analogies have been explored, moving on different levels and in different segments of the legal process. Quite unsurprisingly, where some would locate unity within an apparent variety, others find variety within an ostensible unity. Reconciling these separate lines of inquiry has become so difficult that it is tempting to leave aside the punishingly copious literature the inquiry has spawned. But this temptation is to be resisted: it would seem flippant to suggest new approaches and add to the cacophony of voices without first indicating reasons for dissatisfaction with what has been thought and said before. Hence the fortunes and misfortunes of the most notable families of inquiry must be sketched in the following brief prolegomenon.

i. ADVERSARIAL AND INQUISITORIAL SYSTEMS

One well-trodden path that many have followed is to oppose adversarial against nonadversarial or inquisitorial systems. In the twelfth century the dichotomy was already in use to distinguish a process that required the impetus of a private complainant to get under way (*processus per accusationem*) from a process that could be launched in his absence (*processus per inquisitionem*). In later times this distinction was used by Continental jurists in a variety of contexts and acquired several technical meanings.[1] It is only more recently that it came to be used by comparativists on a broader scale, mainly to express the contrast between Continental and Anglo-American administration of justice. But having escaped from the relative exactness of internal legal usage, each label now denotes distinctive clusters of traits in shifting combinations, not infrequently conflicting with one another. Only the core meaning of the opposition remains reasonably certain. The adversarial mode of proceeding takes its shape from a contest or a dispute: it unfolds as an engagement of two adversaries before a relatively passive decision maker whose principal duty is to reach a verdict. The nonadversarial mode is structured as an official inquiry. Under the first system, the two adversaries take charge of most procedural action; under the second, officials perform most activities.

Beyond this core meaning uncertainty begins. It is unclear how far the adversarial process yields to the wishes of the parties ("how passive the judge?") and how pervasive official control is in the inquisitorial mode ("how active the

---

1. The most important use was to distinguish and explore the relation between two types of the criminal process, one of which (the inquisitorial) prevailed in practice, whereas the other (the accusatorial) was a theoretically superior and preferable form. See A. L. Homberk zu Vack, "De diversa indole processus inquisitorii et accusatorii," in J. F. Plitt, ed., *Analecta iuris criminalis*, 369–72 (Francoforti-Lipsiae, 1791). Until recently, more pragmatic common lawyers have refused to theorize about the administration of justice: the utility of scholarship drifting across the Channel was, on the whole, quite suspect.

officials?"). Each concept is endowed with features of a different shape according to whether discussion focuses on criminal cases, civil procedure, or the administration of justice in general. Particularly confusing is the habit of incorporating into the two models of procedure various traits whose relation to the opposition of contest and inquest ideas is tenuous at best. For example, in the inquisitorial mode one finds features such as a career judiciary, preference for rigid rules, and reliance on official documentation, whereas the adversarial mode embraces jurors as decision makers, discretion in decision making, and an attachment to oral evidence.[2] The more each concept embraces such loosely knit collections of characteristics, the more obvious it becomes that the premises of the opposition are uncertain or ambiguous.

Another dimension is added to the complexity by the inclination of both Anglo-American and Continental lawyers to develop native variations on the theme of adversarial and inquisitorial proceedings. On the Continent, lawyers continue to attribute to the opposition a more technical and descriptive meaning, and they think about the allocation of control over the process—either to the officials or to the parties—within parameters that appear normal to Continentals in light of their historical experience. Matters such as the interrogation of witnesses seem "naturally" to be the responsibility of officials in charge of proceedings, so that alternative ways of proof taking are not included in the contrast of adversarial and nonadversarial forms.[3] To Anglo-Americans, on the other hand, the two concepts are suffused with value judgments: the adversary system provides tropes of a rhetoric extolling the virtues of liberal administration of justice in contrast to an antipodal authoritarian process—such as the system of criminal prosecutions on the Continent prior to its transformation in the wake of the French Revolution.[4] Furthermore, matters that can be allocated either to the parties or to the decision maker are imagined in light of Anglo-American experience, so that the adversarial style also includes, among other features, the partisan presentation of evidence.

Much of the resulting confusion is due to the fact that criteria remain uncertain for the inclusion of specific features into the adversarial and the inquisitorial types. Promiscuously intertwined, two basic approaches to this problem can be discerned. One approach is to conceive the two types as portrayals of two distinctive groups, descendants of actual historical systems: one type embraces features common to procedures in the tradition deriving from England, while the other similarly relates to procedures in the Continental tradition. Now

2. See, e.g., A. Goldstein, "Reflections on Two Models: Inquisitorial Themes in American Criminal Procedure," 26 *Stanford L. Rev.*, 1009, 1017–19 (1974).

3. The interrogation of witnesses by the judge came to be viewed as an essential part of the judicial office as early as the twelfth century, so that it appeared "natural" that proof taking be in the hands of the judge in both inquisitorial and accusatorial versions of the legal process.

4. This usage is sometimes reflected in court decisions. See, e.g., *Miranda* v. *Arizona*, 384 U.S. 436, 460 (1966). Viewed against the background of their history, Continental lawyers place their contemporary systems of prosecution somewhere midway between "inquisitorial" (prerevolutionary) and "accusatorial" (reformed) forms. In contrast, common lawyers often refer even to contemporary Continental systems as "inquisitorial": from their standpoint both pre- and postrevolutionary Continental forms easily seem like branches of a common parent stem.

if this implies an attempt to set up models to which all Continental and Anglo-American systems would conform, the task becomes Sisyphean: the lowest common denominators of each system are unstable and constantly changing. As soon as a feature is rejected by a single country, it must be exorcised from its respective model; more trivial tricks of the style cannot be distinguished from its important components. It should scarcely be surprising, then, that those who subscribe to this understanding of the typology offer only "examples" of adversarial and inquisitorial systems and are unable to articulate the respective types as definite compositions of procedural and institutional patterns. To be sure, the first approach can also be understood to comprise only features that somehow "characterize" the Anglo-American and Continental traditions of administering justice.[5] Inevitably, however, the criteria for inclusion of features into the models become numerous and difficult to organize coherently: traditions embrace analytically separate matters pertaining to the structure of institutions, choice of procedural form, and similar characteristics that may coexist in unresolved tension. Doubtless, only some of these multiple characteristics can be related to the theme I have identified at the core of the opposition between inquisitorial and adversarial systems. In short, the typology becomes cumbersome and difficult to employ as an instrument of analysis. It is of very limited use in providing comparativist orientation beyond justice systems in the West.

The other approach to the typology goes a greater distance in detaching the two modes of the legal process from contingencies of history: it involves a search for and the articulation of ideas that are capable of molding forms of justice into recognizable patterns. Once obtained from observation of actual systems, these ideas assume, so to speak, a life of their own. Their implications for procedural form can be consistently traced over a wide range of procedural issues, whether or not any actual system goes so far as to embody all these implications. In their totality, the entailments of the ideas constitute the characteristics of the type. One such idea can be to entrust procedural action to the parties and another, to entrust it to a nonpartisan official: the implications of these two ideas can then be traced out to issues, such as who controls the initiation and the termination of proceedings, their subject matter, the taking of proof, and the like—even if existing systems, in varying combinations, entrust only some of these matters either to parties or to a nonpartisan official. Where this second method is applied, the adversarial and nonadversarial processes become fictitious creatures, seldom if ever found in reality, but under certain conditions useful for analyzing it and making it intelligible. Just as a particular building can be "recognized" in terms of an architectural style, so an existing process can be assigned to a type.[6] Thus conceived, the typology can be used as a neutral map across Continental and

---

5. See, e.g., A. Goldstein, *supra*, n. 2, 1017.

6. Comparison with styles in art can be carried further. To classify a work of art as belonging to a particular style, it is thought sufficient that the work encompass some, though not all, elements of the stylistic ideal. For example, although the Notre Dame Cathedral in Paris, lacking spires, does not fully express the vertiginous, sky-bound drive of other Gothic cathedrals, it is still unmistakably within the Gothic convention. It seldom occurs that a particular work of art fully embodies a style, as Boucher, perhaps, epitomizes the rococo.

Anglo-American countries: adversarial traits can be identified in continental Europe and can even be quite conspicuous in some branches of the administration of justice, while inquisitorial features, sometimes quite conspicuous, can be found in Anglo-American lands. Of course, the typology can also be applied to actual systems outside the Western legal tradition.

The effort to understand forms of justice in modern states is better served by this second approach. But if narrow and sterile constructs are to be avoided, the background against which lawyers oppose contest and inquest, official and party control, and similar structural principles of the legal process must be explored. Moreover, vain attempts to express the core of the contrast between Continental and Anglo-American administration of justice by juxtaposing such concepts must also be abandoned. Most features that constitute the essential contrast cannot be captured by them, especially if one's vision extends beyond the narrow area of criminal procedure.

ii. LEGAL PROCESS AND THE SOCIOECONOMIC ORGANIZATION OF THE STATE

A distinctive family of inquiries into the diversity of procedural forms has emerged from efforts to relate the legal process to the economic and social organization of modern states. Although many aspects of the administration of justice can profitably be studied from this perspective (e.g., how haves and have-nots fare in the courts), it has proved exceedingly difficult to relate the *design* of the legal process to any presently available classification of states according to socioeconomic variables.

This can be illustrated best by misfortunes that have befallen studies inspired by Marx's distinction between various "modes of production" (feudalism, capitalism, socialism, and the like) as ultimate determinants of social institutions, including the legal system. It was hoped that reliance on these categories would provide the Ariadne's thread by which to find one's way out of the labyrinth of procedural diversity: in theory, it should be possible to identify a basic feudal, capitalist, or socialist form of administering justice that, albeit permitting internal variation, provides the necessary orientation and possesses the greatest explanatory power.[7]

But the insights promised by this alignment of legal systems with Marxian categories turned out to be illusory. The immediate problem was how to account for strikingly similar procedural styles found in categorically different socioeconomic environments, and for strikingly dissimilar styles in categorically identical ones. Consider the obvious, if elusive, difference between common-law

---

7. Karl Marx himself never attempted to link his broad models of socioeconomic structure to formal aspects of the legal process. In the Soviet Union, however, especially during Stalin's rule, belief in the possibility of establishing this link became part of the canon, and all sorts of opportunists set out to discover it. The cogency of Vauvenargue's dictum was soon vindicated: "When the great minds have taught the lesser how to think, they put them on the road to error" (*Réflections et Maximes*, no. 221, Charbonnel, ed. [Paris, 1934]).

and civil-law systems: both sprang from the same socioeconomic subsoil of the waning Middle Ages (feudalism), and they continue to divide capitalist countries. Of course, arguably feudalism and capitalism differed on each side of the Channel; but if different feudal and capitalist settings produced different forms of the legal process, then this internal variation should be attributed to some other factor (or factors), rather than to feudalism or capitalism as such. Perhaps more important, it has proved insuperably difficult to articulate an overarching difference among forms of capitalist, socialist, or feudal justice in comparison to which contrasts such as those between common- and civil-law proceedings would pale into insignificance.[8] On the contrary, the conventional contrasts continue to loom large and to intrigue lawyers in European socialist systems: despite the fact that they could point to some novel "socialist" forms,[9] many important aspects of their legal process, when compared to puzzling common-law arrangements and institutions, appeared to exhibit a strong resemblance to conventional Continental systems. The essential structure of trials was similar, and so were the basic outlines of the preliminary and the appellate process, modes of proof, and a great number of more specific arrangements. There was clearly no way out but to acknowledge that such similarities bridge the divide that separates continental European states coordinated by plan from those dominated by capitalist markets.

The solution to this predicament has been to proclaim that the apparent similarities among procedural systems with different substructures in economic organization are merely superficial: similar formal arrangements, it has been said, are permeated with a different meaning or purpose and are recast into a new ensemble according to the economic substrate. Likewise, differences of procedural form among jurisdictions sharing the same socioeconomic organization have been explained away as merely shallow: here, variation in form is said to conceal important identities of purpose and of meaning. Justice—imagined as the instrument of a group dominating the socioeconomic formation—retains its identity, even as the shape of the instrument changes. Although this argument has been misused as an ideological elixir, it still deserves to be taken seriously. To consider forms of justice in monadic isolation from their social and economic context is—for many purposes—like playing *Hamlet* without the Prince. It is also true that an identical social policy can be realized, to a degree, through very different procedural arrangements and that very different policies can be imple-

---

8. For unsuccessful attempts in the Soviet literature and for some crudities of this enterprise, see, e.g., M. Cheltzov, ed., *Ugolovnyi Protsess*, 425–40 (on socialist procedure), and 440–56 (on capitalist systems) (Moscow, 1969). Differing views have been expressed by Soviet scholars on the relation between adversarial and nonadversarial forms and the opposition between capitalist and socialist procedure. Whereas some commentators, including the famous Pashukanis, thought that the adversarial idea was "bourgeois" and the nonadversarial "socialist," this identification was denied by others.

9. I do not here suggest that peculiar traits of Soviet justice could always be attributed to the economic dimension of Soviet life with any degree of plausibility. While a historical link to economic organization is in some instances quite obvious (e.g., with respect to ways of settling disputes between nationalized firms), more often than not a relation to ideology and politics appeared more direct and plausible.

mented in similar proceedings. Here, where the subject of inquiry is diversity of procedural form *tout court*, this argument misses its mark—except, perhaps, insofar as it suggests that interest in procedural form is a preoccupation with surfaces.[10] What is tacitly conceded is that no new leaves are turned in the strange album of procedural form as society moves from one "mode of production" to the next. Because most questions relevant to the study of procedural diversity lie beyond the opposition of capitalism, socialism and similar vague socioeconomic concepts, inspiration for a scheme useful for our purposes must be sought elsewhere.[11]

iii. LEGAL PROCESS AND THE CHARACTER OF GOVERNMENT

If socioeconomic criteria are of little help, can political factors provide more illumination? This approach is hardly novel and has been explored on a great variety of topics. The study of affinities between the legal process and dominant currents of political ideology appeared particularly promising: after all, it was thought, political regimes legitimate themselves through the administration of justice that they establish. Mining this vein, numerous writers have contended that the design of proceedings is sensitive to particular shifts in prevailing ideology, especially to oscillations between individualistic and collectivistic, liberal and authoritarian, or similarly labeled positions. In the civil process, it has been argued, these shifts have a direct impact on the question of how much power private individuals should have to direct the course of lawsuits—undoubtedly an important question in the choice of procedural form.[12] In the criminal process, it was similarly argued that ideological shifts affect the degree of protection accorded the defendant from the state: the comparatively peculiar position of the

10. This is probably what Marx and Engels actually thought: the form of law—even the forms of political regimes—were far from the center of their interest. Law was seen as an instrument for the attainment of specific substantive ends, in particular, class domination. The shape of this instrument, the contour of legal form, was of minor importance and largely disregarded. Yet the concept of ties between substance and form lingered in the background. In an interesting letter to Mehring, the aging Engels acknowledged this narrow focus and tried to justify it. See K. Marx and F. Engels, *Selected Correspondence*, 459 (letter of July 1893) (Moscow, 1955).

11. Even in countries where Marxism is the official state ideology, some sophisticated thinkers now acknowledge that links between the legal process and economics are "mediated" by political variables, so that the latter have a greater explanatory force. The economic sphere determines procedural form only "ultimately" or "in the last instance." See, e.g., I. Szabó, *Les fondements de la théorie du droit*, 66 (Budapest, 1973). The causal primacy of economics remains undiscussable, like Helen beckoning to her bed.

12. A long tradition of Continental legal scholarship maintains that ideologies penetrate the civil process by changing ideas on the applicability of "private" as opposed to "public law" style. See, e.g., F. Klein and F. Engel, *Der Zivilprozessrecht Oesterreichs*, 162 (Mannheim, 1927). The theme is developed in a comparative context by M. Cappelletti, *Processo e Ideologie*, 11–20 (Bologna, 1969). However, many writers have discerned "ideologically determined" variations within both public and private law styles. See G. Foschini, *Sistema del diritto processuale penale*, 226–30 (Milan, 1965); M. Taruffo, *Il Processo civile "Adversary" nell' esperienza Americana* (Padua, 1979).

accused in the Anglo-American criminal prosecution has time and again been linked to tenets of classical liberalism. [13]

In the writings of others, relationships of political power received more emphasis than the role of pure political ideology. Thus, for example, important changes in the design of the legal process were traced to differing degrees of centralization, to the participation of laymen in the administration of justice, and to similar factors. [14] Many insights generated by such studies, mostly of historical nature, were used by social theorists—most notably by Max Weber—to suggest an apparatus for more systematic understanding of procedural change. Weber developed "ideal types" of authority and suggested that the diversity of power relationships can explain important differences among legal systems, including their administration of justice. [15]

In this volume, proposals about linkages between politics and justice will be taken seriously: hence, factors from the political sphere will be recruited in the search for a scheme capable of making the striking variations in modern forms of justice more intelligible. Much of the discussion about politics and justice circles around two themes that command our attention. The first concerns the structure of government—more specifically, the character of procedural authority; the second concerns the legitimate function of government—more specifically, views on the purpose to be served by the administration of justice. In much of what has been said thus far, these two themes have been interlaced and confounded: certain engagements of government were invariably associated with certain kinds of governmental organization. I shall attempt hereafter to develop each theme separately, seeking in each a distinct coherence that can link procedural arrangements into identifiable associations. A context will thus emerge within which to associate a great deal of procedural diversity—and its puzzles— with the changing structure and function of contemporary states.

The Apparatus of Government

The organization of procedural authority leaves some marks on the legal process which are fairly obvious and often noted. For example, many distinctive traits of the Anglo-American style have been related quite persuasively to the division of the tribunal into judge and jury. While other marks are more remote and speculative, it can scarcely be disputed that even such intangibles as the more or less personal tone of proceedings, or divergent attitudes toward documents and deadlines, may be influenced by a particular character of authority (e.g., by degrees of

13. See, e.g., J. Griffiths, "Ideology and Criminal Procedure," 70 Yale L.J. 359 (1970); M. Taruffo, supra, n. 12, 259–301; S. Kadish, ed., Encyclopedia of Crime and Justice, vol. 1, The Adversary System (1983).

14. See, e.g., J. P. Dawson, A History of Lay Judges (1960); F. Wieacker, Privatrechtsgeschichte der Neuzeit, 183–89, 243–48 (Göttingen, 1967).

15. M. Weber, Economy and Society, vol. 1, p. 215, vol. 3, p. 1059 (1968). See also Max Rheinstein, ed., Max Weber on Law in Economy and Society, 349–56 (1966).

bureaucratization). In the first chapter I shall suggest a framework within which to study these linkages between authority and the legal process in a more systematic way. To facilitate this task I shall assemble into models or "ideals" those characteristics of procedural officialdom that seem relevant for the forms of justice. To keep the problematic within manageable proportions, I shall construct only two such ideals of officialdom, building the two models from major features that seem to distinguish the machinery of justice on the Continent and in lands of the Anglo-American tradition. But because these two ideals will exaggerate certain tendencies (e.g., hierarchical ordering of courts in Europe, less rigid hierarchization in Anglo-American countries), their use as instruments of analysis or as sources of empirical hypotheses will not be limited to the contrast of civil- and common-law systems. Indeed, as will be seen, aspects of the Soviet system and technocratic tendencies in the West will also be reflected in some aspects of the two ideals.

The implications of these two ideals will largely concern important aspects of procedural design, such as the varying structure of the trial, its relation to the process as a whole, preferences for alternative proof-taking techniques, and the like. Other implications will concern more general subjects in regard to which existing systems have been observed to differ: for example, how the way in which the apparatus of justice is organized affects the prevailing perspective on issues (more or less abstract viewpoints), or how the relative attractiveness of discretion in decision making contrasts with preference for rules.

Before the second chapter comes to a close, two distinctive styles of administering justice will thus emerge, capturing much of the observed difference between common- and civil-law systems apart from the customary contrast of contest/inquest forms or the adversarial/inquisitorial modes. To be sure, the two styles will include some traits found in one or another version of these conventional concepts, but while these traits are only loosely attached to conventional categories they will have firmer moorings in this scheme.

It is important not to misconceive the relation of the two styles to Continental and Anglo-American systems of procedure. As I have pointed out, the two styles will be constructed against the background of models of authority which exaggerate or stylize contrasts among judicial organizations in Continental and Anglo-American states (such as attitudes toward hierarchization or toward lay decision makers). In consequence, the two styles will also intensify or magnify trends and features of existing procedures. Actual Anglo-American and Continental procedures will be seen to belong to one or another mode, as buildings can be said to belong to one or another architectural style.

Functions of Government

My second theme demands that connections be established between the design of legal proceedings and dominant views on the role of government in society. Such connections can be established in several ways, but I shall mainly trace them as mediated by changing ideas about the purpose to be served by the administration of justice: dominant ideas about the role of government inform views on the purpose of justice, and the latter are relevant to the choice of many procedural arrangements. Because only some forms of justice fit specific purposes, only certain forms can be justified in terms of prevailing ideology.

If this path is to be followed, the great wealth of ideas on the mission of the state in society must somehow be absorbed and arranged for the needs of this study. One solution is to see these views as embodying two contrary inclinations, each rarely strong enough totally to displace the other: the one is to have government manage the lives of people and steer society; the other is to have government maintain the social equilibrium and merely provide a framework for social self-management and individual self-definition. In the third chapter I shall approach the preserves of political theory to inquire into the ideological background of these contrary inclinations. Where government is conceived as a manager, the administration of justice appears to be devoted to fulfillment of state programs and implementation of state policies. In contrast, where government merely maintains the social equilibrium, the administration of justice tends to be associated with conflict resolution. In chapters 4 and 5 I shall use these two contrasting purposes of justice—refracted, as it were, in the lenses of the ideological tenets that support them—to articulate two archetypes of the legal process: one devoted to conflict resolution, the other to policy implementation. This undertaking involves a search for arrangements that are either implicit in the animating purposes or suitable to their realization, while compatible with ideologies that lie at their base.

As this study progresses, it will more clearly appear that the policy-implementing mode is partial to inquest, while its antipode is similarly biased in favor of contest forms. That is to say, a kinship will thus surface between the archetypes on the one hand and adversarial and inquisitorial systems on the other. Three main points of difference from conventional thought should be noticed at this early point. First, as such, inquest and contest arrangements are conventionally thought of as structural alternatives to achieving the same end.[16] In America, for example, they are usually imagined as alternative designs for conflict resolution. But where the opposition is imagined as two alternative routes leading to the same destination, the two sets of arrangements to which the opposition relates cannot properly be distinguished without ambiguity. Second, our two modes of legal proceedings, each predicated on a different purpose of justice, embrace only characteristics that can be related to a particular procedural goal, and exclude others that reflect a particular structure of authority. For example, whether judicial, prosecutorial, or other authority is more or less centralized will be irrelevant for the purpose of opposing our two archetypes. A price

16. As suggested *supra,* n. 12, an ancient line of Continental thought suggests in an implicit and oblique way that the two forms serve different purposes: one form is said to fit civil cases (or private law matters), while the other fits criminal cases (or public law matters). This view was already current in the fourteenth century. See, e.g., A. de Butrio, *Super Prima Secundi Decretalium Commentaria,* Tomus 3, *Rubrica de Judiciis,* 2 (Venice, 1628). For differences between this line of thought and the approach proposed in the text, see *infra,* ch. 3, n. 42.

must be paid for this self-imposed abstention, but as I shall suggest in the next section, it will prove illuminating in the end.

Finally, the policy-implementing and the conflict-solving processes arise against the background of two extreme views about the role of government—views in which the roots of the conventional opposition of inquest and contest forms are perceived. This link to political ideology provides the context in which I shall address the issue of how far the twin themes of party dispute and official inquiry can be pressed in modern states. Further, a perspective will be obtained that will reveal—and in revealing, expand—the limits of conventional analysis. For example, sharply divergent ideas on judicial independence, and on the sacrifice of accurate judgments for the sake of preserving the integrity of the legal process, can both be related to the opposition of policy-implementing and conflict-solving procedures.[17]

This brief synopsis of the proposed archetypes discloses that they embrace legal arrangements in pure or ideal form, but that these terms are meant to denote not a perfect or wished-for procedural design but rather a design detached from historical contingency by an urge to analyze and to identify. The relation of the archetypes to actual proceedings parallels the relation of governmental functions they each presuppose to the function of existing or historic governments. As the function of government includes both the maintenance of social equilibrium and programs of social transformation, rather than only one or only the other, so actual legal proceedings exhibit both conflict-solving and policy-implementing forms, often in complex and ambiguous combinations. Of course, in pronouncedly managerial states such as China or the Soviet Union, one should expect a heavy layer of policy-implementing characteristics in all spheres of the administration of justice. But in classical Western systems—be they of common- or civil-law variety—more equivocal compounds are likely, with the flavor of the blend depending on the particular proceeding. Anglo-American systems have no monopoly on conflict-solving (thus also adversarial) features; Continental systems have none on policy-implementing (thus also inquisitorial) characteristics.

So, the analytical scheme opens the possibility for finding some conflict-solving features in Europe that are missing from Anglo-American jurisdictions, and some policy-implementing features in the latter that are absent from European law. In brief, characteristics of the two archetypes should not be understood as repositories of essential facets of *existing* procedures in civil- and common-law countries. They are meant to be used in seeking to understand the complex mixtures of arrangements, as means to analyze them in terms of their components, as one would study compounds in analytical chemistry.

17. The "inquest-contest" dichotomy, so habitual with lawyers, is sometimes linked to ideological tenets. See *supra*, n. 12. However, on the whole, ideological positions relevant to the dichotomy have not been sufficiently purged of inconsistencies and obfuscations that characterize many prominent political doctrines. Inquiries into the political assumptions of the inquisitorial form have been particularly deficient. However, seeds of a polarization of ideologies useful for our purposes can be found in C. Lindblom, *Politics and Markets*, 248 (1977).

Proposal for a Unitary Scheme

Having developed two different perspectives on the administration of justice in modern states—one focusing on its relation to the structure of state authority, the other centering on its relation to the function of government—I shall then attempt to bring the two perspectives together, in order to observe the panorama, so to speak, bifocally. It will be doubted, however, whether the policy-implementing and the conflict-solving processes can freely be combined with arrangements adapted to structures of authority. Are not *some* functions of the state invariably associated with certain structures of government? Is it not true, for example, that states bent on effecting a far-reaching transformation of society require a centralized and professional government, so that their programs—in Lenin's phrase—are not applied differently in Kaluga and Kazan? And does it not therefore follow from this that policy-implementing forms of justice should be associated only with forms adapted to a centralized bureaucratic machinery of government?

It cannot be denied that certain enterprises of government will not be contemplated at all, or will remain pipe dreams, in the absence of a minimally capable apparatus of rule. But short of such extremes, there seems to be no necessity that a particular conception of the mission of government must be accompanied by a particular structure of implementation. An intensely managerial state can be ruled by decentralized amateurs—a situation, for example, like Iran governed by the Shiite clergy[18]—and a state with a proclivity for laissez-faire can have a centralized bureaucratic government—a situation reminiscent of many Continental states in the nineteenth century. It can be argued, of course, that realization of certain objectives of the state is better served by particular organizations of authority, or that certain types of governmental organization impede the smooth realization of particular objectives. A state with many independent power centers and a powerful desire to transform society can be likened to a man with ardent appetites and a poor instrument for their satisfaction. But this argument does not deny the reality of such combinations; it implies only the observation that some combinations are harmonious while others create dissonance, stress, and tension.[19] Similarly, policy-implementing and conflict-solving forms of justice can be combined with forms adapted to various structures of

18. In a lay illustration, the Yugoslav model of socialism combines pervasive social programs with the ideals of decentralization and of Jacksonian rotation of citizens in office.

19. In the presence of such mismatches, structuralists tend to diagnose a dismantling (*décalage*) of the structure and functions of government (N. Poulantzas, *Pouvoir politique et classes sociales de l'état capitaliste*, 303, 388 [Paris, 1968]). The presence of a décalage does not inevitably indicate an undesirable state of affairs: for example, the dilatory effect of decentralized lay officialdom on the realization of some programs can be assessed, on balance, as a salutary check on hasty realization of ill-conceived projects, or as justified by the observance of some "expressive" value (e.g., maintaining the judgment of one's peers despite cost and delay in the administration of justice). Automatic condemnation of "dysfunctions" and "inefficiencies" may in fact tacitly recognize bureaucratic inclinations, themselves objectionable in certain types of governmental organization.

authority, but while some combinations can be viewed as stressful mismatches, others can be assessed to successfully dovetail procedural functions and procedural authority.

The remainder of this volume will then attempt to interlace the two sets of models in a unitary scheme and suggest ways in which the resulting ensemble can be used to analyze the diverse arrangements and institutions that characterize the administration of justice in some prominent modern systems. The enhanced perspective will enable us to identify some heretofore obscured differences of degree—such as discrepant conceptions of the judicial office in common- and civil-law countries—and to perceive divergent ideas on the relation between civil and criminal processes. But most of my effort will be not so much to identify new things as to show how my proposed perspective differs from the conventional gloss on them, and how it suggests new meaning for the previously incomprehensible.[20]

The more puzzling forms of American public interest litigation will now appear as complex and equivocal blends of policy-implementing and conflict-solving modes, interacting with arrangements and institutions adapted to an apparatus of authority that still "in principle" rejects bureaucratization and hierarchization of judicial authority. Genuinely "Soviet" arrangements will be seen as combinations of features attractive to an intensely managerial state and features associated with centralized and bureaucratized procedural authority. I shall pay particular attention to those aspects of traditional Anglo-American authority that create stresses and tensions with contest forms, and those aspects of Continental authority that facilitate their implementation. Thus, certain adversarial arrangements unknown to Anglo-American procedure have flourished in some spheres of the Continental administration of justice: this paradox—to conventional theory—can in turn be explained as an interaction of procedural authority with certain objectives of proceedings.

Although the foregoing sufficiently marks the route to be traveled in this volume, a word of caution remains to be addressed to the reader. Adjusted to the broad comparative scale, my scheme must always suggest how things appear

20. My main purpose will be to show how certain ideas on the mission and shape of government justify or support particular clusters of procedural forms, thus providing means whereby recognizable patterns of procedural arrangements can be composed. By and large I shall refrain from making stronger claims that these ideas actually caused certain procedures to be what they are. However, such stronger claims will occasionally be made: some forms seem inextricably linked with specific purposes of justice, or with specific structures of procedural authority. Some procedures have also had demiurges who showed little respect for preexisting form, and who tried—whenever possible—to shape it in accordance with ideological preconceptions. I shall make some methodological observations, but attempt no full account of the precise nature of links or connections between politics and justice. Greater precision would risk delay on the barbed edge of complicated philosophical issues: whenever human purposes and perceptions constitute links among phenomena, staggering methodological problems arise. Even if they could be resolved, the lever would be weightier than the load, and I would never get on with my story.

from the outside—to a peregrine from another world,[21] rather than to one whose roots are firmly planted in a particular country. Discrepant viewpoints can lead to serious misunderstandings: what appears from within as pronounced bureaucratization of authority may seem on a larger scale as a merely insignificant departure from prebureaucratic arrangements; a government that is experienced domestically as managerial (activist) may seem from a broader perspective laissez-faire. Such varying assessments can be reflected, of course, in variant characterizations of forms of justice as they relate to the structure and function of a particular government. Inevitably, then, the perspective that my scheme opens upon some systems will appear iconoclastic and bizarre, even offensive to a parochial legal sensibility. Also inevitable, from this perspective, is a detachment from domestic commitments, depreciation of internal disagreements, and— more generally—a dispassionate attitude of neutrality, violently suspect in some quarters. As a result, the illumination provided here will be at best like the winter sun: emitting light but little warmth. Before embarking on the intellectual adventure I propose the reader should be aware of the unavoidable costs of looking at things from the outside: it is hard to be at once comfortable everywhere and at home anywhere. *Quisquis ubique habitat nusquam habitat.*[22]

---

21. The allusion is to all denizens of *civitas peregrina*, who are no more than transient aliens in existing states. See P. Brown, *Augustine of Hippo*, ch. 27, 322–25 (1967).

22. "One who lives everywhere lives nowhere" (Martial, VII, 73).

I Organization of Authority: The Hierarchical and the Coordinate Ideals

i. TWO IDEALS OF OFFICIALDOM

Systematic study of features impressed on the legal process by state officialdom requires a scheme to identify and describe different modes of organizing procedural authority. Although there is ample and rapidly growing literature on structures of authority in general, the peculiarity of the role of law does not permit the luxury of relying on established theory with only minor modifications. Hence I shall begin by developing a distinctive analytical framework.

The conceptual elements needed for this framework correspond to three questions often asked in confronting an organization of authority; the first concerns the attributes of officials, the second, their relationship, and the third, the manner in which they make decisions. Thus separated out, these three aspects of authority have long been suspected of influencing the shape of the legal process, and I shall use them as dimensions along which to define our categories. On the first dimension, the usual focus is on the distinction between professionalized, permanent officials and those who are untrained and transitory. On the second dimension, two lesser configurations deserve special consideration: under the first, officials are locked into a strict network of super- and subordination; under the second, they are rough equals, organized into a single echelon of authority. On the third dimension, the critical distinction is between decision making pursuant to special or "technical" standards, and decision making informed by undifferentiated or general community norms.

It is easy to see that these three larger aspects of authority are analytically independent, so that smaller variables from each dimension can be combined in various ways. For example, there is no necessary connection between the attributes of officials and their interrelations. Classical bureaucracy has been defined in terms of a professionalized corps of officials composed in a pyramid of authority; however, a "nonhierarchical" bureaucracy can be imagined where professionals pursue an ordered sequence of activity, each performing a segment of the common task, with no superior review of any prior decision: each decision in this cumulative and linear process is final.[1] Nor is there a necessary connection between hierarchical ordering and professionalization: lay officials too can be situated in a network of subordination.

Variables from each dimension could be assembled in a great number of ways, and their implications for procedural form examined in a complex classificatory scheme. But such extensive taxonomic exercises are not required: our theme permits selection of only two composite structures of authority from a larger number of possibilities. The first structure essentially corresponds to conceptions of classical bureaucracy. It is characterized by a professional corps of officials, organized into a hierarchy which makes decisions according to technical standards. The other structure has no readily recognizable analogue in established theory. It is defined by a body of nonprofessional decision makers, organized into a single level of authority which makes decisions by applying undifferentiated community standards. The first structure I shall call the *hierarchical* ideal or vision of officialdom, and the second I shall term the *coordinate* ideal.

The reason for this narrow selection has been suggested: the two ideals of officialdom can be used to organize into new configurations many scattered but widely shared observations about salient differences between two important judicial organizations developed in the West and disseminated through the world—the traditional judicial apparatus on the European continent, and the traditional machinery of justice in England. To the extent to which the organization of judicial authority influences the design of the legal process, the hierarchical and the coordinate ideals thus offer a convenient perspective upon the always intriguing, never fully grasped contrast between Continental and Anglo-American styles of administering justice.

It hardly needs saying that actually extant features that distinguish the Continental and English judicial organizations will not be fully captured in these two constructs. This is because tendencies observed in actual organizations—for example, the tendency toward professional decision making in one and the tendency toward lay decision making in the other—become constitutive elements of these two ideals even if these tendencies were never fully realized on the Continent and in the British Isles. It is precisely this relationship between reality and these two constructs that permits the use of the hierarchical and the coordinate ideals to illuminate reciprocities between procedural authority and procedural form on a scale broader than the conventional opposition between common-law and civil-law systems. For example, in most communist countries judicial organizations have carried tendencies toward overall hierarchical leadership further than have traditional Continental systems, so that the ideal of a hierarchical apparatus may help in analyzing some characteristics of the socialist legal process as well.

1. See S. Ackerman, *Corruption: A Study in Political Economy*, 168–69 (1978). Given advanced information technology, future organizations are likely to find many presently important levels of supervision unnecessary and to replace them with such sequential structures.

The special emphasis here on traditional organizations of authority may come as a surprise. It is often said that broadly similar circumstances in contemporary states have brought the judicial organizations of various countries closer together than they were in the past. Pronounced trends toward professionalization, centralization, and organized expertise have been reported everywhere, so that some have even predicted that centralized bureaucracies will inherit the earth. Is it anachronistic, then, to dwell on the recessive contrast between bureaucratic and nonbureaucratic authority rather than on internal variations of modern bureaucracies? The short answer is that modern pressures toward bureaucratization of the machinery of justice interact with inherited structures in complex ways and produce hybrids that can hardly be analyzed without regard to their historical antecedents. Nor have traditional structures become totally obsolescent, or surrendered to modern trends in equal measure. The American machinery of justice, for example, while increasingly professionalized and centralized in this century, continues to be more deeply permeated by features embodied in the coordinate ideal than are judicial administrations of any other industrial state in the West. These perduring features not only account for some perplexing tensions in the modern American administration of justice but may also illuminate, in part, the widening gap between American and British legal sensibilities.

Let us then take a closer look at the hierarchical and the coordinate ideals of officialdom by concentrating on those aspects most relevant to the study of procedural form.

ii. THE HIERARCHICAL IDEAL

First, what are the main implications of professionalization, vertical ordering of officials, and attachment to technical decision making that characterize the hierarchical vision of authority? Most of these implications are widely recognized and quite uncontroversial. However, under analysis, contours will emerge of an institutional ambience which the traditional Anglo-American decision maker[2] would profoundly dislike, while his Continental counterpart would find this ambience much more congenial, even if it caricatures the environment in which he is accustomed to operate.

Professionalization of Officials

Permanently placed officials carve out a sphere of practice which they regard as their special province. Over time, they also develop a sense of identity with similarly situated individuals, so that lines become rigid between "insiders" and "outsiders." If outside participation in the making of decisions is imposed upon

2. Who should be regarded as the paradigmatic decision maker will be discussed later in this chapter. In the view of a comparativist, this question has a far less obvious answer than domestic vision assumes.

such officials, it is viewed, at best, as meddling which deserves to be contained and made innocuous. How this official exclusivity affects procedural form will be a recurring theme throughout this volume.

Long terms of office create the space for routinization and specialization of tasks. Routinization of activity implies that issues that come before the official are no longer apprehended as presenting a unique constellation of circumstances calling for "individualized justice." Choices are also narrowed: while there may be many ways to go about solving a problem, only one emerges as habitual. A considerable degree of emotional disengagement also becomes possible. Specialization implies, of course, that only certain factors—those within a narrow realm—play a part in decision making. As a consequence of habitualization and specialization, a professional's official and personal reactions part company: he acquires the capacity of anesthetizing his heart, if necessary, and of making decisions in his official capacity that he might never make as an individual.

This schism between office and its occupant promotes institutional thinking: impulses to bypass institutional interests and to consult one's conscience are too "protestant" to be tolerated. Judgments become pronouncements of an impersonal entity (a curia) even where a single individual is entrusted with their rendition. And because the institution must be univocal so as not to be equivocal, the announcement of a judgment made by several officials nullifies prior internal dissent: those who disagree must now repress their feelings. In the vision of officialdom now under discussion, the widespread failure of Continental jurisdictions to publish dissenting opinions—or sometimes even to disclose the names of judges who voted for a decision—far from being undesirable, can assume a sort of melancholy dignity. Like drones who die having fertilized the queen bee, so dissenting and concurring voices, instrumental in the formation of an institutional decision, should not survive its announcement.

Strict Hierarchical Ordering

Officials are organized into several echelons: power comes from the top, trickling down the levels of authority. Great inequalities among officials at different hierarchical positions are characteristic. At the lowest level are petty officials—*parvuli*, in medieval Continental legal texts—with limited responsibilities of doing the spadework for the organization. However, they jealously guard their bailiwick against outsiders, no matter how modest the qualifications for the job may be. (Serving documents and minor ministerial tasks are examples of such duties.) Each successive higher echelon carries considerably greater responsibility and prestige. Officials of the same rank are equals, but where a conflict among them arises, these "homologues" are not authorized to settle it by themselves through accommodation and compromise. Contested matters must be referred to the common superior for disposition. It is only at the top of the authority pyramid (assuming it is not monocephalous) that clashes of opinion are necessarily resolved by accommodation.

Cementing the components of authority are a strong sense of order and a desire for uniformity: ideally, all are to march to the beat of a single drum. In larger organizations, of course, the supreme authority cannot keep all decisions to itself, charging lower echelons with only their preparation and execution. Of necessity, subordinates must be empowered to make first-order decisions, or, to use characteristic Continental terms, to decide "in the first instance." But the logic of strict hierarchization requires that such decisions be subject to superior review on a regular and comprehensive basis: wide distribution of unreviewable authority to lower levels would strain the animating assumptions of the whole authority structure. Understood in this sense, official discretion is anathema.

It is important to observe the tension between individualized decision making and comprehensive superior review. If administrative incapacitation is to be avoided at the top echelon, where there are fewer decision makers than at the base, superior audits must be restricted to a limited number of points, preferably those that lend themselves easily to verification. In other words, high authority expects lower levels to schematize the complexity of matters they are called upon to decide. Of course, this schematization is facilitated in hierarchies that also insist that officials be professionals: routinization of activity increases one's capacity to "typify" situations. However, this capacity is not equally distributed across the hierarchical apparatus. Initial decisionmakers are closer to the messy details of life, including human drama, and therefore can less readily be immunized from individual aspects of cases. Meanwhile, higher officials face realities prepackaged or edited by their subordinates; individual destinies are less visible. Because of this mediation, higher-ups can more easily disregard the "equities" of the cases they must decide. The advantage of their insensitivity to individual circumstances is that they are free to concern themselves with correcting inconsistencies in low-level decisions and with cultivation of broad ordering schemes for decision making. As in the ordering of angels, then, the superiority of officials increases in proportion to the greater generality of their knowledge. It is in this sense that, as some students of bureaucracy have claimed, "the top understands universals; the lower echelons understand particulars."[3]

Because it implies differentiation of functions among specialists, professionalization—the first dimension of the hierarchical ideal—can promote dis-

---

3. See K. Marx, *Critique of Hegel's Philosophy of Right*, 46 (1970). The reference to heavenly hierarchization is not necessarily farfetched. The Continental judicial apparatus was developed in the Church of Rome whose ideas on proper ordering of terrestrial authority were believed to reflect the celestial order. On the bases for the hierarchization of angels, see M. J. Adler, *The Angels and Us*, 49–51 (1982). Where hierarchical concerns for unity and consistency should give way to the greater sensibility of low-level officials for individual circumstances permits no easy solution. But however the top chooses to define the focus of lower officials, hierarchical judicial organizations develop mechanisms to narrow the gap between more individualized initial and more generalized subsequent decision making. Some mechanisms originate from the top: for example, the training of officials can screen out persons overly sensitive to particulars. Other mechanisms come from the bottom: those familiar with Continental judicial practice can testify to the skill of trial judges in writing opinions so as to mask their characterization of events to conform to the decision-making models of reviewing authorities.

cord. When professionals are stratified in a chain of subordination (the second dimension of the ideal) and thus are under pressure toward unity and obedience, then the possessive "turf" psychology of specialists is mitigated. The specter of superior audits promotes an ethic of cooperation, and the dynamics of hierarchical promotion contribute to a spirit of "team playing." Those officials whose desire to make a special impact obstructs the harmonious functioning of the organization are likely to be bypassed for advancement.

Technical Standards for Decision Making

Two basic approaches to technical decision making should be distinguished, although they are often combined in judicial organizations. One approach is for officials to assess the consequences of alternative decisions and then to choose the alternative that seems most attractive in terms of a posited organizational goal: the decision is justified with reference to the desirable consequences believed to flow from it. Self-consciously formal techniques have been developed to assist the decision maker in performing such consequentialist (instrumental) calculations, and the influence of such techniques is growing. This first approach, which I shall call the technocratic orientation, will remain on the periphery, nevertheless. I shall consider this orientation only in discussing aspects of the legal process in some intensely activist states where matters that come before the courts increasingly require technical expertise of this consequentialist sort.

The second approach is prevalent in traditional apparatuses of justice. Under this approach, which I shall call the legalistic, officials are expected to make a particular decision when facts are found that are specified under a normative standard. In contrast to the technocratic orientation, the attainment of desirable consequences is not an independent justificatory ground. The propriety of the decision is evaluated in terms of fidelity to the applicable standard. This is not to imply that the legalistic approach is indifferent to consequences resulting from official action: those who fashion the standards are expected to make the necessary instrumental calculations and to design standards capable of advancing organizational goals. Moreover, even specific rules necessarily contain an element of indeterminacy and can be interpreted in light of underlying goals so as to lead to desirable outcomes.[4]

If the language of standards were infinitely flexible, space would exist for consequentialist and legalistic approaches always to meet in harmony. But hierarchical bureaucracies set limits on the arbitrary Humpty Dumpty attitude to-

---

4. The distinction between decision making by instrumental (means-end) calculations and by adherence to standards has figured prominently in Max Weber's discussion of bureaucracy. See M. Rheinstein, ed., *Max Weber on Law in Economy and Society*, 355 (1967). It is still often used by legal sociologists. See, e.g., N. Luhmann, *Legitimation durch Verfahren*, 2d ed., 130, 210 (Darmstadt, 1975); T. Eckhoff and K. Jacobsen, *Rationality and Responsibility*, 9, 17 (Copenhagen, 1960). The internal division in utilitarian philosophy between "act" and "rule" utilitarianism can be traced to a similar differentiation. See *infra*, n. 6.

ward the language used in standards: conventions are established that foreclose many theoretically possible paths of interpretation which easily occur to an institutionally unrestrained legal imagination. A point can thus be reached where adherence to a standard can frustrate the achievement of a desirable end. At this point, the distinctive nature of the legalistic orientation surfaces: the standard must be applied, even if it produces negative results.[5]

It is necessary to distinguish here two modal variations of legalism. One variant views social life as being so complex and fluid that decisional standards are targeted to narrow areas, referring to concrete sets of facts. Preferably, such decisional paradigms are in the form of examples telling how concrete life situations should be treated. Confronted with a case—a life situation—the decision maker compares it to the standard example, and the closer the similarity between the two, the greater will be the guiding force of the standard. Plainly, such standards cannot be detached from the pragmatics of their application to specific cases. Indeed, they are so deeply enmeshed in detail that a relatively minor change in circumstance makes standards only partially applicable. The technical character of this variant of legalism—which I shall call pragmatic—resides mainly in the skill of making subtle distinctions.

The other variant is partial to sweeping ordering schemes, and attached to standards that are more context-free and therefore more general: a network of interlocking principles and rules tends to be created. Inevitably, decisions made under this second branch of legalism which I shall call logical, cannot take into account many concrete aspects of cases that the pragmatic orientation easily accommodates. However, this is not viewed as disturbing: "individualized justice" is readily exchanged for a greater consistency of decision making across large classes of cases. Both formulation and application of standards become more detachable from the details of life than a pragmatist is willing to concede.[6] In other words, the ordering function of decisional standards is stressed. What

5. Of course, no real-world organization is prepared to insist on absolute fidelity to norms under any circumstances, no matter how disastrous the consequences of the resulting decision. *Fiat justitia, ruat caelum* (let justice be done though the heavens fall) is a motto that makes unrealistic demands of the legalistic orientation. Nevertheless, judicial organizations vary according to the degree to which they are prepared to insist upon adherence to predetermined standards even at the cost of precipitating negative results. Those who neglect these differences of degree miss important contrasts among actual judicial organizations. For example, they lump together "revolutionary legality" and the classical liberal "rule of law." For arresting observations on this theme from a nonlawyer, see C. Milosz, *The Captive Mind*, 30–31 (1953). See also *infra*, ch. 3, n. 17.

6. Similar distinctions between pragmatic and logical legalism appear in a variety of comparative contexts. For a related opposition between the "science of the concrete" and "canonical science," see C. Geertz, *The Interpretation of Cultures*, 352 (1973). Max Weber tried to express internal variations of Western legal thought in terms of a similar dichotomy between thought relying on "the external characterization of facts" as opposed to a thought involving "the logical interpretation of meaning." See M. Weber, *Economy and Society*, vol. 2, pp. 655–57 (1968). For a somewhat different distinction, see C. Schmitt, *Ueber die drei Arten des rechtswissenschaflichen Denkens* (Hamburg, 1934).

precisely they command often seems less important than the fact that a matter is clearly and consistently regulated by them.[7]

It should be plain that pragmatic legalism must clash with hierarchical ordering; where original decisions are engrossed in details, regular and comprehensive superior audits become well-nigh impossible. It should be equally obvious that tall pyramids of authority find logical legalism attractive. When reality is observed from a distance, from hierarchical *hauteur*, one's sight becomes selective: the complexities of problems can be absorbed to a far greater extent than is possible at close range. Information transmitted up to top officials—ultimate decision makers—already conforms to restraints imposed on the more inclusive vision of intermediaries: the facts of the case are pruned and neatly arranged according to criteria on relevance (ordering criteria) imposed from above. The image of decision making as a somewhat mechanical process of relating facts to norms can thus acquire plausibility.[8]

It is normal in hierarchically structured organizations for the logically legalistic attitude of high authority to set the tone: dominant views are formed at the top and percolate down to lower officials, otherwise more vulnerable to the layman's call for individualized justice.[9] In short, a version of the hierarchical ideal truer to its premises is obtained when one combines the vertical ordering of professional officials with logical rather than pragmatic legalism. Henceforth I shall focus on this "purer" version of the hierarchical ideal and in the next chapter, begin to play out the implications of this vertical ideal for the legal process with this purer variant in mind. However, I shall not ignore pragmatic legalism, but invoke it when I refer to horizontally structured judicial organizations.[10]

iii. THE COORDINATE IDEAL

The ideal to which I now turn envisions an amorphous machinery of justice. There are few sharp and obvious lines that separate its officials and its attitudes

7. To a mind imbued by hierarchical values, the ordering component in law is not merely a regrettable concession to human frailty and wickedness, unnecessary among the virtuous or in heaven "where the lion lies down with the lamb." Contrast the views on the need for law among the virtuous of G. Gilmore in *Ages of American Law*, 111 (1977) with those of Marcilio Ficino in K. von Montoriola, *Briefe der Mediceerkreises*, 103 (Berlin, 1926). See also G. Radbruch, *Rechtsphilosophie*, 6th ed., 172 (Stuttgart, 1963).

8. In consequence, varying ideas about the nature of the "judicial process" are not unrelated to differences of institutional perspective, and should not be used uncritically across legal cultures.

9. Some mechanisms generated by hierarchical organizations to reduce the discrepant outlooks of original and reviewing decision makers have been discussed (*supra*, n. 3). Faced with uncertainties of how to weigh "equities," properly indoctrinated lower officials may welcome resolution of their doubts by applying a clear, albeit somewhat Procrustean norm. They may even come to accept a hierarchy of knowledge, whereby higher authority also possesses more valid insights. Nevertheless, lower officials remain more "pragmatic" than those in upper reaches of authority.

10. Provided that decision making requires, at least to some extent, the application of technical standards.

toward decision making from the rest of society. Yet, under scrutiny, this ideal reveals a distinctive institutional framework in relation to reality, which I shall examine before this chapter ends. In anticipation, let me suggest that the character of authority which this ideal invokes contains little that would shock or surprise the citizens of Attica, or Romans of the classical legal period, or—if the reader will suspend his disbelief—those accustomed to the workings of the traditional Anglo-American machinery of justice.

Lay Officials

Ideally, power is vested in amateurs who are called upon to perform authoritative functions *ad hoc*, or for a limited time. Where the apparatus of authority is in the hands of such temporary officials, there is little opportunity for a spirit of exclusivity to develop. Insiders and outsiders in relation to the judicial apparatus are not sharply distinguished, and the distinction is likely to be of little importance. Few serious obstacles exist to block officials from delegating some action to persons without authoritative functions. After all, officials themselves are without initiation and training, recruited into the administration of justice for a limited purpose only. In the next chapter, it will be seen that this readiness to delegate or "farm out" action holds the key to many distinctive procedural arrangements.

Characteristics that I have earlier associated with professionalization are here conspicuous by their absence. Given short terms of office, routinization of activity has little chance to develop: neophyte officials confront their jobs green—with ample room for spontaneity and improvisations, for reacting emotionally and acting *ex abundantia cordis*. Issues can hardly be disentangled from personalities. Where the terms of office are longer, some hardening of ways may set in, but personal and official attitudes still do not separate so sharply as they do with career officials. Nor is there enough time for long-term differentiation of functions and specialization to evolve. Indeed, both developments are likely to be resisted by laymen in positions of authority who bring to their office ordinary "generalist" attitudes. That the resulting fusion of functions will affect procedural form is, of course, straightforward.

With no sharp discontinuity between personal and official spheres, institutional thinking is quite rudimentary. Verdicts, judgments, or other authoritative determinations, whether individual or collective, are not conceived as pronouncements of an agency independent of the individuals comprising it, and remain highly personal. In fact, the demand that individual opinions be repressed or forgone for the sake of a single overall view seems to invite spineless attitudes, and is tantamount to an affront to the personal dignity of lay officials. When unified into panels, they thus retain their individual voices, even if the result implies—as in Pirandello's plays—that there is no single, official story of the group. Nor does a lone dissenter from the majority opinion—a protestant—feel bound by this opinion in the future: he feels free to repeat his dissent over and over again.

A major difficulty facing such organization of temporary officials is how to develop a reliable memory—how to handle complex problems and function continuously rather than periodically. Such difficulties provide a fertile soil for the appearance of a caste of professionals who make it their business to interact with lay officials. These professionals assist the "inexperienced" decision maker, supply him with information, and maintain tenuous continuity within the apparatus of authority. Specialization, while absent from the apparatus of authority, can be found in their midst. In short, a symbiotic relationship thus develops between a cast of nonauthoritative professionals and the amateurs in positions of power.

Horizontal Distribution of Authority

The ideal now under consideration envisages a wide distribution of authority among roughly equal lay officials: with no one clearly superior to others, there is essentially a single stratum of authority. The question immediately arises whether such an arrangement is compatible with a unitary apparatus of authority, especially where decision makers have a weak sense of institutional loyalty, or a strong *libido dominandi*. It has been said that where there is no ultimate authority, things fall apart and anarchy is loosed upon the world. For a moment, however, let us continue to contemplate a purely horizontal configuration of authority—a web without a spider sitting at its heart.

How can the unity of this structure be protected from various centrifugal forces? External factors, such as a common purpose, may supply the necessary cohesion, as in David Hume's metaphor of several people rowing a boat. But I seek the possibility of a cohesive force generated *within* the single layer of authority. To understand its origin, consider that parallel lay officials are bound to have overlapping, even completely duplicating jurisidictions in a lay organization that is not a well-ordered sequential bureaucracy. Accordingly, decision makers situated in parallel can easily frustrate or nullify the fruits of one another's efforts: one official can protect a party from the enforcement of another official's judgment (for instance, the traditional English chancellor) or can refuse, in his discretion, to extend assistance. Alternatively, one official can decide to institute proceedings in a matter which is already pending before parallel authority, causing all sorts of problems within coordinate structures. These and similar possibilities of frustration of one another's efforts may raise fears of retaliation and lead to mutual adjustment and cooperation. In other words, not unlike the situation in the international arena, the fear of reciprocity becomes a cohesive force, replacing the duty to submit to the imposed and the ordained that prevails in hierarchical organizations.

It may be wondered how consistency and predictability of decision making can be preserved within such a single echelon of authority. Characteristic instruments are again voluntary adjustment and harmonization of otherwise independent activity: coordinate officials can convene and adopt common guidelines or standards in certain spheres of their jurisdictions. It is also true that regulation imposed from without on the official apparatus (e.g., legislation) can contribute to uniformity of decision making, although the impact of such regulation should not be exaggerated. Decision makers who are free from superior controls retain "the discretion to disobey"[11] or to nullify the regulation's mandate.

No doubt, all such devices for ensuring unity seem weak and inefficient to a believer in hierarchical ordering. But it should not be assumed that the desire for order is identical in hierarchical and coordinate organizations. To begin with, the process of taking consistent positions is not exactly parallel, so that the very *possibility* of decision making being consistent is assessed divergently in the two settings. Consider that, in contrast to the hierarchical apparatus, all decision makers in a horizontal configuration of authority remain close to the concrete, factual situations of life. As they make their way through the thickets of detail, they are driven to make fine distinctions. Seldom are two cases alike; identity is elusive, and divergent dispositions can easily be justified. What is lacking is the hierarchical distance, capable of generating a remote, bird's-eye view that absorbs so much situational detail that simple ordering schemes can be fashioned, and rough similarities and differences easily identified. But there is more. A cast of mind that aspires to the ideal of coordination must be prepared to tolerate inconsistencies—and a considerable degree of uncertainty—more readily than one attached to the hierarchical vision of authority. A certain amount of disorder must be accepted as the price of the fundamental commitment to a wider distribution of power.[12]

I shall now turn from an ideal of extreme coordinate apparatus for justice and introduce a modicum of subordination in order to come closer to existing judicial organizations. In this modified environment, the first level of authority continues to set the tone: vertical ordering, by voluntary transfer or otherwise, is mild and only sporadically exercised. Original decision makers are like Olympian gods—free and powerful, albeit loosely subordinate to Zeus: positions of sub- and superordination are not sharply delineated; higher and lower officials are essentially homologues with similar prestige and power. Indeed, they can be the same persons changing roles. The absence of distinctive rank removes pressure for submission generated by the prospect of hierarchical promotion and demotion: one is not climbing up or down a ladder. Superior audits are exceptional events, and under lay authority, also an unsystematic enterprise. In consequence, the whole apparatus of justice is permeated by attitudes characteristic of the original decision makers. There are few pressures to simplify decision making and to disregard particulars for the purpose of making the tasks of audit and review easier. I shall later examine not only the procedural implications of pure

11. See S. Kadish and R. Kadish, "On Justified Rule Departures by Officials," 59 *Calif. L. Rev.* 905, 925 (1971).

12. Observe also that ad hoc lay officials have no time to acquire the career bureaucrat's sense of continuity, so important for the capacity to detect inconsistencies. To assume that notions of order and tolerance of disorder are constants across judicial apparatuses is a mortal sin of the comparativist. Warnings against this assumption, which obscures so much comparative discourse, shall be one of the leitmotifs of this study, a caveat to be repeated at its conclusion.

coordinate structures, but also the marks that such an "Olympian," loose hierarchization of officials leaves on procedural arrangements.

Before turning to the last aspect of the coordinate ideal of authority, I would observe a characteristic impact of conjoining its first two aspects. When lay officialdom is placed in a horizontal order, a striking contrast with the hierarchical apparatus of authority emerges. While the latter is characterized by separation of functions (owing to professionalization) and also by the fusion of power at the top (owing to strict vertical ordering), the coordinate apparatus is characterized by fusion of functions (owing to the *absence* of professionalization) and also by wide dispersal of power (owing to horizontal distribution of authority). Furthermore, much as fragmentation of authority within a judicial organization can lead to redundancies and jurisdictional overlaps, so the fusion of functions can lead to the blending of administrative, legislative, and strictly judicial activities.

Substantive Justice

The coordinate ideal rejects any approach to decision making that would require officials to apply standards divorced from prevailing ethical, political, or religious norms, or would compel them to reach results unsupported by common sense. In other words, "technical" approaches to decision making appear undesirable—a deviation from the ideal situation. But the mixture of undifferentiated community standards which coordinate officials apply should not always be identified with the *nomos* generally prevailing in society. While such identification is possible, especially in communities organized around values immemorially posited, an alternative possibility is that officials be guided by the values and policies of a ruling elite or group. In the latter case, decision-making standards need not mirror widespread social convictions and expectations, but may rather reflect precepts of "the good life" shared by only a narrow elite. Rather than sanctioning inherited practice, decisions can be inspired by the elite's vision of a better society, or by its propulsive *rêve de société*, believed capable of radically transforming social relations. [13] Hereafter, when I begin to combine an activist vision of justice with the coordinate judicial apparatus, this latter possibility must be remembered.

It will be convenient to use a unifying term for the characteristic mélange of decisional standards of coordinate officials, in which practical common sense and prudence mix with ethical, political, or religious norms. I shall refer to this complex mixture under the collective term *substantive justice*, wherein the adjec-

13. One historical illustration of this possibility is the reaction in German lands to the transforming spirit of "rationalization" that began to radiate from the Church of Rome in the late eleventh century, undermining older medieval forms of justice. No longer were judgments based on unreflected tradition of the German communities: new "oracles of the law" became members of an elite (*scabini*) whose "rationalizing" views were integrated into the administration of justice. See F. Wieacker, *Privatrechtsgeschichte der Neuzeit*, 2d ed., 112 (Göttingen, 1967).

tive indicates hostility toward the more formal models of decision making. It stands to reason that this mélange carries a heavy load of unreconciled group values and objectives. Standards of substantive justice are open-ended, and can be only imperfectly embodied in textually fixed rules. Like folk poetry or jazz music, they are subtly betrayed if forced into rigid notational systems. Quite naturally, those provisions that purport to codify precepts of substantive justice employ vague terms such as "reasonable" or "fair," terms which allude to old unwritten and amorphous community standards. However, imperfect expression in terms of rules does not mean that the hall of coordinate judicial apparatus is always dimly lit: decisions need not be totally unpredictable, nor incapable of justification in terms of rational discourse. Instead, their transparence depends on the clarity of consensus in the community or in the dominant group. To take an elementary example, a provision that refers to "obscenity" or to "reckless driving" is textually vague, but can have a clear meaning in a homogeneous community—or on its highways. On the whole, however, an officialdom oriented to substantive justice cannot aspire to the degree of firm predictability that could be achieved if technocratic or legalistic models of decision making were adopted. Nor is such predictability likely to be desired in an apparatus composed of horizontally arranged lay officials.

There is no inherent necessity that community norms be applied by lay officials: indeed, career bureaucrats can also be instructed to make decisions according to norms prevailing in a community. But where this occurs, the apparatus of justice may be torn by tensions. A body of knowledge developed by professionals may conflict with substantive justice. Nor is there a necessary connection between lay officialdom and the application of community norms; decision makers can be given ad hoc instructions in the relevant fragments of a technical discipline. But a tension again arises: laymen dislike being bound by technical criteria, not only because they do not always understand them, but also because such criteria may dictate results at odds with their ideas about the appropriate solution of the case—ideas likely to be generated by feelings about substantive justice. If external pressures nevertheless impose a degree of legalism on coordinate structures, the kinship of these structures with pragmatic legalism is far closer than their kinship with logical legalism. This is because the legalist of the pragmatic persuasion and the layman attached to substantive justice both demand close attention to concrete particulars. To both, *le bon Dieu est dans le détail*. On the other hand, the regulation that appeals to logical legalists is alien to laymen. It displays insensitivity to the singularity of human drama, and its capacity to assure principled decision making leaves laymen unimpressed. They are likely to prefer warm confusion to cool consistency.

A more harmonious vision of coordinate authority appears as one envisages an organization of lay officials applying standards of substantive justice rather than an organization of these officials using technical norms. And in this vision of authority, vague standards of substantive justice combine with the absence of hierarchical supervision to ensure that the theme of official discretion becomes the essential accompaniment of coordinate judicial organization.

iv. THE HIERARCHICAL AND THE COORDINATE IDEALS IN HISTORICAL CONTEXT

Having defined the requisite categories and outlined two ideals of officialdom, I might now begin to spin out their implications for procedural form. Yet this abstract discussion must be interrupted for an explanation, necessary at this point. Narrow focus on two particular structures of authority has been justified, in part, by claiming that these two patterns capture—albeit in exaggerated form—the most striking differences between the traditional judicial organizations on the continent of Europe and in Anglo-American lands. The preceding depiction of the two structures of authority has been interspersed with more or less thinly veiled allusions to Continental and common-law jurisdictions. The time has come to offer support for these implicit claims, which perhaps have taxed the reader's credulity: *hic Rhodus hic salta*. To this end I shall attempt a swift retrospect of centuries of historical development. Of course, the selectivity required by such a compressed excursus must be drastic, but I shall make an effort to center throughout on issues widely regarded by comparativists as important to the development of the Continental and the Anglo-American administrations of justice. In this sense, then, my selection of data, while it may appear arbitrary to some, will not be unexpected to cognoscenti. However, the following rearrangement of known data in new ways as suggested by my analytical categories will be unusual. Whenever possible I shall try to imagine how a development in one setting would appear in the perspective of a visitor from the other. This will be done in order to avoid conventional reassessment of known events, reassessment imprisoned by either a parochial Continental or a parochial Anglo-American viewpoint.

Continental Machinery of Justice

Tracing the genesis of the Continental apparatus of justice[14] does not require consideration of the judicial bureaucratization in Roman-Byzantine antiquity. It will suffice to begin with the fresh outbreak of bureaucratization in the late eleventh century when the movement toward unity within the Roman Catholic church gained momentum. What was then the dominant view on the proper ordering of authority in the church? As expressed by another product of that century—the upward swing of the Gothic cathedral—the ordering was to be pyramidal and hierarchical. The very term *hierarchia*, unknown to classical Greek,[15] was coined by a Syrian monk to express the perfect structure of celestial government as well as the ideal organization of ecclesiastical authority. It is thus quite unsurprising that the successful drive of the church toward greater unity produced a hierarchical structure of its officials with the pope at the top of the pyramid of authority.

14. I speak loosely of the European continent; Scandinavian lands and parts of Eastern Europe were only marginally, or quite recently, affected by developments I discuss in this section.
15. See W. Ullmann, *Law and Politics in the Middle Ages*, 230 (1975). Ranks of super- and subordination were discussed in different terms by Aristotle and other Greek philosophers.

In the legal literature of the period there is hardly a theme more fascinating, none more intensely relevant to the administration of justice, than the theme of the *officium judicis*—the office of the judge. It is under this rubric that one finds the first clear traces of the separation of the office from the person who exercises its powers. The prevailing opinion was that private and official knowledge should not mix, and that decision making was to be based only on officially acquired information. The judge was expected to keep separate what he knew as a person (*ut homo*) and what he had learned in the performance of official duties (*ut judex*).[16] Under the influence of this theory, adjudicative and testimonial functions were separated in the courts of the church as early as the twelfth century—a striking fact in comparison with the English jury, as it functioned well into the sixteenth century.

At this early period the view also prevailed that judicial administration called for special expertise, not only for the resolution of legal issues, but also for fact-finding activities. The debate with the unknown which is implicit in fact-finding was not to be left to the guess of the untutored: complicated rules were devised, for example, for the weighing of evidence (legal proof). Quite naturally, the participation of laymen in adjudication appeared less and less desirable. Whenever possible, these *judices idiotae* (in the jargon of the period) were replaced by trained professionals or required to seek advice from the learned. Within the corps of permanent ecclesiastical officials, there were unmistakable signs of functional differentiation: special investigators were attached to courts, and the forerunners of public prosecutors appeared (*promotores fidei*).[17]

The hierarchical ordering of authority implied reliance on a comprehensive and regular system of appellate review, almost totally unknown to medieval society, and indeed to England until the end of the nineteenth century.[18] So important was superior review that it was often doubted whether city ordinances or local customs could validly abrogate the right to appeal. Officials who frustrated the transfer of cases to higher authority were in some instances liable to serious punishment.[19]

What special knowledge was required to guide officials? Decisional standards were to be found in scattered texts of canon law, such as conciliar decrees or

16. On the separation of private and official knowledge in the administration of justice of the period, see K. W. Nörr, *Zur Stellung des Richters im gelehrten Prozess der Frühzeit*, 43, 71 (München, 1967). For one spillover effect of the ecclesiastical theory of *officium* on secular political theory, see E. H. Kantorowicz, *The King's Two Bodies: A Study in Medieval Political Theology*, 5, 13 (1957).

17. On pristine forms of the ecclesiastical process with the participation of the *promotor fidei*, see C. Lefèbre, *Juges et Savants en Europe*, 22 Ephemerides Juris Canonici, 76, 96 (1966). On the rise of other specialized officials (*auditores*, investigators, etc.), see id., 102. See also *infra*, ch. 5, n. 15.

18. It is fair to say that appeals were reinvented in the twelfth century. The term *reinvented* applies because the origin of superior review in Europe goes back to the Roman-Byzantine idea that authority is exercised by delegation from the emperor. See T. Mommsen, *Römisches Strafrecht*, 980 (Leipzig, 1899). The continuity of development was interrupted in the Middle Ages when the main remedy against adverse judgment was to sue the judge before his lord in separate proceedings. For the absence of regular review in England, see *infra*, ch. 2, n. 22.

19. See H. de Marsiliis, *Consilia et Singularia Omnia*, vol. 2, *Consilium 84*, 11 (London, 1537).

papal pronouncements, and to some degree, also in the sixth-century compilation of Roman law by the Byzantine emperor Justinian. Most important for our purposes is the approach that developed toward these texts. Of course, these texts, dating from different periods and social settings and inspired by diverse worldviews and social policies, were more often than not widely discordant. But the regnant philosophy was that all such disharmonies and apparent inconsistencies were only superficial, and that a rational order lay close beneath the surface waiting to be discovered. The attitude thus developed that the search for the right solution implied reliance on textual analysis and logical penetration of its meaning. Law came increasingly to be regarded as a self-contained, or closed system— a "science."

The origin of this approach to law—I have termed it logical legalism—is usually attributed to the rise of Italian universities in the late eleventh century. They provided an ambience where schoolmen, insulated from the messy details and responsibilities of legal practice, could indulge in the luxury of treating texts of classical antiquity with dispassionate erudition as objects of intellectual inquiry. But it must not be overlooked that students of canon law had also engaged in the activity of seeking "concordances" among "discordant canons" by means of an essentially similar method of logical analysis. Their activity was motivated not by the desire to confect theories or to deliver coherent lectures but by the eminently practical purpose of assisting high ecclesiastical authority in running its emerging apparatus.[20] One might thus conjecture that a variety of logical legalism—albeit not distilled so much from the grapes of Roman-Byzantine law—would have emerged within the church even in the absence of the undeniable contribution of academic lawyers (*legistae*). As it is, the birth of the typically Continental approach to law may have been overdetermined by the confluence of both academic and hierarchical distance from the immediate complexities of decision making. This approach to law conjures up not only the schoolman's lamp but also the quiet shuffling of documents by officials at the top of the pyramid of authority.

Before we leave the period in which distinctive contours of the Continental machinery of justice first begin to appear, it should be emphasized that many features which I have incorporated into the hierarchical ideal were less than fully developed in the ecclesiastical judicial organization of the period. It would be both anachronistic and inaccurate to attribute rigid institutional thinking or inflexible legalism to judicial authority in the waning Middle Ages. As befits a system of

20. An excellent account of the emergence of this approach can be found in H. Berman, *Law and Revolution,* 120–85 (1983). Scholarly ordering of the law was especially influential in the sphere of procedure, where legal imagination was constrained by venerated texts of antiquity much less than in substantive law. The learned *summae* and treatises on various procedural problems that began to appear in the twelfth century (mainly by canon lawyers) were truly unequaled in prior legal history, and were to have no real counterpart in England. See M. Damaska, "How Did It All Begin?" 94 *Yale L.J.* 1807, 1816 (1985). From the standpoint of modern conceptions, the "systemic" efforts of early legal scholars should not be exaggerated. While they ordered the law by developing abstract concepts, they seldom used these concepts as building blocks to construct a systematically interrelated body of law on the pattern of seventeenth-century Continental lawyers. See H. Coing, *Geschichte und Bedeutung des Systemgedankens in der Rechtswissenschaft* (Frankfurt, 1956).

sacred law, judges of the church were expected to temper the rigor of rules with considerations dictated by conscience (*aequitas, arbitrium*). Yet the resulting dispensation from rigidity should not be interpreted as an apostatic deviance of ecclesiastical authority into unstructured and unreviewable discretion: departures from the norm had to be exercised "in conformity with reason" and were subject to review by superiors.[21]

The next step in the development of the Continental judicial organization was taken by the kings of France. Starting in the thirteenth century, the Capetians began to build a stratified corps of professional officials better to assert and extend royal power. Instead of entrusting local potentates with independent authority, they chose to dispatch their own agents to perform a variety of local functions. Often of lowly origin and dependent on the king for their livelihood, these royal officers were loyal to the center and relatively immune from local pressures. Divided into ranks, they were interconnected by a system of review: appeals from *prévôts* went to the bailiffs and from the bailiffs to the central royal authority. The resulting administrative apparatus became quite popular as a model for aspiring princes in other Continental lands.

There were also significant developments in the chief court of the land, the Parlement of Paris, in which trained lawyers gradually displaced magnates of the realm as decision makers.[22] Following the lead of ecclesiastical judicial organization, the principal task of this high court became the review of decisions rendered by inferior judicial authority, including a mosaic of seigneurial courts.[23] But even when the Parlement exercised original jurisdiction, the judges came to be removed from activities associated with trials (such as proof taking, for example), and were deprived of the fresh scrutiny characteristic of original decision making. The material needed for decision was gathered in documentary form and neatly arranged for decision makers by a variety of specialized judicial officials.[24] One among them, charged with safeguarding the royal interest, ultimately became the public (state) prosecutor, an office widely copied in other lands.[25] Functional differentiation affected the decision making panel as well: one judge was assigned to sift through documents and report to his colleagues about the case. Following

21. See N. Horn, *Aequitas in den Lehren des Baldus,* 153 (1968). Pronounced hostility toward unreviewable discretion and its association with tyranny clearly surfaces in the fourteenth-century work of the famous jurist Bartolus. See Bartolus, *Opera Omnia,* vol. 11, 326 (Basle, 1588).

22. The history of this displacement is recounted in great detail and with little sympathy for lawyers by the duke of Saint-Simon in his memoirs. See *Historical Memoir of the Duc de Saint-Simon,* ed. and trans. L. Norton, vol. 2, 367–71 (1968).

23. See M. Fournier, *Histoire du Droit d'Appel,* 231–32 (Paris, 1881).

24. In contrast to England where central courts would formulate issues and let the countryside render the verdict, the parlement had official investigators perform their *enquêtes* locally, reserving the power for decision making to itself. See also J. P. Dawson, *A History of Lay Judges,* 53–60 (1960).

25. It is often said that the forerunner of the modern public prosecutor was the French *procureur de roi,* who then influenced the church's *promotor* or *procurator fiascalis.* See, e.g., P. Hinschius, *System des Katholischen Kirchenrechts,* vol. 6, 12, n. 2 (Graz, 1959). In fact, a promotor appears in ecclesiastical proceedings at least at the time of Tancredus in the twelfth century. See Lefèbre, *supra,* n. 17, 104. The French *procureur général* developed his own hierarchical organization, known metonymically as the *parquet.*

the rendition of the decision, based in important ways on his report, the *rapporteur* was required to draft the judgment of the court. (Incidentally, the style of the judgment became increasingly formal, calling for special initiation and training). In the course of the fourteenth century a clearly defined ranking of officials emerged within the parlement, and with it also the possibility of internal appeals. In short, emergent processes of hierarchical bureaucratization were unmistakable.

But it was not until the strengthening of princely absolutism in the sixteenth and seventeenth centuries that centralized bureaucracies started to dominate the governmental apparatus in the influential Continental countries. Even language was now affected by pressures toward regimentation. Official discourse was to be conducted in rigidly structured speech forms, dry, Latinate, and "abstract" in comparison with the colloquial private idiom.[26] The idea of impersonal office was extended to the very heart of government. Despite the famous later dictum of Louis XIV, "*l'état c'est moi,*" it is in this period that the idea of the state became detachable from the personal status of the ruler and converted into an institutionalized (impersonal) locus of allegiance.[27]

In the great majority of Continental countries judicial officials became career professionals. Lay participation in the legal process, where it survived at all, was reduced to insignificance or to a ritual. No longer were judicial functionaries, now organized into a hierarchy, perceived as unrelated to the center of state power. And unlike the judges of the church, secular adjudicators were no longer permitted to mold ordinances and other legal sources to conform to their conscience. The integrity of a powerful central authority was thought to require strict governance by rules. Highly placed judges found the resulting shrinkage of discretionary space quite acceptable: they became accustomed to deciding on the basis of orderly documents that screened out "messy" situational and personal nuances likely to exert pressure toward leeway in decision making. As a bureaucratic maxim of the period asserted, *quod non est in actis non est in mundo* ("what is not in the file does not exist").

The attachment to rules also affected attitudes toward judicial precedent. Decisions of high courts, whether binding or not, were not treated as exemplars of how a life situation had been resolved in the past so that the case sub judice could be matched with these examples of earlier decision making.[28] Rather, what

26. On the seventeenth-century regimentation of the French language, see G. Steiner, *After Babel*, 365 (1975).

27. On the contribution of impersonal bureaucratic thinking to the emergence of the modern concept of the state, see P. Frölich, *1789, die grosse Zeitwende: Von der Bürokratie des Absolutismus zum Parlament der Revolution* (Frankfurt, 1957).

28. When the role of precedents is discussed comparatively, the question of whether they are formally binding or not comes up so quickly that one loses sight of varying conceptions of what "precedent" means. Anglo-American and Continental legal cultures probably differ more in how they *conceive* of "precedents" than in the actual binding force of prior adjudication. The attitude toward decisions that seeks symmetry of life situations (a pragmatically legalistic approach in terms of our categories) is more characteristic of Anglo-American than Continental courts. That continental courts of last resort were an influential authority in several legal systems of the ancien régime is often ignored. See G. Gorla, "La communis opinio totius orbis," in M. Cappelletti, ed., *New Perspectives for a Common Law of Europe*, 45 (1978).

the judge was looking for in the "precedent" was a rulelike pronouncement of higher authority, the facts of the case stripped to their shadows. Thus what conventional common-law doctrine would devalue as mere dictum was welcome precisely because it stood independent of the concrete constellation of facts in the case. Montesquieu perfectly expressed this "logically legalistic" Continental attitude toward precedent by asserting that prior judgments are merely a "more precise text of the law."[29] In sum, long before the French Revolution the Continental judicial apparatus came to incorporate features I have associated with the hierarchical ideal. The administration of justice was permeated by attitudes springing from professionalized decision makers, saturated by ramifications of multilayered authority, and redolent with logical legalism.

This characterization may be challenged on the ground that the legal system in countries of the ancien régime remained imperfectly centralized. It is well known that even in absolutist France, the most important court—the Parlement of Paris—shared supreme judicial authority with provincial parlements. Voltaire's hyperbolic lament, directed at this feature of the legal landscape, became famous: "There are as many interpretations of the law as there are cities" (il y ait autant des jurisprudences que de villes). Remnants of feudal privilege and practice, such as the sale of judicial offices, weakened the dependence of judicial functionaries on the center of state power: judges were not yet les employées. Substantive law was also not yet unified: a kaleidoscope of local customs continued as an important source of legal authority.

That said, however, a strong attachment of the judicial apparatus to hierarchical bureaucratization cannot be denied. At this point, a view from across the channel would be revealing, but because I shall turn to the English machinery of justice only in the next section, let it suffice for the moment to register the impression of a well traveled sixteenth-century Englishman, Thomas Starkey. Although the English are said to have centralized their legal system as early as the Angevin rule, Starkey still found his own law "without order and end," comparing it unfavorably with the orderly "civil law" on the Continent.[30] Even in the absence of a comparative perspective this curious impression can be partially explained: it can be demonstrated that incomplete centralization of judicial administration in Continental lands detracted little from a strong commitment to the ordering of the law and the hierarchization of the judiciary.

Much as the existence of a single central forum within a country does not presuppose rigid judicial hierarchization, so the existence of several independent tribunals does not rule it out. High Continental courts first and foremost exercised appellate jurisdiction. They were located on top of small judicial hierarchies, exercising strong overall leadership over the lower judiciary. Moreover, it would be a mistake to imagine local coutumes as a disorderly and amorphous agglomeration of poorly articulated norms. As of the fifteenth century, Continental

29. "Les jugements ne soient jamais qu'un texte plus precis de la loi." De l'esprit des lois, Liv. 11, ch. 6.

30. See T. Starkey, A Dialogue between Reginald Pole and Thomas Lupset, Burton ed., 173 (London, 1948).

princes—primarily the kings of France—insisted that customs be drawn up in writing, and sometimes even provided elaborate formal procedures for the promulgation of *coutumiers*.[31] Continental legal scholarship (legal science) supplied a categorical scheme for simplifying and organizing customary rules, so that the internal arrangement of coutumiers did not vary greatly and lawyers could find their way in them with relative ease.[32] In fact, one can discern in this drive to written texts more than faint heralds of the codification movement that would sweep Continental countries at a later period. Already in seventeenth-century France it seemed fashionable to seek "principles" common to various local customs, so that *une seule coutume* could ultimately be promulgated by the king.[33] And it is only a short step from this search for unifying principles to the attitudes that generated the classical Continental codifications—those crowning achievements of Continental logical legalism. What was common to both movements was the belief that society is governed by a few unalterable principles from which clear rules can be deduced so that the law can be made surveyable. Both movements shared the belief that legal decision making can be organized as a process of relating context-free rules to clear facts. In this connection, it is noteworthy that the first codifications on the Continent antedated the nouveau régime: they were enacted by absolutist rulers in German lands who desired clear guidance for their judicial bureaucracies.

In assessing the disunity of the law during the ancien régime there is another consideration that deserves mention: as of the sixteenth century, with the decline of the *denunciatio canonica*, there was no true counterpart in Continental legal systems to the split between law and equity that continued to characterize the English legal landscape. It would seem that an apparatus of justice attached to order is disturbed less by the plurality of sources from which to choose the standard for a stable decision than by the possibility of one court of last resort destabilizing the decisions of the other. The law during the ancien régime did not lack a "stable ground to lean unto," as the situation in their own country was diagnosed by some Englishmen familiar with Continental (civil) law.[34]

31. See A. Esmain, *Cours élémentaire du droit français*, 2d ed., 750 (Paris, 1895). It is also true that kings would sometimes determine which customs were applicable over what areas (F. Olivier-Martin, *Histoire du droit français des origines à la révolution*, 114 [Paris, 1948]).

32. One frequent blueprint was a part of Justinian's codification containing a systematic treatment of Roman law for educational purposes. See A. Watson, *The Making of Civil Law*, 66 (1981). The strong influence of the scholarly "Roman" approach to analysis of legal problems was deplored by believers in the native French legal tradition. It is attested, for example, in Montaigne's laments against the encroachments of "Roman law," and it found its classic expression in Hotman's *Antitribonian*.

33. Codification as an act of sovereign ruler was first clearly spelled out in the sixteenth century by Jean Bodin. See Q. Skinner, *Foundations of Modern Political Thought*, vol. 2, 289 (1978). On the search for "a single custom," see P. Viollet, *Précis des Institutions Politiques et Administratives de la France*, vol. 1, 173 (Paris, 1890).

34. Starkey, *supra*, n. 30. In assessing the author's diagnosis of Continental law as very orderly, one must bear in mind that while Starkey studied law in a Continental law school, he had no practical experience. Even allowing for distortion stemming from familiarity with only "professorial" law, there is yet a measure of truth in his comparative observations, to which I shall return in the next section.

The growth of governmental centralization after the French Revolution is known too well to need rehearsal here. After a brief prelude, the plurality of legal orders was abolished and courts too became unified. The hierarchical features of the inherited judicial apparatus remained essentially intact, although some aspects of this hierarchization, such as the role of the chief judge, now elude parochial Continental vision—an eye examining itself.[35] But certain reforms inaugurated in the electric air of those turbulent times had the potential to undermine or seriously weaken the bureaucratic hierarchical structure of judicial authority. Although judges now became *les employées,* they were accorded special status among civil servants, a status entailing a characteristic loosening of the chain of hierarchical command. Legal opinions of superior courts were proclaimed to be not binding on subordinate judges, even on remand of a case to the court below for reconsideration. More conspicuous was the injection of a lay component into adjudication: while civil justice remained as before the exclusive province of professional judges, their monopoly was broken in the trial of most serious criminal offenses. A lay jury, transplanted from England, came to share decision making powers with three professionals.

No matter how significant these reforms may have been in some respects, their potential to destabilize judicial hierarchies, or to curb the dominance of professionals, has never been fulfilled. Native bureaucratic forces soon reacted against this transplanted organ, endeavoring to expel or at least to neutralize the foreign body. The belief continued to prevail that administration of justice is a sphere of specialized practice in which vigorous assertion of untutored views equals arrogance. The main form of lay participation in criminal cases came to be a mixed bench, on which lay and professional elements sit and decide jointly and on which the professional component exercises decisive influence.[36]

Reforms that sought to loosen the chain of hierarchical rank have fared not much better. While formally free to disregard legal opinions of their superiors, judges continued to look to high courts for guidance. Although many factors conspired to preserve this deference to superiors, the attitude can most easily be explained as caused and nourished by recruitment, training, and promotion policies, all congenial to hierarchical organizations. Typically, the beginning of a career on the bench was also the beginning of the professional career for a young lawyer, fresh from a period of internship in the judicial apparatus. Rarely was a judge someone entering a second career. The first appointment (or election) was to the lowest court, a position carrying little prestige, and promotion depended at

35. The "supervisory powers" of the chief judge in some Continental systems (e.g., West Germany) can include criticism of his judges for poor preparation of cases for trial or disqualification of his judges for bias. While perfectly normal in the Continental legal tradition, such powers easily appear excessive to the Anglo-American judiciary.

36. Thus problems of controlling an independent lay panel which decides sitting alone are absent from the Continental administration of justice. On empirical studies confirming general impressions about the limited influence of lay assessors on decision making in mixed panels, see M. Damaška, "Structures of Authority and Comparative Criminal Procedure," 84 *Yale L.J.* 480, 498 (1975).

least in part on the approval of those who regularly reviewed lower courts' decisions. In this situation it is hardly surprising that assertion of independence on the part of lower judiciary, even where formally possible, remained quite aberrational. Firmly tied to the mast of civil service, lower judges could hear the seductive music of freedom as Ulysses heard the singing of the sirens.[37]

In a somewhat roundabout and latent fashion, the very doctrine of judicial freedom from higher legal opinion has found its spiritual home in the environment of logically legalistic officials: it requires the exaltation of context-free norms and belief that norm creation and norm application can be sharply separated. I shall briefly suggest the connection. Even prior to the revolution, it was widely believed by Continental judicial authorities that normative standards could be developed with such clarity and precision that their application to individual cases would require a mere "subsumption" of facts to norm with no further elaboration (interpretation) on the part of the adjudicator. However, while the old regime did not oppose the unabashed creation of norms by the apex of the judicial pyramids (arrêts de règlement), the revolutionary doctrine of separation of powers called for a change. The judicial branch was now to be limited to norm application and completely forbidden to intrude upon the policy-making function of the legislature. In theory, courts were prohibited even such interstitial creativity as is required by the interpretation of statutes: the judge was to be only la bouche (the mouthpiece), not le cerveau (the brains), of the law.[38] Now if law creation is ultra vires for the judiciary, it follows that there can be no hierarchical ranking of judges with respect to this issue: all are equally—and solely—subordinate to the legislator.[39] And while the higher court can

37. It is worth noting that a doctrine of formally binding precedent would be far more rigid in Continental than in the common-law institutional framework. The primary reason is not so much the greater spirit of obeisance to superiors in the former than in the latter as the different understanding of precedent. See supra, nn. 28–29 and accompanying text. The Continental judge does not weigh the symmetry of factual situations which, under the aegis of stare decisis, permits fine distinctions and thus assures the flexible growth of the law. Instead he seeks ever more concrete rules in prior decisions, disregarding the enveloping factual context. Assuming the binding nature of this progressive norm concretization, decisional standards would in time become intolerably rigid, each new decision a drop in the formation of an ever longer stalactite of norms. In short, while a judicial organization composed of loosely hierarchical judges may require a doctrine of binding precedent as an internal ideological stabilizer, a hierarchical career judiciary may well be better off without it.

38. In 1790, while the tocsin of the revolution was still sounding, two decrees of the Assembly forbade courts any interpretation of laws: where uncertain about the import of legislation, judges were expected to refer the matter to the lawmakers. Similar unrealistic bans on judicial interpretation were imposed by absolutist rulers from Justinian to Frederick II of Prussia to Joseph II of Austria. For lucid comments, see F. Neumann, The Democratic and the Authoritarian State, 38, 141 (1957). It hardly needs saying that all such prohibitions were of short duration.

39. The doctrine that judges are never bound by internal (judicial) interpretation of the law was soon abandoned with respect to high courts. These courts traditionally had a large number of judges divided into specialized sections, each section further subdivided into numerous panels. Thus the danger was always present that separate panels would deliver themselves of conflicting opinions on the same point of law. To prevent this, various mechanisms were developed to ensure internal consistency, one of which deviated from the above doctrine: if a panel of the court of last resort (often also a panel of an intermediate appellate court) wished to deviate from an opinion already announced

disagree with the court below on the interpretation of a rule, it cannot require adherence to its views; the strength of its legal pronouncement derives solely from supporting arguments, and it is worth only as much as can be proven by reason (*tantum valet quantum ratio probat*). As could be predicted, this revolutionary ideology not only failed to destroy respect for the legal opinions of higher judicial authority, but also failed to discourage Continental judges from self-consciously engaging in norm-creating activity. However, in keeping with the hierarchical structure of authority, such conspicuous norm-generating judicial activity remained the province of higher courts.

The turn of century has ushered in a serious weakening of logical legalism, with corresponding changes in the tone of judicial bureaucracy.[40] Despite all such changes, the Continental judicial apparatus has nevertheless retained a very pronounced bureaucratic hierarchical flavor, especially when observed from the common-law perspective.

Anglo-American Machinery of Justice

The relationship between the traditional Anglo-American apparatus of justice and the coordinate ideal may seem much more problematic than the relationship between the hierarchical ideal and Continental judicial organization. But it will suffice to change the usual foci of attention only slightly in order to realize that those features that characterize Anglo-American judicial organizations—when these organizations are observed from the Continental mainland—can meaningfully be expressed as a strong affinity toward the values and attitudes I have conceptualized in the coordinate ideal of authority.

Let us begin with the ideal's preference for lay decision makers. English polity has always manifested a close collaboration in power among well-to-do classes.[41] The Norman kings who began to build (on Anglo-Saxon foundations) a relatively sophisticated administration as early as the twelfth century left important governmental functions in the hands of local gentry, so that these local potentates, although acting upon royal commission, dispensed justice largely free from royal supervision and interference. Mechanisms of regular superior review, so important to the ecclesiastical authority, did not evolve. In central royal courts, judges acted in partnership with local juries composed of members of the landowning class. The working of the English adjudicative centaur—part profes-

---

by any panel of the supreme court, the matter had to be certified to a superpanel for a decision binding on all judges of the supreme court. Ironically, the doctrine of "sole" subjection to the law continued to apply only to trial judges.

40. For a perceptive analysis of these changes, see N. Lühmann, *Rechtssystem und Rechtsdogmatik*, 11–14 (1974); G. Schmid and H. Treiber, *Bürokratie und Politik*, 204–24 (München, 1975). The infusion of broad political considerations, necessitated by expanding judicial review of the constitutionality of statutes, was quite damaging to the "closeness" of the logically legalist universe.

41. There is a vast literature on this topic. See, e.g., P. Anderson, *Lineages of the Absolutist State*, 115–16 (1974); M. Bloch, *Feudal Society*, vol. 2, 331, 424 (1961); J. R. Strayer, *On the Medieval Origins of the Modern State*, 36–37, 47 (1968).

sional, part lay—is usually expressed by saying that the adjudicative function was in the hands of the judge who took his facts from the jury.[42] But is this the way in which the allocation of functions would appear through the lens of Continental legal scholars? By the thirteenth century, the essence of judicial activity was identified with the process of relating law to ascertained facts, and accurate fact determination (*ventilatio veritatis*) became an indispensable part of the judicial office (*officium judicis*).[43] From the Continental perspective, then, the English royal judge would appear to be more like the moderator of a judicial conference, or perhaps a supervisor of fair proceedings, the announcer of their outcome and the enforcer of judgments, rather than the quintessential decision maker. In this perspective, the real adjudicators would seem to be the jurors. This interpretation would remain unchanged even if a Continental observer were informed that royal judges could pressure jurors to decide a case in a particular fashion. There were precedents for this on the Continent: Carolingian barons too could manipulate a court, and yet "the court passed the judgment not the Lord." Sir Thomas Smith, trying in the sixteenth century to explain the English mode of criminal trial to the French, was acutely aware of these long-standing divergent perspectives on the judicial office. "Judex is of us called the judge," he remarked, "but our fashion is so diverse that those who either condemne or acquite the man for guiltie or not guiltie are not called judges but twelve men."[44]

From the Continental standpoint, then, the real decision makers in the traditional English apparatus of justice were laymen—either justices of the peace or jurors. Having placed such significant powers in the hands of lay gentlemen, the English apparatus of justice failed to develop many features that I have earlier associated with bureaucratic structures. A telling example is the comparatively slow differentiation of functions, including such elemental matters as the separation of testimonial from adjudicative tasks. As late as the fifteenth century, Fortescue still celebrated the self-informing Angevin jury in which jurors could decide a case on the basis of their "private" knowledge of relevant facts, or on the

42. See, e.g., R. Pound, *The Spirit of the Common Law*, 170–71 (1921). The conventional analysis relates to the jury after its sixteenth-century transformations, but it also applies mutatis mutandis to the older, self-informing jury referred to in the text.

43. See, e.g., the opinion of the famous jurist Baldus de Ubaldis, as gathered from a conspectus of scattered relevant utterances in N. Horn, *supra*, n. 21, 140. It could even be claimed that in the early period it was more important for the judex to ascertain the true facts than it was for him to be a repository of legal knowledge; in complex cases he was expected to consult legal scholars (*juris periti*). But in the Roman Catholic church the emphasis on legal expertise emerged quite early. As of the second half of the twelfth century, bishops (*judices ordinarii*) would appoint as their "vicars" persons from their entourage who were learned in the law. See Lefèbre, *supra*, n. 17, 101. The view that "essential attributes" of judicial powers do not include fact-finding is still often proclaimed by American courts. For a recent example, see *Northern Pipeline Co. v. Marathon Pipeline Co.*, 458 U.S. 50 (1981).

44. See T. Smith, *De Republica Anglorum, Lib. II. Cap. 8*, ed. L. Alston, p. 66 (1960). Modern analysis subscribes to the view that jurors are more than mere fact finders, at least in a typical case where they deliver a general verdict. To return such a verdict facts and law must be related, that is, mental operations must be performed that are at once nonmechanical and essentially adjudicative.

basis of their own private inquiries.[45] It is no exaggeration to say that the English jury became a purely adjudicative body only after its sixteenth-century transformation from a group of neighbors and witnesses to a panel of disinterested persons to whom facts had to be proven in court.

Another example of delayed bureaucratization is the slow and imperfect separation of office from incumbent. Acting in the performance of their duties, English officials continued to be treated as ordinary people long after their Continental counterparts had acquired a special status. Thus while grievances came to be lodged against Continental *offices* (not their holders), English officials continued to be enjoined and mandamused in their personal capacities. Of course, they also exercised their authority in a highly "personalized" way, traces of which survive in the judicial apparatus of Anglo-American countries to the present day.[46] The uncertain line between public and private law enforcement is also related to the prebureaucratic English environment. Private individuals could sue at once in their private capacity and in the public interest (*qui tam* actions), or in the public interest alone (criminal prosecution in the name of the king), even as Continental judicial bureaucracies established a virtual monopoly of action in the public interest.[47] Another example of the interpenetration of official and private spheres is that members of the English bar could easily be enlisted ad hoc to serve as judges of the central courts.[48]

The distribution of authority in the traditional English judicial apparatus also deserves a fresh look: salient features of coordination may be obscured by undue emphasis on the centralization initiated by the Angevins. What tends to be lost from sight is that the disposition of most criminal cases remained in the hands of local justices of the peace, acting alone or in partnership with the local jury, with minimal interference from the central royal authority. Accordingly, an important sector of the administration of justice was a remarkable "essay in decentralization."[49] Only when attention is riveted by civil cases do central royal

45. J. Fortescue, *De Laudibus Legum Anglie, Cap. 26,* ed. S. Chimes, p. 62 (Cambridge, 1949). Much later, Sir Matthew Hale still defended the commingling of testimonial functions (private knowledge) with adjudicative responsibilities. See M. Hale, *The History of the Common Law of England,* Runnington 6th ed., 348, 353 (London, 1820).

46. The notion that judges owe institutional responsibility to the court is not nearly so strongly developed as it is among the Continental civil service judiciary. Nor has the idea taken hold in all Anglo-American countries that the court as a unit has spoken when a judge belonging to its bench has rendered his decision. For example, the denial of bail or of a stay by one American judge does not prevent his colleague on the *same* court from granting such relief.

47. On *qui tam* actions, see W. Holdsworth, *A History of English Law,* vol. 4, 355 (1924). Note that the English system of private prosecution was not limited to the victim of crime: any citizen could bring a criminal action on behalf of the Crown. Contemporaries were well aware of differences between England and Continental lands in the degree to which they tolerated private enforcement of criminal law. See W. Fulbecke, *A Parellele or Conference of the Civil Law, the Canon Law and the Common Law of this Realme of England,* 64–65 (London, 1618).

48. This enlistment, continuing into the present century, was facilitated by the fact that royal judges came to be selected from members of the bar.

49. See T. Plucknett, *A Concise History of the Common Law,* 5th ed., 169 (1956).

courts become as prominent as they are in conventional writing. But unlike the situation on the Continent, these courts were mainly exercising, or—more accurately—participating in the exercise of *original* jurisdiction. There was no clear rank among them: the same individuals moved in and out of various positions, serving different judicial bodies. Where the bringing of an appeal was possible, the appeal would go between courts at the same level (common pleas and king's bench) rather than from an inferior to a superior court. Some tribunals, such as the Court of Exchequer Chamber, were more like committees of parallel judges than a superior court.

Hence while it is true that the Norman kings launched a process of centralization before the Continental secular rulers did so, this precocious centralization, limited mainly to civil cases, was not achieved by way of hierarchical ordering of judicial authority. In short, it can be said that Angevin kings established a single layer of central courts for matters of greatest interest to the landowning class, leaving the rest to local nobility which never developed multi-layered tribunals. Thus the administration of justice was organized around a single plane of authority. Attitudes I have identified as characteristic of this pattern of judicial organization flourished; attitudes I have associated with the vertical ordering of the judiciary found no fertile soil in which to grow.

How could the necessary unity be maintained in this institutional framework? Thanks to the comparatively small scale of operations, royal judges formed a small, closely knit group, regularly engaging in informal consultations and exchange of views.[50] The occasional discord between parallel central courts was resolved in a typically coordinate style: undesirable decisions were not directly invalidated (as a superior court would do), but their enforcement was frustrated indirectly in a variety of ways (e.g., intercourt injunctions). Ironically, as notions of unitary sovereignty fully emerged in the sixteenth century, the center of English justice continued to embrace two separate normative systems—common law and equity—two voices in need of harmonization and adjustment.

There is little doubt that decision making by local justices of the peace was strongly influenced by prevailing community norms rather than by technical legal rules detached from their social matrix. Even if numerous manuals for lay justices are regarded as a variety of technical literature, it is difficult to imagine that the few substantive standards for decision making set out in them exercised a powerful influence on lay potentates whenever such standards deviated from prevailing notions of fairness, common sense, or similar considerations. The informality of proceedings and the absence of lawyers and of regular channels of review provided ample room for "discretionary" departure from instructions contained in the manuals. When one turns to view the central royal courts, however, the affinity of decision making with precepts of substantive justice seems highly problematic. True, the court of equity's stress on ethical values, its

---

50. On various techniques used to develop unity of law within royal courts, see M. Hale, *The History of the Common Law of England*, 251–52 (1820).

personal, almost confessional atmosphere, as well as its flexible remedies, bespeak an attachment to nontechnical decision making.[51] But what about the
operation of the celebrated common-law courts and the formidable technicalities
with which their operation is associated?

The search for an answer demands that we examine the function of the
technicalities generated by common lawyers. In the early period of the self-
informing jury, the principal business of lawyers was to formulate through the
mechanism of pleading the most appropriate questions to be addressed to the
decision maker—the lay jury. In their origin, then, the technicalities of common
law concerned the formation of issues rather than their resolution.[52] When juries
gradually ceased to be self-informing and facts had to be proven to the jurors in
court, an additional task emerged for lawyers—to the extent to which they were
allowed to participate in trial proceedings.[53] They began to control the flow of
information to the jury, and to ensure that the evidence was sufficient to warrant
submission of an issue to them. It is clear that rules regulating this activity were
again addressed to matters *preceding* actual adjudication rather than to adjudication directly. In moving from the vestibule to the penetralia of decision making,
the proper question to ask is what standards guided the *jury* in returning their
verdict, rather than to inquire what rules controlled the behavior of *lawyers*.
When the inquiry is refocused in this way, it becomes apparent that even the
justice administered by royal common-law courts was strongly influenced by
prevailing community norms. Facts and norms were frequently intertwined, as
in negligence cases, and treated as a matter for laymen to decide; instructions to
the jury regularly encompassed vague terms that enabled jurors to inject into the
verdict their notions of propriety, fairness, and similar undifferentiated community standards.

It is for this reason that common law could be associated with the slow
process of gradually accumulating experience and with custom growing spontaneously from social circumstances rather than with obedience to rigid technical
rules. And it is this openness to ordinary community judgments that may well be
more deeply engrained or more canonical in Anglo-American legal culture than
the more visible arabesques of pleading, or the exquisite refinements of evidentiary rules.[54] I would not wish to overstate the proximity of traditional decisional

51. Despite much talk about indisputable ecclesiastical influences on the chancery, the operation of the court of equity would easily have been more perplexing to Continental lawyers than the
complexities of common law, at least after the sixteenth century. Explaining the relation of law and
equity to Europeans is still one of the comparativist's most challenging tasks.

52. See S. Milsom, *Historical Foundations of the Common Law*, 37, 75 (1969). Fulbecke, an
early English comparativist, related the common law to the pleading stage of Continental civil
proceedings, virtually neglecting the contrast between English jury trials and the adjudicative stages
of the process before Continental hierarchical bureaucracy. See Fulbecke, *supra*, n. 47, 77.

53. The rule forbidding legal counsel to the accused in felony cases started to break down only
in the eighteenth century. See J. Langbein, "The Criminal Trial before the Lawyers," 45 *U. Chicago
L. Rev.* 263, 307 (1978).

54. The association of common law with custom and slow organic growth is a theme master-
fully developed by J. Pocock, *The Ancient Constitution and the Feudal Law*, 36 and passim (1967). For

standards to the demands of the coordinate ideal: a technical component in these standards cannot be denied. But it is important to notice the peculiar character of this technical component, for it presents a striking contrast to the Continental judicial apparatus. As befits a judicial organization without tall pyramids of authority, technical aspects of the common law were deeply immersed in the pragmatics of litigation and responsive to concrete particulars of cases. In other words, the flavor of the technical component was closer to pragmatic than to logical legalism.

To carry the story forward I need not speculate on what peculiar forms of bureaucratization English absolutism might have eventually generated, had the civil war of the seventeenth century not aborted the fledgling institutions of central royal authority. The fact is that professionalization and centralization of the ruling apparatus were arrested: leading members of the local gentry remained the pillars of government. And while the bureaucratic tone of Continental officialdom continuously grew in intensity, the English official style was not free from notions of sport, appropriate to the activity of gentlemen of leisure bent on converting life into something of a game. Central English institutions also continued to embrace attitudes and forms from an earlier age.

The halcyon period of this official apparatus continued throughout the eighteenth and into the early nineteenth century.[55] Paradoxically, even as the British Empire approached its apogee, England was seen as hardly a "modern" state by those who associated modern government with a hierarchical bureaucratic organization. And to those who understood modern law to be systematic legislation, the English legal system was an anachronism, a chaotic jungle with judicial precedent its principal fauna.[56]

Important departures from inherited patterns of authority began to be implemented only in the second part of the nineteenth century with the rise of the professional civil service. The apparatus of justice was not impervious to change: the province of local lay magistrates was narrowly circumscribed, and the lay jury went into a general decline, especially in civil cases. Regular appellate courts were set up at the turn of the century, and a space was thus created for the development of more rigid hierarchical relationships. A series of reforms, most of them in the present century, streamlined and simplified the court system, bringing it closer to the Continental model. Informal ways of assuring unity of

---

a view somewhat similar to the one presented in the text, see R. David, "Les caractères originaux de la pensée juridique anglaise et américaine," 15 *Archives de la Philosophie du Droit* 6 (1970).

55. On features of English local administration, see L. Namier, *England in the Age of the American Revolution,* 2d ed., 3–41 (1961). Continental visitors were amazed that England managed to preserve order without centralized and professional police until well into the nineteenth century. See F. de la Rochefoucauld, *A Frenchman in England 1784,* 125 (London, 1935); C. Cottu, *The Administration of Criminal Justice in England* (London, 1822). It is also noteworthy that the House of Lords has continued into the modern era as both a legislative body and a high tribunal, with peers trained in the law sitting with their lay colleagues on this important court.

56. Hegel described the common law as an "Augean stable" in dire need of cleansing, or a "jungle" in need of replacement by legislation "framed predominantly on general principles" (*Political Writings,* 300, 310 [Oxford, 1964]).

decision making were replaced in the nineteenth century by the normativistic doctrine of stare decisis,[57] and the duality of law and equity was abolished. In short, there occurred a dramatic swing in the direction of hierarchical bureaucratization.

Yet, in spite of momentous changes occurring over a century and a half of dynamic development, the existing English judicial organization remains a palimpsest from which the past has been only partially erased. To get a better sense of surviving traces of traditional arrangements, it is again useful to take a look from the Continental perspective: to know things is to watch them from the outside. Even today visitors from across the Channel are struck by features of the English judicial organization attributable to the ideal of coordinate officialdom. For example, while the Continental lower judiciary consists of young professional judges on the first rung of the hierarchical ladder, the English lower judiciary is still often composed of lay magistrates. Even professional English judges should not be identified with a separatist governmental organization in the Continental sense: they are all people in their second career, barristers of long standing, formed within an independent guild and sharing its ethos. It is also true that the relative informality of internal procedures in English high courts continues to baffle Continental lawyers familiar with bureaucratic routines of the Continental judiciary.[58] While examples are easily multiplied, it will suffice to suggest merely the flavor of contemporary hybridization of traditional prebureaucratic and modern bureaucratic elements in the English judicial apparatus, given that this chapter concerns the historical roots upon which more recent forms have been grafted.

In America, circumstances were from the outset especially propitious to a coordinate mode of organization. The colonists were intimately familiar with English local administration; there was little in their experience and nothing in their situation to recommend a hierarchically structured, bureaucratic judiciary. Government itself was widely viewed as no more than a necessary evil: it was not only the Age of Jackson that strove to make all official functions so plain and simple that any person of average intelligence could serve a temporary term or "rotation" in office. To identify law with proclamations of authoritative institutions, staffed with experts, was alien to people already conditioned to discover law in ordinary community standards. In fact, it can be said that if ever there was a general political consensus in America, it was—and perhaps still is—an antipathy toward bureaucracy, hierarchical ordering, and the conception of law as a technical discipline, that is, an antipathy toward all the essential aspects of the hierarchical ideal.[59]

57. On the relatively recent rise of the stare decisis doctrine, see A. Simpson, "The Common Law and Legal Theory," in *Oxford Essays in Jurisprudence* (2d ser.) 77 (1973).

58. Some of the residual differences between internal procedures in English and West German courts are reviewed in J. Henkel, *England, Rechtsstaat ohne gesetzlichen Richter* (Frankfurt and Berlin, 1971).

59. See S. P. Huntington, "Paradigms of American Politics," 89 *Pol. Sci. Quarterly*, 1, 20–22 (1974). Ironically, this antipathy survives into the present where there is growing reliance on the state for solution of a multitude of social problems.

Some salient characteristics of coordinate structures in the traditional American apparatus of justice may be briefly observed. From the start, the system relied heavily on local juries which, at least for some time, were much more independent of judicial influence than was usual in England. The central role of the jury was enshrined in the Constitution and thus rendered immune from undoing by simple legislative reform. Trial judges were often amateurs, as is sporadically still the case with village and town justices. But even as judges came to be chosen more often from the ranks of lawyers, political service proved to be a more important prerequisite for getting on the bench than professional legal skills or the extent of professional experience.[60] In this context it was considered normal that legal expertise be supplied from the outside, and that outsiders be enlisted to perform a variety of tasks that would fall within the compass of Continental judicial monopoly. In another contrast to the Continent, specialization on the bench continued to be viewed as a vice rather than a virtue.[61] Finally, a vigorously personal style of exercising authority remains a hallmark of the American judiciary, even when observed from England.[62]

Because appellate courts appeared much earlier in America than in England, it may perhaps be inferred that hierarchization of the judiciary has progressed further than in other common-law countries. The truth is, however, that hierarchical instruments and the hierarchical spirit have remained quite embryonic. Even now there are few American jurisdictions in which the courts form a pronounced and cohesive hierarchy. Nor should this cause much surprise. Trial judges are frequently political figures, more inclined to heed the opinion of their constituencies than the opinions of superior courts, even if these opinions are technically binding. The prospect of promotion to a higher court is not nearly so potent a device for instilling hierarchical discipline as it is in Continental judicial systems because even the lowest rung in the American hierarchy of courts is already a very prestigious occupation.[63] Furthermore, American appellate review is not nearly so comprehensive as it is on the Continent, so that lower court judges retain vast "discretionary" or virtually unreviewable powers. Inevitably, the demands for unity in decision making are comparatively weak.[64]

60. This stands in stark contrast to the French judiciary, for example, where law school graduates aspiring to a career on the bench must attend a special school (École Nationale de Magistrature). In England, all higher judges must be qualified barristers of at least ten years standing. See Supreme Court Act, 1981, ch. 54, para. 10.

61. Contrast the American situation with a typical Continental country, where judges of the highest court of general jurisdiction (to say nothing of specialized court hierarchies) sit in specialized divisions, sometimes even in specialized panels within a specialized division. On the other hand, the narrow specialization of the American bar (not only over legal areas but also with respect to the plaintiff's or defendant's side) has no close analogue, even in those Continental systems that carry the specialization of the bar relatively far.

62. This is apparent, for example, in the greater frequency of dissenting opinions in American than in English courts. See P. S. Atiyah, "Lawyers and Rules: Some Anglo-American Comparisons," 37 *Southwest L.J.* 545, 549–52 (1983). As previously noted, most Continental systems do not even permit the publication of dissents.

63. On factors weakening hierarchical relationships in the American judicial branch, see P. S. Atiyah, *supra*, n. 62, 554.

64. Even in the federal system, existing differences among the case law of various judicial

The continuing importance of the lay jury ensures that the American orientation to substantive justice remains strong and vital. Nor will judges who view themselves as political figures be likely to espouse a conception of the law in which political, ethical, and technical-legal considerations are sharply separated. True, the fact that American judges are regarded as guardians of the Constitution—the pivotal legal document—has often been seen as injecting legalistic attitudes into American social life. Many have observed that Americans tend to convert all sorts of problems into legal issues: even matters that are elsewhere perceived as not "legal" at all end up in American courts. In this Tocquevillian sense, American legal culture is undeniably "legalistic." But in a sense more germane to comparative concerns, it is the very centrality of the American Constitution that reinforces general antipathy to conceptions of the law as noncommunitarian, specialized technique. It is precisely the Constitution, a document studded with broad standards of ethical and political significance, that makes sharp separation of the ethical, political, and legal-technical domains both unnatural and impracticable. Even today a fundamentally nontechnical conception of the law manages to hold its own in the struggle with the strong technocratic tendencies of an increasingly interventionist state.

Contemporary transformations of the American judicial apparatus will be addressed in the last chapter and need not be considered here. Suffice it to say that despite the trend toward bureaucratic centralization, coordinate features remain much more viable in America than in England. Indeed, if one were to set aside the broader comparative viewpoint, much of the difference between the English and the American judicial apparatuses could be expressed in terms of the opposition between hierarchical and coordinate structures: the English procedural authority is far more professionalized, hierarchically ordered, and committed to a technical conception of the law.[65] It is only when the horizons are further expanded that conspicuous internal differences between English and American judicial authority begin to recede and their family resemblances clearly emerge.

My purpose in the preceding section has been to show how the conceptual framework established earlier in this chapter can be used to shed new light on features that distinguish the Continental from the Anglo-American apparatus of justice. Having both defined the relevant categories and established a pied-à-terre for them in historical reality, the groundwork has been laid for the study of my central theme—the influence of procedural officialdom on the shape of the legal process. Reciprocities between procedural authority and procedural form will now be explored in more systematic fashion.

---

districts are as frequent as they are long-lasting. More important, even *within* a circuit, discrepancies of the case law are not a major cause of dismay, and accordingly internal mechanisms of the circuit courts designed to remove disagreements among its panels are quite weak. See *infra*, ch. 6, n. 113.

65. See P. S. Atiyah, *supra*, n. 62, 552–55.

II Process before Hierarchical and Coordinate Officialdom

This chapter will inquire first into procedural arrangements suitable for a hierarchical judicial apparatus, and second, forms suitable for an apparatus conforming to the coordinate ideal. What features of the legal process, or elements of its design, can be attributed to specific characteristics of hierarchical and coordinate organizations? What bearing do attitudes prevailing in one or another setting have on procedural form? These are the primary questions here. In pursuit of answers to these and similar questions, contours of two distinctive procedural styles will gradually come into view. I shall call one of them the *hierarchical* and the other the *coordinate* process, because their constituent elements will be "derived" from each respective type of authority.

The two styles, applicable across the lines that separate criminal, civil, and administrative proceedings, will not be related to the distinction between a process designed as an inquiry and a process designed as a contest of two sides before the decision maker. Although throughout this chapter I shall stress the level of ideal theory, I shall make sufficient reference to real-life proceedings to illustrate how the hierarchical style reflects salient characteristics of the legal process rooted in the Continental tradition, while the coordinate style similarly mirrors features of the legal process in the English tradition. More specific references to actual systems will be postponed until the final chapter. The discussion here seeks to demonstrate how the structure of procedural authority impinges on the legal process, and how wrong it is to focus on the desirability of procedural form without asking whether such form is compatible with a particular judicial apparatus. The question is not only what sort of procedure we want but also what kind of officialdom we have.

i. PROCEDURAL IMPLICATIONS OF THE HIERARCHICAL IDEAL

Methodical Succession of Stages

Let us begin our inquiry by considering one of the most obvious implications of the hierarchical apparatus for the design of the legal process: because hierarchy is multilayered, proceedings must consist of several stages. And because this apparatus is also partial to functional specialization, it is normal to expect that the stages be assigned methodical subtasks. One stage can be devoted to the gathering and organization of relevant material, another to the initial decision, still another to hierarchical review, and so on, depending on the number of levels in the pyramid of authority. Accordingly, proceedings before the initial decision maker (trials) are merely one episode in an ongoing sequence and are thus an inept symbol for describing the total effort. In the hierarchical setting, Kafka's hero is not "tried," he is implicated in "proceedings."[1]

The Impact of Superior Review

Equally obvious is the connection between vertical ordering of authority and hierarchical review, a connection to which I have previously alluded. Here I shall look more closely at various ramifications of regular superior audits: not only do they reveal characteristic aspects of the hierarchical style, but they also prevent us from mistakenly extrapolating, from identical verbal formulae, true hierarchical review from its apocryphal forms, such as can be found in predominantly coordinate judicial organizations. This confusion is endemic to discourse between Continental and common lawyers, although it often passes unnoticed.

The first important point to recognize is that the reviewing stage is conceived not as an extraordinary event but as a sequel to original adjudication to be expected in the normal run of events. In well-integrated judicial hierarchies, such as the Soviet, supervision by higher-ups need not be conditioned—as it is in classical Continental systems—upon an appeal by a disaffected party; it can also take place as part of the official duty of higher judicial authorities. Far Eastern systems have been known to go even further: original decisions were treated as mere drafts of judgments that could be announced in definitive form only by superiors.[2] Observe that where review is routine, it is also normal to postpone enforcement of the original decision until the highest authority has spoken. Thus, in contrast to the situation in coordinate systems, where the initial decision is presumptively final, there is no need expressly to ask the primary adjudicator to postpone (stay) the execution of his decision pending review: until hierarchical supervision has been given the chance to run its course, the decision is not yet res judicata.

Hierarchical review is not only regular, it is also comprehensive. There are few aspects of lower authority's decision making that are accorded immunity

1. Characteristically, the standard translation of Kafka's *Der Prozess* into English is "The Trial." One perceptive English observer of Continental trials has noticed their character as stages in an ongoing activity and was somewhat shocked by this discovery. See S. Bedford, *The Faces of Justice,* 123 (1961).

2. See M. Shapiro, *Courts: A Comparative and Political Analysis,* 180 (1981). In all countries that follow the Soviet model, chief judges of high courts can cause reconsideration of lower decisions *motu proprio.* See *RSFSR Code of Crim. Pro.* art. 371. Similar provisions exist for civil proceedings as well.

from supervision: fact, law, and logic are all fair game for scrutiny and possible correction.[3] Where reconsideration by superiors is so pervasive, it makes sense to require lower authority to make clear exactly what it has determined and why. Perfunctory and conclusory statements of grounds, so prevalent among trial judges in common-law jurisdictions, invite rebuke and reversal in a hierarchical judicial system.[4]

Once a lower official has spoken, the procedural episode conducted before him comes to an end (*functum officio*): corrections of his decision, if needed, can now be made only by higher-ups in the organization. Requests to reconsider addressed to the initial adjudicator are therefore misplaced; such requests will be seen to characterize the coordinate style. Simultaneous review of a judgment by different echelons of authority violates the hierarchical sense of order and rank: were such parallelism permitted, subordinates could try to conceal their mistakes or render the work of their superiors superfluous by setting their own decisions right. However, reversal or modification of a decision does not necessitate a finding that the subordinate decision maker had erred or committed a fault; even if impeccable at the time of rendition, a judgment can be changed by superiors. Thus if new evidence is discovered pending an appeal (casting doubts on the propriety of a decision, but no blame on the decision maker), it must be submitted to the reviewing authority rather than to the original adjudicator. Of course, if fault is found, hierarchical organizations have a battery of instruments at their disposal to teach the errant official a lesson. Given such great disciplinary powers, there is less need in hierarchical than in coordinate organizations to resort to the costly reversal of an otherwise proper decision in order to discourage official misconduct, but the calculation of the costs and benefits of such a reversal is not exactly alike in the two settings of authority. I shall return later to this point in several contexts.

The great significance attributed to "quality control" by superiors in a hierarchical organization inevitably detracts from the importance of original decision making: the latter acquires an aura of provisionality. It is thus a mortal sin for a comparativist to assume that the significance of trials is identical in proceedings before an officialdom gravitating toward the hierarchical or toward the coordinate ideal. On the other hand, the importance of quality control explains why a regular and comprehensive system of appeals is typically regarded in hierarchical judicial organizations as an essential guarantee of fair and orderly

---

3. In Continental systems, "logic" is tested in reviewing the reasons trial judges must advance for their findings of fact. Although there are no longer *legal* rules that can be violated in weighing evidence (the principle of free proof), grounds offered for reliance on one witness rather than another can be weak or incoherent, inviting reversal on grounds of faulty logic. The evaluation of evidence is truly free only in the very limited sphere of the surviving criminal jury, where jurors are invited to weigh evidence according to their unreviewable "intimate conviction." Of course, there are limits on effective supervision of fact-finding by lower officials: subordinates learn how to justify their decisions in ways that can "withstand" review by their superiors. This problem was noted in the first chapter, with regard to internal tensions between original and reviewing officials.

4. For the situation in American trial courts, see *infra*, n. 22 and accompanying text.

administration of justice, or as an essential component of personal "due process." It should not be surprising, therefore, to find the right to appeal enshrined in several constitutions as one of the basic rights of citizens.[5]

The File of the Case

A multistage hierarchical process needs a mechanism to integrate all its segments into a meaningful whole. Material gathered over time by various officials must be assembled for decision making, and traces of official activity must be preserved for future audits. Officials in charge of procedural stages are therefore expected to maintain files to ensure completeness and authenticity of documentation. Like tributaries of an ever larger river, files kept by lower officials are incorporated into the evermore encompassing files of their superiors.

In order not to confuse the file of the case with its false cognates, it is important to realize that hierarchical officials prefer to decide on the basis of written records. Documents contained in the file are not internal official documents, helping a particular official to organize his activity, but rather sources of information on which to base both original and reviewing decisions.[6] The higher the authority, the greater the ratio of information from the file to the total data base. And while the accuracy of information in the file is not unchallengeable, it commands considerable weight. Indeed, unless such weight were attributed to it, the very foundation of the hierarchical process would begin to tremble: a multistage process is put at risk if its main integrating mechanism is seriously questioned. In fact, a good test to assess the intensity of hierarchical attitudes is to propose the reduction of the evidentiary significance of official documentation. The greater the intensity, the more vehemently such reform proposals will be opposed. If the evidentiary significance of the file is totally and effectively denied, the hierarchical process is no more.

The previous chapter demonstrated that the top of the hierarchical pyramid cannot afford to be submerged into the sea of details of cases decided below, as is reflected in the character of documents contained in the file. They are succinct, summarized, whenever possible, and set out in standard sequences to facilitate quick handling. Brief accounts of interrogations performed are preferred to full transcripts. But even if full transcripts were made of all interrogations, the spoken word would still be replaced by a substitute text whose language is devoid of behavioral cues and traits, so that decision making on the basis of the "cold"

---

5. See, e.g., the *Yugoslav Constitution* of 1974, art. 180(2); compare also the *International Covenant on Economic Social and Cultural Rights*, art. 14(5), adopted by the UN General Assembly in 1966. For America, see *infra*, n. 22.

6. Anglo-American commentators easily fall into the trap of associating the continental file of the case with files kept in America by officials participating in proceedings (e.g., by the public prosecutor in criminal prosecutions). See A. Goldstein and M. Marcus, "The Myth of Judicial Supervision in Three 'Inquisitorial Systems': France, Italy and Germany," 87 *Yale L.J.* 240, 255 (1977). For the widespread Continental practice of using the *whole* dossier of a case as evidence in another litigation, civil or criminal, see R. Schlesinger, *Comparative Law*, 4th ed., 423, 458 (1980).

file still implies substantial mediation of experience. Where only short summaries are drawn, the stylization of experience is, of course, quite considerable. And where experience is thus simplified and mediated by a text, decision making more readily lends itself to logical analysis than does dense, direct experience. From a slightly different angle, this confirms my previous suggestion that the higher reaches of procedural authority are easily attracted to syllogistic models of decision making and to logical legalism.

It will be claimed that modern recording technologies which minimize mediation (e.g., videotapes) may soon replace old-fashioned dossiers, so that hierarchical insulation from the unruly mass of data will inevitably come to an end. But in judicial organizations where superior review is at once regular and comprehensive, the hierarchical summit may be expected to develop new instruments of condensation to protect itself against the danger of drowning in the sea of details generated by proceedings before lower officials. It is only in systems where review is sporadic and limited in scope, as in American law, that one can more freely engage in the luxury of full transcript and the exposure to particulars.

While few would be prepared to deny that the reliance on terse documents gives the Continental appellate process its distinctive tone and flavor, the role of the file in first-instance proceedings is more uncertain, even controversial. I shall return to this theme after considering the mode of trial that suits judicial hierarchies.

Piecemeal Trials

Two designs for first-instance proceedings can be distinguished. In the one variant, which I shall call the "day-in-court" model or "trial" strictly speaking, all material bearing on the case is preferably considered in a single block of time. In the other variant, proceedings develop through separate sessions at which material is gradually assembled in a piecemeal, or installment style.[7] This latter style presupposes the capacity of the official apparatus for sustained action and requires that the results of scattered and temporarily discrete activities be preserved. Bureaucratic organizations are capable of meeting both requirements, and it may seem at first that they should be indifferent to which of the two alternative trial designs is employed. Yet closer scrutiny of the corollaries of judicial professionalization suggests a different answer.

A genuinely concentrated trial, even if well prepared, requires that decisions be based largely on fresh impressions, including surprise, shock, the spell of superficial rhetoric, and perhaps even theatrics. A bureaucrat dislikes to decide on such grounds. He fears that first impressions might collapse like a soufflé upon unhurried reflection and that additional investigation or argument may be necessary. It seems preferable to him to proceed as would a dentist—in discrete installments: after a matter has been considered at one session, new points can

7. See A. T. von Mehren and J. R. Gordley, *The Civil Law System*, 2d. ed., 203 (1977).

emerge to be the subject of another session, and so on, until that issue seems thoroughly clear. A final session can then be devoted to pulling all strands together, reviewing interim results, and calmly reaching a decision. But even this last session is only presumptively final: any sudden development or surprise can necessitate a postponement and still another session. This bureaucratic preference for the installment style is reinforced by the existence of regular review mechanisms. It makes little sense to require the early crescendo of a day-in-court trial if it is routinely to be followed by the diminuendo of appellate procedural "rounds." Accordingly, unless concentrated trials are imposed on judicial bureaucracies, they are likely to adopt the piecemeal style.

Extreme examples of first-instance proceedings without concentrated presentation of evidence and similar "trial" activity are found in the Far East,[8] but for more common cases it is enough to cast a quick glance at continental European systems where since the Middle Ages the installment style has predominated in both civil or criminal cases. The passing of the initial judgment was typically preceded by a conference among professional judges who debated material in documentary form as generated by episodic judicial inquiries. The file of the case was generally proclaimed to be the vehicle of the judge to arrive at the decision (*vehiculum judicis ad sententiam*). In civil cases, this traditional arrangement survived the reforms of the French Revolution and still flourishes in Continental systems. Since civil justice remained the exclusive domain of the professional judiciary, this is scarcely surprising.[9]

In criminal matters, the situation is more complex. The ideological currents that led the revolutionaries to import the criminal jury from England mandated that a public trial be made the focal point of the whole process. So strong was the revolutionary ideology that even where the jury trial was not adopted, professional judges were no longer permitted to decide solely or even primarily on evidentiary items contained in the file. The principle was adopted that all evidence had to be adduced in original form rather than in distilled documentation. What followed illustrates the destiny of procedural arrangements transplanted to an inhospitable environment: outwardly, the doctrine reigned supreme that witnesses must be heard by the trial court, but the record of preliminary proceedings continued nevertheless to play a crucial role. Presiding judges would study the file and at trial make frequent reference to material contained in it. As any visitor to a contemporary Continental courtroom notices, examination of witnesses is still routinely conducted so that information from

8. For Communist China during Mao's rule, see W. C. Jones, "A Possible Model for the Criminal Trial in the People's Republic of China," 24 *Am. J. Comp. L.*, 229, 232 (1976).

9. Only very recently, experimentation has begun in a few Continental jurisdictions with concentrated trials for simple cases of little importance, always on condition that complexities not suddenly arise in the course of proceedings. This recent development is linked to the overcrowding of dockets and corresponding pressures for efficient case-flow management. For experimentation in West Germany, see R. Schlesinger, *supra*, n. 6, 440–41. See also the West German Code of Civil Procedure, ¶272, as amended in 1977.

the written record must almost constantly surface. What has been well said of the Russian procedure applies with minor modifications to classical Continental systems as well: the file remains in the wings of the trial like the prompter at an amateur play. [10] The Continental trial is, then, actually not the doctrinally proclaimed event of paramount importance that generates all material for disposition of the criminal case quite independently from prior (piecemeal) proceedings. This fact is especially striking to Anglo-American observers to whom the European trial appears to be essentially an audit of work done before or an appeal from the findings of preliminary investigation. [11] Not unexpectedly, there are few unforeseen developments in the courtroom, and if surprise should mar the orderly progress of the trial, continuances are readily granted until the dust has settled.

Sporadic suggestions for effectively lifting the documentary curtain have been vigorously resisted by the Continental law enforcement machinery. Officials argue that observations made at trial must be checked against information methodically assembled over time and preserved in the written record. To decide independently from the file, solely on first impressions, is to decide with inadequate preparation, on flimsy and uncertain grounds.

Exclusivity of the Official Process

Hierarchical officialdom is subject to Parkinson's law and tends to expand its sphere of activity. Because it sharply separates internal from external spheres, it strives to monopolize procedural action: the "farming out" of procedural steps is considered a dereliction of responsibility. Members of the private bar are denied a variety of functions in the legal process which, in proceedings before coordinate authority, are routinely performed by lawyers. Nor do other functionaries of ambiguous status—part private, part official—find a niche in the hierarchical process: the "private attorney general" and similar procedural actors are creatures of a coordinate setting of authority.

Such is the bias of bureaucratic sentiment that private procedural enterprise is generally discouraged. It is seen as too much tainted by possible self-interest to be credible, perhaps not sufficiently "serious" for such an important pursuit as the meting out of justice. For example, if a witness is interviewed by private lawyers, his testimony is viewed with great suspicion—he has been "tampered with." It is no coincidence, then, that Continental lawyers seldom

---

10. G. Feifer, *Justice in Moscow*, (1964). Even in those Continental systems that are least permissive in the use of materials from the file, at least some documents can be used for substantive rather than mere impeachment purposes. The extent to which evidence allegedly used for mere impeachment *actually* influences the substantive decision remains an open question. On the so-called principle of immediacy, see M. Damaška, "Evidentiary Barriers to Conviction," 121 *U. Pa. Law Rev.* 506, 517 (1973). For contrasts with America, see R. Schlesinger, *supra*, n. 6, 458, n. 5; 31 *A.L.R.* 913 (1984).

11. For this external perspective on Continental trials, see, e.g., J. N. Hazard, *Settling Disputes in Soviet Society*, 26 (1960).

engage in independent investigative activity, even if clearly permitted to do so, as they are in civil cases.[12] Nor is it surprising that expert witnesses are seldom called by private parties, even where this possibility exists on paper. "Experts" are treated as judicial assistants, and it seems normal that they be appointed by the judge, preferably from among persons accustomed to bureaucratic court routine—hence, Continental "permanent" or professional court experts. Where higher courts retain their own experts, a veritable minihierarchy of court assistants can arise: "superexperts" review the estimates and opinions of ordinary experts.[13]

With the ethos of official exclusivity stifling private procedural action, the hierarchical apparatus seeks to develop proper incentives for professionals to perform their functions. In cases where interests of the state are engaged, these incentives are not lacking, but difficulties can arise in matters of narrow private concern. Here, officials continue to enjoy the monopoly of procedural functions, but can be inert or otherwise ineffective. Supplementing inadequate official motivations with private action creates problems reminiscent of difficulties that arise in economic affairs when state monopoly is combined with admixtures of private enterprise. Private actors either can be unaccustomed to take initiative or can be frustrated by the pervasive official monopoly. Some perplexing aspects of the Continental civil process can be explained in terms of such "lazy" official monopolists, as subsequent chapters will show.

One final consequence of official exclusivity deserves attention here: the hierarchical legal process is identified with action performed by officials personally in charge of a procedural segment or at least with activity performed in their presence and under their direct supervision. It follows that actions performed in their absence are not part of the hierarchical process. One example is depositions taken from witnesses by lawyers, even if in the presence of a court reporter. Nor should the implications of this understanding of legal process be taken lightly: where procedural authority is wedded to logical legalism, logical entailment of certain "principled" positions can assume a persuasive power unequaled in more pragmatic official environments.

Logical Legalism and Procedural Regulation

In a hierarchical organization where the spirit of logical legalism reigns, it is considered ideal that the legal process be regulated by an internally consistent

12. In criminal cases, once an official investigation is under way "private" interviews of witnesses by lawyers come close to the dangerous zone of criminal tampering with the administration of justice. It is plain that a hierarchical authority is opposed to the role private bail bondsmen play in the American criminal justice system: my comments about bureaucratic hostility to private enterprise in matters of justice apply as well to bondsmen and their power to bring a fugitive to justice.

13. Institutions such as medical schools are favorite superexperts in many Continental countries, with "institutional" opinions signed by the director. Given the penchant for documentation, expert opinions are typically in writing. The oral examination of the expert then proceeds in court against the background of this document.

network of unbending rules. In reality, of course, there is no denying that one must often make do with mere guidelines—directive rather than mandatory— or, worse yet, that some matters have to be left unregulated—in the official's discretion. But in a logically legalist milieu such guidelines and discretion are tolerated only as a regrettable means of last resort, and only so long as satisfactory rigid regulation cannot be devised. The example of regulating the weight of evidence is instructive here. I have observed that early on, the Continental judicial apparatus developed quite elaborate rules of proof necessary for fact-finding in both civil and criminal cases. Legalistic attitudes mandated that the cogency of evidence not be left for the adjudicator freely to determine. When rules of legal proof were finally discarded, this was not a retreat from bureaucratic-legalistic attitudes, but more than anything else an act of despair. It was realized that, for the moment, it was impossible to determine in advance the specific impact of various concrete configurations of evidence.[14] Contrary to what is often said, even today the Continental "free evaluation of evidence" is not really free: as befits the hierarchical process, trial judges are required to justify their findings of fact, and the cogency of their reasoning is scrutinized by appellate courts. Clearly, if there were no regularities to be observed in finding facts, appeals for "factual error" would be deprived of any basis.[15]

If officials are to be guided by rules and if the exercise of official discretion is to be contained, then the regulation of the legal process must be highly differentiated and well adjusted to the goals pursued. Otherwise, the rigidity of procedural regulation could lead to unacceptable results. As an illustration, consider the regulation of discovery. An organization that welcomes official discretion can be satisfied with according officials sweeping powers to enforce discovery requests, leaving it to their judgment to decide when broad discovery is in harmony with procedural goals and when not. A logically legalist organization, however, requires more differentiated regulation. To the extent it can be predicted that broad discovery would advance the policy-implementing goal, but could be counterproductive for the resolution of disputes (that is, the information sought could broaden the conflict), procedural regulation will expressly permit sweeping discovery for the former but not for the latter class of cases.[16] In subsequent chapters, this characteristic of logically legalistic regulation will assume importance for analysis of activist and reactive legal processes. The internal variations of activist and reactive justice can be explained in terms of the different character

---

14. This attitude was shared by both Jeremy Bentham and Montesquieu. See *Works of Jeremy Bentham*, vol. 6, 216 (London, 1838–43); Montesquieu, *De l'esprit des lois*, book 12, ch. 3.

15. See *supra*, n. 3.

16. Another example is adjudicative power to grant relief. A system less attracted to rules can simply provide that a civil judge has discretion to grant relief which a plaintiff has not requested, leaving it to the judge to decide when this is appropriate. Judges will seldom take advantage of this possibility in those cases where they believe they are confronted with a self-contained, private dispute. A logically legalist regulation is likely to be more discriminating, expressly prohibiting the adjudicator from disregarding prayers for relief in private law litigation.

of officialdom, and therein a key to several bizarre comparative law paradoxes will be obtained.

Because logical legalism aspires to principled consistency, inherited procedural arrangements vulnerable to serious analytical criticism have little santity and slim chances of survival: pressures mount to overhaul the system. To illustrate the point, imagine a logical legalist confronted with an arrangement whereby a person can be arrested upon probable cause that he committed a crime and is then detained, but must invariably be set at liberty if bail is posted. The arrangement would be criticized as incoherent, especially in a society that values liberty. Of course, probable cause that a person has committed a crime justifies the initiation of criminal proceedings against him, but not his arrest and detention. These drastic measures require additional supporting grounds, such as the danger of flight, intimidation of witnesses, and the like. If arrest is to serve a symbolic function underscoring the state's assumption of jurisdiction, so that all suspects should be arrested, the arrested person should be released—without bail—as soon as the symbolic message has been brought home. The automatic release on bail would also come under attack, because the mere posting of security need not be an antidote for those dangers that can truly justify pretrial detention. If told that in such cases the judge could adjust the amount of bail so that the suspect cannot post it, the logical legalist would respond that this is a roundabout way to achieve what can be gotten more directly by "rational" regulation. We need not follow the argument further to recognize in it the Continental critique of the traditional American law of arrest and the apology usually advanced for traditional Anglo-American arrangements.[17]

Summary

In retrospect, thus far this chapter has provided the outline of a legal process adapted to the spirit and methodology of hierarchical authority. The distinctive mark of such hierarchical proceedings is that they are structured as a succession of stages, unfolding before officials locked in a chain of subordination. Original decision making is not a focal point, overshadowing in importance whatever preceded it and whatever might follow it. The file of the case is the nerve center of the whole process, integrating various levels of decision making. If, as a case moves from one stage to the next, information contained in the written record were to be cut off from officials, the hierarchical process would become disoriented. The equation of procedural action with action under direct official superintendence is also typical of hierarchical proceedings. Delegation of any procedural step to outsiders is inappropriate or even repugnant. Private procedural enterprise is thus almost an oxymoron in the lexicon of hierarchical authority.

17. It should be noted that traditional arrangements are increasingly transformed by statutes. See, e.g., the Federal Bail Reform Act of 1984, 36 CrL 3017 (1984). For a further illustrations of logically legalistic criticism of American procedural arrangements, see *infra*, n. 31.

ii. PROCEDURAL IMPLICATIONS OF THE COORDINATE IDEAL

Concentration of Proceedings

When judicial authority is structured as a single undifferentiated echelon, there are no specialized court officials charged with the preliminary task of gathering, sifting, and preserving procedural material, nor are there higher officials before whom proceedings continue after the initial judgment has been rendered. An essentially homogeneous single level of authority spawns proceedings that center around the original and presumptively final adjudicator. In short, trial is a proper synecdoche for the legal process as a whole.

The affinity of the Anglo-American administration of justice with such a compressed procedural model is still striking to a foreign observer. He perceives at once not only the relatively weak character of appellate review but also the conspicuous absence of a stage truly comparable to the preparatory proceedings on the Continent. The historical roots of this contrast lie in the traditional structure of procedural authority. As I have noted, the Continental judiciary had already evolved its own investigative branch in the late Middle Ages: in both civil and criminal cases, specialized court officials were charged with gathering material for the decision, including technically competent evidence. This evidence was "frozen," as it were, in the file and thus preserved for later use by the decision makers.[18] England followed a different path. Only a moderate degree of investigative elements was injected into criminal prosecutions by justices of the peace, who were charged with binding suspects over for trial; on the whole, they were more like traffic controllers at the gates of the justice system than investigators assiduously collecting evidence. Police and prosecutorial functions remained mainly in the hands of private individuals until the middle of the nineteenth century.[19] In the civil process, preparatory stages (pleadings) were concerned with the formation of issues rather than with the search of material to resolve them. Information-gathering activities were again in private hands.

Because of this absence of official investigators, the preparatory stages of the Anglo-American process in both civil and criminal matters were never as tightly integrated into the subsequent proceedings as was the case with Continental preliminary stages. Even today it is difficult in common-law systems to generate competent evidence out of court in advance of the trial. Investigative

18. In most Continental criminal justice systems, investigating judges seem of late to have lost ground to police and prosecutorial investigators. Nevertheless, the tradition continues that the products of investigative labors constitute usable evidence and can be "introduced" in the formal process. In civil matters many Continental jurisdictions continue to charge a single member of the court with gathering evidence (*juge en charge de la mise en état*), while the judgment is rendered by a panel of judges.

19. See J. Langbein, "The Origin of the Public Prosecution at Common Law," 17 *Am. J. Leg. Hist.* 313, 326 (1973).

action still leads more often to information of use in obtaining evidence than to evidence itself, properly speaking.[20]

Ramifications of a Single Decision-Making Level

Legal remedies against judgments of common-law decision makers are a bizarre world for Continental lawyers to contemplate. While much of what they find is vaguely familiar, it is bathed in an atmosphere in which even easily recognizable objects assume a strange surrealist quality. Much of their enigmatic character can be dispelled if Anglo-American legal remedies are interpreted as reflecting a continuing attachment to the ideal of one-level decision making upon which bits and pieces of hierarchical quality control have been grafted. I shall now explore the principal ramifications of single-level decision making in order to convey a sense of the legal landscape into which fragments of hierarchical supervision have been introduced.

In a horizontal apparatus of justice the fact that original decisions are presumptively final does not imply that they are all vested with guillotine finality and immediately enforced. With nobody to look over his shoulder, the decision maker can decide provisionally or conditionally: he can change his mind. Hence, one possibility for altering decisions is to induce the adjudicator to take a second look at his own decision or to permit a new hearing. Motions for reconsideration, so intriguing to one accustomed to a different setting of authority, are as normal and prevalent in the coordinate apparatus of authority as are requests for superior review in hierarchical judicial organizations. Another possibility, even more curious to outsiders, is for affected parties to take advantage of the horizontal relationship among coordinate officials, and to try to frustrate the enforcement of decisions that are immune from "direct" attack. Without waiting for proceedings to run their full course to an anticipated unfavorable outcome, these persons can institute another action, pursuing roughly the same issue before another official in the hope that the second decision, favorable to them, may lead to the nullification of the effects of the first. Observe that in an organization dominated by lay officials the notion of what issues are "identical" to those already pending in court is not likely to be rigid. Yet another strategy is for the disaffected party to request a parallel official to block the enforcement of a decision rendered by a colleague. To a mind accustomed to hierarchical ordering of authority, such procedural moves can be taken as distressing signs of a seriously flawed judicial

20. This is true of course, with only minor exceptions, for depositions of witnesses in the discovery stages of the civil process. Depositions of witnesses made in the preliminary criminal examination can be used with greater ease in English trials than in America, but still with much greater difficulty than in Continental systems. This is especially the case with statements recorded by the police (police records) that still tend to be excluded as inadmissible hearsay. See 31 *A.L.R.* 913 (1984). These residual differences between the Continent and most common-law countries explain divergent attitudes toward actual and potential witnesses. For example, where evidence is "canned" early on, as it is on the Continent, intimidation of witnesses is deprived of much of its motivation: the prosecution can often make its case even if a witness has disappeared or changed his story at the time of trial. See M. Damaška, *supra*, n. 10, 519–20.

organization, but to a mind embracing the ideal of wide distribution of adjudicative powers, such blocking maneuvers are a small price to pay for the realization of desirable power relations.

Despite such instruments for permitting modification of judgments, it is characteristic of the process before a single echelon of authority that procedural devices designed to ensure decisional rectitude (quality control) *precede* rather than *follow* the initial decision. Only at this early point do procedural actors feel they can truly control events; they can ill afford to wait and see whether a procedural lapse will negatively affect a presumptively final judgment, or, in the affirmative, place their trust in later persuading the decision maker to change his mind. A procedural misstep early on can therefore require that a trial be aborted and that proceedings begin anew. The resulting idea of "mistrial" can be puzzling to lawyers used to a machinery of justice that is less in need of such "prophylactic" devices, to whom mistrials and similar mechanisms appear wasteful, merely ritualistic or otherwise irrational.

It hardly needs emphasis that such arrangements, natural in a single-level judicial organization, still characterize the process of many common-law jurisdictions, especially in America. Stepping away from ideal theory, let us now contemplate the impact on legal remedies of the loosely hierarchical, essentially one-level organization I have sketched in the previous chapter. Here the legal process still ends preferably with the announcement of the decision by the primary decision maker. Far from being a regular sequel to the trial, or a normally anticipated further stage of the process, superior review is more in the nature of an extraordinary and independent proceeding. The resulting procedural arrangements come even closer to those that common lawyers usually unreflectively accept, while they strike Continental observers as poor form or as simply bizarre.

Because of the extraordinary character of superior review, it still makes sense to treat the original judgment as res judicata and to permit its enforcement. The sporadic appeal is merely a ground on the basis of which execution can be postponed. It also seems appropriate to let the trial court's judgment lead immediately to a variety of collateral consequences. Because the fundamental notion has not really been discarded that the judgment of the trial court terminates criminal proceedings, review of acquittals is perceived as unfair, new or double jeopardy, rather than mere continuation of the original one. Furthermore, where a conviction is reversed the new trial is regarded as in many senses independent, a new proceeding, rather than as part and parcel of an ongoing process. Thus upon resentencing, the court need not credit defendants for time served under the original sentence: the perception of a single unitary proceeding within which both sentences were imposed is weak or absent.[21]

In this hybrid but basically coordinate system, judgments can be attacked only where the presumptively final decision maker has failed in such a serious way that his decision is in some sense perverse and his jurisdiction, as it were,

---

21. Until recently this was the prevailing American practice. But see *North Carolina* v. *Pearce* 395 U.S. 74 (1969).

forfeited. If decisions could be reversed on the simple ground that they might be wrong, review would of course cease to be an exceptional remedy. An offshoot of this practice of limiting review is that original decision makers are unlikely to be required to provide clear and expansive justifications for their findings, as is still the case with trial judges in most common-law systems. Where supervision is sporadic and confined to the most egregious blunders, fragmentary and conclusory reasons for decision ordinarily suffice. Another consequence of this situation is that where it takes place, review assumes an *indirect* character: rather than directly checking the propriety of reasoned decisions, superior authority tries to reconstruct what was actually decided, and it speculates whether a reasonable adjudicator would have reached the outcome attacked by the appellant.

Significantly, mechanisms for superior review supplement, but do not replace, instruments designed to cause reconsideration by the original adjudicator. It may even happen that he be asked to modify a decision after it has been sustained on appeal—a deplorable form, in the view of hierarchical authority concerned to maintain clear distinctions in rank. New evidence discovered before the time limit for appeal has expired constitutes a ground for reconsideration by the original adjudicator rather than an appellate ground: because the new evidence was not part of the original decision, the adjudicator has not failed at all, let alone so seriously erred that superior review is warranted.

In a very general sense, the right of appeal is not exalted as central to due process. Thus it is not shocking that appeal be made dependent—as it often is in England—on obtaining leave either from the trial or from the superior court. But this hybrid system need not be pursued in tedious technical detail: in what I have suggested so far, a style is clearly visible that is superimposed on a coordinate substratum. This style is distinctively Anglo-American: although obscured by the twisting route by which its implications have been circumvented, Anglo-American jurisdictions still display an attachment to the ideal of one-level adjudication. Appellate remedies came late to the common-law world, and if one is to speak of common-law tradition, it is not one that embraced regular avenues of appeal.[22]

22. As suggested in the first chapter, while regular appellate mechanisms were a feature of the Continental machinery of justice from its inception, in England they were created only by late Victorian reforms. In the sixteenth century, Thomas Smith still proudly proclaimed that there were no "dilatory appeals" in the realm of England (T. Smith, *De Republica Anglorum*, Third Book, ch. 2, p. 111 [London, 1583]). Very limited correction of judgments was possible by way of writ of error, but even this writ did not issue as of right until the eighteenth century. Of course, the finality of verdicts had much to do with the jury, but the whole machinery of justice was essentially a series of single-level courts. In America, appellate courts were established after the revolution; they are comparatively old by common-law standards. Yet they were a far cry from their Continental counterparts and incorporated into an environment hostile to hierarchization, being creatures of statute rather than common law. For their weakness and peculiar features, see L. B. Orfield, *Criminal Appeals in America*, 215 (1939). To the present day, no matter how serious the case, the right to appeal is not regarded as of constitutional stature. See 27 *Stan. L. Rev.* 945 (1975). Nor are various devices to facilitate or encourage appeals nearly so strong as on the Continent. Until very recently, a criminal defendant could receive a harsher sentence upon appeal in almost all American jurisdictions. On the

Reliance on Oral Communication and Live Testimony

Reasons for a preference for live witnesses are not difficult to see, quite apart from a possible belief in greater reliability. In the coordinate process there are no widely scattered procedural steps that must be integrated through a file; traces of prior procedural action need not be preserved to establish a firm basis for superior review. Moreover, in an organization of temporary lay officials, long institutional memory need not be cultivated: consistency is contemplated over relatively short temporal horizons. It may also be true that readiness to decide on the basis of cold files requires skills and dispositions generated only in bureaucratic organizations. To a layman, recorded testimony appears as a lifeless residue of reality. Nor does a coordinate system incorporate a class of minor bureaucrats who can be entrusted with the production, preservation, and retrieval of documents.

Consider some implications of the reluctance to rely on the written record. It becomes difficult or impossible to obtain competent evidence early on, and to disinter it, when obtained, after long entombment in the file. The disappearance of a single witness can ruin even a carefully prepared case. Various mechanisms must therefore be developed to ensure that witnesses are available at the time of trial—hence the notion of "material" witnesses, hardly known in Europe; hence also frequent grants of immunity to witnesses in exchange for their testimony. Unlike the hierarchical process, statements made by a witness at trial cannot be compared with his officially recorded prior declarations in an effort to decide what to believe. Consequently the coordinate process must develop "powerful engines" to challenge witnesses as they testify before the adjudicator. More than does hierarchical authority, coordinate officialdom must also rely on the threat of prosecution for perjury or similar deterrents against false testimony.

For many centuries, Continental and English administration of justice had been strikingly distinguishable on these grounds—the one relying on records in the file, the other on oral communication.[23] Although this contrast has lost its sharpness in more recent times, the degree of rapprochement between them can easily be exaggerated. While it is true that documents have assumed an increased importance in common-law proceedings, no real counterpart has emerged of the official file as the chief repository of information on which the adjudicators can predicate their judgment. The files maintained by officials participating in com-

---

Continent, since the fall of the ancien régime this practice has been branded an unfair deterrent for the accused to take his case before higher courts.

23. Concerning sixteenth-century criminal trials in England, Thomas Smith remarked, "It will seem straunge to all nations that doe use the civill Lawe of the Romane Emperours, that for life and death there is nothing put in writing but the enditment only" (Smith, *supra*, n. 22, Book II, ch. 23, p. 101. On the Continent, the maxim appeared that "what is not in the file does not exist." To compensate for the lack of live testimony, a special file was developed containing observations on witnesses' and parties' facial expressions as they testified (*Gebärdeprotokol*). The greater attachment of Anglo-American systems to testimony under oath will be discussed in chapter 4.

mon-law proceedings (not by judges!) are mainly in the nature of "extraneous" material which merely helps them organize their procedural action.

The "Day in Court"

I have already discussed the concentration of proceedings in connection with the absence of multiple levels of adjudication. Further compression of proceedings results from the character of the officials who compose the single echelon of authority. An organization composed of part-time laymen prefers to dispose of judicial business in a continuous block of time, or at least without lengthy interruptions. The reason for this preference is again not hard to see: if proceedings were of the installment variety, by the time of the next episode it could be inconvenient or impossible to reconvene the officials who sat at a prior judicial installment. Of course, newly recruited officials would be deprived—at least in part—of the benefit of live proceedings. Chopping up the trial into separate sessions is thus not an ideal arrangement in the coordinate process.

The day-in-court trial can be packed with excitement and drama: the vivacity of first impressions is not adversely affected by a documentary curtain over the trial. Surprises and unpredictable turns of events are commonplace, but coordinate officials are accustomed to deciding on the basis of what might be called "astonished reflection." The dramatic courtroom atmosphere is enhanced by the possible finality of the trial court's judgment: no punches can be pulled in reliance on a next procedural round before a higher authority. Another complex facet of the trial deserves attention here. The fact that the adjudicators are unfamiliar with the case, as well as the fact that the trial is a continuously unfolding event, makes the cognitive needs of both the decision maker and the attending public identical: informing and persuading the former implies informing and persuading the latter as well. Under favorable conditions, trials can thus truly become events where, in the setting of a public performance, social norms are articulated, or those already articulated are solemnly affirmed.

The link between the traditional attachment of Anglo-American justice to day-in-court proceedings and the trial by jury has often been noted. But it can also be argued that justices of the peace, acting alone, were similarly attracted to concentrated trials. Alternating between private and official pursuits, they must have favored prompt disposition of cases. Private individuals, on whose participation at trials they counted, were also not easy to reassemble for several discrete trial episodes.

The more recent professionalization of the judiciary and the complexities of contemporary litigation have combined to produce installment-type trials in some Anglo-American countries. Nevertheless, piecemeal proceedings are here not a reflection of an ideal of gradual and methodical action, but a concession to necessity. Nor is the tendency to proceed in installments so widespread and deeply ingrained as it is in the setting of the Continental career judiciary.[24]

24. For contrast with civil proceedings in Europe, see *supra*, n. 9 and accompanying text.

Legitimacy of Private Procedural Action

Amateur officials draw no rigid lines between official and private domains. Accordingly, procedural steps can be taken informally in a private setting and can be interlaced with unofficial activity. An early example of this pleasant mix of *otium* and *negotium*—play and work—was the business transacted by the English country gentlemen commissioned by the Elizabethan chancery to examine witnesses: they would set about their work in country inns, with frequent interludes of wining and dining.[25] But this example draws attention to another facet of coordinate proceedings—the readiness of the apparatus of authority to farm out procedural actions. As suggested in the previous chapter, if paradigmatic adjudicators are themselves amateurs, recruited to dispense justice ad hoc, there can be little principled opposition to expanding "adhocracy" a little further.

Where the private bar exists, its members are obvious candidates to whom procedural steps may be entrusted. Many ministerial functions that are the exclusive province of minor bureaucrats in hierarchical systems can thus be transferred to lawyers. For example, American attorneys can issue summonses, take depositions, command the assistance of local sheriffs, and even be relied upon to prepare orders and judgments for the judge to sign.[26]

The task of enforcing state policies in court can be entrusted to private individuals with much greater ease than in systems possessed by the spirit of official exclusivity. Relator actions in England and Australia, or private attorneys general in America, illustrate this tendency.[27] Various amici curiae are welcome assistants rather than somewhat tiresome meddlers disrupting official routine.

Almost naturally, the coordinate apparatus comes to rely upon private parties to prepare the material for consideration at trial. In the absence of official investigators, there would seem to be no other alternative. And since the decision makers themselves are unprepared, the parties also assume important functions at the trial in presenting the material they have assembled. Evidence produced by one party can be challenged by the other, who can in turn produce his own evidence, and so on. Of course, where a case involves a very serious clash of interests, the trial can produce heated and noisy arguments, especially where the production of evidence is in the hands of the interested parties rather than their lawyers. A good example of this style of proceeding was the English criminal trial before lawyers were permitted to participate. Thomas Smith described such trials to his French audience quite aptly as "altercations."[28] However, when lawyers assume control over the presentation of the assembled material, proceedings can

25. See W. J. Jones, *The Elizabethean Court of Chancery*, 240, 287 (1967).

26. For semiofficial activities of American attorneys, see *In re Griffith*, 413 U.S. 717 (1973). Lawyers not only draft judgments and orders, but often also submit drafts of findings of fact and conclusions of law to the judge. See *Railex Corp.* v. *Speed Check Co.*, 457 F2.d 1040, 1041–42 (5th Cir. 1972).

27. See M. Cappelletti, "Governmental and Private Advocates for the Public Interest in Civil Litigation," 73 *Mich. L. Rev.* 794, 849 (1975).

28. Smith, *supra*, n. 22, Lib. II, ch. 23, p. 100.

be transformed—as they were in England—into an exquisite minuet of confrontational steps.

A general consequence of the interpenetration of official and private action in coordinate proceedings deserves to be emphasized. It is often exceedingly difficult to state without equivocation when the proceedings commence, or what is, strictly speaking, part of the legal process. In contrast to the hierarchical mode, proceedings cannot clearly be identified with each step taken under direct supervision of authoritative governmental officials.

Substantive Justice and Procedural Regulation

In coordinate systems, one often finds complex technical rules regulating the conduct of trial protagonists before the lay decision maker. The genesis of these rules is related to the symbiosis of coordinate authority with a cast of professional advocates, a phenomenon of which I have already spoken. Growing out of eminently practical concerns and reflecting minutiae of accumulated professional experience, these rules defy easy summation and can be called unsurveyable, even arcane. However, in contrast to rules regulating the conduct of forensic actors in the hierarchical setting, such rules of practice and evidence are not unbending. The official presiding over proceedings can refuse to enforce them if he thinks it best under the circumstances. His refusal can be motivated by feelings of propriety or even by emotional factors such as compassion. For example, whereas the rule may require testimony from a witness who has validly waived his privilege against self-incrimination, the official can exercise discretion not to enforce the rule if he sympathizes with the motives that have led the witness to waive his privilege (e.g., by beginning to testify) and then to experience a change of heart.[29] Vigorous insistence on adherence to clear technical rules can easily backfire, especially if powerful and autonomous coordinate officials suspect that a party, although "technically correct," has pressed a point for ethically inferior reasons or has come to court with "unclean hands." Departure from technically mandated procedures is further facilitated by the absence of bureaucratic routine in the coordinate apparatus. As I have suggested, lay officials are willing to innovate and to experiment. In short, the filigree of technical rules does not prevent the impact on proceedings of standards of substantive justice.

As distinguished from rules governing the conduct of lawyers and parties, few rules bind the behavior of presiding officials. That they possess discretion to refuse to enforce the normative regime is only one aspect of their freedom. Those few rules which are addressed to them are vague and leave a substantial margin for additional, textually unexpressed authority. Nor should it be surprising if coordinate officials are authorized to enact their own rules concerning proceed-

29. From the perspective of a rigid hierarchical organization, there would be no point in having a regulation which can be so readily defeated. "All is lost if the judge wants to be smarter than the statute." See H. Drost, *Das Ermessen des Strafrichters*, 88 (Berlin, 1930). The phrase is attributed to Abbé de Mably.

ings in "their" court.[30] But unlike the situation in a hierarchical judicial organization where rules regulating official behavior are applied more mechanically, the coordinate apparatus, while according vast powers to its officials, relies on their discriminating sense to decide when to exercise such powers. Even textually identical rules can thus have a vastly different impact in the coordinate and the hierarchical environments. If a judge in the coordinate apparatus is empowered to call witnesses on his own, for example, it would not be unusual if he actually did so only on the rarest of occasions. It is difficult to imagine that a judicial organization comprising such officials would support attempts to streamline procedural arrangements into an intellectual structure consistent with a few principles—a structure in which absence of logic and incoherence in procedural convention would cause great concern.[31]

In conclusion, as one would expect in an apparatus comprising powerful and independent officials, the progress of proceedings—no matter how minutely regulated at the surface—greatly depends on the manner in which these officials choose to exercise their vast "inherent" authority. Official discretion remains a keynote. As a turn-of-the-century German observer of English magistrates wondered from his perspective, can these officials be likened more appropriately to constitutional monarchs or to enlightened despots?[32]

Summary

Let us briefly pause and take stock. Proceedings adapted to the needs of coordinate officials center around the single echelon of authority: the trial is the focal point of the whole process, and it unfolds preferably without interruption. Its preparation is not the responsibility of a specialized branch of the judiciary or of other specialized state officials, but is relegated to the parties involved in the case. Decision makers thus necessarily come to the case unprepared and are unable to take charge of proof taking and similar activity—at least initially. As a result, those who prepare the trial—the parties or their forensic assistants—also present the evidence before the decision maker. Live testimony and oral communication are preferred over evidentiary records (documentary evidence) and written submissions.

Without regular mechanisms of review, parties dissatisfied with the decision must attempt to persuade the adjudicator to reconsider, or try to frustrate the enforcement of the decision in collateral proceedings. The easy blending of official and private action renders the outer boundaries of the process indistinct

---

30. American judges, even single judges in a multijudge court, are often accorded the power to adopt rules of decorum in their court. These rules can be fashioned ad hoc to fit a particular occasion. See *United States* v. *Barcella*, 432 F.2d 570, 572 (1st Cir. 1971).

31. For example, coordinate officials are singularly unimpressed by the "conceptualist" argument that it is inappropriate to let the defendant plead guilty and to delete the guilt-determining stage of the trial process because guilt is a matter for the adjudicator to decide in "creative" ways, by fine-tuning the law to the circumstances of the case. See *infra*, ch. 3, n. 43 and accompanying text.

32. See A. Mendelssohn-Bartholdy, *Das Imperium des Richters*, 120 (Strassburg, 1908).

and encompasses elements of private procedural enterprise. Moreover, although aspects of the trial may be subject to extensive technical regulation, this regulation can easily be displaced by norms invoked by coordinate officials in their own discretion.

iii. COMMENSURABILITY OF THE HIERARCHICAL AND COORDINATE PROCESSES

By playing out the procedural implications of the hierarchical and the coordinate ideals, elements of two distinctive procedural styles have now been obtained. But in showing how the character of authority impinges on procedural arrangements, I have also implicitly suggested the difficulty of comparing procedural problems across the divide that separates them. Otherwise similar forms of justice in the two institutional settings may differ in ways not easy to define, and forms of justice natural in one setting can elude description in terms of categories habitual in the other. Surely, Continental and Anglo-American lawyers find it more difficult to develop a common language in matters of procedure and evidence than in other areas of the law. Some problems of relating the divergent outlooks deserve a cursory review.

Single and Multiple Echelons of Authority

We saw that appeals, natural to hierarchical officialdom, are no longer the same when grafted upon a predominantly coordinate judicial organization, and that coordinate-style trials do not retain their identity when incorporated into a multistage process. While it seems normal in one system to enforce the trial court's judgment even before all legal remedies have been exhausted, this procedure appears "unnatural" and grotesque in the other.[33] Of course, where decisions are based on live testimony in one system and on the written record in the other, perceptions of a variety of problems must begin to diverge. We are all sufficiently McLuhanesque to suspect that form is likely to have an effect on the manner of viewing its content. Subtle but far-reaching differences in attitude arise from the absence in coordinate structures of a vision congenial to distant officials in tall pyramids of authority: where a more concrete and inclusive vision would locate a chance to attain "individualized" justice, a more abstract and selective vision would find dangers to consistent and predictable decision making. As a result, a large number of procedural problems is approached from different positions, and many procedural devices are assessed differently in the two official organizations. Like Don Quixote and his squire sensitized to different aspects of reality, so lawyers socialized in different settings of authority can look at the same object and see different things.

---

33. To the bewilderment of Continental lawyers, American courts are tempted to enforce foreign judgments before appellate remedies have been exhausted. See *Hearst* v. *Hearst*, 150 N.Y. 2d 764 (Sup. Ct. 1955). To make such a "mistake" seems almost unthinkable to Continental lawyers.

Unequal Degrees of Bureaucratization

One particularly troubling problem is that of relating a system that equates the legal process with steps taken by officials to a system that readily delegates procedural action to outsiders.

Consider an example. While to coordinate authority it is perfectly acceptable to allow private attorneys to take oral depositions in their private offices, the hierarchical process does not even have a categorical niche to classify this practice. At first, when viewed through the spectacles of hierarchical authority, the taking of oral depositions appears as a mere private interview aimed at developing the lawsuit. This is because depositions are taken without direct judicial superintendence, and because the results are not competent evidence to be incorporated in the official file of the case. But this categorization falters when it appears that deponents can be compelled to appear, can be impeached, and are obliged to respond truthfully to questions. In the end, the practice is neither fish nor fowl in the conceptual scheme of the hierarchical process. Yet because more than a private interview is involved, depositions tend to be viewed as an arrogation by private persons of action that must be reserved for governmental officials. Quite predictably, attempts by American attorneys to conduct depositions on the Continent are treated there as offensive to the prerogative of the state to administer justice and are now outlawed in several European countries.[34]

Forms of justice are not likely to be integrated similarly in a judicial apparatus that strives toward specialization and one that fuses functions. This gives a clue to the puzzlement of Continental lawyers looking at the branches of the American administration of justice and their mutual relation. The civil process, for example, seems to them to be much too diffuse, encompassing forms that seem more appropriately to belong to the administrative process, general administration, or even the legislative process. On the other hand, criminal prosecutions embrace many arrangements that seem "natural" only in the context of civil litigation.[35]

Substantive Justice and Technical Legalism

It is not easy to establish a community of discourse for those attached to substantive justice and those inspired by legalism. While one disposition strives to keep

34. France now prohibits pretrial discovery *à l'Americaine* even if it is part of an effort to obtain evidence for a lawsuit that has already begun in earnest, rather than (as often happens) solely for purposes of "fishing for information." See *Law* No. 80–538 of July 16, 1980. English authorities also disapprove of American pretrial discovery tactics, but they are not likely to regard such practices as violative of sovereignty, or even as reprehensible, provided the lawsuit has earnestly begun. For further examples of "privately" undertaken American litigation activity which Continentals find offensive, see H. Steiner and D. Vagts, *Transnational Legal Problems*, 669 (1968).

35. See chapter 6 passim. Even in England, Continentals find that the line between civil and administrative proceedings is drawn with insufficient clarity. See V. Varano, *Organizzazione e garanzie della giustizia civile nell'Inghilterra moderna*, 271 (Milano, 1973). From the Continental viewpoint, English criminal process also seems saturated with forms that "ontologically" belong to civil justice.

political, ethical, and legal issues distinct, the other finds this separation artificial and inappropriate. The problem can again be illustrated in the example of Continental and Anglo-American legal cultures. Continental judges are ideally still expected to anchor their decisions in a network of outcome-determinative rules; they are reluctant to "politicize" or "moralize" matters that come before them.[36] To the extent that they participate in decision making at all, laymen are pushed into relatively innocuous roles: vigorous advocacy of independent views on their part is readily branded as an arrogant display of dilettantism. By contrast, more potent forms of lay participation in the Anglo-American administration of justice (jurors, lay magistrates) continue vigorously to infuse precepts of substantive justice into the courtroom.[37] The American professional judiciary is notoriously politicized and expected to consider "the equities" of cases so that the door remains open to the consideration of various extralegal factors. Even in England, where professional judges are much more technically oriented than in America, Continental lawyers register their surprise at the apparent flexibility of the judiciary to respond to contours of individual cases in commonsensical ways.[38] Divergent attitudes surface also in the adjudication of constitutional issues—that is, in the area where law and politics inevitably merge. It is well known that several Continental countries have adopted mechanisms of judicial review, in some instances under the obvious influence of American constitutional law. Yet so deeply ingrained is the fear of unduly "politicizing" the administration of justice that it appeared undesirable to empower ordinary (real) judges to strike down unconstitutional statutes. Instead, this power has been vested in a highly placed and specialized tribunal, regarded not so much as a true court of law but as a superlegislative body.[39]

As this study proceeds, the difficulties of making hierarchical and coordinate proceedings truly comparable will persist. Like concepts of organic and geometrical beauty, the two procedural modes seem to elude a common Vitruvian measure. But because this study seeks to illuminate differences more than to

36. The tendency of the Continental career judiciary (and the legal culture as a whole) to separate legal and political questions more sharply than is usual in Anglo-American systems has often been noted. See M. Cappelletti, *supra*, n. 27, 865; K. Mannheim, *Ideology and Utopia*, 105 (1949); H. Spiro, *Government by Constitution*, 285 (1959).

37. Mendelssohn-Bartholdy has characterized decisions of English law magistrates as "Solomonic" (*supra*, n. 32, 161). Although the technical component of decision making has increased considerably in this century, lay magistrates, even if assisted by "technicians," should not be equated with the lower civil service judiciary on the Continent.

38. Flexible judicial supervision of every phase of trust administration as well as many "equitable" doctrines are telling illustrations. See R. Schlesinger, *supra*, n. 6, 736 (n. 3). The institutional merger of the judiciary and the legislature in the House of Lords is also surprising. As between the legal sensibility of professional judges in England and on the Continent, the main contrast is one between a more "pragmatic" and a more "logically ordered" brand of legalism. Many legal principles, dear to Continentals, appear across the Channel as airy generalizations linked, like so many captive balloons, by the most tenuous ties to the cases beneath.

39. On Continental constitutional courts as "superlegislatures," see J. Esser, *Vor-verständnis und Methodenwahl in der Rechtsfindung*, 201 (Frankfurt, 1970). For the special case of Greece, see F. Spiliotopoulos, "Judicial Review of Legislative Acts in Greece," 56 *Temple L.Q.* 463, 496 (1983).

identify common grounds, I shall not inquire here whether a scheme can yet be formulated in which procedural conventions in the two settings of authority can be made easily translatable.

iv. RELATIONSHIP TO CONVENTIONAL CATEGORIES

The core of the contrast between the Anglo-American and the Continental styles of administering justice is conventionally expressed by opposing the "inquisitorial" process of continental Europe to the "adversarial" process of countries whose systems derive from England. I have evoked this contrast, however, by juxtaposing the hierarchical and the coordinate styles. Clarification of the relationship among these categories requires that I revert to and expand upon certain themes sounded in the Introduction.

It should be clear that the hierarchical and the coordinate styles can each be employed either to adjudicate a bipolar adversarial dispute or to establish whether legal preconditions exist for the enforcement of some state policy or program. A controversy between two parties can be decided either by professional or by lay judges; the contest can unfold in written form (exchange of briefs) or orally; adversaries can be pitted against each other in a single "round" or in several, and argue before a single or several levels of authority. Conversely, an inquest with a view toward law enforcement can be conducted by professional or lay officials; it can rely on documents as well as on live testimony; it can implicate single or multiple echelons of judicial authority. The hierarchical and coordinate styles can thus be used across the lines of civil, criminal, and administrative proceedings— lines that are variously drawn in different legal cultures.

The possibility remains open that a particular organization of authority is better suited or more efficent to conduct an inquest, and another to conduct a contest, but there is no necessary relationship between the organization of procedural authority and the object of proceedings. Now if the adversarial system is understood to be a process designed as a bipolar dispute and the nonadversarial system is associated with a procedure of inquest (which seems to be the prevailing view), the two procedural styles I have described in this chapter are independent of the conventional dichotomy. The hierarchical style can be combined with *both* adversarial and nonadversarial forms, and the coordinate style possesses the same valences. To phrase the matter differently, the hierarchical and the coordinate authority can each develop its own adversarial and nonadversarial proceedings.

It is precisely because inquest and contest forms have actually been adapted to the indigenous organization of authority—coordination in Anglo-American lands and hierarchy on the Continent—that conceptions diverge in the two settings with respect to the constituent elements or necessary ingredients of adversarial and nonadversarial proceedings. As a result, there is presently no concept of the adversarial and nonadversarial modes that can be applied "neutrally" across the line that divides the two families of law shaped by different traditions of organizing judicial authority: forms of litigious and inquest procedure are desperately entangled in hierarchical and coordinate incrustations.

Can they be unraveled? If one is to begin to approach an answer to this question, the background of the contrast between contest and inquest forms of justice must be examined. Heretofore I have discussed connections between the administration of justice and the *structure* of authority. Controlling now for this variable, I shall examine in the following pages how different conceptions about the *function* of government can affect the shape of the legal process.

III Two Types of State and the Ends of the Legal Process

In search of a basic orientation, I shall explore how the legal process can be affected by two contrasting dispositions of government: the disposition to manage society and the disposition merely to provide a framework for social interaction. Some governments chose to be almost totally uninvolved in certain spheres of social life and to be quite managerial in others; they can embrace one disposition as a regulative ideal and temper it with the other; again, they may be profoundly torn between the inclination to stay at arm's length, and the duty to assume responsibility to steer society. They thus occupy a wide range on a continuum stretching from one theoretical end point—a state that fully penetrates social life—to the other theoretical terminus—a state that is truly laissez-faire.

It might be thought possible to obtain a double vision of an interventionist and of a laissez-faire administration of justice sufficiently polarized to cover existing systems, without including the end points of the continuum and thereby avoid considering extreme political doctrines. In short, to uncover the assumptions of these two visions it may be thought sufficient to analyze those proceedings in which *moderate* governments seek to implement programs, and those proceedings in which such governments provide a forum for the resolution of social problems. This approach can be restated in slightly different form: even if managerial and laissez-faire impulses lead to different ideas about the design of the legal process, such ideas are indifferent to the changing scope of government. As managerial concerns of the government expand, forms of the laissez-faire process remain unaltered; only the range of their applicability decreases. Conversely, as the agenda of government shrinks, forms of the interventionist process remain unaltered; only the domain of its applicability narrows.

On closer inspection, however, this argument has little to recommend it. The spheres in which moderate governments choose to assume managerial responsibilities and the spheres where they opt to be uninvolved are not hermetically sealed; rather, they interpenetrate and influence each other. The dominant conception of the role of the state—the idea of limited government, for example—more or less openly affects the legal process even in those spheres where the state departs from its ideal. One is thus more likely to find hybrids and contamination rather than pure forms. It is only in the ideological arsenal of extreme political theories that one finds adequate support and justification for the properly polarized visions of the laissez-faire and managerial administrations of justice.

But before I consider extremes of uninvolved and interventionist government, it will be useful to make a few general remarks on the nature of the polarity and on some problems it entails.

The bifurcation is predicated on two contrary interpretations of the relation between state and society. According to one position, the task of the state is to support existing social practice. It is improper for the government to embrace views of what the desirable way of life is and to lead citizens toward its ideals: society should be immune from self-conscious governmental direction. The other position authorizes the state to pursue and impose particular views of the good society and to lead society in desirable directions. According to the progressive variant of this position, existing social institutions can be transformed according to the goals espoused by the government; according to the conservative variant, spontaneous social change can and should be resisted if it detracts from governmental conceptions of the good life. Among interventionist political doctrines, those of special interest here invest the government with a pervasive program permitting its penetration of all spheres of social life; among ideologies of limited government, those of special interest here limit the function of the state solely to the maintenance of social equilibrium. Clearly, both groups of political doctrines are not without overtones of utopian thought: whereas one group contemplates an omnivorous state—a Leviathan ready to swallow civil society completely—the other envisages a vanishing state—a political Cheshire cat. I shall call the one extreme the reactive state, and the second, the activist state.

These terms may cause misunderstanding that must be anticipated and removed at this point. It has gained currency in many quarters to refer to variously defined extremes of minimalist government as the reactive state and to call a state activist even if it uses its managerial potential sparingly and continues to regard the absence of governmental direction as an overall ideal.[1] This convention should not be confused with the one proposed here: a limited activist state may come closer to a laissez-faire than to a truly managerial government when it is observed from the broader perspective required by comparative horizons.[2]

---

1. The doctrine of liberal activism in America is a case in point. According to this doctrine, the autonomy of the individual and the limited interference of government in social life continue to be regarded as desiderata, but at the same time governmental responsibility for the solution of social problems is increasingly recognized, mainly for dealing with a narrow set of market imperfections. See B. A. Ackerman, *Reconstructing American Law*, 1–6, 32 (1984).

2. Governmental programs can be devised to correct failures of "the invisible hand" (the market), thus to reduce the need for the intervention of "the visible hand" (governmental management of large segments of social and economic life).

Devotees of such limited activism may nevertheless resent the comparativist's usage: "activism" is associated with a state that deeply penetrates social life and therefore the term conjures up the specter of totalitarianism. But I do not mean to imply that the expansion of the agenda of government inexorably leads to oppressive managerial regimes: stable intermediate positions may exist. In seeking a proper balance between activist and reactive impulses, it is misleading to invoke the *bête noire* of an extreme uninvolved government while closing one's eyes to the precise character of an extremely intrusive state. In a historical period when it becomes increasingly important to seek acceptable middle positions between governmental direction and individual self-definition, one must strive to define properly the poles of the debate.

i. THE REACTIVE STATE

General Characteristics

The task of the reactive state is limited to providing a supporting framework within which its citizens pursue their chosen goals. Its instruments must set free spontaneous forces of social self-management. The state contemplates no notion of separate interest apart from social and individual (private) interests: there are no inherent state problems, only social and individual problems. It is often said of such "minimalist" government that it does only two things: it protects order, and it provides a forum for the resolution of those disputes that cannot be settled by citizens themselves.[3] But the task of protecting order—especially insofar as it shades into preventive action—can lead to a considerable extension of managerial activity. Accordingly, genuine extremes of reactive ideology tend to collapse the protection of order into dispute resolution. The principal strategy is to argue as follows: because the state has no interests apart from society, it also has no rights as such that can be violated apart from the violation of a "private" right; any breach of order originates in a violation of somebody's right, so that the state springs into protective action only when somebody complains, seeking redress, and somebody else refuses to meet his demands. To protect order is therefore to settle disputes.

It is also true that the state superficially appears as guardian of an interest all its own. Actually, however, its function is surrogate: the state acts only to protect those interests that would ideally be urged by individuals or groups of citizens. State protection of the interests of individuals who are not—or are not

---

3. The external function of the state in national defense and in war is deliberately neglected here. Astute theorists have not failed to observe that war invests the state with a common purpose and managerial tasks which tend to subvert its abstentionist posture. Michael Oakeshott has articulated a distinction between two "characters" of the state which can be classed as variants of activist and reactive ideology, and he has rightly pointed out that the state as a "civil association" (reactive state) moves toward an "enterprise" or "managerial" association (activist state) in time of war and in preparation for it. See M. Oakeshott, *On Human Conduct*, 146, 272 (1975).

yet—capable of independently structuring their personal affairs is a case in point: vis-à-vis the child or the mentally incompetent, the government assumes the role of parent substitute. But whenever the state acts in this capacity, the interests it represents retain their individual identity; they are never placed on a more exalted plane, over and above private interests.

The vision of such a state obviously lacks any transforming power: it appears uninspired, almost lifeless. Civil society, split off from the state, becomes the center of political action: values, initiatives—even projects for New Jerusalems—originate here. And it is in civil society that individuals—sovereign in determining what to do with their lives—can, should they so desire, form communities devoted to the promotion of common goals, even including common annihilation. In civil society the voice of men and women can be choral.

This aspect of the reactive state requires a brief digression. Because the most important variants of the doctrine now under consideration arose in the context of societies organized around capitalist markets, it has been forcefully argued that, rather than promoting a variety of organic groups or free associations, ideologies of governmental noninvolvement promote a society of competitive or "possessive" individuals.[4] But there is no necessary connection among the reactive posture, capitalism, and individualism. The ideal of the minimal state constitutes part of an important socialist tradition: its anarcho-syndicalist variant envisages a society composed of *mutualiste* associations in the context of an "abstentionist" form of government. This vision, although overshadowed by statist socialism, continues to influence contemporary political ideologies even in countries where the progenitors of anarcho-syndicalism are criticized and ridiculed. For example, embedded in one strand of Marxist thought, the Yugoslav doctrine of self-management calls for a minimalist government and has in fact produced a dramatic reduction in the scope of government.[5] It is also worth remarking that reactive governments have existed by force of circumstance (before the advent of political ideologies) in settings wherein independent associations played an all-important role. Prior to the rise of capitalist markets, central governments of medieval Europe were predominantly reactive. Their agenda was limited to the prevention of hostility through peaceful settlement of clan disputes. Society, however, was then anything but atomistic. In brief, ideologies of reactive states or even reactive governments need not be always associated with support of private markets, nor always be treated as smoke screens through which the economically powerful validate the status quo.

4. The phrase is from C. Macpherson, *The Political Theory of Possessive Individualism* (1962). With an eye on claims of classical liberal ideology, many have argued that there never was a laissez-faire state, markets never were truly self-regulatory, and the boundaries of state activity never so restricted. But even within the Marxist tradition it is frequently recognized that during certain stages of modern history some countries approximated an "autonomous market society," with the sphere of government relatively insignificant and with actual social power vested in the successful components of "civil society." The more successful the market, the more the state retreated to a position of uninvolvement. See, e.g., G. Lichtheim, *From Marx to Hegel*, 133 (1971).

5. For an extensive collection of literature on Yugoslav self-management in English, see C. Lindblom, *Politics and Markets*, 387 (1977); D. Rusinow, *The Yugoslav Experiment 1948–1974*, 32–245 (1978).

An important implication of the reactive state's refusal to embrace any independent theory of what is good for society can now be considered. By virtue of its own abstention, the state can encompass and include associations and individuals with widely disparate objectives. When individual or group conflict arises, the state can claim a neutral position: amidst storms and strife in society, it can profess calm objectivity—*tranquillitas in undis*. Its citizens are not linked to it by mutual desire to achieve a common end; rather they are connected to the state primarily in its capacity as a neutral forum for dispute resolution. As in the formative period of the modern European state when princes integrated a fragmented society by providing a common court and were conceived essentially as judges, the reactive state is first and foremost an adjudicative body. All other state activities are an extension of and subordinated to dispute resolution.[6] Far from being the least dangerous branch of government, the judiciary is—with little exaggeration—indeed the only branch of government.

Although the reactive state need not necessarily espouse epistemological skepticism, it seems most comfortable when anchored there. Where it appears that no wholly objective means exist to determine what values deserve to be promoted, perhaps even no objective way to establish which scientific views accurately mirror reality[7]—a firm predicate for the formulation of state goals is missing. By default, as it were, the definition of life ambitions must be entrusted to individuals who, it is hoped, relish the excitement of choosing for themselves. By following their preferences, indirectly, individuals may perhaps contribute to the well-being of all: when the rose embellishes itself, it also decorates the garden.

The Law

Where the government celebrates self-regulation by members of civil society, the mainspring of the law tends to be outside of the state or "above" it. And where individual preferences are sovereign, the most suitable norm-creating devices are various types of agreement, contracts, and pacts.[8] Even Mephi-

6. Although Western princes have legislated since the Middle Ages, they continued to be conceived primarily as judges until the sixteenth century. See Q. Skinner, *The Foundations of Modern Political Thought*, vol. 2, 289 (1978).

7. The skepticism toward values of laissez-faire doctrines has often been noted; this skepticism can be extended to facts as well. An example is the recent attempt to link the general distaste for epistemology with a mode of political association where the populace is united in terms of "civility" rather than in terms of common goals. See R. Rorty, *Philosophy and the Mirror of Nature*, 318 (1979). This extension of skepticism is interesting, for it can be an influential factor in fashioning fact-finding techniques for the legal process.

8. In the theory of Proudhon, for example, enterprises become important social cells based on contracts with the workers. Larger units are formed through agreements among economic sectors and broader pacts involving state authorities. See G. D. H. Cole, *Socialist Thought: The Forerunners: 1789–1850*, vol. 1 (1953). The Proudhonian distinction between pacts among sectors of the economy and broader pacts involving the state has been almost exactly reproduced in the Yugoslav experiment to replace state legislation by "self-managing agreements" (*samoupravni sporazumi*) and "social compacts" (*društveni dogovori*).

stopheles—otherwise so independent and overpowering—submitted to the magic rule of contract.

To say that law emanates from social intercourse and thus empoverishes state lawmaking is not to suggest that there is no room left for legislation. Consider substantive law first. Not all conflict-causing behavior can be anticipated by an actual contract or pact that will define substantive rules for its disposition. If actual prior agreements were in fact prerequisites for permissible conduct, private activity would be intolerably restricted.[9] Furthermore, even where a dispute is preceded and anticipated by a contract, the agreement's terms may be vague, ambiguous, or ragged on the edges, so that the state must address uncertainties or gaps in private contractual arrangements. But the tenor of state law is not to announce what citizens should do substantively; rather, it is to set forth procedures which make such arrangements binding and enforceable. In other words, the state does not so much tell citizens what they should do or agree upon as tell them how to seek agreements, make them binding, and behave in case of conflict. But how are legal standards—substantive or procedural—to be formulated? Where the state embraces no independent value system or policies, its law plainly cannot embody and express state values and policies. The only legitimate route the lawgiver can take is to try to determine how citizens would have agreed to resolve a matter had they anticipated it; social expectations must be captured and defined. Accordingly, even state law is affected by the imagery and hermeneutic of agreement, albeit in a somewhat subterranean fashion. At bottom, all state law can be regarded as a "hypothetical" or "model" contract. And being a surrogate for an actual agreement, in principle it can be displaced and modified by the actual "private" arrangements of individuals and groups. Thus a vast expanse of yielding law (*loi suppletive, jus dispositivum*) characterizes the legal culture of the reactive state; absolute prohibitions or injunctions are anomalous.[10] Whether state law is promulgated or "codified" in advance of an actual dispute or in the context of its resolution is a problem related to the structure of state authority and need not be discussed here.

The relation of state law to state mission should now be clear: the law facilitates and supports autonomous regulation by members of civil society in its creation of "bargaining chips" for transactions among citizens. Participants in negotiations realize that unless they reach agreement, one side can invoke the state forum, which is apt to impose the "model" arrangement.

The centrality of the contracting mode is closely related to another feature of the legal culture in the reactive state—the apotheosis of private, individual, or

---

9. For an argument along these lines, see R. Nozick, *Anarchy, State and Utopia* 72 (1974).

10. Thus criminal law prohibitions can readily be converted into licenses purchasable at a price: citizens of the reactive state can imitate Lucius Veratus, who is reported to have wandered the streets of Rome and slapped people he did not like in the face, offering to pay the fine for battery on the spot. See Aulus Gellius, *Noctes Atticae* 20, 1, 13. Because the mission of reactive governments is never *completely* provisional, its advocates concede the existence of a small core of provisions that cannot be altered by citizens' voluntary transactions. This grudging and somewhat embarrassing admission is reflected in attitudes toward the waiver of procedural rights, discussed *infra*.

group rights. Because both contracts and pacts are devices for the allocation of rights and duties, any state regulation can readily be translated into a network of personal rights and duties. No "objective" regulations, addressed to state officials, are exempt from this transformation. If a judge is directed to acquit a defendant who committed an illegal act under duress, it seems natural to conclude that such an individual has a personal right to commit an otherwise illegal act if he finds himself under certain kinds of compulsion. How deeply alien is this move in the legal culture of activist government will soon be seen. But the apotheosis of rights does not imply only that all law is transformed into a bundle of rights with corresponding obligations. It is only in the ideological ambience of the reactive state that the assertion of rights can be severed from assessment of the consequences of such assertion. The state embraces no aggregate policy vision in light of which the ripple effects flowing from the assertion of rights could be evaluated. Like trees or flowers on medieval manuscript margins, rights are treated in monadic isolation—that is, in their strongest, absolute sense.[11]

Administration of Justice

Can the reactive state be associated with a particular design of the legal process? Suggesting an affirmative answer, I shall show, first, how minimal government colors the perception of what it means to administer justice and, second, how such perceptions can affect choice of the basic structural principle for design of the legal process.

It has been pointed out already that in the optic of reactive ideology, all state activities become inseparable from the resolution of conflict. Being merely reactive, the state cannot legitimately respond to a crisis in civil society unless and until disputants have engaged its forum: its legal process necessarily presupposes an instance of *actual* dispute. To the extent that the state engages in residual administration, that too becomes intertwined with litigation. If the administration desires to act in a way opposed by somebody, it must initiate some sort of "civil" prosecution before a court, rather than simply carry through its plans and thereby place the burden of engaging the forum on the aggrieved citizen.

Disputes that come before the courts of the reactive state involve not only individuals but also voluntary associations. It is precisely because the government is uninvolved that both space and reason are created for vigorous conflict-

---

11. The adjective *absolute* can be understood here in its original etymological sense as "free from effects" (*absolutus ab effectu*). Rights can also be treated as truly personal or "subjective," that is, as something that inheres (*subjacet*) in an individual by virtue of his being an end in itself rather than as something that is thrown (*ob-jectum*) before him and accorded him conditionally. Perhaps we have moved, in most spheres of social life, to a point where it is difficult to imagine rights in this strong "abstract" sense, so natural to thinkers such as Leibnitz, Locke, Spinoza, and especially Kant. But even in late twentieth-century America, aspects of social experience exist where the opposite difficulty is experienced—the difficulty of thinking of certain rights as dependent on social benefits resulting from their exercise. On the relatively recent and resolutely Western origin of strong notions of the right, see M. Villey, *Seize Essais de Philosophie du Droit*, 140–77, "La Genèse du droit subjectif chez Guillaume d'Occam" (Paris, 1969).

entailing activity by citizens' groups. Now group litigation can have a wide-ranging impact that extends into areas which most states tend to regulate in light of policies they espouse. It is difficult to "depoliticize" such group conflict and to view it as self-contained, narrow, or "private." But not so in the optic of reactive ideology: here, there are no policies in whose context broader effects of group disputes could be measured, and the dispute thus treated as an occasion for implementing governmental policy. Even in this situation, the idea that to administer justice is merely to resolve a dispute can be maintained.

In those exceptional cases in which the reactive state functions as a surrogate for an underrepresented interest, it appears that the state must develop "policies" concerning the interest it would safeguard or promote. When an official "promoter" comes in conflict with a citizen or an association, it seems at first that the legal process can no longer be conceived as engagement in pure dispute resolution. Remember, however, that these policies are not "independent," and that the surrogate state interest is placed on an equal plane with private interests: the state official must sue to enforce just such interests, and must be treated in court on an even footing with his private opponents. In other words, the relationship between the surrogate state official and the private individual or group is "horizontal"—both are parties to a dispute—so that even surrogate state activities are annexed to dispute resolution. Of course, the tenability of the litigational frame—the equal treatment of both sides—will be questioned because the state is at once a contestant and an arbiter of the contest—that is, the judge in his own cause (*judex in causa sua*). Whatever the ultimate answer to this question, observe that an extreme reactive state provides relatively the most propitious environment for taking the litigational frame seriously, even in this situation. Where the state adopts no theory of good life and is engaged in only fragmentary and surrogate projects, a certain equanimity or *nonchaloir* with respect to the outcome of any given case acquires maximum plausibility. As I have observed, the state can continue to profess impassivity—*tranquillitas in undis*—rather than demand involvement from adjudicators.

Having shown that in the lens of extreme reactive ideology, to administer justice is always to engage in dispute resolution, I now want to suggest ways in which master questions of procedural design can be affected by this particular perspective on the purposes of the legal process.

Where the legal process involves a dispute over rights, it involves two sides—group or individual—advancing contrary claims and pressing for incompatible dispositions of the case. Should conciliatory or confrontational forms be chosen for the resolution of the controversy? Again the answer must follow from the character of the reactive state. Its ideal of self-management prompts it to place primary reliance for dispute resolution on civil society: if disputants belong to the same association or are part of the same social institution, their disagreements are best settled internally. In this setting, dispute resolution can be understood to involve a search for middle positions between competing claims, for reconciliation and mediation: appeals to shared goals or exhortations to mutual sacrifice for the sake of preserving valued relationships take their rightful place. Recourse to a state forum is imagined only as a means of last resort, to be employed in the event that less drastic "private" means have failed. But when a disputant decides to take his case before the state judge, his cause of action indicates refusal to subordinate his claim of right to shared values and goals or to acknowledge a middle ground. A state that refuses to espouse any independent theory of the good life cannot provide the missing common ground to reunite the litigants. Moreover, a state tribunal's quest for the middle ground can easily be interpreted in ways damaging to the mission of reactive government. In controversies involving claims of right—dichotomous issues—any independent activity on the part of the adjudicator can be interpreted as partiality. In urging compromise, he may appear to pressure a disputant to give up what is his due according to law.[12] To the extent that the reactive state wants its courts to strengthen and further elaborate the normative framework (bargaining chips) for social self-management, another objection to mediative dispute resolution arises. Conciliation results in a decision that does not reflect the law as related to the issues in controversy: the judgment is an accommodation, which seldom provides fixed reference points as to how future cases would be decided in the absence of private ordering.

For all these reasons, when a controversy is brought to a state court, conciliatory morphology is no longer appropriate. The arrangements that pit the disputants against each other in a courtroom contest now become attractive as a peaceful substitute for a violent encounter between those who acknowledge no common ground. In the end, the fundamental structural principle upon which the procedural edifice of the reactive state is erected thus becomes the idea that proceedings are a contest of two sides. To imagine, however, that the ideal of self-management is wholly discarded once the jurisdiction of state courts has been invoked would be wrong: like the phoenix, that ideal can rise from its own ashes. If the disputants reach an out-of-court settlement of their difficulty, legal proceedings lose their underlying animus and come to an end; agreement between former litigants overrides prior judicial rulings. As expressed in an old adage, dating from a time when the primary objective of courts was the prevention of clan warfare, *pactum vincit legem et amor judicium* (an agreement prevails over law and love over the judgment).

How far the combat motif can be carried in the legal process depends on the degree to which intervention by a third side—the state adjudicator—is permitted. The more limited the opportunity for intervention, the more pronounced the combat motif. It is therefore clear that extreme variants of reactive ideology buttress an extreme combat design: here, the state's detachment includes minimal interference with the way in which disputants manage the forensic combat. Adjudicators merely preside over the disputation of the adverse parties and intervene in the process only insofar as intervention is required to monitor and to

---

12. Compromise may also be regarded as an inadequate disincentive for breaches of right: if the aggrieved and the transgressor are pressured to settle, each giving up a little, the transgressor's violation of the law may pay off to a degree, unless the aggrieved as plaintiff properly overclaims. For example, if A illegally obtains $100 from B and the compromise is that he return $80, he has gained $20, unless A inflates his claim in anticipation of the compromise.

ensure the fair disposition of incidental controversies. The verdict follows the close of the contest, and if the contest was fair and the decision maker has not compromised his neutrality, the loser has little reason to suspect the legitimacy of his defeat. He has mainly himself to blame for the adverse decision, and even if he rebels, society as a whole maintains its faith in the neutral administration of justice. Disputes thus can be "absorbed" by a legal process carrying the contest idea to its limits.

In the next chapter I shall explore how far the connection between the reactive state's ideology and the shape of the legal process can be pursued. But even this first approximation reveals that the legal process of the reactive state resembles what is called "the adversarial process" in common-law cultures and the "party-governed," "contradictory," or "accusatorial process" in Continental legal culture.[13] In order to avoid their misleading connotations in conventional analysis, I shall reluctantly discard better known labels and call the process predicated on reactive ideology the "conflict-solving process." Of course, those in the habit of identifying the legal process with conflict resolution will find this terminology pleonastic. But disapproval should be suspended until after a different vision of justice has been outlined, a vision fitting the ideology of activism.

ii. THE ACTIVIST STATE

General Characteristics

Let us focus our attention now on the other end of the ideological spectrum—on the extreme activist state. Such a state does much more than adopt a few propulsive policies and welfare programs. It espouses or strives toward a comprehensive theory of the good life and tries to use it as a basis for a conceptually all-encompassing program of material and moral betterment of its citizens.[14] All spheres of social life, even matters that take place *in pianissimo*, can at least potentially be evaluated in terms of state policy and shaped to its demands.

Existing social institutions and social practice command little deference: as it exists, society is defective and in need of improvement. With civil society stripped of legitimacy, projects and perspectives that arise spontaneously among citizens are suspect, for they may clash with those favored by the government,

---

13. "Party-dominated proceedings" (*Parteiverfahren*) and "the contradictory process" (*procédure contradictoire*) are terms employed primarily in discussing the civil process, whereas "the accusatorial process" appears mainly in the analysis of criminal justice.

14. Although some aspects of this program can be linked to the hereafter, in what follows only secular goals are intended. A possible tension must be acknowledged, even in this more limited domain: material betterment, with its emphasis on the exploitation of natural resources, tends to produce instrumentalist approaches even in settings not dominated by rational bureaucracy. On the other hand, the task of improvement of moral welfare pushes toward expressive or noninstrumental values even in bureaucratic environments. This tension can be reflected in the legal system, where two different paradigms of the law clash and vie for primacy.

may weaken commitment to state goals, and sap confidence in its actions. Accordingly, voluntary associations should either be dismantled or placed under supervision. It is hardly an exaggeration to say that civic associations, even if superficially independent, become annexes of state agencies—conduits through which governmental ideas are imparted to the populace. The state becomes the sole forum for political activity and the exclusive locus of allegiance: society is "statized"—swallowed by the state. Thus social problems and social policies are dissolved into state problems and state policies.

Relationships among people and their ties to the government can be variously characterized, but common to all formulations is a strong emphasis on a shared sense of citizenship, on harmony and cooperation rather than on dissonance and conflict. People should be linked by their efforts to achieve common goals, each subordinate to the overriding state interest. The government regards itself not as a neutral conflict resolver but rather as a manager of joint pursuit.[15] Its task is to bring people together and to devise incentives to mobilize inert individuals. Those who believe that work on civic projects and participation in public ceremonies take too many evenings are singled out for special scorn: mere indifference to state programs can appear rebellious. Inevitably, the possibilities are reduced for citizens to do what they want. But in the light of state philosophy, this is not cause for concern: government subscribes to Rousseau's opinion that the more time citizens spend on civic matters and the less on their own private affairs, the better.

Needless to say, individual autonomy is far from sacrosanct. To an activist government, individuals need not even be reliable judges of their own best interest: their self-perception, shaped by a defective social practice, may be faulty and incorrect. Of course, the more citizens are changed according to the image of governmental theories, the easier it becomes for the government to allow greater self-definition: what citizens want becomes increasingly what the state intends them to want. I shall return to this point, but only briefly to glance toward the distant horizons where individual and state desires closely converge. Waiting for this state of affairs could be like waiting for Godot.

Unlike a reactive polity which is suffused with skepticism, the activist state bristles with optimism. Its mission presupposes the intellectual capacity to discern goals worthy of pursuit and to formulate policies correctly geared to their attainment. The more encompassing and ambitious the government's programs, the more crucial this optimism becomes: uncertainty about the powers of inquiry and analysis can chill governmental action.[16] Skepticism would also impede translation of the state's proclaimed goals into resolute state action. Skeptics not

15. Where the existence of antagonistic classes is recognized *rebus non iam stantibus,* as a vestige from the past, the government still does not view itself as a neutral umpire in the resulting class conflicts, but rather sides with the class favored by its theory of the good society. The state may even occasionally be tempted to devise a separate expanding law for "us" and a separate receding one for the zone of class conflict ("them").

16. See C. Lindblom, *supra,* n. 5, 248–49.

only seldom become architects of programs for social change; they also seldom rush to mount the barricades.

The Law

Rather than emanating from civil society and mirroring its practice, activist law springs from the state and expresses its policies. The controlling image of law is that of the state decree, wholly divorced from contractarian notions. Insofar as the state's objective is to increase material welfare, its decrees spell out programs, assign tasks, or distribute shares of the common pie to citizens. Insofar as the state aims to promote moral welfare, its decrees are a collection of directives for proper conduct and right attitudes, or cautionary examples of bad behavior and objectionable tendencies. In contrast to law in the reactive state, whose stress is on defining forms in which freely chosen goals may be pursued, activist law is directive, sometimes even hectoring: it tells citizens what to do and how to behave.

While activist law cannot be modified by the preferences of those whose conduct it purports to regulate, it is malleable and flexible in a different sense, changing in turn with each failure or success in carrying the government toward its ideals. Whether it takes the form of objective regulation or model of conduct, it cannot be permitted to be so firmly fixed as to stand as an obstacle to the realization of state programs. It must be modified whenever found ineffective or counterproductive. If its interpretation in light of policy considerations fails to render a provision in accord with state policy, the provision must be disregarded.[17] The best example is criminal law: a miscreant should not be permitted to escape conviction simply because his conduct, found dangerous or harmful in light of state policies, does not fall within one of the established categories in the catalog of crimes. The maxim *nullum crimen sine poena* (no crime without punishment) prevails over *nullum crimen sine lege previa* (no crime without prior definition in law). If necessary, then, existing criminal prohibitions must be extended by analogy to reach the dangerous or harmful conduct.

Nevertheless there are constraints on the freedom to peer behind legal provisions to examine whether desired goals have been achieved in particular cases. This is so because the effort to attain state objectives without interposition of relatively stable standards can be a task of unmanageable complexity, creating dangerous levels of uncertainty and ample room for arbitrariness. While the all-encompassing theory of activist government often provides some guidance, its postulates cannot always be translated into clear and coherent practical action. Thus even if its ruling apparatus appears not to set great store by order and uniformity, the activist state is driven to respect a degree of fixity in its law,

---

17. This hermeneutic step beyond theological interpretation is often considered by Soviet commentators to distinguish bourgeois (formal) conceptions of legality from "socialist legality." See F. C. Schroeder, *Rechtstaat und sozialistische Gesetzlichkeit, Aus Politik und Zeitgeschichte*, vol. 3, 7–8 (Bonn, 1980). Compare *supra*, ch. 1, n. 5. This view is no longer advanced with the vigor and conviction that characterized semiofficial pronouncements during the first four decades of the Soviet rule.

thereby tempering the law's instrumental character.[18] Yet the resulting separation of legal standards from underlying policy goals creates a regrettable strain in the administration of justice. Defining the limits of this separation is a serious problem for all truly activist legal cultures. The predicament they experience is analogous to that experienced when a reactive legal culture is forced to acknowledge some outer limit to independent ordering by members of civil society.

Activist law is not readily translatable into personal claims of citizens implicated in regulatory schemes. Many decrees spell out the tasks of governmental officials in implementing state programs and thus are not addressed to citizens at all. To repeat an earlier illustration, if an official is directed to acquit a defendant who committed a crime under duress, it would seem absurd to interpret the resulting situation as creating a personal entitlement—a "right"—of the individual to break the law under those circumstances. The answer would be to say that the state official is obliged to exempt a citizen from punishment for breaches of the law committed under certain types of compulsion. This approach is reflected in the optimal strategy employed by the citizen to realize an advantage he perceives in a regulatory scheme. To aggressively insist on personal entitlement does not get him very far: it is more in harmony with activist legal culture for him to insist that officials perform their duty as prescribed under a decree, and thereby act in a way that the citizen finds personally beneficial. As in jujitsu, it is best for the citizen to use the weight of an "objective" regulation in order to realize his personal interest. In short, attitudes normal in a reactive state—where law can always be transmogrified into a bundle of personal entitlements—should not be projected into the different legal environment under an activist government.

Nor should claims flowing from state decrees, even though routinely designated "rights," be equated with personal entitlements congenial to reactive ideology. The citizen of the activist state possesses no rights accorded by virtue of his being an end in himself.[19] No right is absolute or abstract, in the sense that its exercise can be abstracted from its broader impact. Further, because the policies and programs of the activist state are theoretically all-encompassing, broader implications can be detected anywhere: all rights are at least potentially subject to qualification or denial. This concept is often expressed by saying that no right may be exercised so as to infringe on state interests. The idea of "full mastery over rights" is repugnant, because it contradicts the avowed supremacy of government and raises the specter of personal autonomy vis-à-vis the state—a "filthy disgrace" to activist ideology.[20] Strictly speaking, then, personal claims based on activist law are mislabeled if characterized as rights. To underscore the

18. One can imagine a technocratic extreme of activist government wherein state decrees discard normative regimes in favor of technocratic formulae for the calculation of optimal outcomes in light of state goals in each and every case. Of course, in this technocratic scenario law would shade into a variety of technical disciplines (cost-benefit analysis, etc.). Compare *supra*, ch. 1, n. 4; see also the discussion of the nature of activist procedural regulation, *infra*, ch. 5.

19. See *supra*, n. 11.

20. See G. Radbruch, *Rechtsphilosophie*, 6th ed., 224 (Stuttgart, 1963). Similarly, Lenin's letter to his justice commissar Kursky, V. I. Lenin, *Sobranie Sochinenii*, vol. 44, 396 (Moscow, 1949).

contrast with personal entitlements in an extreme reactive state, it would be better to invent new terms—to say that activist decrees accord conditional privileges, create roles, assign tasks, give each their just share, and the like.[21]

A further distinction from the situation in the reactive state needs emphasis here: in the perspective of extreme activist ideology, "rights" shade into obligations. Thus a decree may specify the right to health care, but at the same time obligate all to take care of their health and subject all to mandatory measures such as inoculation. The right to education can be coupled with the duty to go to school, or the duty to go to a school of a particular kind.[22] Nor is this commingling perceived as anomalous or regrettable. On the contrary, activist ideology may welcome it as a harbinger of a better future in which individuals will improve and be related to one another in more harmonious ways. For the moment, it may be conceded, the identification of rights and duties may bespeak aspiration more than reality. But as their level of consciousness continues to rise, citizens will begin to perform their duties almost as readily as they exercise their rights. Eventually, as in the *concordia* of knowledge and feeling contemplated by Augustine of Hippo, all alternatives for action other than those a person *should* take must become unattractive: right and duty coalesce in an indivisible whole.[23]

Administration of Justice

In considering the impact of activist ideology on the shape of the legal process, a convenient starting point is to show how the activist state's conception of law as an instrument for the realization of its policy makes the legal process independent of dispute resolution.

Requiring a controversy as a general prerequisite for the institution of the legal process clearly makes no sense to an activist government. Disputes do not miraculously arise whenever a social event suggests the need to enforce the law and thus to realize a policy goal in the concrete circumstances of a case. In fact, absence of controversy—social stasis—may itself be a cause of concern to a government seriously engaged in the transformation of society. Activity between consenting adults—a contract they entered into, or a mode of their sexual

21. It is sobering to note that the managerial governments of imperial China and Japan produced cultures in which there was no precise equivalent to the term "right" (*jus, dikaion, droit subjective*) as used in Western legal systems. Even in the West, the strong concept of right is not so old as often thought. See M. Villey, *supra*, n. 11.

22. The interpenetration of rights and obligations characterizes Soviet legislation in many areas. See *Fundamental Principles of Legislation of the USSR* and *Union Republics on Public Health*, art. 3 (1979) in *Collected Legislation of the USSR and the Constituent Union Republics*, vol. 3, ed. W. Butler (1983). In Communist China, work, education and even family planning are constitutional duties. See "Constitution of the P.R. China arts. 42, 46, 49," *Beijing [Peking] Review*, Dec. 27, 1982.

23. For a recent account of Augustinian *fundatissima fides*, see P. Brown, *Augustine of Hippo*, 365–75 (1969). An argument reminiscent of the Augustinian *concordia* is frequently made in Soviet legal writing, and also appears in the charter of the Soviet Communist party. See V. M. Chkhikvadze, *The State, Democracy and Legality in the USSR: Lennin's Ideas Today*, 47 (Moscow, 1976); N. Aleksandrov, ed. *Teoriya Gosudarstva i Prava*, 2d ed., 652–53 (Moscow, 1974).

behavior—while it sparks no disturbance in society at large and while it fully gratifies the participants, may nevertheless be regarded by state officials as a threat to the improvement of economic or moral welfare. Individuals may need to be protected from their own folly or from the distorting screen of their "false consciousness" that blocks the realization that they are being victimized in consensual transaction or in voluntary sexual relations.[24]

It cannot be denied, however, that a dispute is often a good indication to officials that governmental intervention is needed. One might thus be inclined to believe that, at least in those cases which come up in the form of a dispute, activist legal process is devoted to dispute resolution. This matter deserves closer scrutiny and requires that distinctions be drawn among disputes between citizens, between citizens and officials, and between officials themselves. Each situation shall be examined in turn.

When a dispute between citizens is viewed in the context of state policy, either one or both litigants can be found deserving of punishment. (For example, they may have concluded a contract harmful to the state's economic plan.) In this situation, to institute an independent criminal prosecution can easily appear cumbersome and time-consuming. To switch from the civil into the criminal mode within a *single* proceeding becomes an attractive possibility. Where this occurs, of course, the object of the "unitary" proceeding is necessarily bigger than mere dispute resolution. Because the truly activist state often detects broader and sometimes ominous implications beneath what appears on the surface to be the narrowest of controversies, this Saul to Paul transformation of the case can occur in any civil dispute.[25] The original litigational frame can also be transcended in other ways. Through the lens of activist policy, a dispute between private individuals may appear to be symptomatic of a larger difficulty (e.g., institutional corruption) best tackled within a single proceeding. Thus a procedural vortex can be created and all those strategically placed for the solution of the difficulty drawn into the enlarged lawsuit. Or the state may want to use a narrow controversy as an exemplum through which to drive home a lesson to a larger audience: citizens may be invited—or required—to assume a variety of roles that have nothing to do directly with the resolution of the original dispute. They may become a chorus in the forensic drama.

Even if not expanded or transposed to another register, the proceedings triggered by a dispute between private individuals are not really aimed at its resolution, at least not in the strict sense compatible with a reactive state. Observe that activist government has little reason to tailor a lawsuit to the precise contours of an interpersonal controversy: indeed, the correct disposition of the

24. The legal process may be independent of dispute resolution in yet another sense, especially so long as class conflict is still recognized. As instanced in certain periods of Chinese managerial socialism, some "struggles" among people may be regarded with favor: like sand in a shell, such struggles can be viewed as irritants capable of producing social pearls. Of course, those victimized by social pressure cannot bring their injunctive or compensation claims before state adjudicators, since disputes arising from such "struggles" are not cognizable in state forums.

25. Illustrations of this metamorphosis will be found in chapters 5 and 6, *infra*.

case in light of state policy can require that matters be considered that are not in issue between the litigants. Observe also that prayers for relief may have to be disregarded, since plaintiffs do not always know what is best for them. The original dispute is thus not much more than a mere precipitating event of limited significance to the subsequent progress of the legal process. Put differently, the interpersonal dispute becomes a pretext for finding the best solution to a social problem brought to the knowledge of authorities by a conflict between the plaintiff and the defendant.

What has been argued so far about disputes between private individuals applies with much greater force to proceedings involving a dispute between a private individual and a representative of the state. To imagine that such proceedings are devoted to the resolution of a dispute between the individual and the state is to smuggle ideological assumptions of the reactive state into a hostile environment. The very idea of granting a citizen standing to set up his self-interest in opposition to the state's interest runs counter to fundamental premises of activist government. The state interest is lexically superior, indeed supreme, rather than on the same plane with individual interests wherein the two could be "balanced."[26] The refusal to place the representative of the state in a position parallel to a private individual should not be understood to imply an automatic decision in favor of the former: the state official may have interpreted the prevalent interest incorrectly, or he may be wrong on the facts. But for the sake of argument, assume that the activist government's repugnance to legitimating a clash between individual and state interests is somehow overcome: now another serious obstacle to conceiving the lawsuit as devoted to the absorption of a dispute arises—a neutral adjudicator is nowhere to be found. In a state that fulfills its activist potential, as in the war between God and Satan, there is no room for neutrality. Indeed, *vae neutris* (woe unto the neutrals)!

Can the legal process be aimed toward resolving a conflict between two representatives of the state, each advocating a different interest or a different version of the same interest? Where the governmental machinery of an activist state is hierarchically organized, it is unlikely for such an official dispute to become the subject matter of a lawsuit. It is more probable that the issue will be solved by submitting it to the mutual hierarchical superior. In a coordinate activist apparatus, however, where disagreements over state policy can be rampant, the possibility of resolving the conflict through litigation cannot be precluded. Suppose, then, that two state officials disagree over what should be done with a miscreant—one official favoring incarceration, another release on probation. Since both officials are committed to realization of the criminal policy of the state, it may well happen that as the proceedings progress their originally discrepant views begin to converge. But the dissipation of the original controversy does

---

26. While some sort of "bargaining" between the citizen and the representative of the state, or some sort of "balancing" of state and individual interests, can still be found useful (or efficient) by those who operate an activist judicial apparatus, nevertheless such bargaining remains unacceptable, because contrary to intrinsic (noninstrumental) values of activist government. See *infra*, pp. 94, 95.

not signal the end of proceedings. There can still be more work to be done to arrive at the best sentencing decision. As the former disputants now join hands in a cooperative search for optimal solutions, the epiphenomenal character of the official dispute surfaces: at bottom, proceedings were all along but a vehicle for realizing the criminal law policy of the state. Appearances should not deceive us.

Leaving the full argument for a subsequent chapter, I shall now recapitulate the discussion thus far. Although the administration of justice in a truly activist state may involve an official or a private dispute, it is actually independent of dispute resolution per se. The true procedural objective is to *apply* law in the context of contingent circumstances: it must be ascertained whether conditions exist that require official attendance, and if so, measures must be chosen that best advance the interests of the state. Inasmuch as activist law mirrors governmental policy, it can be said that the ultimate purpose of activist justice is to implement state policy on cases that come before the adjudicator.

What does this imply about procedural form? Divorced from dispute resolution, activist justice is also free from the controlling image of a lawsuit as a symbolic contest—two sides pressing discordant claims before a decision maker in the classic triadic relation. The legal process may be a bipolar affair between a state official and a single individual, or an affair implicating a great number of protagonists advancing a variety of disparate views—a polygonal relation. Of course, the litigational (triadic) form can also provisionally be maintained. But whether bipolar, triadic, or polygonal, activist proceedings must be structured so as to permit a search for the best policy response to the precipitating event. It is also clear that control over this search must be vested in state officials; first, private individuals, driven by self-interest, might thwart the realization of state programs; second, facts and interests other than those urged by private actors must often be considered in the forensic drama. Hence, animated by its perception of the objective of administering justice, an activist state must seriously consider designing its legal process as an inquiry controlled by state officials. In lieu of privately controlled contest, the idea of officially controlled *inquest* epitomizes the procedural style.

The more fully a state realizes its activist potential, the narrower the sphere in which the administration of justice can be understood as dispute resolution, and the more the legal process is pruned of procedural forms inspired by the key image of a party-controlled contest. How far official inquiry—the now dominant theme—can be carried will depend on the intensity of governmental activism. It is only in the tenets of extreme activist ideology that one finds support for the most incisive inquest forms, and thus for a pure investigative model of the legal process. I shall attempt to make a detailed statement of such a model in a later chapter, but it is already clear that this model will be cognate to what is conventionally termed "inquisitorial," "nonadversarial," and sometimes (mainly on the European continent) also called "officially dominated" procedure.[27] The

27. This last term is used in countries influenced by German legal scholarship. See, e.g., E. Kern and C. Roxin, *Starfverfahrensrecht*, 9th ed., 42 (München, 1969).

discrepancy between conventional images of nonadversarial procedure and the one I shall soon describe in some detail requires that I depart from terminological convention. In order to avoid misleading connotations of common terms, especially of the phrase "inquisitorial process,"[28] I shall label the procedural model that conforms to activist ideology "the policy-implementing process."

iii. CONFLICT-SOLVING AND POLICY-IMPLEMENTING JUSTICE

Two Faces of Adjudication

Two ways of conceiving the office of government have now been outlined, which generate two contrasting ideas about the objective of the legal process. According to one, the process serves to resolve conflict; according to the other, it serves to enforce state policy. I have shown these contrasting ideas to be pregnant with implications for the choice of procedural form: while the one favors the contest morphology, the other prefers the morphology of inquest. Common opinion to the contrary, then, a process organized around the key image of contest and another organized around the key image of inquest are not in fact structural alternatives for achieving the same objective. Each, in pure form, is directed to a separate end.[29]

Serious doubts must be anticipated at this point, especially in America, as to whether a process devoted to implementation of state policy qualifies as an *adjudicative* engagement. It will be argued that an official entrusted with realizing a state objective can be required to follow the law, and that persons implicated in proceedings he directs can be permitted to advance proof and argument. Yet these conditions need not be deemed sufficient to supply the bare minimum of "judging": if administration under the rule of law satisfies these conditions, it is not thereby converted into an adjudicative activity. The specific character of judging—its *differentia specifica* in relation to administration—resides in a relation of two sides and a court, a relation associated with the settlement of a contested matter. Uncontested matters are not for judges to decide.

According to a strictly analytical notion of adjudication, this argument is correct. In fact, in portraying the ideology of a fully activist state I have already

28. A pejorative aura surrounds the term "inquisitorial procedure." It is due to its association with harsh and cruel criminal prosecutions during the ancien régime, and it is due also to the confusion of ordinary secular proceedings of the period with those of the Inquisition. See M. Damaška, "Evidentiary Barriers to Conviction and Two Models of Criminal Procedure," 121 *U. Pa. L. Rev.* 506, 558 (1973). Voltaire, who contributed greatly to this aura by exaggerating the vices of ordinary criminal proceedings (for laudable political reasons), nevertheless acknowledged the difference between them and Inquisition writ large. See Voltaire, *Dictionaire Philosophique,* tome 6, 127–32 (Amsterdam, 1789).

29. See *supra*, Introduction, text accompanying n. 16. The discrepant objectives can be conflated by using the term "conflict resolution" so broadly that it covers not only the absorption of actual disputes, but also events that can precipitate state intervention in the absence of any dispute among persons against whom proceedings are directed. For an example of such usage, see, e.g., M. Wolf, *Gerichtliches Verfahrensrecht* (Hamburg, 1978).

made this concession. I pointed out that adjudication and administration tend to converge as a government begins to approach its fullest activist potential. Whereas all activities of a radically laissez-faire state, including administration, acquire a flavor of adjudication, all activities of a fully activist state, including adjudication, acquire a flavor of administration. But it would be parochial to assume that this narrow concept of adjudication covers activities that are perceived as instances of "judging" or even activities that are thought to be quintessentially judicial, in all legal cultures of the world. In old China, for example, the enforcement of imperial regulation was at the heart of the administration of justice, and in contemporary communist systems the identification of adjudication with dispute resolution is dismissed as a mystification of reality, especially with respect to criminal justice.[30] But it is unnecessary to invoke exotic chinoiseries or communist jurisdictions in order to prove the narrowness of the analytical concept of adjudication: the end wall of the Sistine Chapel presents a famous Western example of how a broader concept of adjudication—believed normal in mundane matters—was projected to heavenly affairs. Would proceedings on Doomsday have to be contested to be classified as adjudicative? Did Michelangelo really want to depict an administrative engagement rather than the Last Judgment? It is true that earlier, the twelfth century schoolmen who founded Western procedural theory tended to associate court proceedings with an interaction of *trium personarum* and with a contest.[31] But this view began to lose ground on the Continent quite early on, owing to the rapid expansion in the thirteenth century of self-initiated investigations by courts of law. A *judex* who launched an inquiry into a suspicious event without a complainant, or who decided a criminal case on the basis of an unilateral inquiry, continued to be regarded as engaged in an eminently adjudicative activity. This is still the prevailing view on the Continent: the idea that to adjudicate need not necessarily imply resolution of contested matters continues to appear natural to lawyer and layman alike.[32]

30. On the allegedly "bourgeois" character of this identification, see T. Szabó, *The Unification and Differentiation in Socialist Criminal Justice*, 13 (Budapest, 1978).
31. For a compendium of authority, see K. Nörr, *Zur Stellung des Richters in gelehrten Prozess der Frühzeit*, 8 (München, 1967). The reasons for this attitude are related to the political panorama of medieval Europe prior to the centralization movement. See *infra*, text accompanying n. 33.
32. This view has its stronghold in the domain of criminal justice. For an example of the typical reasoning on this point, see K. Peters, *Starfprozessrecht*, 30 (Karlsruhe, 1952). For contrast with an influential strand in American legal thought, see J. Thibaut and L. Walker, "A Theory of Procedure," 66 *Calif. L. Rev.* 541, 566 (1978); A. Goldstein, *supra*, Introduction, n. 2, (the adversary and nonadversary forms of criminal justice are "methods of conflict resolution"). While acknowledging that even uncontested matters are fit objects for judicial process, some Continental commentators like to argue that "real" criminal proceedings come into being only after a "triadic" relation is constituted between the judge, the prosecutor, and the defendant. The pragmatic undertheme here is the desire of liberal lawyers to challenge the validity of evidence gathered by police (or a prosecutor) during their unilateral inquiries. But the frail scholarly lances of these commentators have barely scratched the surface of practical administration of justice. For an example of such barren scholarly reasoning, see D. Dimitrijevic, "Handlungsbegriff und Rechtsverhältnis im Strafprozess," in J. Baumann and K. Tiedemann, eds., *Einheit und Vielfalt des Strafrechts*, 253, 258, 262 (Tübingen, 1974).

It is important to recognize that the long association of adjudication with conflict resolution exercises a strong hold on the legal imagination, especially in those legal cultures where the posture of government (either actual or ideologically proclaimed) tends to be of a more reactive than activist kind. Such was the case in the dawn of modern Europe as the central governments were barely emerging—in the wake of the papal revolution[33]—from their limited role as peacemakers in the endemic feuding of clans. It was also true in the nineteenth century when laissez-faire reached its apogee on the Continent. The comparatively striking readiness of the Anglo-American legal mind to associate adjudication with dispute resolution can be partly attributed, I shall argue, to the paucity of managerial concerns of government in the English tradition.

To sum up, if in his wanderings from culture to culture, a comparativist were to use the narrow analytical concept of adjudication, many activities widely perceived as instances of adjudication would elude him. Accordingly, he must adjust his concepts and expand the idea of adjudication: to him, justice must become Janus-faced. In his vision, the objectives of the legal process must encompass not only the resolution of disputes but also enforcement of the law, or—ultimately—the implementation of state policy.

An Excursus on Anglo-American and Continental Systems

In the preceding chapter I attributed the major part of the contrast between Continental and Anglo-American styles of administering justice to differences stemming from variation in the structure of the judicial apparatus. This does not mean that aspects of this contrast cannot also be attributed to divergent ideas about the function of government, including its role in the legal process.

In fact, it seems probable that the traditional roles of Continental and Anglo-American governments were not exactly alike. One indication is that so many Europeans, looking at England and America through the prism of their experience, were struck by the relatively modest role played by the state in managing the affairs of society. While Continental rulers continuously expanded the agenda of government—from the army to the maintenance of internal order, to education, even to public health and social security—England and America seemed until recently to rely to a far greater measure on private or "voluntaristic" action for the fulfillment of social needs.[34] Outsiders marveled about the

33. The expression "papal revolution" is borrowed from H. Berman, *Law and Revolution* (1983).

34. Tocqueville viewed voluntaristic action as the inner dynamic of American society: the important things are not those that the public administration does, but what is done "without it or outside of it." *Democracy in America*, vol. 1, 252 (1945). Concerning nineteenth-century America, Karl Marx wrote that the state there was reduced to the very minimum possible in "bourgeois" society. See F. Mehring, ed., *Aus dem literarischen nachlass von Karl Marx, Friedrich Engles und Ferdinand Lassale*, vol. 3, 438 (Stuttgart, 1902). For the comparison between England and the Continent, see M. Oakeshott, *supra*, n. 3, 301. The "activism" of the citizenry and the passivity of the state were especially striking to Russian visitors; there, owing to the absence of a large middle class, the idea that the government should be the instrument for the fulfillment of social needs was particularly strong. Even the question of "who keeps order" here was a mystery to nineteenth-

feasibility of such "minimal statism" and proposed a variety of theories to explain the mystery. One theory that has gained wide currency attributes the comparatively minor importance of government in Anglo-American lands to the allegedly greater success there of capitalist markets:[35] The more pervasive and effective the mechanisms of the market, it is said, the lesser the need for direct governmental involvement; power can be exercised mainly in the economic and social spheres, and the state apparatus can often be bypassed.

Now if the managerial concerns of English and American government were truly more limited than in Europe,[36] then Anglo-Americans could have indeed drunk more deeply from the Pierian spring of laissez-faire. They could have been more receptive to the view that the state need not initiate and implement social programs, and that the primary office of government is to arbitrate conflict among citizens and their voluntary associations. Administration of justice could also have been associated with conflict resolution on a much broader scale than on the Continent; a lawsuit involving a matter that came to be regarded as governmental responsibility across the Channel could continue to be interpreted in England as devoted to the resolution of a conflict among people engaged in civic activity rather than as entailing an official effort to realize the goals of the state.

However, a difference in ingrained Continental and Anglo-American attitudes toward the adaptation of procedural form to perceived objectives of the legal process should not be overlooked. Recall that from its inception the traditional Continental machinery of justice tended to shape procedural arrangements according to a limited number of principles inspired by the purposes of justice (logical positivism). The Anglo-American apparatus, on the other hand, was traditionally addicted to slow organic growth, and it opposed "instrumentalist" streamlining of procedural arrangements to fit clearly defined procedural functions.[37] This difference suggests another hypothesis. Owing to the legacy of more managerial government, Continental lawyers—even where inspired by laissez-faire—could imagine the legal process as an engagement in conflict resolution only in a comparatively restricted area. But where they did so imagine the legal process, the area was well defined, and procedural arrangements were invented with comparatively great consistency to fit the notion of legal process as

---

century Russian liberals. See A. Schrier and J. Story, *A Russian Looks at America; The Journey of A. B. Lakier in 1857,* xxxviii, 66, and passim (1979).

35. The greater success of markets is in turn attributed to a more thorough destruction of peasants (small-scale producers who own productive wealth, or the means of production) in England than on the Continent. With nothing to sell but their labor potential, former agricultural producers contributed to a larger and much more mobile work force, giving capitalism more room for development than in countries like France. See N. Poulantzas, *Pouvoir politique et classes sociales de l'état capitaliste,* 182 (Paris, 1968).

36. Because the administrative functions of the English state increased during the laissez-faire period, this may be doubted by some. See K. Polanyi, *The Great Transformation,* 139 (1957).

37. It is well known that many archaic procedural ideas, some of them vestiges from the Middle Ages, survived in England until the nineteenth century. Dressed in modern garb, some still exist— for example, the mechanism of pleading in criminal cases, or rigid requirements for the personal presence of procedural protagonists. On slow organic growth, see, e.g., R. Caenagem, *The Birth of the English Common Law,* 84 (1973).

a dispute-absorbing forensic contest. However, Anglo-American lawyers could expand the conflict-solving image of proceedings even to areas where this expansion looked inappropriate to Continentals; but they were much less concerned about adjusting procedural form to its animating purposes. This possibility should be remembered in succeeding chapters where I consider several puzzling relationships between civil and criminal procedure in both Anglo-American and Continental systems.

Mixtures of Activist and Reactive Justice

This excursus on common-law and civil-law procedures provides an illustration of actual governments' oscillation between managerial and arm's-length impulses, and thus suggests the possibility of combinations or mixtures of procedural arrangements suited to the two contrary tendencies of government. It is, of course, premature to dwell here on such mixed forms before the pure activist and reactive styles have been sufficiently described in the next two chapters. However, two different dynamics in which these mixtures can develop must briefly be outlined here.

One possible path for such mixtures of reactive and activist forms to develop opens up when a state, heretofore strongly committed to the ideal of limited government, acquires an increasing appetite to intervene in the circumstances of social life. A dissonance or a tension must now be expected to arise between legal procedure conceived as a privately controlled contest and the novel objectives of the legal process. Increasingly, the inherited dominance of private parties over procedural action and traditional insistence on controversy as a prerequisite for a lawsuit will clash with the state's growing desire to enforce its own policies through the legal process. Contest forms, forms fitting justice in the reactive state, will begin to recede or erode in those spheres where activist postures are adopted.

Various patterns of this decay deserve brief mention. One pattern is for old forms to undergo, more or less covertly, an adaptation to changing needs. For example, although a dispute continues to be required for proceedings to commence, controversies are artificially created and sustained. Private parties are used as instruments of activist government: an individual may engage an antagonist in a dispute in order to reform him in the image of state values. Alternatively, litigants who have settled their differences out of court may be prohibited from leaving the forum so that the judge can decide the case in the manner that accords with state policy rather than in the interest of the original disputants. The offshoot of these changes is that legal process begins to serve policy-implementing objectives while outwardly retaining features of the contest style. Another possible response to new activist tendencies—a possibility not mutually exclusive from the one just described—is for the process to retain its inherited forms in relative purity, but to be used less and less frequently, or in an ever decreasing segment of the administration of justice. The contested trial, for example, may come to be displaced by alternative modes of processing; while still celebrated as an ideal, it can actually be relegated to an oubliette in the fortress of justice.

Both strategies of adaptation are likely to appeal to an authority that prefers incremental change to change resulting from comprehensive planning, and both can therefore capture the dynamics of developments accompanying the rise of the welfare state in countries of the English political tradition. In the welfare states of Western Europe, where authority is more affected by rationalist-bureaucratic attitudes, a different strategy might be contemplated. In spheres where activist postures seem desirable, inappropriate components of the reactive procedural order would be openly abandoned and replaced by arrangements more suitable to the image of an officially controlled investigation—the now dominant inspiration for the choice of procedural arrangements. Here, the policy-implementing face of justice is not hidden behind the conflict-solving mask. It comes more plainly into view.

Thus far I have suggested some implications for procedural form of the movement from reactive to activist government. But mixed forms can also develop as a result of drift in the opposite direction. A state that aspires to manage virtually all aspects of social life and is ready to intervene in virtually all types of proceedings may find that its reach exceeds its grasp. Cases that implicate no readily identifiable policy and therefore no firm ground for governmental intervention come before its courts. A dispute that initiates policy-implementing proceedings, for example, may fail to reveal the contours of any larger problem requiring official attendance. Like blades of grass peeping through concrete, lawsuits that escape the avowedly larger goals of justice, and are actually devoted to the resolution of "self-contained" disputes, may now appear. Where this occurs, policy-implementing forms will become inapposite or eviscerated: the participation of various specialized officials in proceedings—useful where state policy is at stake—can turn into a costly ritual; potent investigative instruments can be counterproductive and prolong interpersonal disputes ("the greater the truth, the greater the libel"). While it is of course possible that, despite all these "dysfunctions," the original activist procedures will remain mired in the old rut, it is more likely that some adaptation of pristine arrangements will occur and that mixtures of activist and reactive forms will emerge.

Various strategies of adaptation can again be contemplated. Some elements of the contest design can be woven into the fabric of the dominant policy-implementing process, or special subsystems can be developed for the processing of "narrow" cases, leaving the rest untouched. Again, changes can be more open, or relatively subterranean. I shall allude to such resulting pastiches of procedural form at several points hereafter, but mainly in discussing certain aspects of the administration of justice in Communist China and the Soviet Union. Illustrations of forms that develop in the wake of such a move from a pronounced to a more moderate activist government will be presented there.[38]

38. Retreats in communist systems from extremes of activism in the area of substantive law will be set aside. Perhaps the most widely discussed example here, grossly overrated in terms of its practical importance, is the 1958 Soviet rejection (preceded by the Yugoslavs in 1952) of the doctrine that conduct can constitute crime even if not specified in a criminal statute prior to commission.

Pure Forms of Activist and Reactive Proceedings

In this chapter I have sought to show how two different purposes of justice, as envisaged by two extreme political doctrines, affect the choice of major structural principles for the design of legal process. But even if it is true that the polarities of political ideology provide an orientation and a basis for understanding the lawyer's opposition between proceedings designed as a private contest and proceedings designed as an official inquest, the question still remains open: how can more detailed procedural arrangements in the contest and inquest styles be discerned against this background? What criteria does this insight provide for selecting features to include in a pure conflict-solving mode of proceedings (arising against the background of a reactive state) and those chosen in a pure policy-implementing mode (arising against the background of an activist state)?[39]

Three ways can be distinguished in which procedural arrangements can be said to "follow" from ideologically tempered ideas about the purpose of the legal process. One is that these arrangements can be understood to express fundamental tenets of a political doctrine. When I turn to the portrayal of the conflict-solving mode, it will shortly be seen that many of its features reflect the notion that the parties to the contest have the ultimate say as to matters involved in managing the lawsuit; they are *domini litis* (masters of litigation). It is easy to see that this notion simply transfers the ideal of personal autonomy, so central to the laissez-faire ethos, from the sphere of political ideology to the administration of justice.[40] Because personal autonomy is axiomatic to reactive ideology, procedural arrangements expressing it serve the advancement of no ulterior ends. Even if some of them, such as the criminal defendant's right to self-representation, seriously strain the process patterned on the idea of party contest—the contest may well be lopsided—nevertheless they continue to be regarded as necessary in a pure model. Similarly, when I attempt a detailed statement of the policy-implementing mode, there will be encountered many arrangements that transpose to the domain of justice one of the fundamental assumptions of the fully activist state—the notion that the state interest prevails over private interests. If a procedural arrangement cannot be reconciled with this fundamental tenet, such as "bargaining" between private individuals and the representatives of the state interest, the arrangement is not part of a pure policy-implementing process, even if otherwise arguably efficient.[41]

In another sense, a form can be said to follow from the procedural purpose

39. Conventional theories about the inquisitorial and adversary process are silent on this point. I have elsewhere tried to reconstruct the methodology implicit in most prominent approaches. See *The Encyclopedia of Crime and Justice*, vol. 1, 25–29 (1983).

40. In fact, Kant's teachings on personal autonomy were a direct inspiration for the architects of the German nineteenth-century civil process. See H. Kiefer, "Der Einfluss Kants auf Theorie und Praxis des Zivilprozessrechts im 19. Jahrhundert," in Blühdorn and Ritter, eds., *Philosophie und Rechtswissenschaft*, 3 (Frankfurt, 1969).

41. Bargains may be efficient because they can lead to quicker disposition of cases or similar savings of resources.

if it is conceptually implied in it. Where such conceptual entailment can be shown, procedural forms are unpacked from the underlying purpose like a set of Russian dolls.[42] As an example, consider devices, such as pleadings, designed to assist in the formation of issues. Such devices are necessary, even implicit, in the objective of the conflict-solving mode of proceeding: they enable the judge to ascertain the existence and the limits of the dispute he is called upon to resolve. Absent such mechanisms, the process becomes disoriented and incoherent. In a policy-implementing process, by contrast, pleadings and similar mechanisms have no deeper justification. I have already noted that a lawsuit must continue, regardless of whether the subject matter involved in it is contested or not. Take the example of the guilty plea in activist criminal prosecutions: where guilt equals the presence of conditions justifying application of criminal policy measures, guilt must be determined by the state adjudicator. The question "are you guilty?" ("how do you plead?"), if it is asked at all, is not a vehicle to ascertain whether a process-sustaining controversy exists, as it is in the conflict-solving mode. Instead the question is no more than an invitation addressed to the defendant to confess to the facts of the crime. Whether his confession is credible, and whether the facts as confessed make the defendant guilty under state law, is for the judge and not the defendant to decide. Most of the time, the latter does not even know whether he is guilty.[43] And even if the answer "guilty" is obtained from him, proceedings must continue—albeit perhaps in a less demanding form, reserved for cases in which fact-finding is comparatively easy. In sum, pleadings are not mandated by the procedural purpose of the policy-implementing process. To be incorporated in a pure model, they must be supported on some other ground, provided that they do not appear objectionable in terms of activist ideology. Incidentally, this can easily occur because verbal formulae used in pleadings evoke a setting in which private individuals are empowered to determine the forms to be used in lawsuits implicating them (simple or more complex), whereas an activist state insists that such determinations be in the hands of state officials.[44]

42. The quest for conceptual entailments attracted Continental scholarship from its inception in the twelfth century and reached its peak in the work of the natural law scholars of the late eighteenth century. See K. Nörr, *Naturrecht und Zivilprozess*, 47–49 (Tübingen, 1976). See also *supra*, Introduction, n. 16. This approach, somewhat refined, still underlies Continental thinking about basic principles of the civil and criminal process. The questions that continue to be raised are not "what is entailed in the purpose of resolving disputes and what is the purpose of implementing state policy," but rather what is entailed in the public as opposed to private law character of a lawsuit. Because a public matter may also give rise to a dispute, the approach suggested in the text and the venerable Continental approach are overlapping rather than identical.

43. In the 1970s, an instructive anecdote circulated on the campus of the University of Pennsylvania, involving one of its professors who had come to the United States from abroad. Arrested for speeding a short while after his arrival, he was arraigned before a magistrate and asked to plead. The professor was perplexed and asked what this meant; when told that he must state whether he was "guilty" or not, he replied: "This, your honor, is a question for you to decide, not for me to comment upon." According to the story, he was promptly cited for contempt. *Se non e vero e ben trovato.*

44. If ideologically objectionable, the verbal formulae of pleadings cannot be retained in a pure model—even for mere decorative purposes, like gargoyles on old churches.

The third and last sense in which forms can be linked to objectives of the legal process remains. Although not necessarily implied in these objectives, forms may advance them more effectively than available alternatives. If these procedural forms are then included in a model of procedure, their inclusion is based on real or assumed empirical relationships rather than on results of conceptual analysis. As an illustration, consider two alternative techniques of examining evidence: according to the first, evidence is adduced bilaterally through direct and cross-examination, while under the second, it is adduced unilaterally by a single individual or a group. It is clear that techniques of direct and cross-examination are not conceptually implied in the conflict-solving purpose of the legal process. A dispute can be resolved by assigning fact-finding tasks to a third person or to a research group. It is equally plain that the bilateral style of proof taking is not conceptually incompatible with the policy-implementing objective. An investigation can be organized so that two officials present evidence to the fact finder, each official focusing on bringing out information to support a different factual hypothesis. However, assume that the bilateral style advances the conflict-solving objective better than the unilateral, while the unilateral method proves superior in the policy-implementing context: each proof taking style can now be assigned to its respective model because it best advances the model's objective.[45]

These two types of the legal process will be constructed so as to incorporate procedural forms in all three senses that I have just described. But what shall ultimately prove to bind them together are tenets of activist and reactive ideologies. In a more or less obvious way, these tenets influence the search for conceptual entailments—even the formation of empirical hypotheses—and thus justify the preceding pages' preoccupation with the polarity between laissez-faire and managerial governments.

---

45. Or, in another illustration, whether participation of lawyers is part of the conflict-solving model may be thought to depend on whether such participation contributes to the parties' control over the process—a matter for empirical obervation. This method of determining what arrangements are part of the procedural model is exemplified in the work of J. Thibaut and L. Walker, *supra*, n. 32. See also their book *Procedural Justice* (1975).

IV   The Conflict-Solving Type of Proceeding

This chapter attempts to make a detailed theoretical statement of a mode of legal proceeding that conforms to the ideology of a radically laissez-faire government. Expressed in conventional terms, this project entails the search for a pure adversarial process. It is worth repeating here what has already been said about the relation of the hypothetically pure conflict-solving process to actual procedural systems: just as the state concerned solely with dispute resolution is a theoretical limiting case, so likewise is the procedural style which would conform to the understanding of legal process in such a state. No existing system can be expected to duplicate fully all the features of the pure model. An objection must therefore be anticipated: if the conflict-solving process is based on extreme variants of the reactive state, is the resulting polarity not so remote that it is of no use in analyzing procedures in the real world? Before I go further, this question should be answered.

While it is true that no extant system completely reproduces the model to be depicted in the following analysis, its building blocks are not mere figments of legal imagination. Features to be assembled in the model—its constituent fragments, as it were—are widely dispersed among existing systems. These features interact there with arrangements which restrain or weaken their impact, producing a great variety of attenuated or diluted conflict-solving procedures. Without some idea about the essential concentrate itself, the great variety of such diluted forms can hardly be compared with respect to the intensity and proportion of the conflict-solving element each contains. Nor can real life mixtures be assessed in terms of their relative proximity to an undefined conflict-solving standard. Nevertheless, many lawyers debate procedural change and compare actual systems by invoking "the adversarial system" while remaining reluctant to define its pure form. As a result, such discussion often proceeds in the hazy atmosphere of half sense, as in the predicament of one trying to express the finely shaded nuances of cappuccino with only vague notions about coffee and milk. Here, the detailed statement of the pure conflict-solving model assembles scattered fragments of conflict-solving features into a theoretical edifice which is intended to remedy this difficulty and to clarify the comparative analysis to come. The model is a construct to provide orientation for confronting various mixtures of procedural form which are the norm in actual systems. Whether or not I shall polarize to excess will depend on how many aspects of actual procedural systems find support only in extreme laissez-faire ideas, rather than in more moderate variants of reactive ideology. If a sufficient number of such aspects are identified, and if only extremes of laissez-faire can link them into a meaningful whole, the resulting polarity will be vindicated: the conflict-solving model will then not be a mere fictitious creature which belongs in the pages of a bestiary of procedural forms rather than a volume interested in living forms of justice.

It would be vain to expect, however, that I shall look for the scattered building blocks of the pure conflict-solving process only in countries that belong to the Anglo-American tradition. That such building blocks can be found elsewhere will surprise only those who imagine the adversary system as the epitome—no matter how ambiguous—of the common-law procedural tradition. Indeed, there is no reason to believe that pure conflict-solving forms ("adversarial" features in conventional terminology) must *always* have the common-law pedigree, unless one believes that this tradition's multiplicity of factors must inevitably have enabled procedural forms for dispute resolution to evolve. The possibility must even be contemplated that some aspects of Continental procedures might be more "adversarial" than their Anglo-American counterparts, and that some aspects of common-law justice might—*horresco referens*—be more "inquisitorial" than their civil-law analogues.

i. THE CHARACTER OF REGULATION

It will be remembered that in the reactive state the legal process takes the shape of forensic contest. This contest must somehow be regulated: unregulated, like war without rules of combat, it would provoke reprisals, spinning off additional conflict rather than containing or absorbing the existing one. The character of such regulation is seldom discussed in the theory of the adversarial process, and deserves a closer look.[1]

Yielding Nature

As with all law in the reactive state, regulation of the legal process is largely a problem of identifying the implicit terms of a model contract. The lawgiver must imagine how potential litigants would reasonably and fairly have agreed to behave in the event of a future lawsuit. If actual litigants wish to alter the terms

1. "Regulation" should not necessarily be imagined as a comprehensive code with rules that are relatively context free. As noted in earlier chapters, while hierarchical authority leans toward comprehensive guidance in advance, coordinate authority demands that due process be determined "as the particular situation demands." See, e.g., *Morrissey* v. *Brewer*, 408 U.S. 471, 481 (1972). Because the character of officialdom in the reactive state is temporarily left an open question, procedural regulation can be here envisaged in either form.

of this hypothetical contract—the procedural law in the reactive state—there is no firm basis on which the state can insist on the unbending nature of its law. This is especially conspicuous where the alteration contemplated is by way of bilateral stipulation, and it also holds true for unilateral waivers. As I have pointed out, the ideology of reactive government favors the conversion of law into rights personal to citizens. And because citizens are sovereign in determining their own interests, including their chances of success in litigation, they are in principle free to renounce rights accorded them in the legal process. Rights can thus be used as bargaining chips in negotiations between procedural parties. In the end, the state's regulation of the legal process is not much more than a baseline from which litigants can depart when and if they so choose. Breach of a procedural regulation is in itself not sufficient to provoke remedial action by the state. Only when a litigant objects to the breach must the adjudicator intervene to settle the collateral conflict; therefore, absence of an objection can be interpreted as tacit consent to departure from a norm.

To be sure, some outer limits on displacement of regulation are recognized, even by rigorous proponents of procedural laissez-faire. Thus, in accord with the notion that a citizen cannot contract himself into slavery, the state normally refuses to permit waiver of the right to be charged with a crime: an individual cannot choose to go directly to a penal institution (*nulla poena sine processu*). The fact remains, however, that such immunity of regulation from private alteration is the exception, not the rule. The law of waiver is hence largely unconcerned with the substantive question of what can be waived and what not; rather, the tenor of this law is to elaborate second-order procedures for valid renunciation of rights.

Such easy displacement of procedural regulation may seem fantastic to a lawyer from a Continental or communist system. He may be tempted to view it as an example of polarizing beyond need. But, consider the contemporary American scene. In spite of the much heralded decline of laissez-faire values, the extent to which litigants are still free to choose a particular procedural form remains quite remarkable. That a person can waive his right to be notified of the institution of civil proceedings or to be heard before judgment is rendered[2] surprises outside observers, even those from systems that normally have few compunctions to proceeding ex parte. It is equally surprising to foreigners that some fact-finding techniques—inadmissible because of their dubious reliability—can be employed in America if the litigants so stipulate.[3] In some American states, the prosecution and the defense can agree to submit a case for trial on evidence contained in the transcript of the preliminary hearing alone, with the result that oral testimony—normally so typical of the common-law style—is displaced in favor of a procedure reminiscent of the written process in Continental countries

2. The reference is to the so-called *cognovit* mechanism. See, e.g., *D. H. Overmeyer Co. v. Frick Co.* 405 U.S. 174 (1972).

3. This is true, for example, for the admissibility of testimony of "lie detector" experts in some American states. See P. Thomas, "Compulsory Process and Polygraph Evidence," 12 *Conn. L. Rev.* 324, 338 (1980).

prior to the French Revolution (*transmissio actorum*). But most intriguing to outsiders is the power of the criminal defendant to affect the selection of procedural form, even in cases of most serious crimes. Remember that his plea of guilty or nolo contendere is taken as a waiver of the right to trial, so that this most prominent part of the criminal process need not take place at all. The defendant can also affect the choice between bench and jury trials by waiving his right to be tried by his peers.[4] And, albeit submerged and combined with other factors, notions of waiver still lie at the core of the requirement that the affected litigant must first object to a violation of procedure before the judge will react to it.

As the spirit of laissez-faire weakens, it is less readily assumed that the goals of justice can be attained when litigants are left free to select the form of procedure which best suits their interests. This tendency is clear not only in cases where both sides are self-seeking individuals, but also where one party is a public official expected to protect the public interest (e.g., the state's attorney). Vast judicial powers, heretofore seldom exercised, are now being increasingly employed to supervise the displacement of procedural regulation. Waivers, whether genuinely unilateral or induced by party negotiation, are more regularly subjected to judicial scrutiny. The requirement of immediate objection to a procedural misstep is also losing ground with the spread of the doctrine that an appellate court can reverse a judgment for procedural "error" to which no exception was taken at the trial.[5] These developments emphasize the tension between the still prevalent rhetoric of "personal" procedural rights and the power of the judge to disregard them.

Nevertheless, the significance of these recent trends can easily be overdrawn. Judicial scrutiny of waivers is often perfunctory or limited to the question of their voluntariness, and refusal to ratify the parties' negotiated agreements remains an unusual event.[6] Even if it cannot be said that litigants alone determine the procedural form, it is striking from a comparative perspective that they have any voice at all in the choice of a wide range of procedural issues. The juxtaposition with Continental jurisdictions is again illustrative. Even as the ideology which extols individual autonomy achieved its apogee in Europe, and aspects of legal process could now more easily be imagined as the continuation of

4. A useful catalog of waivable rights can be found in E. Rubin, "Toward a General Theory of Waiver," 28 *U.C.L.A. Rev.* 478 (1981). Except in a few states, most waivers require judicial consent, to be discussed later.

5. The so-called plain error doctrine is still used sparingly and only in exceptional circumstances. See, e.g., *F. R. Crim. P.* 52(b).

6. Although guilty pleas, whether negotiated or not, can be subject to close scrutiny, they are still almost routinely accepted by most judges. Similarly, although the defendant's choice to waive the jury requires the court's consent in almost all jurisdictions, such consent is usually given. See "Note, Government Consent to Jury Trials under Rule 23(a) of the Federal Rules of Criminal Procedure," 65 *Yale L.J.* 1032 (1965). Judges are especially reluctant to engage in detailed scrutiny where waiver of a right by one party is unopposed by the other. Where the court intervenes, normal procedural arrangements are seriously strained, in that a process supposedly fueled by the parties' contest is deprived of its vital energies. "Public interest" litigation presents sui generis problems to be discussed in the last chapter.

private dealings in a forensic setting,[7] few deviations from the procedural norm through party choice were permitted—most of them minor, and in the contentious civil process. The law of criminal procedure remained quite unbending: that the defendant could waive trial or a particular composition of the tribunal, whether such waiver were subject to judicial approval or not, was so alien an idea to Continentals that it was never seriously advanced.[8]

The reasons for the greater rigidity of Continental regulation are complex and cannot be pursued here. But in thinking about the power of the parties to affect procedural arrangements, the divergent institutional environments must be borne in mind. In common-law systems, the parties (through their counsel) perform a number of activities that are intrinsic to the office of the judge on the Continent. Thus, while the waivers and stipulations of Anglo-American litigants mainly affect their own forensic conduct, similar transactions would affect ingrained patterns of judicial behavior in Europe. Furthermore, as I have suggested in earlier chapters, the Continental civil service judiciary is far less hospitable to disruption of its routine than are Anglo-American adjudicators. *Ceteris paribus*, then, it is easier to let the parties improvise in the context of coordinate authority than in the context of hierarchical authority.

Procedure as Substance

Proceedings conceived as a contest of two adverse parties before a neutral conflict resolver generate structural pressures toward judgment in favor of the party who wins the courtroom disputation. The conflict resolver is therefore put into a position similar to that of the judge in a debating society who, unconcerned about the issue under discussion, concentrates dispassionately on the display of forensic skills. Judgments tend to be justified procedurally—that is, by victory in the forensic contest. In this context the observance of rules regulating argument assumes great importance. Procedural law, whether prefabricated by the state or tailored ad hoc by the litigants, acquires its own integrity and independence from substantive law. But no matter how strong the pressure exerted by the design of the contest, the decision maker remains but loosely bound by the stress on procedural legitimation of verdicts. The administration of justice cannot be completely separated from substantive notions of right and wrong or wholly associated with a game or debating society activities. Hence a serious problem arises whenever it appears to the judge that the result which reflects the view that prevailed in the contest does not coincide with the proper outcome on the merits; the more accomplished forensic performer need not necessarily represent the position consistent with the better reading of substantive law. The decision

7. Some nineteenth-century Continental commentators began to regard civil proceedings as an essentially private transaction.

8. Although the English jury trial was transplanted to the Continent after the fall of the ancien régime, and despite the enthusiasm for English legal institutions which characterized the period, both waiver of the jury and waiver of trial (by way of a guilty plea) remained unknown to French or any other Continental criminal procedure.

maker now confronts discordant procedural and substantive voices: he cannot honor Artemis without slighting Aphrodite. While reluctant to disregard what to him appears right according to the merits, he cannot abandon the procedural perspective: if the verdict goes against the apparent winner of the contest, the process structured as a contest has defeated its own principles. Not only is the character of the contest's incentives negatively affected, but more ominously, the impartiality of the conflict resolver is beclouded: it will appear that he has sided with the loser.

The conflict-solving process is thus characterized by a variety of procedural mechanisms designed either to prevent such a dilemma from arising or, if need be, to resolve it without undermining the integrity of proceedings organized around the contest motif. An example of the first type of mechanism is the strict requirement that all information in the dispute be presented to the decision maker in the presence of the litigants, and that it be immediately—before the dust has settled—subject to their argumentation. Where no source of information is independent of the party contest, chances are minimized that the adjudicator might arrive at a view different from the one supported by the winner of the argument. Later in this chapter, as I canvass the ideal position of the conflict resolver, it will be seen how many features of the pure model can be attributed to this requirement that all information be "filtered" through the partisan dispute.

An example of the second group of devices are the various forms of mistrial. These help preserve the dominance of the procedural perspective without completely neglecting the substantive issues. Where a litigant commits a serious breach of procedural propriety, proceedings must be discontinued even if the breach imparts accurate and decisive information on the merits of the case. But the right result will not be totally sacrificed; assuming that there is no special bar which precludes repetition of the contest, proceedings may begin anew. Appellate review contains similar mechanisms: if on appeal a decision can be traced to a procedural error as its source, the decision will be reversed despite the possible accuracy of the outcome in terms of the applicable substantive law. This conception, natural to American lawyers, has no place in proceedings designed for the expeditious implementation of state programs in many foreign countries.

It is important to recognize that the underlying philosophy of reactive government creates an ambience which supports the procedural legitimation of judgments. Where the object of adjudication is to resolve disputes, and where the judge is not supposed to advance independent policies or values, insistence on the substantive accuracy of verdicts loses much of its raison d'être. If a decision is capable of absorbing a conflict, the deviation of this verdict from the result required under substantive law causes little concern: after all, the procedural objective has been fairly obtained. The more rigidly this view is implemented, the easier it is for the judge to permit deviant results on the merits. And the more nearly a reactive government approximates the reactive ideal, the stronger is the temper of skepticism that permeates reactive ideology and makes the judge wary of seeking "right" results. The reactive ideology reinforces a procedural perspective on the administration of justice: in brief, how a decision is reached counts as much as what it says.[9] In the limiting case of a purely reactive government, procedural questions almost totally eclipse substance.

Imagine now that a state begins to use the legal process, or a part thereof, as an instrument to advance values and policies broader than the resolution of a particular dispute. To the extent to which these transcending objectives require verdicts to be substantively accurate, it becomes more and more costly to sacrifice such verdicts for the sake of procedural integrity. The dilemma of which I spoke a moment ago becomes more and more intense. And where the judge perceives the right solution on the merits, he is increasingly inclined to see to it that this solution is incorporated in the judgment notwithstanding the vagaries of the litigants' procedural fortunes. The image of the judge as neutral arbiter of a debate—indifferent to the issue debated—becomes inapposite, perhaps even repulsive. The contest structure of proceedings tends to be weakened, and departures from the pure conflict-solving mode are accepted.

Balancing Advantages

If the procedural legitimation of decisions is to be sustained, the rules of party contest must not only be observed but also be fair. Now, whatever else the idea of fairness might require in a comparative context, it surely entails arrangements intended to afford equal chance of victory to the contestants. A system similar to *jeu-parti* (jeopardy), or to a game with even chances, flows from the association of procedural law with a model contract in the reactive state: there is no good reason to depart from procedural parity where those who contemplate the possibility of litigation are equally ignorant of the ways in which various substantive alternatives might affect their self-interest. In short, the perennial problem in regulating the conflict-solving process is to balance the advantages of litigants to provide them with equal weapons.

The balancing act poses special problems where one party to the proceedings is a state official. Here, the full strength of the contest motif can be sustained only if he is treated as representing a citizen's interest or that of a citizens' group rather than as spokesman for the aggregate state interest. In a criminal case, for example, the image of proceedings as a contest can be preserved in its purity only if the public prosecutor is regarded as a representative of the victim. But as soon as the prosecutor is equipped with power to disregard the interest of the victim for the sake of broader concerns, the premises of adversarial arrangements are weakened: the proceedings no longer involve the clash of two partial (partisan) interests, but rather a clash between the aggregate interest of the state and the partisan interest of an individual. Why should partial interests be placed on the same plane with aggregate interests—and balanced? Why should the

9. "Any treatment that would have been just according to an independent criterion for assessing just outcomes is in fact unjust if performed without employing an appropriate judicial process" (D. Resnick, "Due Process and Procedural Justice," in J. R. Pennock and J. W. Chapman, *Nomos*, XVIII, 213 [1977]).

process be organized as a combat between the state and individuals—with equal chances of success? The answers to such questions are far from self-evident to many political doctrines, but easy in the reactive state. Here, the interests of the state are treated by analogy as private interests, and the legal process cannot legitimately be used to promote the policies and values of government.

But because state officials normally occupy a position superior to that of ordinary litigants, how are advantages to be balanced in this special situation? It seems fair to handicap the superior contestant: state officials should be denied at least some procedural rights that are accorded their private adversaries. This handicap undeniably reduces the symmetry of procedural rights that characterizes the pure conflict-solving model in disputes between members of civil society. But where a state official is a party, especially in criminal matters, full procedural symmetry is seldom attainable: the public prosecutor is not laboring under the threat of detention and punishment, conversion into the role of witness (which would imperil his control over the lawsuit), and similar burdens.[10] It seems advisable, then, to relax further the demands of rigid parallelism in order to achieve the more basic goal of proceedings organized as a contest—that is, to equalize the contestants' chances to prevail. How far to deviate from symmetry can be a difficult and delicate enterprise—it has been likened to that of entertaining a nun. Yet it is plain that the balancing of advantages is affected by the structure of the judicial apparatus. If the state official in the role of the party is hierarchically linked to the center of government and if the adjudicator belongs to a hierarchically organized civil service, the contest structure of proceedings is much more difficult to maintain than in a machinery of justice where officials are decentralized and the adjudicators are temporarily enlisted citizens. It should be expected that it is much easier in Anglo-American than in Continental systems meaningfully to employ contest forms, even in those segments of the legal process where a state official appears as a party.

ii. THE PARTIES: PREMISES OF THEIR STATUS

Strong Concept of Autonomy

As I have pointed out, the reactive state, reluctant to embrace any philosophy of the good life, allows individuals to be sovereign in the management of their own concerns. Transposed to the administration of justice, this sovereignty requires that a party be recognized as the master of his lawsuit (*dominus litis*), entitled to conduct it as he pleases, in most cases choosing even the form of the proceedings. Whether he conducts his case well or not is hard for presiding officials to deter-

---

10. In the Middle Ages the system of private criminal prosecution carried the idea of symmetry so far as to require that an unsuccessful private prosecutor be subject to the same punishment that a defendant would suffer in the event of conviction. See P. Fournier, *Les officialités au Moyen-Age*, 255 (Paris, 1880). Although in a less drastic form, the idea that private prosecutors should share the burdens of the defendant continued to influence the criminal process of the ancien régime.

mine. A state that recognizes no *index veri* is ill-suited to proclaim that any particular action of a litigant is harmful to his interests. What to do if a person manages his case badly is thus a question that does not arise with the frequency or intensity which it would present to activist government. Assume nevertheless that an official of the reactive state is convinced that a litigant is not competent to realize his self-interest. Should the official now engage in some corrective action to protect the party from his own foolishness or ineptitude? Even here the price of corrective action can be too high: the reactive ideology is wary of permitting any move that might lead to an overbearing officialdom bent on "coercive paternalism."

Indeed. so seriously is autonomy taken in the reactive state that it is protected even in those instances where the parties' exercise of autonomy seriously strains the optimal functioning of legal process designed as a contest. A telling illustration is the right of the citizen to self-representation—a clear entailment of individual self-definition. Where a pro se litigant lacking forensic skill insists on personally managing his case, the courtroom contest is seriously skewed, and even officials of the most rigidly passive governments find at least some consequences of such lopsided litigation hard to swallow. For example, that an innocent citizen can freely choose to go to the gallows is an intolerable proposition, even to such a government; yet this could be precisely the result of an inept defense against criminal charges. Notwithstanding the seriousness of such consequences, the right of the parties to self-representation is likely to prevail: to force counsel on an unwilling defendant is offensive to the very foundation (noninstrumental values) of reactive ideology.

So far I have dealt with parties who play the forensic game badly. But a litigant may be stricken with such debilitating incapacity that his forensic activity—even if nominally opposing the adversary's claim—no longer qualifies as argumentation: rather than being played badly, the forensic game is not being played at all. Under such circumstances proceedings must be discontinued until the party has regained his capacity, or, where postponement is not feasible, a substitute must be appointed to represent the incompetent's interests. What deserves to be noted here is that choosing the second alternative poses serious difficulties in the reactive state, most particularly in those proceedings where the adverse party is a state official. It is feared that the mechanism of substitution itself can provide a foothold for activist conceptions of the legal process. It is not easy to ascertain the personal interest of the citizen declared incapable of defining it for himself, and the officers of the justice system may be tempted to appoint a guardian *ad litem* who shares their own educational, curative, or other views. The guardian could then join hands with the adversary of the person stricken with incapacity and (under the guise of conflict-solving forms) conduct a search for the best policy response to the problem sub judice. Under such circumstances, procedural arrangements suitable for dispute resolution would lose much of their meaning and become readily dispensable as empty formality; courts would become dispensers of education or medicine—coercively paternalistic. In this parade of horribles a worse possibility is that litigants whose understanding of their own interests differs from the views of government could be declared incapable of self-representation and be replaced by surrogates whose views are amenable to authority. Managerial concerns of the state could now be run under the guise of conflict resolution.

In order to avoid such problems of substitution, the legal process imbued with reactive ideology is characterized by low demands for procedural capacity. Even those persons who suffer from serious disorders are not denied procedural autonomy; they may even be left free to decide whether or not to argue their own insanity. Where even minimal requirements of capacity cannot be met, the justice system is prepared to go a long way toward indefinitely postponing the legal process.

Lest it be thought that no real-world system displays symptoms of such strong conceptions of procedural autonomy, cast a fleeting glance at the American scene. The American criminal defendant has the constitutional right personally to defend himself even against the most serious charges.[11] Although various palliative measures have been adopted to relieve the resulting strain on normal trial procedures, the balancing of advantages can still be seriously affected by the defendant's stubborn refusal to accept the assistance of legal counsel. Outsiders invariably ask, "How can a citizen have so much power to influence the outcome of criminal proceedings?" The answers are seldom satisfying. Nor do strangers cease to wonder over the exclusive right of criminal defendants in some American jurisdictions to raise and to argue the issue of insanity.[12] From the perspective of uninvolved reactive government, however, these and similar arrangements are justified and acceptable.

Equality

I noted earlier that the conflict-solving process is regulated so as to accord equal rights to the parties. Of course, because the parties are actually different, providing them with equal procedural weapons does not ensure their equal ability to pursue litigative interests effectively. Does the pure model still call for adjustment and compensatory mechanisms where the inequalities of the litigants stem from sources other than regulation of the forensic contest? To phrase the question differently, is another concept of party equality required, other than the "formal" one emanating from the regulation of a fight with equal procedural weapons?

The question must again be examined in the perspective of laissez-faire ideology. A truly reactive state is hard put even to identify these additional

_____

11. See *Faretta* v. *California*, 422 U.S. 806 (1974). In the words of one dissent, the court bestowed a constitutional right on the defendant "to make a fool of himself" (Id. at 821). In prosecutions for serious felonies, however, the right has been laced with so many exceptions and reservations that the whole body of law is immersed in a welter of confusing and sometimes self-contradictory language.

12. See Model Penal Code, §4.03 (Tentative Draft No. 4, 1955). For a recent case, see *State* v. *Jones*, 99 Wash. 2d 735 (1983).

aspects of inequality, let alone to devise a scheme for their reduction or elimination. This is because it claims neutrality vis-à-vis competing visions of the good life that exist in civil society. By refusing to adopt any one official position on matters such as the desirable distribution of power in society, it deprives itself of secure criteria to establish whether a particular inequality of litigants, in terms of their wealth, natural endowment, and the like, constitutes a mismatch which should be classified as unacceptable. All litigants must be treated as equal for the purpose of allocating procedural weapons, just as all voters must be considered as equal for the purpose of regulating the ballot (one person, one vote). In other words, parties are treated "abstractly," in isolation from their personal (substantive) differences, and as equivalent bearers of procedural rights.[13] Predicated on these ideological principles, the pure conflict-solving model begins to resemble the model of a perfectly competitive market—that is, a market satisfied with any allocation of resources which produces an equilibrium and which, where equilibrium exists, does not require redistribution. Like the statue of the goddess with the scales who personifies justice, the decision maker in the pure model is blindfolded. Inequalities which spring from sources other than "abstract" procedural rules do not enter the balance.

Can deviations from extreme laissez-faire positions affect the purity of the conflict-solving mode? Suppose that state officials are ready to identify unacceptable substantive mismatches of litigants and that they are willing to consider taking corrective action. Two strategies come to mind. One is to activate the judge who presides over the party contest: he is expected to intervene where parties are not evenly matched (although supplied with equal procedural weapons) and to assist the weaker side. But where this occurs the judge is no longer a perfectly impartial conflict resolver; he can no longer easily decide who wins a debate in which he himself is entangled. And the opponent of the assisted party, if the loser on the merits, may easily suspect that the verdict went against him not because his claim of right was unfounded or because he managed his case badly but because the adjudicator favored the adversary on the basis of some extraneous consideration (e.g., his poverty). The more the judge injects himself into procedural matters, the more the usual contest style and its accompanying structure of incentives are weakened.

An alternative corrective strategy accords better with the contest design of proceedings: instead of activating the adjudicator, the state tries to redress the substantive inequality of the parties by providing the weaker with assistance of counsel, required to pursue the case effectively. But even this alternative strategy ultimately must dilute the purity of the conflict-solving style. Assume that the state decides to assist those parties who face wealthier adversaries. As is natural in a process whose outcome depends primarily on the activity of private parties, vigorous pursuit of partisan interest—especially by high-powered counsel— opens up a variety of effective but costly activities, so that in a world of limited

---

13. Of course, any system of rules disregards (abstracts from) some aspects in which persons differ from one another.

resources, one must now expect conflict between the extent and the quality of assistance made available by the state to the financially weaker litigant. Unless the state is able and willing to spend enormous resources to subsidize litigation, it must impose limits on the expenses incurred by the parties it chooses to assist. But in many instances these limits will leave unacceptable mismatches in place: the wealthier litigant can price his opponent out of the justice system. Hence a state that takes seriously the transcendence of formal equality is also driven to impose expenditure restraints on the private financing of lawsuits. Costly procedural techniques will have to be outlawed. Unable to guarantee a litigational Cadillac (as it were) to all citizens, the state must contemplate banning their manufacture altogether in favor of the more modest procedural vehicle available to all. The full-fledged party-dominated mode of proceedings is thus restricted, placed in the state's straitjacket. At this point, an even more dramatic departure from the contest form could become attractive: if the inequality of the parties is so troublesome, why not reduce its significance by transferring the performance of most of the procedural action from the litigants to a nonpartisan agency that can also decide on the acceptable level of cost? Or, to stretch the analogy a little further, should not public transportation replace private automobiles? In brief, while the first corrective mechanism (activating the judge) may make the parties doubt the decision maker's neutrality, the second strategy (subsidizing the weaker contestant) may end up impoverishing the arsenal of adversarial techniques. In either case, the party-dominated mode of proceeding has been distorted.

It goes without saying that departures from pure adversarial form can be, in Horace's phrase, all unwept. In fact, powerful ideological currents of our age demand increasing sensitivity to the substantive inequality of litigants, especially to inequalities that arise from differences in wealth. Like welfare economists, judges are supposed to be on the lookout for failures of forensic competition and ready to correct deficiencies where they occur. A perfect conflict resolver is not necessarily an ideal judge, so that departures from pure conflict-solving forms can be a cause for rejoicing rather than an elegiac occasion. But it must be recognized that approval of such departures goes hand in hand with a decreasingly roseate view of governmental noninvolvement.

It may then be objected that the pure conflict-solving model sets up an unrealistic polarity. If modern states are increasingly activist, if they engage more and more in social engineering, then procedural forms predicated on strong laissez-faire attitudes must be defunct. That this is false, however, can again be shown by turning to the example of the American administration of justice. The American legal process allocates an unusually wide range of procedural action to the adverse parties, especially in trial preparation, creating opportunities for free procedural enterprise unparalleled in other countries. In this environment, the inequality of the parties has a more powerful effect and looms larger than in systems that rely less on the initiative of the litigants: a party assisted by skillful counsel, or capable of absorbing huge costs of pretrial discovery, has a significant advantage over his weaker opponent. Indeed, a financially weaker litigant can be driven out of the justice system altogether. Nevertheless, until about two decades ago, the primary impulse of the American legal imagination was to expand and refine the arsenal of procedural weapons in benign neglect of the fact that their users—the litigants—possess unequal litigative capacities. No wonder, then, that many substantive mismatches of the parties remain uncorrected to the present day. It is true that indigent criminal defendants now have the constitutional right to the assistance of counsel, but indigent civil litigants are still not entitled to the assistance of counsel as a matter of right.[14] Small claims courts, contingent fees, class actions, and similar mechanisms are only partial remedies, so that situations still exist where the system is satisfied with the merely abstract equality of the litigants, or, to phrase the matter differently, the formal guarantee that equal procedural weapons are available to all legitimates the system.

A vision of the conflict-solving process that would require something more than formal party equality would provide no place for arrangements that actually exist in the adversarial style. This is a clear indication that this vision, no matter how attractive,[15] is not acceptable for comparative purposes. Only against the background of an extreme laissez-faire ideology—that is, one satisfied with mere formal equality—can one conceive of a more properly drawn polar vision, one in which existing adversarial forms can be included within the termini of the polarity and thus find a place in the total scheme.

iii. PARTY CONTROL OVER PROCEEDINGS

The dominant feature of the conflict-solving process is that it vests control over procedural action in the parties. This is hardly a novel proposition, and party control over the lawsuit is widely accepted as a major characteristic of the adversarial system. But there are considerable disagreements over the precise scope of party control ("How far can the dominance of litigants go?") and over the relative importance of its various aspects.

Existence of the Lawsuit

That parties decide upon the commencement of the lawsuit is necessarily implied by the objective of conflict resolution: until a party complains, there is no indication of a conflict ripe for resolution. At least this much has been generally conceded from the earliest theoretical reflection on forms of justice devoted to the resolution of disputes. Similarly, it would seem that party control over termina-

14. Some courts have discretionary power to appoint counsel for the indigent civil litigant, but they seldom use it. See, e.g., *Dreyer* v. *Jalet*, 349 F.Supp. 452, 486 (S.D. Texas, 1972). That the indigent civil litigant should be constitutionally entitled to the assistance of counsel is an idea encountered occasionally in dissenting U.S. Supreme Court opinions. For a survey of the problem, see "Note," 76 *Yale L.J.* 545 (1967).

15. This vision can be useful, for example, as an expression of desired changes of the legal process in the climate of a limited (liberal) activist state. Where government has historically been limited and markets have produced great inequalities of wealth, the move toward substantive equality assumes both urgency and ethical appeal.

tion of the lawsuit is implied by the procedural objective: if, having been apprised of a civil claim or a criminal charge, the adverse party decides to concede it in full, a process designed to settle disputes loses its reason for being and the court must accept the declaration of "no contest." Or, if at any stage of the lawsuit the adversaries agree to withdraw their dispute from the adjudicator, the court has no legitimate ground for insisting that the wheels of justice remain in motion. Even so, the initiation and the termination of an "adversarial" lawsuit have often been treated differently, and a pure contest style has been thought reconcilable with judicial control over the end of proceedings. Once proceedings are under way, it has been argued, party control over the life of the lawsuit is no longer sacrosanct. The prestige of the state adjudicative system is now at stake, and the litigants can disengage themselves from the process only by leave of court.

Various compelling arguments can be made in favor of authorizing the court to deny a withdrawal of demands or a dismissal of charges in the interest of the sound administration of justice. But no matter what these arguments may be, they will exceed the goal of conflict resolution: since one or both adversaries are no longer willing to engage in disputation, continued proceedings can be propelled only by the state's desire to fulfill some larger aim of government—a desire suspect to laissez-faire ideology. To its extreme variants, closing the exit from the forum is a cause of gravest concern, even of *Torschlusspanik*. Private ordering appears no longer supreme; citizens may hesitate to submit their disputes to state courts, anticipating that larger policy concerns may overwhelm their narrow controversy. In fact, the existence of an unqualified right of the litigants to withdraw from the state forum, even at the cost of conceding the opponent's demands, is an important indication that the legal process is actually driven by energies that do not exceed the goal of dispute resolution. Even if, in a mixed system, most other procedural arrangements are in some sort of inquest style, the inquiry can always be frustrated if the parties retain mastery over the right to terminate proceedings. A lawsuit can never be switched from the conflict-solving into the policy-implementing mode against the will of the litigants. It is for these reasons that a process that requires no judicial consent for withdrawal from the forum is closer to the pure conflict-solving "adversarial" mode than a process that calls for a leave of court.

Modern Anglo-American and Continental systems are inclined to accord control over the life of the lawsuit to the parties in comparable situations. Since the early nineteenth century, Continental authorities have acknowledged the indisputable right of civil litigants to terminate proceedings, whenever the case involves an issue amenable to out-of-court settlement.[16] In the same period also

16. This acknowledgment is linked to liberal recognition of individual autonomy in the sphere of private law. Prior to the revolutionary period, in the ancien régime the situation was different. It is true that even the earliest Roman-canonical law authorities made general pronouncements to the effect that the judge should never act on his own motion in private lawsuits (*judex ex officio non procedit*), but once a lawsuit began, the judge enjoyed important powers to "see that justice be done." Thus the practical import of such general pronouncements was reduced mainly to the commencement of lawsuits (*nemo judex sine actore*). For the seventeenth-century civil process in Saxony, see B. Carpzov, *Jurisprudentia Forensis, Pars I, Constitutio 23, Def. 1, Rub. 15, 16* (Leipzig, 1663).

the principle was adopted that the initiation of a criminal case requires the prosecutorial charge. In some European countries so strong was the enthusiasm for adversarial form that the criminal judge was given no choice but to discontinue proceedings if the public prosecutor decided to desist from prosecution.[17] The situation in America is essentially similar, although perhaps less clearly expressed. In a garden-variety civil case, the judge has no power to compel litigants to continue their contest.[18] Somewhat surprisingly to Europeans—who often expect to find extreme adversarial forms in common-law proceedings— most American jurisdictions empower the judge in a criminal case to review and to reject a plea of guilty negotiated between the prosecution and the defense.[19] In exceptional situations, then, where the plea is not accepted, the public prosecutor and the defendant may be compelled to do battle in the courtroom against their expressed desire, or a special prosecutor willing to do battle with the defendant may be appointed.

Framing Factual Issues

Who should be sovereign in deciding what facts are to be determined in a lawsuit—the parties or the adjudicator?[20] The answer again is implicit in the purpose of the conflict-solving process: since the procedural aim is dispute resolution, the parameters of the dispute should be set by the disputants. The plaintiff or the prosecutor chooses what to allege, and the defendant, what to contest and what to admit: what is not contested should not be made an object of proof. True, the judge may have good reason to look at facts other than those in dispute between the parties, but in doing so he would become "inquisitive" on his own and no longer limited to resolving the controversy. Where the judge is permitted to range beyond the allegations of the parties, the state interest in implementing its policies and programs can trump the interest of the parties in having their dispute resolved.

Although persuasive in broad outline, this reasoning may be questioned upon closer examination. Facts constitutive of a disputed right (e.g., the taking of a sum of money as a loan) may be distinguished from "exceptions"—that is,

17. This is still the case in some central European jurisdictions (e.g., Austria). However, the influential West German system permits the judge to overrule the public prosecutor.

18. Settlements leading to dismissal of a case are said to be regarded as private contracts, so that the judge will refuse to recognize them only if they contravene "public policy." This view extends to consent judgments. Of course, where the consent judgment can implicate the judge in the enforcement process, party arrangements may require judicial consent. Observe, however, that an increasing number of issues now seems affected by the public interest so that the universe of cases amenable to free settlement has become less clearly defined than it used to be.

19. See A. Goldstein, *The Passive Judiciary*, 9–24 (1981). I have noted that this power is seldom exercised (*supra*, n. 6).

20. My present concern is with allegations of fact on which substantive claims are directly based (that is, "ultimate facts"). A separate problem (canvassed later) is the allocation of control over facts of mere evidentiary significance (e.g., circumstantial proof, such as alibi). Here, the concern is with the *scope* of facts to be established rather than with the *manner* in which facts should be ascertained.

facts negating or restricting such a right (e.g., the payment of a debt in full or in part). While party control over the determination of constitutive facts cannot be challenged in a conflict-solving mode of proceeding, the case for party control over the exceptions seems less compelling. It might be argued that while the decision maker could be denied power to define on his own what issues will be resolved, he must retain the power necessary for accurate adjudication, and thus also the power to introduce exceptions whenever the case, as framed by the parties, raises the probability that such exceptions exist. Thus if a debt has been paid, there is no longer a contractual obligation; if a homicide occurred in self-defense, no crime has been committed. This reasoning can be supported by more technical arguments. It can be urged that the exceptions are implicitly or tacitly introduced into the case by the party who alleges a constitutive fact: if the prosecutor charges a person with homicide, he is implicitly alleging all facts necessary for the accurate adjudication of this charge, including the absence of circumstances establishing self-defense. Thus in extending the scope of adjudication to exceptions on his own, the decision maker still in fact stays within the bounds of the controversy as delineated by the parties.[21]

This argument has little persuasive force in an extreme laissez-faire polity. The argument presumes a justice system which seeks factual accuracy as a goal independent of the resolution of disputes between members of civil society. But the reactive state has no such interest: if a litigant—for some reason best known to himself—decides not to raise an available exception, the judge has no legitimate ground to raise the issue himself.[22] The autonomy of the parties in managing the lawsuit should not be interfered with, nor should the tactical interests of the litigants, as they perceive them, be second-guessed, even if this autonomy results in substantial distortion of what the adjudicator takes to be proper factual determinations.

Despite the recent trend in America toward greater judicial involvement in the conduct of the litigation, extreme reactive attitudes die hard, and vestiges of pure conflict-solving arrangements are still much in evidence. Surprisingly, they surface even in criminal matters where one would expect a relatively strong insistence on the accuracy of outcomes. Instead, the criminal justice system often seems satisfied with establishing merely a rough basis for punishment—sometimes a mere torso of actual wrongdoing—leaving the more precise delineation of factual parameters to the initiative of the parties. The primary vehicle for achieving this result is the bargained guilty plea. Following a deal between the prosecutor and the defense, a lesser—sometimes even a different—crime than the one actually committed may become the basis of a criminal conviction. While the judge can refuse to accept the deal, he is usually satisfied with persuading himself

21. For a sophisticated and detailed account of this argument, trenchant in justice systems that have departed from laissez-faire, see M. Cappelletti, *La testimonianza della parte nel sistema dell' oralità*, vol. 1, 353–75 (Milano, 1962).

22. The reactive state acquires an independent interest in the accuracy of judgments if a decision may send false signals about the meaning of law. But this danger is not present in the area of *factual* allegations.

that there is *some* factual basis in wrongdoing for the negotiated guilty plea. But even if a matter comes up for trial, vestiges of the control of private individuals over the parameters of fact determination can be found. Although judges are now increasingly empowered to introduce exculpatory matters (affirmative defenses) on their own initiative, there remain matters intimately related to guilt and innocence which can be put in issue only if the defendant raises them. His decision that certain determinations not be made is honored, even if the verdict is thereby distorted; his tactical choices are respected, even if public policy as expressed in substantive law is negatively affected thereby. For example, although in most legal systems of the world criminal liability and the insanity defense are related as a constitutive fact is related to an exception, in some American jurisdictions the court is prohibited from raising the insanity defense *sua sponte.*[23] Thus, even where the factual grounds supporting the finding of insanity are overwhelming, so that a verdict of not guilty by reason of insanity seems appropriate, the defendant who fails to raise the defense can be convicted. The situation is similar with the defense of duress, which is not extraneous to culpability (as is entrapment, for instance).[24] In consequence, and as strong laissez-faire philosophy permits, even exceptions to a charge may remain in the control of a private individual.

One might object that American criminal law, unlike most modern systems, recognizes a generic difference between criminal liability and defenses such as duress or insanity. In America, one might argue, an insane defendant or a defendant who acted under duress is still guilty, so that these defenses should not be treated as true exceptions to a criminal charge. Setting aside the pedantic rejoinder that the successful interposition of these defenses leads to a verdict of "not guilty," instead consider what is implied in the claim of an underlying generic difference between criminal liability and these special defenses. The claim amounts to a tacit acknowledgment that the system of criminal justice ordinarily is satisfied with crude notions of liability and that it entrusts the fine-tuning of liability to the free enterprise of the parties. In a rough sense, an insane defendant may be "guilty"[25] (he may have perpetrated the act described as a crime), but in a more refined sense—upon which he can insist—he may well be innocent. That a private individual should decide whether criminal law should use a crude or a refined measure of liability is clearly an idea from the ideological storehouse of laissez-faire government: individuals can themselves decide whether to go to prison or not.[26] *Volenti not fit iniuria.*

23. See *supra*, n. 12.

24. See P. Johnson, *Criminal Law*, 2d ed., 738 (1981).

25. The idea is sometimes expressed oxymoronically as a finding of "factual guilt" ("oxymoronically" because guilt is an evaluative, not a factual concept).

26. With the defense of duress, the situation is clear cut: if proven, the defense of duress calls for an acquittal. Because the verdict of not guilty by reason of insanity may automatically result in commitment, it may be argued that the defendant is given a choice only between punitive and curative modes of confinement. But even this choice is not likely to be offered to a private individual in a state that uses the legal process to seek and apply the optimal reaction to an example of crime: it is a decision that should be entrusted to an official.

Framing Legal Issues

It may appear that control over the legal parameters of the lawsuit is always vested in the court, without regard to whether the legal process is devoted to the resolution of disputes or to the realization of state policy. The judge must always determine the range of legal theories that will inform the disposition of the case; he takes "judicial notice" of the law. But is it so? There is something dubious on its face about a procedural system that leaves the definition of factual parameters to the parties and the definition of legal parameters to the court. Even in legal cultures where the distinction between factual and legal questions has been finely chiseled in theory, the two kinds of questions remain so closely intertwined in practice that one wonders how a process which treats control over them in radically different ways can be made operational. The problem deserves a closer look.

The parties to a conflict-solving process, as sovereign shapers of factual issues, must orient themselves in deciding strategy: what to contest and what to admit. Since it is impossible to have such an orientation without a legal theory of the case, the parties are impelled to advance legal arguments and to extend their dispute to legal issues as well. At least in the early stages of a lawsuit, the adjudicator has little opportunity to participate in the formation of legal issues: he is unfamiliar with the facts. But suppose that after a while he begins to chart his own course, reaching outside the legal parameters drawn by the litigants, searching for the best legal theory of the case. But because he is limited to the facts alleged by the parties, his independent legal research will often be futile. His theory may require that facts be ascertained which the litigants refuse to introduce into the case. Even if he remains strictly within the factual limits of the dispute, his abortive venture beyond the legal theories advanced by the parties can undermine the integrity of the conflict-solving process. Whenever he expands the scope of the legal issues, potentially dispositive elements enter the case independent of party contest and the side disfavored by the adjudicator's pet theory may believe that the decision maker has unfairly aided the adversary. While it is true that the potential damage could be contained by subjecting the adjudicator's independent theory to party contest, the favored side need say nothing about that theory: "the balance of advantages" has already been tilted in its direction by the court's independent action. In short, a procedural system that entrusts the definition of factual issues to the parties and the formulation of legal issues to the adjudicator (or some other third party) invites serious trouble. If all the forensic actors, each in their allotted domain, vigorously exercise their prerogatives, the legal process will likely be paralyzed. It is thus more probable that someone will yield. Either the adjudicator will refrain from researching the law on his own or the litigants will bow to judicial pressure to introduce facts required by the court's legal theory. It is clear which alternative is closer to the ideology of the reactive state: to submit to judicial pressure is repugnant to a doctrine that extols the litigants' autonomy; making the judge passive is not. Nor is the power of the parties over the range of legal theories anomalous, in the perspective of reactive government. In that light, parties are sovereign in defining what rights are to be vindicated; if a plaintiff invokes contractual recovery and the judge independently finds that a tort is involved, a dispute over rights has been adjudicated different from the one originally contemplated by the litigants.

Initial impressions about the responsibility for framing legal issues in the pure conflict-solving process must therefore be corrected: the more the court relies on the parties to define legal issues and to supply applicable legal theories, the more the lawsuit approximates a pure conflict-solving mode. Ideally, the judge decides the case within the legal limits the parties have prescribed.

Those inclined to believe that this ideal is not reflected in real-world procedures should consider the extent to which common-law judges still regularly rely on the parties (that is, their counsel) to supply them with legal authority and to develop legal arguments. Even if judges can "take notice" of domestic law, this doctrine has never acquired the strong sense of *requiring* self-propelled legal research on the part of the judge, especially at the trial-court level. Instead of embarking on voyages of legal discovery of their own, judges still expect counsel for the parties to develop the law for the case through adversary briefing and argument. Until quite recently, it was a serious question in many common-law jurisdictions whether a judge may invoke legal authority that the parties have failed to cite. Many English judges still regard it as improper to rely on a precedent or a legal argument that counsel for the parties have not canvassed; if the judge thinks that important authority has been overlooked by the litigants, he will schedule the case for further hearing.[27] Failure to raise a point of law at trial can often still bar a party from urging legal error based on the omitted point on the appeal of the case.[28]

The continuing influence of counsel on shaping the legal instructions that American judges give to the criminal jury is comparatively striking. For example, where counsel agree that a particular instruction should not be given, the judge typically honors that understanding, even if facts supporting this instruction are clearly in evidence. Nowhere is this better illustrated than in homicide prosecution: if the defense opposes an instruction on manslaughter—and the prosecution does not object—the judge will seldom give this instruction on his own. He will respect the tactical interest of the defense in gambling that the jury, when confronted with the stark alternative either to convict of murder or to acquit, will choose the latter, while otherwise they could settle for a manslaughter conviction. Again, if the litigants themselves do not insist on fine-tuning the law applicable to the case, the system is satisfied with a very rough outcome.[29] In

27. See P. S Atiyah, "Lawyers and Rules," 37 *Sw. L.J.* 545, 549 (1983); J. P. Dawson, *The Oracles of the Law*, 98 (1968).

28. See McCormick, *Evidence*, 3d ed., 939 (1984).

29. If the gamble is reasonable but fails, appellate courts in some American jurisdictions will refuse to reverse the murder conviction by virtue of the "invited error" doctrine. See P. E. Johnson, *Criminal Law*, 435, n. 4 (1975).

short, the bulk of legal information, as well as the facts of the case, reaches the Anglo-American judge through the filter of party argument.[30]

In contrast, on the Continent independent judicial input into the legal premises of judgments increased in proportion to the number of legally trained professionals on the bench. *Da mihi factum, dabo tibi ius* (give me the facts, I, the judge, shall give you the law) had become a maxim of Continental jurisprudence at least as early as the sixteenth century.[31] Observe, parenthetically, that the maxim would have had to be reversed in English jury trials, where the adjudicator (lay jury) then could be imagined as saying: "Give me the law, I shall give you the facts." One implication of the Continental legal maxim was that the court was justified in deciding a case on a theory neither party had advanced. In many Continental systems, moreover, the judge could legitimately decide a case on a legal theory that had not been subjected to the argument of counsel: *jura novit curia*. Significantly, however, in the wake of nineteenth-century liberal reforms, some Continental countries began to require that judges be confined to legal theories advanced by the litigants.[32] Nevertheless, it always remained the duty of the judge—part of his *officium*—to assemble the legal authorities relevant in light of these theories. On this point, then, it was the character of traditional judicial authority on the Continent that impeded fuller realization of procedural arrangements corresponding to the conflict-solving ideal.

The Personal Scope of Litigation

The conflict-solving process is characterized by high barriers against extension of the lawsuit by the court to persons other than the original parties. Standing to sue is strictly related to the violation of personal rights; a general stake in the procedural outcome is not enough. Joinder of parties is limited mainly to situations where the original disputants share a substantive right with other persons, so that the extension of the lawsuit cannot be avoided. In effect, a good sign that a process is losing its conflict-solving character is the weakening of rigid standing requirements, with accompanying power permitting the court to draw additional parties into a lawsuit.

30. The role of the parties in supplying the applicable law is even greater in issues of foreign law. See, e.g., J. H. Merryman, "Foreign Law as a Problem," 19 *Stan: J. Int. L.* 151, 170 (1983). However, I do not mean to suggest that the common-law judge is *equally* dependent on party argument with respect to both factual and legal issues; the somewhat lesser reliance on disputation of legal issues cannot be denied.

31. The maxim originally applied only to Roman and canon law in which judges were trained, not to customary law or city ordinances, in which they were not. The origin of the view that judges should make their own inquiries into the law independently of litigants goes back to the legal scholars of the twelfth century, who already distinguished the power of the judge to "add" (*supplere*) to the legal theories of the parties, and to add to their factual allegations. See K. W. Nörr, *Zur Stellung des Richters im gelehrten Prozess der Frühzeit*, 18 (München, 1967).

32. See R. Schlesinger, *Comparative Law*, 3d ed., 304 (1970). In criminal cases, the judge came to be bound only by the factual premises of the charges, not by the prosecutor's "legal classification" of these facts.

This reluctance to overstep the personal parameters of the original dispute can again be related to the vision of justice administration in the reactive state. When additional parties are introduced into proceedings by the judge, those whose controversy first sparked the lawsuit may lose control over procedural actions. Newcomers can insist on litigational strategies that clash with those adopted by the initiators of the case. Where the rights of original and new parties become closely intertwined, the original parties may even be forbidden to withdraw their suit from the court, because their decision to exit the forum no longer affects their interests alone. But this is not all. Unless kept within narrow bounds, judicial power to expand the litigation can have ominous implications for believers in passive government. Having adopted some vision of the good life, the judge may identify broader social problems of which the precipitating dispute seems but a symptom, and may then seek to remedy some such problem by selecting as additional parties individuals who are most instrumental with respect to the promotion of the larger good he perceives. In an extreme scenario, the judge follows a vision of the good life espoused by the government: larger implications are systematically detected in almost all disputes, and the judge becomes a Prometheus unbound.[33]

Relief or Sanction

Where the violation of a right has been ascertained, the conflict-solving process typically extends from dispute over the right to dispute over the proposed remedy.[34] And just as the judge cannot overstep the parameters set by the parties for the first level of their dispute, so he cannot disregard these parameters in the second stage of the controversy. Were he to exceed the range of the proposed award or sanction, or otherwise attempt freely to choose the appropriate remedy, he would cease to be a mere conflict resolver. Again, the ideology of the reactive state supports the purity of the conflict-solving process. Within certain statutory limitations, citizens who initiate a lawsuit are sovereign in deciding what form of

---

33. The general twentieth-century trend toward more active government was accompanied by relaxation of standing requirements; as larger implications of litigation become visible, various forms of intervention into lawsuits expanded. Yet where judicial authority is of the bureaucratic hierarchical type and especially where logical legalistic attitudes survive, attempted enlargement of lawsuits encounters serious obstacles. Where permitted at all, judicial enforcement of larger interests seems more naturally to be the monopoly of a specialized bureaucracy or of various ombudsmen. The fear is that to bring large numbers of individuals into the litigated issue might pyramid containable legal disputes into broader conflicts and unduly "politicize" the administration of justice. For West Germany, see, e.g., N. Luhmann, *Legitimation durch Verfahren*, 2d ed., 122 (Darmstadt, 1975). In America, where judicial hierarchization is comparatively modest and the recruitment of private individuals in the justice system retains much of its traditional force, the seeds exist for liberal expansion of lawsuits (class actions, etc.) and thus also for the easy enlistment of contest forms of justice in the service of larger interests.

34. Following the determination of an injury, if the demand for redress remains uncontested, it becomes enforceable without independent proceedings, for the indispensable engine of proceedings—a dispute—is missing.

relief suits their interests. Were a state official permitted to second-guess the propriety of demands for redress, the litigant's interest could always be trumped by the desire of the state to realize some vision of the public good. The legal process would then no longer serve as a device for the resolution of disputes in civil society and become an administrative endeavor or an occasion for realization of state policy.

But more than the litigant's control over the remedial process flows from the ideal of minimal government. This ideal also entails preference for remedies that do not require a continuing line of conduct from the losing party. To ensure such conduct—*cogere ad actum*—calls for ongoing supervision and for a variety of incidental measures, thus implicating the state in administrative activity. This, of course, would depart from the ideal of a state that imagines itself an arbiter, not an administrator. Injunctive remedies aimed at transforming society are clearly repugnant to such states: reactive government purports to support existing social practices and expectations, rather than engage in shaping new ones.[35]

On the Continent, civil litigants' control over the remedial process was undisputed long before the rise of liberal ideology. Medieval scholars already thought that this control was "natural" in the context of civil justice and axiomatic in proceedings designed for dispute resolution. *Ne eat judex ultra petita* (the judge should not exceed the prayers for relief) became one of the few unchallenged adages of Continental civil justice. Only after the advent of communist governments in Eastern Europe were judges given powers to disregard the demands of civil litigants—powers related to the ideologically motivated denial that any legal controversies exist that do not affect the larger interests of the state.

Surprisingly, the allocation of control over the remedial process is more uncertain in Anglo-American countries. Equitable relief (which must be regarded as a component of civil justice) was always very flexible: the chancellor could fashion or prescribe his decree quite independently of the parties. Following the merger of equity and common law—which to many outsiders appears a victory for equity[36]—it became difficult to identify any firm rights of litigants in the remedial process: the rigid legal norms which could generate such rights were softened by ubiquitous judicial discretion. At present, in civil proceedings American judges have discretionary power to award damages in excess of amounts requested, and they may even grant relief that was not explicitly demanded.[37] Is it possible, Continentals wonder, that American civil procedure—supposedly the repository of pure adversarial forms—on this point deviates dramatically from arrangements in the contest mode? But the deviation is more apparent than real:

35. Where some kind of injunctive relief seems necessary, it should be kept to the very minimum, that is, to immediately impending threat of injury to a clearly defined right.

36. See the poignant observation on this score of A. Pekelis, "Legal Techniques and Political Ideologies: A Comparative Study," 41 *Mich. L. Rev.* 665, 690 (1943).

37. See Fed. R. Civ. P. 54(c), 15(b). Uncertainties as to party control over the remedial process in America are noted in F. James and G. Hazard, *Civil Procedure*, 2d ed., 82–84, (1977).

one should not jump to the conclusion that American judges use their power in ordinary civil cases—that is, in those cases where such judicial activism would strike traditional Continental lawyers as odd. Prayers for relief are disregarded mainly in those lawsuits that are affected by transcending interest (public interest litigation), matters which frequently fall outside the ambit of Continental civil proceedings. Even so, a residual difference probably remains between Anglo-American and Continental systems. On this point, in a process where so much depends on the way in which judicial power is exercised and where so few lines are clear, American judges may occasionally be tempted to disregard the demands of the parties even in cases where such independent action would clearly be prohibited to their Continental counterparts. Here, then, is an example of one aspect of the administration of justice where the character of traditional common-law authority, rather than facilitating the evolution of forms suitable for conflict resolution, actually hinders their development. The boundary lines of party autonomy cannot always be clearly discerned in the chiaroscuro of judicial discretion.

Criminal cases are a different story. It is thought totally unacceptable, even absurd, in Continental systems to let the prosecution and the defense control the choice or the dosage of the criminal sanction. To let the defendant negotiate with state officials on this score seems to compromise the sovereign prerogative of the government to dispense criminal justice. While it is true that in several Continental systems the public prosecutor is expected to recommend a particular sentence, the judge is not bound by this recommendation and assesses the penalty independently. In America, prescribed penalties are bargaining chips openly and freely used by both the prosecution and the defense in arriving at what might be called "the consensual sentence": state interests in the realization of policy toward crime do not trump the interest of the criminal defendant in improving his lot, and the two interests can legitimately be set off against each other, as if two equivalent private interests were involved.[38]

Fact-Finding

It is often maintained that the competitive method of proof taking is so central to the adversarial process that one can hardly discuss it without including such practices as examination of witnesses by the adverse parties.[39] In fact, party control over proof taking is much less crucial to the conflict-solving process than

---

38. While the judge may reject the bargain made between the prosecutor and the defendant, in practice he seldom interferes. In contrast to America, where plea bargaining is above the counter, in England the practice seems to take place covertly. See J. Baldwin and M. McConville, *Negotiated Justice: Pressures to Plead Guilty* (1977).

39. This is so among commentators who view the adversarial process as the repository of features actually adopted by Anglo–American systems. See, e.g., R. M. Jackson, *The Machinery of Justice in England*, 6th ed., 18–19 (1972); M. Taruffo, *Il Processo Civile "Adversary" nell'Esperienza Americana*, 8 (Padua, 1979).

is party control over the definition of factual issues. Where parties no longer decide what the factual issues are, the legal process no longer serves the objective of dispute resolution. But party control over proof taking cannot similarly be related to the animating purpose of proceedings: a lawsuit can remain devoted to dispute resolution even if control over important aspects of fact-finding is taken away from the litigants and transferred to a procedural protagonist independent of the parties, and in this sense impartial. A good illustration is the classical variant of Continental civil procedure: litigants exercise an undisputed control over the factual parameters of the lawsuit, but the judge decides on the sequence in which witnesses will be called, and it is he who interrogates them.[40]

But if the competitive style of proof taking is not a sine qua non of the conflict-solving process conceptually linked to its objective, it can still be viewed as an integral part of this process, belonging to the full panoply of its forms, so long as it advances the objectives of the process better than do available alternatives. Can this be said for party control over fact-finding? Does the process run more smoothly when parties (or their counsel) take charge of proof taking and related activities?

An answer to this question can best be found by examining some difficulties that confront the conflict-solving process if the responsibility for fact-finding is placed in the hands of an independent agency—the conflict resolver or an official who conducts a factual inquiry and then reports to the decision maker. To conduct a focused investigation, he must adopt an initial hypothesis or assumption which—in a dichotomous dispute—necessarily favors one disputant over the other. It is therefore possible that the party disfavored by this assumption views the official's factual inquiry as a subtle *parti pris*. It makes no difference whether the official fact finder seeks confirmation of his initial assumption or (a less likely alternative) engages in a Popperian quest for its refutation. In either case, one party may begin to lose faith in the fact finder's neutrality. This possible erosion of faith accelerates when the official seeks to test the accuracy of information by vigorously challenging its supplier: when he grills a witness testifying in favor of one disputant, the other may think that the official is assisting his adversary.

Perhaps more troubling is the problem of defining criteria for the sufficiency of proof assembled by the official investigator. If standards of sufficiency are very demanding, disputes will remain unresolved and procedural goals unattained, especially in a reactive state where only the residuum of difficult cases comes before the court. Rules for the burden of proof and presumptions must thus be fashioned to help resolve factual uncertainties. Observe, however, that a reactive state can employ these devices only very sparingly: the risk of factually erroneous verdicts cannot be distributed unequally between the litigants on policy grounds—that is, on the basis of some second-order theory of the social

40. For limitations on judicial proof-taking powers in Continental civil procedure, see *infra*, nn. 49, 50.

good. Claiming neutrality in social conflicts, the reactive state cannot adopt even such second-order theories; it refuses to treat one side to a dispute as more valuable or deserving than the other.[41] What remain, then, are burden of proof rules and presumptions predicated on mere probability: facts are sometimes taken as established which—although not fully proven—seem the more likely to be true.[42] But even the use of such devices is somewhat awkward. To base a decision on a burden of proof rule is to say to one litigant that he has lost the contest because he was unsuccessful in carrying his evidentiary load. If he is himself in charge of proving his allegations, and fails, this way of talking makes eminent sense. But as soon as an official takes over the responsibility for adducing proof, it is no longer appropriate—although it is common—to justify factual findings in terms of burdens unsustained or requirements unfulfilled by the litigants. If any procedural protagonist has failed to sustain a burden, it must be the official fact finder himself. In this situation, the loser of the lawsuit is justified in harboring the belief that he could have prevailed if only he had been allowed to handle his own evidentiary case. A procedural system where judgments are legitimated by victory in a fair contest is not likely to take such reactions lightly. The citizens' faith in the effectiveness and fairness of the administration of justice can be adversely affected.

The plausibility of the loser's complaint ("I could have made a better evidentiary case myself") is greatly enhanced by the difficulties in providing incentives adequate for energetic official fact-finding. Remember that the parties retain their mastery in deciding what facts shall be subject to proof and that they can always delete facts that are in the process of being proven from the scope of controversy. Remember also that they can always replace official findings with contrary stipulations of fact. It is not easy for an official to be a dedicated seeker of truth if the litigants can at any moment interrupt his efforts or make the fruits of his efforts worthless; how many officials are capable of combining devotion to a project with Montaignesque nonchalance about its impending futility? It is true that the system may try to compensate for the absence of intrinsic satisfaction in the investigator's work by adequately rewarding him, even if his labors are frustrated. But such rewards are a costly proposition. They make sense only if fact-finding by an impartial researcher is regarded as clearly superior to proof taking managed by the parties. In this connection, it is sobering to note that lawyers with experience in transnational litigation have found fact-finding in

41. The reverse is true, of course, where an activist government tries to advance the interests of certain classes of citizens, if need be at the expense of other classes. Even the presumption of guilt can be justified under some circumstances. "I have discussed soberly and categorically which is better, to put in prison several tens or hundreds of instigators, guilty or innocent, or to lose thousands of workers and Army men. The first is better. The interest of workers . . . must win out" (V. I. Lenin, 23 *Sochineniia*, 3d ed., 241 (Moscow, 1935).

42. What happens if the evidence is in equipoise? It would seem that in this situation a government seeking to maintain social equilibrium is inclined to favor the litigant whose victory entails less change in existing relationships.

Continental civil procedure much less probing and energetic than in common-law countries.[43] While the lesser "inquisitiveness" of Continentals in this sphere can be attributed to a variety of factors, one of them may well be the particular allocation of procedural control between the civil judge and the litigants. While the former monopolizes the interrogation of witnesses, the latter decide which witnesses will be called and are sovereign in determining factual issues.

If the parties, already in control of the factual and legal parameters of litigation, are also permitted to take charge of the processes of proof, the difficulties I have just canvassed do not arise. The impartial position of procedural authority is better maintained if officials refrain from active fact research and merely referee the competitive fact-finding enterprise of the disputants. Troubling questions of proper standards for sufficiency of proof can be more easily resolved; where facts remain uncertain, judgment can be awarded in favor of the party who has made a better evidentiary case. Because processes of proof are propelled by the parties' self-interest, there is no lack of incentive for energetic evidentiary action. There is yet another somewhat hidden advantage. Where parties manage their own evidentiary cases, they may violate the rules of proof taking. If this breach affects the outcome—and in close cases this can plausibly be urged—the judge can sanction the offending litigant with an adverse decision: as if through the courtesy of an invisible hand, he is thus afforded a mechanism for deciding difficult cases without reaching the merits.

But what about the accuracy of factual determination under the party-dominated process of proof? While self-interested litigants obviously do not lack incentives to act, they may also be motivated to hide the truth. Skillful orchestration of proof may obscure rather than clarify what has actually happened. Even assuming that both parties are honest, does not the precision of competitive fact-finding depend on the roughly equal capacity of the contestants to use the evidentiary sources, so that whenever one side is less adroit, the judgment may be erroneous? The answer to these questions leads inexorably to an assessment of the relative merits of partisan and nonpartisan presentation of evidence as instruments in the quest for the truth.[44] Fortunately, this almost intractable problem,

---

43. See, e.g., R. Schlesinger, *Comparative Law*, 4th ed., 328 (1980). Continental criminal prosecutions are a separate matter: there, fact-finding seems relentless to common-law observers, perhaps vigorously probing: "The sporting spirit, the notion of the law as a game of skill with handicaps to give each side a chance, is entirely absent" (S. Bedford, *The Faces of Justice*, 163 [1961]). In criminal matters, however, Continental investigators can call witnesses on their own, party stipulations of fact are prohibited, and more generally, efficiency in crime detection is satisfying to the fact finder.

44. See M. Damaška, "Adversary Presentation of Evidence and Factfinding Precision," 123 *U. Pa. L. Rev.* 1083–1106 (1975). Empirical science has recently joined the fray, but predictably, no clear answer to this complex problem has emerged; ideological assumptions are often smuggled into the design of empirical projects. An overview of recent research can be found in B. Sheppard and N. Vidmar, "Adversary Pretrial Procedures and Testimonial Evidence," 39 *Journal of Personality and Social Psychology* 320 (1980). See also B. Schunemann, "Experimentelle Untersuchungen zur Reform der Hauptverhandlung im Strafsachen," in H. Kernerr, H. Kury, and K. Sessar, eds., *Deutsche Forschungen zur Kriminalitätsenstehung und Kriminalitätskontrolle* (1983).

over which a feud has been raging with undiminished vigor for two centuries, need not be addressed here, because the problem is a mere red herring in the present context. It becomes germane only if it is assumed that a legal process, no matter what its objective or political underpinnings, inevitably favors that fact-finding style which is most likely to yield accurate results. But this is not true. A moment's reflection on the relationship between the desire to settle a dispute and the desire to establish the true state of the world will suffice to confirm this point. It is an old insight that truth can engender hatred and exacerbate a conflict, for to tell the truth is all too often seriously to offend. A legal process aimed at maximizing the goal of dispute resolution thus cannot simultaneously aspire to maximize accurate fact-finding.[45] In fact, this process does not seek precision of factual findings as a goal independent of dispute resolution, even within the narrow compass of issues as defined by the parties. The verdict in the conflict-solving mode is not so much a pronouncement on the true state of the world as it is a decision resolving the debate between the parties, like a peace treaty putting an end to combat. In consequence, even if it were shown that fact-finding dominated by the parties uncovers the truth less effectively than does impartial research, this showing would not of itself preclude the possibility that the competitive evidentiary method might still be the preferable form in the conflict-solving process.

It must be conceded that many influential theories of justice reject this narrow linkage of desirable outcomes to conflict resolution. Prepared to concede that truth is not a sufficient condition for a wished-for result, they nonetheless insist that it is a necessary condition. But again, the ideology of the reactive state lends support to the narrow conflict-solving perspective and therefore also to a pure model of conflict-solving procedure. The possibility that extreme forms of laissez-faire rest on conceptions of the truth as more a product of a debate than as a mirror of reality need not be conjectured.[46] It is enough for my purposes here to recall that the reactive state is never "inquisitive" about the true state of affairs independently of the interaction of its citizens, even within those segments of reality that its citizens choose to bring before its courts as a matter in dispute. The state has no interests to which private self-governance should be sacrificed; individual autonomy is its highest priority, and as a result, it places significant limits on the quest for truth. Moreover, since only difficult cases are litigated, the "truth"—no matter how conceived—tends to appear elusive and ambiguous. Thus, inspired by the ideology of reactive government, the conflict-solving process is indifferent to how it actually was—*wie es eigentlich gewesen*. Having already accorded control over the factual parameters of the lawsuit to the parties, it also permits them to take full charge of proving the facts brought within these parameters.

How does fact-finding in Anglo-American and Continental jurisdictions compare with the pure conflict-solving form? To fully appreciate this problem, its

45. See N. Luhman, *Legitimation durch Verfahren,* 2d ed., 21 (Darmstadt, 1975).
46. See *supra*, ch. 3, n. 7.

scope should not be limited to the most visible stage of proof taking in the courtroom but must also be seen to encompass a motley of earlier activity, such as the selection of usable evidence, planning of the sequence of proof, even the search for information leading to evidence. In Anglo-American litigation, both civil and criminal, all these preparatory activities are firmly in the hands of the litigants rather than some independent investigative agency. Even if the plaintiff or defendant happens to be an official (the police, the public prosecutor) who symbolically serves the public interest, his preparatory activities are invariably influenced by anticipation of the contested trial and thus assume partisan overtones. For example, this official may attempt to keep some important information to himself in order to make the preparation of the other side more difficult. In the American variant of civil discovery, even the search for information becomes a partisan engagement of direct and cross-examination by counsel.

At the trial, the competitive style of proof taking is commonly regarded as a hallmark of common-law procedure. Somewhat ironically, however, it is at this stage that considerable deviation can occur from party-controlled fact-finding. American judges in both civil and criminal cases have power to call witnesses on their own initiative and sometimes inject themselves in the interrogation process; they often proclaim devotion to the discovery of truth, and some even profess to expect objectivity from all officials cast in party roles. But when all is said and done, few would be ready to deny that proof taking in Anglo-American courtrooms remains quite distinctly a party-dominated enterprise. Judicial powers of interrogation and especially those of evidentiary initiative are used only as means of last resort when party-propelled presentation of evidence fails; even then, these powers are used gingerly and within narrow limits. Nor will an official, qua party, be inclined to assume such a strongly nonpartisan posture as to focus on a line of inquiry damaging to his case but propitious to truth discovery. In rare instances where one does, he is usually castigated by the higher court for stepping out of the proper adversarial role.

This reluctance to interfere in the competitive presentation of evidence is due to the difficulty of devising stable intermediate arrangements that mix impartiality with partisan attitudes. Proceedings designed as a contest of the parties have their own integrity or inner logic, so that they cannot be tampered with without cost. It is the image of the pure conflict-solving mode that brings this inner logic to the surface, exposing the problematic nature of mixed arrangements. Imagine, first, that a judge, seeking to discover the truth, takes seriously the objectivity of one contestant but continues to regard the other contestant as biased or driven by self-interest. Now it becomes a natural reaction for the judge to discount the evidentiary case of the "biased" litigant who is, after all, more likely to obfuscate the truth. No matter how natural or reasonable this reaction might be, however, it contradicts the essential demand of the conflict-solving process that parties must be treated equally by the adjudicator: his impartiality presupposes two "partialities." Imagine next that the judge begins freely to intervene in the competitive proof-taking process. If the system is to function properly, the parties must invest in the strategy and preparation of their evidentiary cases; if they are to derive the greatest tactical advantage from their evidence, they must plan what persons to call as witnesses, in what order to examine them, and even what sequence of questions to propound. But even one limited bona fide interference on the part of the judge in this partisan mode of using evidence may render all the pain and travail of the parties useless.[47] If judicial interference can be expected in the normal run of events, the wind begins to go out of the sails of the competitive evidentiary process, and the incentives that sustain it begin to dry up. All told, it is no coincidence that judges in common-law systems only sparingly employ their powers of intervention in the partisan presention of evidence, and that they will disrupt a strongly competitive exercise of proof taking only in exceptional cases.[48]

Anglo-American observers of Continental courts fasten their attention mainly on the most visible aspect of fact-finding—judicial interrogations of witnesses—with the result that they tend to exaggerate the dominance of the judiciary over the fact-finding process. In fact, this dominance is undisputed only in criminal matters, which are not conceived as involving actual dispute resolution. In civil cases, however, judicial investigative powers are considerably reduced. In the classical variant of the civil process antedating the advent of socialist systems, judges are generally prohibited from calling fact witnesses on their own initiative or against the wishes of the litigants, so that on this point judges have fewer rights than their brethren in many common-law jurisdictions.[49] The parties retain control not only over facts to be subject to proof but also over the sources of information to be used in proving these facts. Some earlier Continental systems—especially in Latin countries—went so far as to limit judicial interrogation in civil cases only to questions suggested by the parties,[50] so that there was in these systems only minuscule opportunity left for the judge to be "inquisitive" on his own. Thus, while probing and vigorous in criminal matters, judicial interrogation can be anemic in civil proceedings. Nor is the resulting void filled by party-propelled examination of witnesses, for from the Continental vantage point this practice comes close to usurpation of the *officium judicis*.[51]

47. A former federal judge has vividly illustrated this point. See M. Frankel, "The Search for Truth: An Imperial View," 123 *U. Pa. L. Rev.* 1031, 1042 (1975).

48. English judges may be even less willing to interfere with proof processes than their American colleagues. See *Ali* v. *London Spinning Co., Ltd.*, reported in the *Times* (London), April 30, 1971, p. 9. In America, sustained judicial questioning can constitute reversible error (*People* v. *Rigley*, 359 P. 2d. 23, 98 [Cal. 1961]). At least in criminal cases, it is clearly recognized in America that parties have the right to present evidence in the sequence they find most persuasive. See T. Amsterdam, "A Selective Survey of Supreme Court Decisions in Criminal Law and Procedure," 9 *Crim. L. Bull.* 389, 404 (1973); P. Westen, "Order of Proof," 66 *Cal. L. Rev.* 935, 975 (1978).

49. For a comparative discussion of exceptional cases where the civil judge can obtain expert opinions on its own motion, see W. J. Habscheid, "Richtermacht oder Parteifreiheit," 81 *Zeitschrift für Zivilprozess*, 176 (1968).

50. For Italy, see M. Cappelletti and J. Perillo, *Civil Procedure in Italy*, 223–24 (1965). The more recent trend toward greater judicial powers of interrogation in civil cases coincides with the rise of state activism.

51. For this reason civil litigants (their lawyers) also refrain from seeking and interviewing prospective witnesses. On the Continent sporadic attempts were made to transfer examination of

The Party as a Means of Proof

Is the conversion of the party into an informational source a deviation from the pure conflict-solving process? An answer to this query is sought in vain in Anglo-American writing on the adversarial process; a *tour d'horison* of actual procedures that qualify vaguely as "adversarial" reveals the rich and somewhat perplexing variety of possible regulation of the party's evidentiary status. On this point, no measure is available by means of which to compare extant procedural systems in terms of their fidelity to the contest-solving ideal. A blank page in conventional theory, the topic deserves to be considered in detail.

Compulsory and voluntary transformations present separate problems and should each be examined in turn. So far as the former is concerned, it is easy to see that such transformation of a litigant into a means of proof, whether at the instance of his opponent or on the court's own initiative, creates anomalies in proceedings conceived as a party contest. A litigant who is converted into an object of the process he purports to manage can no longer control his tactical interest in the lawsuit; many aspects of the competitive style, including the rival style of proof taking, will be seriously skewed. To be sure, an assistant to a party can be enlisted to take over the managerial aspects of the party's role, but such substitution entails serious problems of its own, and, most important, this substitution of a "second" cannot take place over the opposition of the litigant who retains his right to self-representation. But even more serious is the subversion of the requirement that each contestant prove his own claims and sustain his own evidentiary burden. It is a curious burden indeed that can be sustained by one side's forcing the opponent to carry the load. As Roman-canon legal scholars liked to say, a party to a contest should not be compelled to become *telum adversarii sui*, that is, an offensive weapon of his adversary. In brief, then, for proceedings structured as a contest to function normally, each litigant must remain both free to choose whether to be transformed into a means of proof and sovereign in deciding at what point in the presentation of his case the conversion should occur. Compulsory conversion of a party into a means of proof is not a feature of the pure contest style.

How do actual systems relate to this requirement of the pure model? In common-law countries, the position of the parties to criminal proceedings approximates the ideal form more closely than the position of civil litigants. This is obvious early in the pleading stage: the criminal defendant's plea of not guilty is not required to be a truthful declaration; he has the right "to put the state to proof." In American criminal prosecutions the defendant's guilt is often conceded in the course of plea bargaining, but if these negotiations fail, the defense

---

witnesses to litigants, but these reforms remained mostly dead-letter law (as in West Germany), or resulted in interrogations far removed from the cross-examination practiced in common-law jurisdictions. The rigor of competitive proof taking was relaxed by letting witnesses present a narrative account prior to interrogation, and by letting transcripts of prior depositions compete with the spoken word of witnesses for the fact finder's trust.

then enters a plea of not guilty almost as a matter of course. This practice is regarded as perfectly legitimate. In contrast, parties to a civil lawsuit have no analogous right to deny allegations they know are true; a party has no recognized right to put his opponent to proof.

This asymmetry continues in the evidentiary process. To permit the prosecutor to call the criminal defendant to the stand is considered perverse: it is the sovereign prerogative of the defendant alone to decide whether and when to testify in presenting his own case.[52] The self-sealing justification is the constitutional privilege against self-incrimination, of course; but if pressed to offer independent support, few common lawyers would fail to deploy arguments related to the contest structure of proceedings. If the prosecution could use the defendant as a witness to establish its own case, burden of proof regulations would be violated. While powerful in criminal cases, these arguments seem without force in civil proceedings. Here, a litigant can call his adversary to the stand to establish his own case. Although this option may seldom be exercised in practice, there are countervailing tactical considerations: it is risky to use an uncoached and hostile witness to make one's own evidentiary points. This is not the only instance in which the civil litigant can be compelled to become a source of information to his adversary. In America, a party can be subject to searching pretrial interrogation by his adversary, protected only by testimonial privileges available to ordinary witnesses.[53] In sum, Anglo-American jurisdictions use more potent instruments to press for the truth in civil than in criminal cases; on this point, civil procedure is more "inquisitorial" and criminal procedure more "adversarial."

Continental systems reverse this relationship between civil and criminal justice. In the still dominant variant of the Continental civil process, parties are used as evidentiary sources with great reluctance and are frequently called upon to testify only as a means of last resort when other evidence does not suffice for a decision. Yet even then, the litigants have the right to refuse to testify, including the lesser right to fail to respond to specific questions.[54] Only those European countries that have moved a great distance toward managerial activism (Sweden and communist systems) have actually shed this reluctance to use party interrogations; however, these systems have also departed far from the classical conception of civil justice as a means for resolving private disputes.[55] In criminal

52. In *Brooks* v. *Tennessee*, 406 U.S. 605 (1972), the United States Supreme Court invalidated a Tennessee statue requiring criminal defendants to take the stand, if they so chose, before any other witnesses for the defense. See also *Illinois* v. *Allen*, 397 U.S. 337, 338 (1970).

53. This is comparatively all the more striking because testimonial privileges are less generous in America than in most Continental jurisdictions. The witness in Continental proceedings is often entitled to refuse to answer not only because of the threat of criminal prosecution against him or persons close to him, but also if to reply would bring him into disrepute or expose him to serious financial loss. This is the case in many Swiss cantons, Austria, and West Germany. See *infra*, ch. 6, n. 55.

54. For an illustration see the *West German Code of Civil Procedure*, §§445–48.

55. The classical regulation persists, curiously, in communist Yugoslavia. See S. Triva, *Gradjansko Procesno Pravo*, 439 (Zagreb, 1965).

cases the situation is quite different, especially if one disregards proclamations of formal doctrine and focuses on what routinely occurs in practice.

Traditionally, the defendant's testimony is eagerly sought: his interrogation is the centerpiece of preliminary investigations, and the trial begins with an extensive interrogation of the defendant by the judge. Although all systems of criminal justice employ some mechanisms to induce defendants to loquacity, these mechanisms are especially effective in Continental countries. Unlike the accused in common-law systems, the Continental defendant cannot choose whether or not to submit to the interrogation process; he is entitled only to refuse to answer generally or in regard to a particular question, but as a practical matter, even this more limited right is largely illusory and regularly waived.[56] In brief, the criminal process is a much more powerful instrument of truth discovery than is civil justice—more "inquisitive," thus further removed from pure contest forms. This relation between the two branches of adjudication appears perfectly sensible to Continentals: in their view, a process devoted to the implementation of state policy toward crime should be more probing than a process designed for the resolution of interpersonal disputes.[57]

So far I have argued that the compulsory conversion of a party into a source of information should not be seen as an integral part of the pure conflict-solving style. What about a voluntary conversion? Initially it might seem that no special problems arise: a litigant who freely chooses to become a source of information should be assimilated to the status of an ordinary witness. On closer inspection, however, significant differences between parties and regular witnesses come into view, which suggest a need for differential regulation. While functioning in his testimonial capacity, the party continues to keep an eye on his tactical interests in the lawsuit, evaluating the information he is expected to give in terms of how it will affect his chances of winning. Some modification of rules applicable to ordinary witnesses may therefore be mandated by the need to preserve the party's mastery over the lawsuit, so crucial to the conflict-solving process. For example, whereas an ordinary witness can be excluded from the courtroom when others testify, a party can hardly be denied continuous presence in court, even though his presence creates the possibility that he will tailor his testimony to that of other witnesses.

Other modifications could be contemplated, based upon the friction between self-interest and the duty to tell the truth—friction that is typically more severe for the party than it is for the ordinary witness. Consider those testimonial

---

56. This problem is considered in chapter 5 in relation to the role of parties in the policy-implementing process. In Continental trials, the guilt-determining and sentencing stages are lumped together so that the taciturn defendant who refuses to respond to the judge's questions may deprive himself of arguments for mitigating the sentence, quite aside from his challenge to judicial authority by failing to respond. Continental defendants who actually exercise their right to silence are few and far between.

57. I shall examine the reasons for the striking differences between Anglo-American and European jurisdictions' regulation of the parties' evidentiary status in civil and criminal cases in the last chapter, invoking the divergent structure of judicial authority. The different conceptions of the legitimate function of government may also be of help in explaining the unequal relationship of civil and criminal justice in Anglo-American and Continental countries.

privileges whose rationale is said to be understanding of and sympathy for the pain of these very frictions. By invoking these privileges an ordinary witness can avoid with relative ease both damage to his interest and perjury: he has no immediate stake in the lawsuit. A party, on the other hand, often fears negative inferences will be drawn from the mere fact that he has invoked a privilege—inferences that can cause him the loss of the lawsuit. All other things equal, then, the party is necessarily more tempted to misinform for the sake of preserving his interest than is an ordinary witness. Should rules regulating party testimony not reflect this significant difference? Should sympathy for the party's dilemma not lead to relaxation of the duty of the witness to tell the truth? In thinking about this distasteful possibility, one should not necessarily imagine a "worst case"—helping a dishonest litigant or a guilty criminal mendaciously trying to avoid a verdict he richly deserves. A party with a meritorious claim may nevertheless fear adverse consequences, should he reply truthfully to a question or a skillfully devised but misleading sequence of questions. Because human discourse is seldom univalently informative, only those innocent in the ways of the world would overlook the possible costs of veracity, costs that did not escape even the medieval inquisitor's attention.[58]

What is the likely position of an extreme laissez-faire government on this point? A regulation that relaxes rules applicable to ordinary witnesses may appear attractive, especially those rules imposing serious punishment for perjury. Where the government promotes no policy to which the self-interest of individuals should be sacrificed, sympathy for behavior driven by self-seeking impulses is at its apogee and the countervailing desire to establish the truth is at its low ebb. Of course, an objection must be anticipated to "liberalization" of the testimonial regimen: will not fact finders be taken in by concocted stories now spun by litigants with virtual impunity? A justice apparatus where fact finders are inexperienced and predictably gullible cannot make light of this possibility. The best solution for this apparatus might be to disqualify the parties from testifying at all, and to direct them to wage their evidentiary contest with means of proof independent of their persons.[59] But where the fact finders are experi-

---

58. While the propriety of misleading questions can be challenged by counsel, such a challenge, even if sustained by the court, can easily damage the party's general credibility as a source of information. ("He must be hiding something from the court" is the fact finder's frequent reaction.)

59. It is well known that parties were held incompetent to testify throughout much of the history of both Anglo-American and Continental systems. Some American states retained the testimonial incapacity of the criminal defendant well into the twentieth century. However, the chief rationale of this incapacity was concern about the reliability of party testimony: self-serving statements seemed probably spurious owing to the pull of self-interest. In addition, Roman-canon ecclesiastical authorities were concerned that, if permitted to testify, the party could perpetrate the mortal sin of perjury. See St. Thomas Aquinas, *Summa Theologica*, tomus III, pars II, quest. 69, art. 1, 403 (Turin and London, 1895). But it would be wrong to assume that unsworn party statements were not in practice a valuable source of information, even if not technical proof. This was especially the case in England, where lay decision makers could not be expected to disregard utterances of a litigant arguing with his opponent in court. Only in the liberal epoch did the principal justification of testimonial incapacity become sympathy for the predicament of a person who can seriously hurt his self-interest by telling the truth under oath.

enced professionals, liberalization of the rules applicable to ordinary witnesses makes sense; even if the testimony of a party is taken to contain an element of potential deceit—as magicians' acts do—such testimony can still be useful because truth may emerge from detected inconsistencies. And because testimonial incapacity of the parties as a mandatory rule will reduce their freedom to interact and to choose weapons for their forensic contest, this second solution better accords with the general character of procedural regulation in the reactive state.

Observe that Continental procedures in fact distinguish between witnesses and parties as evidentiary sources. In the laissez-faire epoch, Continental criminal defendants were absolved of criminal liability for false testimony: it became quite common to speak of their "right to lie."[60] In the same period, it was also widely believed that civil litigants had no obligation to make truthful allegations; civil parties were actually exempt from liability for perjury in a great number of European jurisdictions.[61] To impose on them the duty to tell the truth and thereby to harm their own interests was proclaimed to be inhumane, akin to a form of moral torture, even though civil parties had also acquired the right to refuse to testify.

This cavalier attitude toward mendacity on the stand was alien to the Anglo-American administration of justice, even in the heyday of laissez-faire, and it continues undiminished to the present day. As a matter of legal doctrine, the party on the stand is treated as an ordinary witness. In practice, relaxation of this rigid attitude, bespeaking a greater tolerance of party misinformation, occurs mainly in criminal cases;[62] again, civil justice displays a greater demand for the truth. It is tempting to see in this harsher attitude toward lies a symptom of the characteristic reluctance of coordinate judicial authority to separate legal and ethical obligations. No matter what may be the reason for this difference between Continental and Anglo-American systems, the comparativist is led to conclude that the evidentiary status of the party in common-law jurisdictions—that is, his equivalence with regular witnesses—deviates from pure conflict-solving forms more than does Continental regulation.

---

60. Even now, false testimony by the defendant becomes a criminal offense only in exceptional cases (e.g., false accusation of an innocent person). For West Germany, see K. Rogall, *Der Beschuldigte als Beweismittel gegen sich selbst*, 37–40 (Berlin, 1977).

61. See A. Heffter, *System des römmischen und deutschen Civil-prozessrechts*, 227 (Bonn, 1843). The introduction of criminal liability for false statements by a civil party is basically a twentieth-century development, but even now party perjury is treated as a less serious grade of the perjury offense in most European jurisdictions. For a good comparative discussion, see E. Cohn, *Zur Wahrheitspflict und Aufklärungspflicht der Parteien, Festschrift Hippel*, (Tübingen, 1967).

62. Criminal defendants who testify and protest innocence are convicted every day in Anglo-American courts, yet few are prosecuted for perjury. While it may be said that "punishment" for perjury is tacitly incorporated into the (heightened) sentence, such is actually seldom the explicit purpose of the sentencing judge. But see *United States* v. *Grayson* 550 F.2d 103 (3d. Cir 1977). Moreover, even acquitted defendants whose testimony turns out later to be false are rarely subject to perjury prosecution. For a survey of authority on this issue, see *Regina* v. *Humphrys, Weekly Law Reports* (London), June 4, 1976, p. 890.

Disclosure of Documents and Other Nontestimonial Information

Do parties have a duty to disclose upon request material of potential evidentiary significance? This question can be examined in a setting where fact-finding is the responsibility of some nonpartisan agency (so that disclosure means disclosure to the agency) and in a setting of party-managed fact-finding (so that disclosure means disclosure to the other side). But because the latter method of fact-finding has been found to be in harmony with the pure conflict-solving process, I shall focus only on discovery as between the parties.

Although compelled exchange of information between litigants—forced cooperation—may seem to have no place in a pure contest model, there is actually some room for it even in those procedures that carry the contest theme to extremes. One need not belabor the difficulties of preparing for forensic contest in total ignorance of the weapons the other side proposes to employ; even medieval knights exchanged some information prior to their tournament engagement. Where trials are of the day-in-court variety, some prior discovery seems absolutely necessary to reduce procedural ambush to a level compatible with notions of fair contest.[63] More interesting for comparative purposes, however, is another reason favoring exchange of information, one that can be related to the ideology of reactive government. Even after proceedings have been initiated, the government prefers bargaining and negotiations between the parties to continue, now conducted in the shadow of the ongoing legal process; the more frequently that such negotiations lead to out-of-court settlement and abort official proceedings, the better. This is where discovery fits in: compulsory exchange of information forces litigants to interact, enables them to appraise the relative strengths of their cases, and in doing so encourages settlement. Of course, demands for disclosure can drive up the cost of litigation and give an edge to the financially better situated party, but as I have said, an extreme laissez-faire system is not unduly disturbed by this prospect.

To demonstrate that there is *some* room for discovery in the pure conflict-solving process is not to deny that forced exchange of information can seriously strain it. A process devoted to the absorption of disputes does not tolerate compelled disclosure of material beyond the ambit of the issues defined by the parties: such information can open up new controversies rather than advancing the resolution of the existing one. Therefore, as a prerequisite to involuntary discovery it is imperative that issues in dispute be clearly defined, and that mutual demands for disclosure of information be circumscribed thereby: discovery detached from disputed issues no longer belongs in a lawsuit conceived as an instrument of dispute resolution. But even where the disclosure required from the adverse party *is* closely related to the disputed issue, it can become problematic in proceedings structured as competitive enterprise. For instance, to

---

63. Effective reaction to some procedural moves (e.g., the defense of alibi) requires preparation. Where proceedings are of the installment variety, as in Continental systems, the need for exchange of information acquires a different dimension, and early disclosure is less important.

permit the forced disclosure of information that a litigant has obtained through his own research may impair or even destroy the incentives that sustain the competitive system; just as the requirement that a firm in a competitive market disclose the fruits of its research to competitors may discourage development of new products, so parties accorded the power to pry into their competitors' case may end up obtaining less information. The cost of greater access to information may be loss of the incentive necessary for the development of information. In short, discovery must be kept within narrow bounds: only that information must be exchanged which is indispensable to a fair contest. The exchange should, of course, be mutual. Where one side is permitted to play it close to the vest while the other must tip his hand, the premise of party equality has been violated. Thus if criminal prosecution is structured as a competitive engagement and the defendant is not required to disclose information, the prosecutor may have significant power to keep to himself information he has acquired for the state.[64]

The history of Continental civil procedure suggests a correlation between arm's-length government and the narrow scope of discovery, although on the Continent those pressures for discovery that arise from the litigants' need to carry out an evidentiary contest independently at the concentrated trial are missing. Still, even by Continental standards, the litigants' duty to disclose was singularly limited in the liberal nineteenth century. For example, a party was then obligated to surrender to the court (which implied the right of their inspection by the other side) only such documents as were common to him and his adversary, or where the duty to surrender material evidence was explicitly provided by statute.[65] This frugal discovery was defended by arguments—protection of individual privacy, autonomy, and so on—that obviously sprang from the font of laissez-faire philosophy. Only with the expansion of governmental concerns in the welfare state did special statutes proliferate imposing duties to disclose documents in spheres of social life—for example, consumer protection—where the state had ceased to be uninvolved.[66] But insofar as Continental civil

64. The limited rights of discovery of the American criminal defendant are often unfavorably compared to the unlimited right of the defendant in Continental systems to inspect the file of the preliminary process (containing all the evidence) in advance of trial. See R. Schlesinger, *supra*, n. 43, p. 448. No matter what one may think of the American criminal discovery rules, fair comparison requires that the problem be observed in a larger context: the Continental defendant acquires an unlimited right to "discovery" from the prosecution only after pretrial investigators have had ample opportunity to obtain information from him and to convert this information into technical evidence; since the cat is already out of the bag, the prosecution can well afford to give the defendant a look.

65. This is still reflected in the procedural codifications of several Continental countries. For reasons that cannot be addressed here, the scholarly founders of Roman-canon civil process advocated very limited discovery (*editio instrumentum*), especially to assist the plaintiff in prosecuting his case. In actual practice under the ancien régime, judges demanded broader disclosure than scholary texts suggest. See F. Bomsdorf, *Prozessmaximem und Rechtswirklichkeit*, 57 (Berlin, 1971). Truly meager discovery is thus the product of the postrevolutionary epoch. For a good comparative discussion of discovery problems, see A. Dondi, *Effettività dei Provvedimenti Instruttori del Giudice Civile* (Padua, 1985).

66. Broader duties of disclosure were occasionally inserted into codifications rather than tucked into special statutes. See, e.g., art. 10 of the French Civil Code as amended in 1972. The extent to

proceedings continued to be conceived mainly as a mechanism for the resolution of interpersonal disputes, discovery remained restricted to proof of specific facts in dispute.

Developments in Anglo-American countries also suggest a parallel between oscillations in the scope of discovery and changing views on the mission of government. The common-law process traditionally demanded considerably more exchange of information between litigants than did Continental systems of justice, but discovery was strictly limited to information regarding facts alleged by the parties. It was only as part of the New Deal reforms in the 1930s that American jurisdictions relaxed this limitation: after the parties had broadly delineated the subject matter of the lawsuit in their pleadings, discovery requests pertaining to anything "relevant" to the case were now permitted.[67] Discovery was thus converted into an instrument for conducting a search for information that may expand the existing controversy or lead to another lawsuit. It should not be overlooked, however, that civil procedure came increasingly to be regarded as an instrument for instituting social reform or for challenging existing institutional practices, so that the objectives of civil litigation became complex and multiple. A source of possible confusion was thus created; effective tools of partisan investigation were developed with an eye toward litigation as an instrument of "public policy," but such means could also be used outside of this context in garden-variety "narrow" disputes. Functional in one context, broad discovery requests can be dysfunctional in the other. In this situation, the relationship of reformed discovery to the conventional concept of adversarial proceedings became a bone of contention. It can be argued that broad discovery will compromise adversarial arrangements by converting them into a fragile facade for an essentially policy-implementing process—a process in which nonpartisan or inquisitorial arrangements can eventually appear to be more suitable ("functional"). On the other hand, it can be maintained that wide discovery actually enables adversarial arrangements to survive: limited discovery could prevent the truth from emerging and thus generate pressures for the judge to intervene and take over the fact-finding function.[68] But notice the tacit assumption of this

---

which broader discovery powers are used in practice is a controversial topic; in some countries, old attitudes may persist, seriously limiting the exchange of information possible under the letter of the law.

67. See, e.g., F. R. Civ. P. 26(b) (1). Some limits on discovery were established to protect the product of counsel's research ("attorney work product"). See *Hickman* v. *Taylor*, 329 U.S. 495 (1947). Observe that denials of discovery requests lead more easily to reversal on appeal than do grants of questionable requests, so that there is a built-in incentive for an American trial judge to permit sweeping demands for private investigation. American discovery practice sometimes appears "exorbitant"—"fishing expeditions"—to lawyers in other common-law countries. See, e.g., I. H. Jacobs, "Models of Court Improvement," in *State Courts: A Blueprint for the Future*, 218 (Williamsburg, 1978); *Radio Corp. of America* v. *Rauland Corp.*, Queens Bench Div. 1 Q.B. 618 (1956).

68. For different perspectives on the relation of discovery to the adversarial process, see, e.g., W. D. Brazil, "The adversary character of civil discovery," 31 *Vand. L. Rev.* 1295 (1978); F. Kirkham, "Complex Civil Litigation," 70 *F.R.D.* 199, 209 (1976).

second argument: the judge will tolerate party control over procedural action—even party autonomy—merely on sufferance, for if the litigants' interaction does not lead to outcomes he approves, he is ready to step in and correct the failure of forensic competition. In light of most political ideologies of our time, this may well be the desirable course of action; but it betrays an orientation more activist than reactive—an orientation in which undiluted contest forms of justice become quite precarious. Gone is the ideological climate that offers them maximum support and maintains their purity: *Rome n'est plus Rome.*

Propulsion of the Lawsuit

Where the subject matter of a lawsuit is a dispute over rights and litigants are thus interested in contrary outcomes, it is often very difficult to make decisions concerning the propulsion of proceedings without appearing to take sides. A state whose main function is to provide a neutral forum for the resolution of disputes is likely to shun making a state agency—especially the adjudicator—responsible for giving rhythm and impulse to proceedings. Mechanisms such as pretrial conferences, capable of providing an opportunity for the adjudicator to direct proceedings, can also function as vehicles for the expansion of judicial control. Parties may find themselves pressured into settlement for the sake of larger interests, including bureaucratic concern with smooth case-flow management. Again, such intervention is repugnant to the reactive state.

But if official control over the progress of lawsuits is undesirable, this does not mean that the reactive state permits litigants to stall the proceedings whenever inaction serves their tactical interests. Because the procedural objective is dispute resolution, delay—at least under prevailing notions in Western cultures[69]—is to be reduced to the minimum. Who is then to do the policing? The best solution seems to be to entrust policing functions to the litigants themselves; each party is empowered to invoke sanctions for transgression of time limits against his adversary. Thus if a contestant fails to offer proof on time or fails to give timely notification of certain contemplated moves (e.g., raising the insanity defense or alibi), the other side is entitled to demand that the violator be precluded from offering proof or making certain procedural moves. To be sure, such preclusions can result in the loss of important matter, but where the state is interested not so much in the accuracy of procedural outcomes as in providing a fair forum, that prospect is contemplated with equanimity.

Given the foregoing catalog of issues over which parties exercise control in the purely reactive or laissez-faire process and the apparently extensive dominance of the litigants over the lawsuit, it remains to consider the limited scope of

---

69. This qualification is necessary because anthropologists report on cultures which attempt to resolve conflict by delaying and avoiding decisions. In the context of Balinese culture, Clifford Geertz attributes this technique to different perceptions of time than those prevailing in the West. On the "vectorless present," see C. Geertz, *The Interpretation of Cultures*, 403 (1973).

authority left to state officials, most particularly to the adjudicator. Not enough is known about the dynamics of litigation to support a claim that the decision maker's activity decreases in equal proportion to the expansion of party control, but if it is not zero-sum, there is certainly an inverse relation between the activity of the parties and that of officials in charge of the legal process. Accordingly, where the litigants preempt so much of the action—from investigative work to presentation of evidence to legal research—there is relatively little left for the adjudicator to do. What remains his exclusive preserve? He is restricted to solving incidental conflict of the parties in preparation for the trial (such as motions to supress evidence or disagreements over limits of discovery), monitoring observance of ground rules for party behavior in the courtroom, and, of course, rendering his decision on the merits of the case.

iv. THE IDEAL POSITION OF THE DECISION MAKER

Because my immediate aim here is to describe a style of proceeding that can be employed in a variety of official environments, I shall stick to the conveniently general term "decision maker" rather than use the more specific but potentially treacherous word "judge." As I have earlier indicated, conceptions of the judicial office greatly vary across legal cultures. Even in the West there are significant variations: some activities central to the office of the Continental judge can be exercised by the jury in common-law jurisdictions, with the result that Anglo-American lawyers consider only the residue of activity that cannot be transferred to the jury to be quintessentially "judicial." More or less perceptibly, divergent notions of the judicial office influence one's thinking on a variety of legal problems, and if a problem must be carried across the abyss of different legal cultures, misunderstandings can arise that are not easily tractable. I shall also refrain from characterizing the decision maker more specifically: whether he is individual or collegial, amateur or professional, functionally differentiated or fused, will temporarily remain open; somewhat greater precision need be introduced only sporadically, where demanded by a particular context.

In actual procedural systems, decision makers seldom perform the conflict-solving function alone. Additional demands are placed on their activity, and some of these demands either detract from optimal conflict-solving attitudes or are in direct conflict with them. My purposes here, however, require that characteristics of a pure conflict-solving posture be isolated from the mix of attitudes: in canvassing an ideal conflict-solving process, a decision maker must be imagined to whom all concerns other than the resolution of a dispute pale into insignificance. Clearly, the extreme laissez-faire state provides the best ground on which such attitudes can flourish; such is a state whose paramount task is to provide a forum for the settlement of conflicts in civil society, and whose very legitimacy rests on its image of neutral conflict resolver. What do citizens of such a state expect as they take before the court those disputes that they cannot resolve themselves? They realize that the outcome of the lawsuit is uncertain and that correct results can be elusive; what they expect from the decision maker most of all is equality of treatment—a neutral, objective, or impartial attitude. Now, it is important to realize that the decision maker's neutrality and the substantive accuracy of his rulings are independent variables: a decision maker who announces the right result on the merits may have treated the parties unequally, while one who has treated them equally may have to pronounce an erroneous result. Faced with the potential tension between these two values, the reactive state does not hesitate to place impartiality of process above accuracy of result. If one equates accuracy of outcomes with the attainment of justice, and equal treatment with fairness, one must conclude that the reactive state—and thus the conflict-solving process as well—values fairness above justice.

Procedural arrangements that safeguard and promote an attitude of impartiality must then be more closely examined. It is in these arrangements that the ideal position of the decision maker in the conflict-solving process can be discerned. Minimal requirements of impartiality—such as that the decision maker should have no personal stake in the outcome of the case—may be left to one side; they are not limited exclusively to proceedings devoted to the resolution of disputes, and they clearly do not suffice.

Dependence on the Parties for Information

Suppose that the decision maker chooses to seek information he needs for the disposition of the case from sources other than those channeled to him by the parties. After obtaining some knowledge independently, it now becomes difficult for him to decide the case on the criterion dictated by the conflict-solving process—that is, by determining which side has made a better argument. Swayed one way or another by extraparty information, he may be inclined to rule against a litigant who otherwise would be the clear victor of the courtroom debate. True, the decision maker can subject this extraneously obtained data to partisan argument at a later stage, but even if he does so before the independent information has had time to settle in his mind, the balance of advantages between the parties has been affected by his action. Moreover, the party disfavored by the information is now saddled with the burden of rebuttal, or of removing it from the decision maker's mind. Even if successful in this added endeavor, the party thus burdened may well feel that he was not treated equally with his opponent, and that the other side benefited from his burden. Accordingly, the pure conflict-solving style has no room for procedural arrangements that expose the decision maker to material that has not previously been structured by party interaction and then refined by party contest. The only substantive information he may receive is channeled to him by the litigants and filtered by their debate.

Insofar as reliance on party-structured information is concerned, the Continental understanding of "adversarial" style departs much further from the pure conflict-solving form than do common-law ideas. On the Continent, it is not felt that the contest style has been violated if the decision maker hears an argument ex parte—by one party alone—on the condition that the other side is subsequently permitted to comment and challenge: *audiatur et altera pars* (let the other party also be heard) is all the Continental "contradictory" process demands. In contrast, Anglo-American procedural law is on the whole much less tolerant of any action before the decision maker that does not take place in the presence of both parties, especially where the term "decision maker" includes both judge and jury.

Compare, as well, some techniques of fact-finding. The founders of the Continental law of evidence regarded visits to the locus by the trier of fact—a practice that enables him to acquire independent information—superior to all other modes of fact-finding and the best way of reaching true knowledge (*scientia vera*). The practice still plays an important role in many European countries.[70] In Anglo-American jurisdictions, on the other hand, such visits are permitted only if carefully orchestrated and controlled by the parties: "views" have no exalted status, and there is not even a settled terminology for referring to them. Also revealing are divergent techniques of collecting information from witnesses. On the Continent, witnesses are first asked by the court to present a narrative account of what they know: these stories are interrupted by questions only to help the witness express himself, to clarify a point, or to steer the witness back from the labyrinth of utter irrelevancy. As a result, information which is not relevant or responsive to parties' questions or structured by their interaction can freely be imparted to the decision maker. No doubt, testimony elicited in the common-law style through direct- and cross-examination comes closer to the ideal of information filtered only by the parties. A final illustration of the contrast between Continental and Anglo-American systems on this point is the Continental practice of requiring witnesses whose testimony is conflicting to face each other directly and engage in altercation. While such confrontation was a favorite of Continental triers of fact during the ancien régime and is still used in many Continental proceedings,[71] it is virtually absent from the courtrooms of Anglo-American countries. Again, more information that has bypassed party filters reaches the Continental than the Anglo-American decision maker.

The Ideal of Tabula Rasa

If in the conflict-solving process the decision is to emerge from the dialectic of party debate, ideally the decision maker must enter the case unprepared, unaware of all matters specifically related to the issues. He should have a "virgin mind," to be tutored only through the bilateral process of evidentiary presenta-

---

70. On the importance of *inspectio occularis* in the Continental tradition, see J. Ph. Lévy, *La Hiérarchie des Preuves dans le Droit Savant du Moyen-Age*, 29–30 (Paris, 1939). *Augenschein, descente sur les lieux*, and various similar labels describe essentially the same practice in contemporary systems.

71. Confrontation was especially valued in criminal prosecution as a means to assess the veracity of the defendant's testimony. See G. A. Kleinshrod, *Abhandlungen aus dem peinlichen Rechte, Teil I*, 138 (Erlangen, 1797). In contemporary systems, this particular use of confrontation is in decline; ironically, it now appeals to some American commentators. See L. Weinreb, *Denial of Justice*, 111 (1977).

tion and argument. The desirability of ignorance, of course, does not entail the desirability of ineptitude: the decision maker should be mentally agile, able deftly to manipulate and make sense of the data presented to him. In sum, the judicial tabula rasa must be skillful, intelligent, and wise.

Insofar as this ideal is opposed to acquiring *factual* knowledge extra-procedurally, it is not exclusive to the mode of proceeding now under discussion. Rather, it is shared by proceedings devoted to purposes other than conflict resolution. It must be realized, however, that the disapproval of private knowledge is general only where it springs from concerns about the accuracy of fact-finding; the trier of fact cannot be expected objectively to weigh evidence that clashes with what he thinks he already knows.[72] But as soon as the decision maker's extra-procedural knowledge is widely shared and taken to be accurate, differences begin to emerge between conflict-solving and other modes of proceedings. The policy-implementing process has no problem with a decision maker in possession of such knowledge, because it can empower him to bypass ordinary proof-taking processes and thus declare "notorious" facts encompassed by his private knowledge. But this luxury is not available in the pure conflict-solving mode: because it ranks the integrity of the contest above the efficient attainment of accurate outcomes, it must demand that all facts in dispute between the parties be subject to rival proof taking, without regard to whether some of those facts are notorious or not. The ideal fact finder in this situation is again one with a virgin mind—ignorant of even what is widely known.

On this point, common-law procedure is again more consistently organized around the idea of party contest than is the Continental administration of justice. Observe that disqualification of common-law jurors approximates the strong demand for ignorance which is consistent with pure conflict-solving style; jurors are, above all, the paradigmatic fact finders. Even if one focuses only on common-law judges, the observation still holds, at least to some degree. Although the doctrine of judicial notice has lately been expanded, the range of facts that an Anglo-American judge can thus take notice of remains narrower than the range of facts that a Continental court can declare "notorious." Furthermore, one should not overlook that Continental judges regularly study the files of prior proceedings in advance of trials over which they preside. Indeed, advance preparation is widely regarded as a hallmark of the conscientious judge.[73] In Anglo-American countries, advance preparation has a much more uncertain status, especially so in anticipation of a contested trial. Nor is it difficult to see that preparation necessarily dilutes the force of party contest at trial. The uncertainties of facing a decision maker who is tabula rasa are among the most potent catalysts of vigorous party action, assuming the case goes to trial and is not settled. If these uncertainties are reduced and incentives to party action thereby

---

72. Apart from this, appellate review is complicated where findings resulting from the processes of proof intermingle with the decision maker's "private knowledge."

73. While advance preparation on the basis of a file of prior proceedings does not imply acquisition of "private" but rather of "institutional" knowledge, the fact remains that the decision maker does not come to the case with a "virgin mind."

diminished, a procedure which relies on litigants as propellant forces is endangered. Partisan argument can lose its vitality and turn into ceremonial posturing.[74]

However, in the sphere of *legal* (as opposed to factual) knowledge, the blessing of the decision maker's ignorance must appear mixed, if not patently absurd. Is not knowledge of the law a desirable accoutrement of one called upon to decide a lawsuit? Yet the issue should be reexamined against the background of the conflict-solving ideal.

Where the law is clear, or the belief obtains that legal conclusions are arrived at through some inexorable method, the decision maker's knowledge of the law need not detract from the appearance of his impartiality. Even if he would have otherwise favored one party, it can plausibly be urged, he could not help but reach a particular, because foregone, legal conclusion. In this scenario there is little room left for the parties to argue about the law. Most of the time, however, the law is not so transparent that parties find it unnecessary to argue legal points. As soon as legal argument appears necessary, it stands to reason that litigants prefer a decision maker who comes to the lawsuit with no position on the law applicable to the case, or at least with a position that is still *al dente;* both parties are stimulated to vigorous activity in the belief that their efforts will make a difference, and no party is burdened with the task of dislodging firm opinions— "prejudice"—from the decision maker's mind. Thus, initial impressions to the contrary, the ideal of an intelligent and wise tabula rasa holds, even in the sphere of legal information. The conflict-solving process is "purer," and it operates at a higher pitch, if the decision maker is an empty receptacle for legal arguments of the parties rather than a repository of legal learning.

The Anglo-American administration of justice is permeated by the idea that the decision maker must be tutored in the law applicable to the case. Setting aside as obvious the informational needs of jurors and lay magistrates, even professional judges—especially in American jurisdictions—openly rely on counsel to supply them with legal material applicable to the case. Many pride themselves on being generalists rather than narrowly specialized legal experts armed with ready answers. Indeed, it is doubted that preestablished legal standards exist that can dispose of concrete circumstances in individual cases, so that the role of ad hoc argument in the development of the law is widely celebrated. Caricaturing but little, the law seems to be a collection of contrary arguments waiting for a case and controversy to be deployed.[75]

74. Where Anglo-American judges do prepare for courtroom events, as for sentencing hearings, by studying the presentence report, parties have generally much less to say than at trials. A similar evisceration of vigorous party action can occur in appellate courts if there is excessive reliance on staff research and analysis prior to oral argument. See, e.g., P. E. Johnson, "The Supreme Court of California 1975–76," 65 *Cal. L. Rev.* 231, 250 (1977).

75. In appellate courts where the "legislative" ingredient of adjudication is more pronounced, legal training is more valued, but even here the need for partisan oral argument is probably taken more seriously than in comparable continental tribunals. See the opinion of Rehnquist, J., in *Laird* v. *Tatum,* 409 U.S. 824, 833 (1972).

On this point, the contrast with Europe is particularly striking. The Continental machinery of justice, dominated by professionals who are raised in the spirit of logical legalism, has little use for the ideal of a decision maker who needs to be instructed on the law in the case. On the contrary, the court is *expected* to know the law: *jura novit curia*. Of course, where legal expertise is expected from the judge. vigorous and extensive argument by the parties may seem to be not only superfluous but also disrespectful. As a famous seventeenth-century German judge remarked about lawyers who make lengthy legal arguments, they are "like patients prescribing a cure from Galen to their physician."[76] No wonder, then, that legal issues are seldom as thoroughly and energetically argued in Continental courts as they are in Anglo-American courts.

The Virtues of Tunnel Vision

The pure conflict-solving process demands more from the decision maker than neutrality as between the parties; he must also be blind to any considerations that transcend the resolution of the dispute before him. In other words, he is not supposed to promote any larger goal or value, even if the cost of this promotion would tax both litigants equally. Were such promotion to occur, the parties could leave the forum dissatisfied: they might believe that the decision maker denied them their due, or failed to be responsive to their demands, for the sake of aggregate interests indifferent—perhaps even hostile—to the dispute that impelled them to go to court.

In the limit case of an extreme laissez-faire state, the narrow concentration on the dispute sub judice reaches its strongest form. Here, the decision maker pursues no governmental policies unrelated to the particular objective of dispute resolution, for the state in whose name he holds court has none. In this sense, then, he is in a perfect conflict-solving position.

It hardly needs saying that this attitude seems myopic in the perspective of most current political ideologies. Worse, it appears to some to be a mere smoke screen for the protection of those favored by the preservation of the social equilibrium. But to a truly reactive government. and perhaps even to those who chafe under oppressive regimes, the decision maker's tunnel vision appears to guarantee that their rights will be vindicated in the legal process, *coûte que coûte*.

v. THE STATUS OF LEGAL COUNSEL

Relation to the Model

So far I have considered the parties and the decision maker as the protagonists. Should the availability of counsel be added to the list of essential features that

---

76. See B. Carpzov, *Practica Nova Imperialis Saxonica Rerum Criminalium*, Pars III, Quest. 115, No. 96 (Frankfort, 1678).

characterize proceedings in the conflict-solving mode? As far as the adversarial process is concerned—a process similarly organized around the idea of party contest—conventional wisdom finds the participation of counsel necessary to the mode: only an inquisitorial process, it is said, can refuse to permit representation by legal counsel.[77] But it is plain that a theoretical statement of proceedings in the contest style, and thus of conflict-solving proceedings as well, can be made without reference to professional assistants to the parties. In other words, counsel's participation is not necessarily implied by the idea of proceedings structured as a contest or the idea of a process devoted to conflict resolution. While not conceptually necessary, it can be shown that counsel advance the goal of conflict resolution, especially when the legal process is envisaged against the background of the reactive state. Advice of counsel clearly figures among the baseline arrangements which potential litigants would have agreed to in considering the design of a legal process suffused with laissez-faire ideology.

As self-regulated civil society becomes more complex, its members need the assistance of specialists in structuring social relationships through pacts and agreements. Informed advance planning anticipates and can prevent disputes from arising, so that there is a great need for those skilled in drafting agreements and conducting negotiations. If disputes nevertheless arise and lead to litigation, where victory depends on presenting the better case, the need for capable advocates is particularly pressing. Nor should one forget the silent undercurrent of the lawsuit: it is tacitly hoped that parties will use their lawyers for continuing interaction and bargaining so that settlement may occur, obviating the need for the legal process to run its full course. *Pactum vincit legem et amor judicium.* It is also true that participation of counsel can preserve and fortify the management of lawsuits by autonomous citizens. If each personally manages his own case, the parties inevitably become sources of information concerning facts in issue, even while performing nontestimonial functions. By retreating into background— perhaps even by not coming to court—and letting lawyers argue the case, they can preserve their self-interest and *dominus litis* position while still remaining free to take over the courtroom action personally.

It is now clear how intimate the relationship is between the conflict-solving process of the reactive state and the activity of counsel; in proceedings characterized by the undertow of bargaining, counsel advance the ideal of out-of-court settlement, and in proceedings defined by party control, the participation of counsel is complementary. To place any restraint on the right of parties to retain counsel, or to bar them from any stage of proceedings, is therefore repugnant to the reactive state. The latter is as lawyer-ridden as activist government is saturated with administrators, educators, therapists, and similar managerial types.

Note, however, that the state cannot *impose* counsel on the litigants, for where individual autonomy is extolled, parties must be free to hire and fire their lawyers, no matter how important the issues involved in the case or how skewed

---

77. Even under the *ancien régime*, most actual proceedings patterned upon the idea of inquest in fact admitted counsel in both criminal and civil cases. See *infra*, ch. 5, n. 58.

the proceedings become when a party chooses to manage his case personally. Mandatory assistance is more likely to be found in proceedings organized by an activist state for the implementation of its policies—in those cases, of course, where counsel's participation appears useful to the government.

Proper Role

In approaching this theme, a system of justice must be imagined that is narrowly focused on the resolution of legal disputes and that does not seek to implement transcending programs of the state. Further, imagine a legal process that places the integrity of a fair contest above the integrity of substantive outcome. Last, suppose a state ideology that salutes the flag of individual self-definition. Where all these preconditions are met, an environment is created where the role of counsel as *assistant to his client* can be understood in its strongest possible sense—the sense restrained least by countervailing considerations. Vigorous promotion of the client's interest is not inhibited by concern that the realization of governmental policy will thereby be obstructed. (Observe, parenthetically, that the thrust of counsel's aggressive action in the pure contest mode is directed toward or against the other side rather than toward or against the representative of state authority who controls proceedings.) Strong action on behalf of the client is not tempered by counsel's coexisting obligation to pursue accurate results. Nor is it legitimate for counsel to alter his role as assistant by interpreting the client's interests differently than the client chooses to define them. It is not for counsel to argue at the sentencing hearing that his client (who values freedom) should be imprisoned rather than released on probation because the client's interests—properly understood—would best be served by an extended rehabilitation program in a penal institution.

Stated positively, counsel must zealously advance his client's interests only as the latter defines them. In the sphere of fact-finding, counsel must help the party make the best possible case by whatever means are permitted under procedural regulation. In the sphere of legal argument, he must provide a dialectical counterweight to the arguments of the other side: he must advance whatever intellectually respectable arguments can be made on his client's behalf, even if he himself is not convinced that these arguments constitute the best interpretation of the law, and even if their advancement complicates the lawsuit and delays the moment of decision.

All this is not to say that counsel may take any and all action that will help his client's cause; lawyers operate within the framework of a regulated—fair—contest. But it is important to observe that the limits on what counsel is permitted to do largely coincide with the boundaries of what a party acting alone can do. Thus, for example, because the party has no carte blanche to forge documents or falsely accuse others in order to improve his chance to win his case, neither has the lawyer representing him. This is not the place to dwell in the problem of separating permissible from illegal behavior in litigation, nor the marginal differences between what a litigant personally and a lawyer acting for him can do.

(The lawyer is not in all respects the party's alter ego.) It should be recognized, however, that these problems become increasingly labyrinthine the more a process relies on counsel as managers of lawsuits. As their total activity increases, the areas expand over which dilemmas of proper and ethical behavior may arise. Many of these difficulties cannot be resolved—as they can in systems where officials share more of the burden—by requiring lawyers to remain passive, neither promoting accurate outcomes nor actively advancing the client's self-interest. Selective inactivity of counsel can seriously hurt the client's chances to win or may even communicate to the fact finder that a particular item of his client's evidence is spurious.[78] It is no accident that European observers seldom fully appreciate the quandaries that may plague an ethically motivated lawyer in the American system of procedure, where counsel is both solicitor and barrister to his client.[79]

This fact offers a clue to an apparent paradox. In many jurisdictions where parties—their lawyers—are accorded wide-ranging control, the lawyer's duty as an "officer of the court" is stressed nearly as often as his duty as employed "assistant to the party"; the former characterization inhabits a more exalted ethical plane. America is a telling example: the conspicuous use of attorneys in social life generally and in the legal process particularly would seem to place a premium on celebrating "zealous assistance," yet the lawyer's status as an officer of the court is invested with at least equal if not greater ethical dignity. Several factors may account for this seeming paradox,[80] but only one is of immediate interest here: the role of counsel consonant with a structure of proceeding must not be confused with ethical exhortation designed to prevent abuse of that role. The invocation of counsel as officer of the court is designed to constrain the excessive amalgamation of the lawyer's interest with that of his client and to forestall the transformation of privately managed litigation into a melee of self-seeking. Because the government is actually not overbearing and its interests are not clearly defined, these excesses of identification are understood to be a greater menace than the contrary identification of lawyers' and governmental interests. In contrast, where a strong managerial state uses the legal process for advancement of its programs, different ethical stabilizers are required: the professional ethic now counteracts pressures reflecting the idea that aggregate state interests must always prevail over narrow individual interests of the client. Accordingly,

---

78. Illustrations of this problem are given hereafter in connection with policy-implementing legal process and the comparison of the role of lawyers therein with their role in conflict resolution. See *infra*, ch. 5, n. 54 and accompanying text.

79. In those common-law jurisdictions where, as in Britain, the barrister has few contacts with the party and engages in no investigative action, chances are less than in America that the trial lawyer will be in possession of information that gives rise to the ethical dilemmas of an American attorney. On the Continent, the scope of counsel's activity is altogether more restricted than it is in common-law systems.

80. One factor has repeatedly been mentioned: the American legal profession exercises several powers which in most Continental countries, where sovereignty is less fragmented, are the monopoly of civil servants.

the dignity of acting on behalf of a private individual enmeshed in the machinery of justice is likely to be glorified.

Effect on Proceedings

Over time, the employment of counsel to manage lawsuits leads to refinement of procedural arrangements and sophistication of procedural action: instruments evolve that permit virtuoso performance but that cannot properly be played by persons without special talent and proper training. For common-law systems, it has recently been argued that the technical niceties of the law of evidence are not so much the natural outgrowth of trials before lay juries as they are the product of the "lawyerization" of trials.[81] Quite naturally, counsel's skill can make the crucial difference in the outcome of litigation. In the legal process of the reactive state, parties indeed remain masters of lawsuits, entitled personally to perform the procedural action; even as counsel's handling of the case becomes critical for success, the client's consent still must be obtained for all important decisions. But, uninitiated in the complexities of practice and evidence, litigants readily defer to the judgment of resourceful and skillful counsel: as with Figaro, or servants in the commedia del l'arte, so with assistants in lawsuits nominally controlled by the parties—servants easily end up dominating their masters. Where decision making is in lay hands, even the adjudicative body cannot remain unaffected by these developments. At least part of that body must become famil-iar with the fine points of practice and evidence in order to be able to resolve incidental disputes of counsel over the propriety of their procedural minuet.[82] All told, the need for lawyers feeds upon itself, as if a kind of legal parthenogenesis affects the legal process of the reactive state.

Because it is probable that variation in forensic skill is less marked among lawyers than among the general population, it appears that the lawyerization of party-controlled proceedings contributes to greater party equality, essential in the conflict-solving mode. Yet even if one concedes a rough parity of talent among members of the legal profession, one cannot assume that litigants are equally able and willing to invest in counsel. The side better able to absorb the considerable transaction cost of justice has a clear advantage over the opponent, both in the out-of-court bargaining related to the lawsuit and in litigation itself. But as with the equality of the parties, the conflict-solving process is satisfied with the requirements of formal equality and thus quite undisturbed by this prospect. When the government begins to listen to Gideon's trumpet and be-lieves that the capacity of the parties to invest in forensic disputes should be

---

81. See J. Langbein, "The Criminal Trial before the Lawyers," 45 *U. of Chi. L. Rev.* 263, 306 (1978).

82. From the Continental perspective, the judge in a common-law jury trial seems more to play the role of a lawyer resolving incidental disputes among professional colleagues than the adjudicative role as they understand it.

equalized, a movement is set in motion that eventually must lead away from the model of procedure discussed heretofore. As adequate levels of subsidy to financially weaker litigants prove too costly for the state, it is driven toward expenditure restrictions. As legal proceedings grow simpler, the skill and sophistication of counsel become less important; the parties have been deprived of procedural instruments whose proper handling requires specialized training and skill.

vi. STABILITY OF DECISIONS

Where decisions can easily be disturbed, the legal process cannot absorb the conflict effectively: disputes can drag on and on or can be rekindled. Because substantively correct outcomes are relatively less important to reactive government, it is clear that the conflict-solving style of proceeding is averse to changing decisions—even if they rest on legal or factual error. The desire for stability encompasses a broad preclusion effect on future litigation, not only upon adjudicated claims, but also as to factual issues previously litigated between the parties (collateral estoppel). When this pronounced desire for repose will set in depends to a large degree on the structure of procedural authority. Where there are several levels of officialdom, original decisions can be treated as tentative and the need for stability is felt only after the highest authority has spoken; however, where one-level decision making is ideal, reluctance to change becomes operative as soon as the verdict is returned.[83] But no matter when reconsideration of decisions is permitted, in the pure model it can occur only on the initiative of the parties, not as part of the court's official duty. While even substantively erroneous decisions can enjoy a high degree of immunity from subsequent change, this immunity does not extend to decisions obtained through unfair practice or fraud. Where the winner of the forensic contest has engaged in some sort of "foul play," subsequent discovery and revelation of his misconduct may revive the dispute laid to rest in the decision. Res judicata loses its bindingness when it does not emanate from a fair contest: *fraus omnia corrumpit* (fraud spoils everything).[84]

To an outside observer, a system of justice may seem seriously flawed—perhaps even perverse—where fairness of procedure can justify a substantively erroneous decision and where faulty procedures can undermine substantively correct decisions: the cart appears to be put before the horse. But in a justice administration that values the integrity of the contest above the attainment of accurate outcomes on the merits, this result seems perfectly normal and acceptable. Interestingly enough, traces of this attitude can still be found in some American jurisdictions. Take the example of a convicted person, who in some states must still establish that the prosecutor unfairly suppressed evidence, newly

---

83. In the multilevel apparatus of justice, delay can occur in the process of superior review; in a single-level system, the greatest danger of delay is in the preparation for trial.

84. The phrase is from "The Duchess of Kingston's Case," 20 *Howell's Trials* 355, 537 (1776).

discovered by the defense, in order to invoke the right to a new trial.[85] Where proceedings are more clearly within the policy-implementing mode, as are, for example, European criminal prosecutions, this rule seems close to a travesty of justice.[86] Thus, it again appears that bits and pieces of the pure conflict-solving procedural model still exist in real-life procedures, and that they draw support from the ideology of a truly laissez-faire government.

85. See Carlson, "Why a Need for the Prosecutorial Tie?" 1969 *Duke L. W.* 1171. The civil party cannot offer evidence previously known to him but unfairly kept from the trier of fact.

86. It is hardly surprising that the rule on unfairly withheld evidence was opposed by European authorities during the reign of the historical "inquisitorial" process. See, e.g., A. Bauer, *Abhandlungen aus dem Strafrechte und aus dem Prozesse, Band II*, 355 (Göttingen, 1852). Compare *infra*, ch. 5, n. 66.

V The Policy-Implementing Type of Proceeding

The legal process of a truly activist state is a process organized around the central idea of an official inquiry and is devoted to the implementation of state policy. In contrast to conventional descriptions of inquisitorial procedure, invariably including features associated with hierarchical judicial apparatus, I shall attempt to portray a type of activist proceeding that is stripped of all features related to any one particular character of officialdom, including only forms related to the policy-implementing objective of justice. A special difficulty posed by this approach should be made clear at the outset.

In the preceding analysis, the refusal to consider forms of justice associated with any one particular type of authority did not prevent development of a fairly specific ideal of the conflict-solving style. Because so much activity was carried on by private protagonists, the deliberate failure to specify the precise character of procedural authority did not prove to be much of a problem. But where *officials* are in charge of both process and decision making—as they are in the policy-implementing mode—the optimal shape of proceedings depends far more on the specific character of procedural authority. Ad hoc amateurs and civil servants have distinctively different ways of going about work; an inquiry conducted by a single corps of officials clearly differs from one organized by investigators locked in hierarchical chains of sub- and superordination. As a result, unless the characteristics of the judicial apparatus are specified, a variety of forms may be compatible with the fundamental nature of the legal process as an official inquiry, for a single method can seldom be identified that will be preferred by all types of authority. Because I shall refuse in this chapter to specify the political or social profile of officialdom, recourse will have to be taken to inelegant modes of negative argument and exclusion instead of the direct description of ideal forms of policy-implementing procedure.

The resulting difficulty, however, is not so severe as to make the model completely indeterminate. Despite the fact that many alternative legal procedures may harmonize with activist goals in the administration of justice, some widespread and important arrangements obviously do not; thus, a residue of forms comes plainly into view, a residue shared by procedures devoted to policy implementation in different official environments. It should also be noted that the relative indeterminacy of the policy-implementing process is the vice of the virtue of my comparativist approach, which focuses separately on procedural forms related to the character of officialdom and forms related to the mission of government in society. The indeterminacy which results is but a price to be paid for the development of a type of activist justice that—unlike the conventional inquisitorial model—spans the divide separating legal cultures influenced by divergent traditions of authority. Only a model of activist procedure that is independent of any variation in the structure of officialdom promises assistance in studying activist justice cross-culturally; and only after I have outlined such a model can I begin to address the questions of its internal modalities, owing to differing degrees of bureaucratization, a different sense of proper hierarchization, and similar factors.

The theme of internal variations in activist justice will be taken up in the next chapter, where much of the indeterminacy required to build the model will begin to disappear. As in Proust's image of the Japanese paper flower immersed in water, the presently somewhat shapeless construct will then gradually unfold, to reveal its capacity for definite form and clear contour.

i. THE PROBLEM OF REGULATION

The Adjective Nature of Procedural Law

In the legal process of the reactive state, decisions are justified more in terms of the fairness of procedures employed than the accuracy of results obtained. In contrast, procedural rules and regulation in an activist state occupy a much less important and independent position: procedure is basically a handmaiden of substantive law. If the purpose of the legal process is to realize state policy in contingent cases, decisions are legitimated primarily in terms of the correct outcomes they embody. A proper procedure is one that increases the probability—or maximizes the likelihood—of achieving a substantively accurate result rather than one that successfully effects notions of fairness or protects some collateral substantive value. In this sense, then, the procedural law of the activist state follows substantive law as faithfully as its shadow. And inasmuch as substantive law itself faithfully follows state policy, procedural law is doubly instrumental, or doubly derivative: like art in Plotinus' vision, it can be likened to a shadow of a shadow.

This should not be taken to mean, however, that accuracy of outcome justifies *any* procedure employed in attaining that result. Even in fully activist states, some procedural rules are of a dual nature—dual in the sense that their breach not only disrupts an internal procedural order but also suggests that a substantive policy has been violated. For example, the coercion of a witness to testify in breach of a procedural provision may be classified as a criminal offense:

criminal law may have been violated by forcing the witness to speak, and that violation is not automatically justified, even if the coerced testimony leads to decisive evidence and eventually to the accurate disposition of the case in hand. But it would be wrong to assume that an activist state recognizes as many rules of a dual nature as a reactive government does. An activist government is less ready to acknowledge that individual lives have their own loyalties, or that individuals can assert their self-interest against the state, as well as many other considerations that underlie the procedural rules which make more difficult the attainment of accurate results on the merits (e.g., testimonial privileges and restrictions on searches and seizures). Nor is an activist state—especially in its more pronounced variants—likely to cultivate procedural safeguards that reflect distrust of its officials. The government cannot launch and sustain its ambitious programs of social change if it is haunted by the specter of official misconduct and forever agonizing over *quis custodiet custodes.* The general inspiration for the choice of procedural form is to select those that tend to produce accurate outcomes, and thus to promote the smooth realization of state policy in the circumstances of a case. Occasional collateral values that inspire impediments to attainment of substantively correct results are like eddies in a mighty river: they cannot deflect the flow of proceedings in the direction of the result mandated on the merits.

With procedural regulation adapted to the smooth realization of state objectives, officials are given ample elbowroom to act.[1] The temptation to circumvent or violate procedural regulation should not be exaggerated, because such regulation usually enables them to reach the result desirable on the merits. When a particular breach of a procedural provision is nevertheless established, the decision stemming from the breach—if substantively accurate—is not as readily invalidated as it is in the conflict-solving process. This is true even in those cases where the breach involves more than a disruption of an internal procedural order. If, for example, the guilty defendant has been convicted and given the proper sentence, the judgment will not automatically be reversed even if it transpires that the conviction was based on an illegally obtained confession. In the perspective of activist government, such reversal would be mindless "formalism." The undoing of a substantively accurate decision would require a successful showing that alternative sanctions for the procedural impropriety (such as punishment of the culprit in collateral proceedings) are insufficient to avert consequences harmful to state interests, such as the loss of confidence in its officials. Of course, such a claim requires serious substantiation to produce an effect, for a certain and direct gain—an accurate judgment—should not easily be sacrificed by reason of concern over remote and speculative losses. The defendant's strongest argument by far is to suggest that in the long run failure to reverse a tainted decision could impair the capacity of the justice system to attain accurate results. Thus the strongest argument for reversal of a conviction based

---

1. This latitude can be illustrated by the example of provisions which regulate criminal investigations and impose formalities on use of measures capable of interference with individual freedom (such as the requirement of a judicial warrant authorizing search and seizure), but which also provide "escape clauses" in case of urgent need and lack of time to observe such formalities.

on a coerced but truthful confession is clearly not one from compassion or humanity; rather, it is the claim that failure to reverse will lead to future exposure of the judicial apparatus to unreliable self-incriminations. In other words, procedural safeguards in the activist state are most securely established if they are attached to concern for maintaining a process that maximizes the probability of attaining accurate results on the merits.

Attachment to Flexible Instructions

The architects of the policy-implementing process thus strive to devise procedural rules and regulations that facilitate attainment of accurate outcomes. But no matter how hard they try, it is impossible to devise perfect procedures which, when followed to the letter, inexorably yield the correct result on the merits. Assuming, for example, that the ban on leading questions in direct examination of witnesses is generally a sound rule, still circumstances can arise—and can never fully be anticipated—in which a suggestive query will advance rather than imperil the factual inquiry.[2] For a system in which procedural law is the instrument for the realization of substantive policy, what follows from this insight is quite clear: if there is to be any regulation of procedural action, it must be flexible; departures from rules should be permitted if rigid adherence threatens attainment of the desired result in concrete cases. Therefore, procedural regulation in the model now under discussion gravitates almost always toward cautionary instructions or rules of thumb to be followed in typical situations rather than toward unbending rules.[3]

When should state officials be permitted to depart from procedural instructions? In theory, at least, there is a tidy answer: disregard for procedural form is permissible whenever in the circumstances of the case the disadvantage of departure from the rule (e.g., inconsistency in the application of valid norms) is

2. This can be expressed in more general terms: where an independent substantive criterion of proper outcome exists (e.g., correct implementation of a governmental program), there can be no "perfect procedural justice"—that is to say, a procedure that guarantees, if faithfully followed, the attainment of the desired result. On "perfect procedural justice," see J. Rawls, A Theory of Justice, 85 (1972). Rawls himself doubts whether such justice is possible in cases of much practical interest—that is, in cases of interest here.

3. Instructions in lieu of rigid procedural rules always appealed to revolutionary governments, at least in their Sturm und Drang phases. Thus Soviet authorities viewed the informality of instructions as an ideal throughout their early history. See P. I. Stuchka, Narodnyi Sud v Voproskah i Otvietkah (Moscow, 1918); J. H. Hazard, Settling Disputes in Soviet Society, 25–33, 433 (1960). The crusade against rules in Communist China reached its highest pitch in Mao's Cultural Revolution when the "smashing of all permanent rules," substantive or procedural, became the Communist party's goal. See D. F. Forte, "Western Law and Communist Dictatorship," 32 Emory L.J. 135, 201 (1983).

Bending procedural rules also appealed to enlightened absolutist rulers: this penchant for flexibility is illustrated in legislation of Frederickian Prussia, a state with widespread "activist" programs. The Preamble to the Corpus Juris Fridericianum stated that procedural norms are valid only when "meaningful in light of circumstances." See K. Nörr, Naturrecht und Zivilprozess, 29, n. 92 (Tübingen, 1976).

outweighed by countervailing policy considerations. But the application of this consequentialist calculus expands the field of inquiry exponentially, and can present intractable difficulties of solution. Procedural rules of a "dual" nature are a good illustration. The fact that the manner in which a confession was extracted violates procedural regulation and also falls within the definition of a crime does not necessarily mean that the departure from both procedural and substantive norms was not justified in the concrete constellation of events. Perhaps the state's interest in accurate disposition of a particular case should be ranked so highly that the need for information constitutes an acceptable utilitarian justification for the breach of norms.[4] Obviously, solutions to this consequentialist problem can be of staggering complexity to anyone whose vision does not encompass—as does the vision of Plato's guardian—"concrete totalities." To let lesser mortals freely operate from such broad utilitarian principles opens ample room for bad judgment, arbitrariness, and invidious discrimination. While these dangers are unlikely to pass unnoticed, even in those judicial organizations not wedded to strong notions of order and predictability, the risks can be truly alarming to a hierarchically constituted judicial bureaucracy.

As an example, consider a theme whose complexity plagued authorities on criminal process under the ancien régime in Continental countries. All supported the view that most rules of procedure could be disregarded in exceptional circumstances—in the face of overwhelming "need." But should officials be permitted such an escape clause concerning *all* procedural provisions? Should they be permitted to dispense with the proper *figura judicii*, even when what is at stake is as important as abiding by the rules that regulate legitimate means of compelling testimony? Significantly, even extreme proponents of crime control among legal authorities of the period hesitated to give a positive answer.[5]

The deceptively simple utilitarian calculus is, therefore, of little help. For this reason, even extremely activist governments fail to convert all procedural regulation into instructions or mere strategies for the direction of official thinking. A limited number of provisions assume some degree of rigidity and therein also a measure of independence from subservience to the state's goal of attaining correct dispositions on the merits. As a further consequence, at least some

4. There are systems of criminal justice where it is contemplated that an act, otherwise criminal, may be justified if committed to counteract a danger to the state's interest. For Soviet law, see N. A. Belyayev and N. D. Shargorodsky, eds., *Kurs Ugolovnogo Prava*, pt. 1, 536 (Moscow, 1968). More common are necessity justifications predicated primarily on protection of more tangible individual or group interests.

5. A famous example of this problem, debated for several centuries, was the question of whether rules of legitimate judicial torture could be disregarded in the case of most heinous and dangerous offenses. Very few authorities were prepared to give an affirmative answer by applying to this procedural problem a doctrine developed in a different context by early civil and canon lawyers. See B. Carpzov, *Practica Nova Imperialis Saxonica Rerum Criminalium*, Pars III, quest. 102, no. 68, 16 (Frankfort, 1677): "Notissimum est quod in delictis atrocissimis propter criminis enormitatem jura transgredi liceat." On the more general (and older) topic of permissible departures from rules (*transgressio legis*), see E. Lefebre, "Morale et droit positif: Une institution disparue, la "transgressio legis,'" in *Miscellanea Moralia in Honorem Eximii Domini Arthur Jansen*, 381 (Louvain, 1949).

breaches of procedure merit automatic reversal. Much as the conflict-solving model gravitates toward procedural legitimation but stops short of purely procedural justice, so the policy-implementing process, while preferring substantive legitimation, stops short of justifying its decisions solely in terms of accurate results. But sacrifice of substantive accuracy for the sake of procedural regularity remains a somewhat embarrassing anomaly; it smacks of the "formalism" so alien to the ideology of the activist state, and so, in most instances, procedural regulation remains pliable.

It is important to distinguish this pliancy from the yielding nature of rules and regulations in the conflict-solving model: whereas the latter reflect the autonomy of private parties, the former mirrors the primacy of state interests. The distinction comes into sharp relief with recognition that the addressees of regulation are not identical in conflict-solving and policy-implementing processes. In the former, regulation is primarily directed to the private parties who control the litigation; they acquire waivable procedural rights. If they choose to assert these rights, the assertion cannot be denied on the basis of some overarching state interest. In contrast, in the policy-implementing process of the activist state the primary subjects of regulation are officials in charge of proceedings, who are given tasks to perform and duties to fulfill. True, many provisions directed to them can be interpreted as *indirectly* according "rights" to persons implicated in the process. Suppose, for example, that an official has missed a prescribed deadline to make a procedural move detrimental to a private individual. It may now be said that this individual has a "right" to oppose an extension of the deadline to permit the omitted step to be taken. But this interpretation would fail to capture the reality of the situation: the individual can argue only that extension of the deadline is for some reason contrary to state interest, and thereby seek to use the weight of this interest to protect his own. As argued before, to convert procedural regulation of the policy-implementing process into a bundle of rights is to transpose the legal idiom of the reactive state into an alien environment, where (strictly speaking) there are no personal procedural rights.

ii. NONAUTHORITATIVE PARTICIPANTS

Parties

If the term *party* is used in the strong sense applicable to the conflict-solving context—that is, to designate a private individual or group who is an autonomous shaper of procedure—then there are no parties as such in the policy-implementing model. To be sure, a case may concern some advantage or benefit that the activist state confers upon a citizen, an advantage conventionally referred to as a personal right. Yet even in such a case, the citizen of an activist state is not sovereign in asserting or waiving the entitlement which constitutes the content of the cause of action. If he is unwilling to assert his claim, state policy may demand that a state official do it for him. For these reasons it would perhaps be more appropriate to talk not about "parties" but about "main procedural participants": those who, although denied mastery over procedural action, are most directly affected by the decision in which the process culminates. Having noted this qualification, I shall nevertheless abide by conventional and therefore more convenient usage.

In analyzing the conflict-solving process, I have indicated the prominence of the issue of the party's legal capacity to undertake procedural action. In contrast, in the model now under consideration, this issue is almost insignificant: according to activist ideology, citizens are not necessarily the best representatives of their own interests, properly understood—that is, their interests as they appear in the light of state values. The resulting attitude toward the party may indicate, when observed through different ideological spectacles, that people are treated as less than fully adult, almost *in statu pupillari*. However, this is something of an exaggeration: the state treats minors and adults in different ways.[6]

Denial of a *dominus litis* position to a party does not imply that he is not accorded an opportunity to present his views or to offer proof: a requirement that affected citizens must be heard is perfectly compatible with a pure policy-implementing model. However, the purpose of providing a hearing is primarily informational rather than protective of individual self-interest. The party is a precious source of information needed by officials in order to reach the right decision; that is, the presentation of the party's views may assist them in formulating and implementing the best policy response to the problem the case presents.

Other Participants

As I have pointed out, the truly activist state tries to seduce citizens away from private concerns and to mobilize them in pursuit of governmental goals.[7] Quite understandably, then, the state encourages a variety of forms of citizen involvement with the administration of justice—forms other than classical testimonial roles or classical modalities of narrow technical intervention in the pending process.[8] Citizens are permitted to come forward as amici curiae to voice opinions on matters before the court, so that new channels of procedural input are carved out, exceeding the bounds of mere character witnesses. Groups of citizens can be entrusted with a wide range of ancillary, nonauthoritative tasks, such as monitoring the behavior of parties implicated in proceedings. Citizens can also be made captive audiences to court proceedings that promise to have a didactic impact.

6. One perceptive American commentator looking at the "activist" Soviet administration of justice has characterized it as "parental." See H. Berman, *Justice in the USSR; An Interpretation of Soviet Law*, 363–68 (1963). While he was quite right from the American perspective, from their point of view Soviet scholars vigorously protested: Soviet law, they asserted, regulates proceedings involving adults and minors quite differently.

7. For the duty of Soviet courts to educate citizens in the spirit of loyalty to the cause of communism and other state values, see *RSFSR, Law on Court Organization*, art. 3; see also H. Berman, *Soviet Criminal Law and Procedure* (1966).

8. Temporary enlistment of citizens as ad hoc officials (petty or grand jurors, etc.) is not considered here.

It may be wondered why one finds little evidence of such citizen involvement in the administration of justice in the period of Continental absolutist
regimes, often thought to be progenitors of "pure" inquisitorial systems. The
mystery is dispelled if one realizes that, with minor exceptions, those regimes
were much more concerned about threats to their authority than about managing
the lives of their subjects.[9] Moreover, the judicial apparatus—dominated by
professional bureaucrats—was inclined to regard the administration of justice as
a technical pursuit, unsuitable for dilettante meddling, even if dilettantes were
given no share in decision-making authority.

iii. OFFICIAL CONTROL OF THE PROCESS

Beginning and End

It stands to reason that where the administration of justice is a vehicle for policy
implementation, the state must retain the choice over whether to activate proceedings. Were private individuals permitted to coerce state action at their will,
they might provoke proceedings where unnecessary or thwart warranted state
intervention. One can argue with equal force that the termination of the process
should also be officially controlled: were private individuals allowed to withdraw
a matter from official examination, they could in effect nullify state action or
preclude communication that the state regarded as important. Or, if they were in
the position to insist that proceedings continue although state officials had decided that such was undesirable, private individuals could prolong an inquiry that no
longer served state interests and thereby squander state resources. Private control over the beginning and end of proceedings could be acceptable only in the
instance of a substantial congruence of private and official motivation for policy
implementation: in the resulting idyll, as private and state viewpoints greatly
converged, citizens in lieu of state officials could make procedural decisions.
However, so long as people have not sufficiently internalized official standards,
the state needs to retain the ultimate power of choice over the vehicles for policy
implementation.

Monopoly control by state officials does not mean, however, that private
individuals should be accorded no voice in the aubade and in the serenade to the
policy-implementing process. Quite the contrary—there can be plenty of room

9. It is true that theorists of eighteenth-century absolutism developed the idea that the state
should be responsible for improving the well-being of citizens; they lauded the Chinese style of
government which, they thought, was responsive to such managerial urges. See J. H. G. von Justi,
*Vergleichung der Europäischen mit den asiatischen und anderen vermeintlich barbarischen Re-
gierungen* (Berlin, Stattin, and Leipzig, 1762). Yet eighteenth-century absolutist practice was on the
whole far from comprehensive social engineering. Calvin's Geneva was a polity with encompassing
controls over the population and widely ranging programs of citizen's improvement; it can be viewed
as one of the exceptions referred to in the text—a Western precursor of truly activist government. In
his *Civitas Solis Poetica*, Campanella offers an early example of educational and parental procedural
forms, dreamed up while the author was languishing in the dungeons of the Spanish Inquisition.

for useful participation of private citizens at both points. Citizens (e.g., victims of crime) can supply important information, signaling the need for governmental intervention. Their rage can be harnessed to convert legal proceedings into a vivid morality play; the change in their attitudes may suggest that proceedings are no longer warranted, and so on. But their value to the justice system is as suppliers of information required by officials in order to decide on the institution and termination of proceedings. It must be recognized that mere informants may superficially *appear* as private plaintiffs or prosecutors with powers to coerce the institution of the policy-implementing process. The main reasons for this illusion are that information supplied by private informants requires some preliminary checks and screening to determine whether the wheels of justice should be set in motion, and that these preliminary checks can be mistaken for the legal process, properly speaking. Especially in the unmethodical and informal environment of a coordinate machinery of justice, it can be very difficult to draw a clear line between preliminary checks and the "formal" initiation of proceedings. The clarity of that line is adversely affected by the propensity of lay officials to entrust private individuals with various tasks, so that mere informers can be required to appear with witnesses and thus leave the impression that they are private prosecutors. Of course, in the more methodical action of hierarchical bureaucracies, the line between mere informants and real private accusers is much less tenuous. Here, the question of whether grounds exist to initiate proceedings can become the special preliminary task of an official Cerberus at the threshold of the justice system,[10] and while the private informants may play a role in this preliminary screening, they have no right to demand that proceedings in the strict sense be instituted and the threshold crossed.

This difference in the clarity with which informants can be distinguished from parties with control over the existence of proceedings can be a source of confusion in cross-cultural studies. At the point where an official in a methodical authoritative apparatus finds no grounds to *commence* proceedings, properly speaking, his colleague in a less methodical milieu determines that already instituted proceedings should be *discontinued:* a private individual, equally powerless to coerce official action, may be perceived as a mere informer in the one setting and as a private accuser in the other. The Continental informer of the

10. In the criminal process of the ancien régime, the investigating magistrate was not supposed to begin proceedings unless and until specific grounds had first been established for a criminal prosecution. These grounds were to be ascertained in a secret, relatively informal inquiry, so that a malicious informant could not damage the reputation of an innocent person. Contemporary visitors to England, even if otherwise enamored with British institutions, disapproved of the power of private individuals to subject others to criminal process through "private prosecution": men of little character, they thought, could destroy reputations and expose to "ignominy" even those later acquitted of "private charges." Lies, even if disproved, leave a damaging residue. See D. Hay, "The Meanings of the Criminal Law in Quebec," in L. A. Knafla, ed., *Crime and Justice in Europe and Canada* (1980). Faint traces of the old distinction between an informal (general) inquisition and proceedings proper (special inquisition) survive to the present day in some Continental jurisdictions, which distinguish two types of preliminary inquiry and which spell out "legal grounds" for setting criminal prosecutions in motion. See the *RSFSR Code of Crim. Proc.*, arts. 5, 108.

ancien régime may not have been as different from the English "private accuser"as conventional wisdom would have us believe.[11]

How should control over the life of the policy-implementing process be allocated among officials? Several alternatives can be contemplated. One is to vest control in the official who is also charged with rendering the decision on the merits; another is to accord control over initiation and termination to a specialized official "promoter"—a state attorney or prosecutor. In the latter scenario, he becomes an expert, an input-output specialist, who identifies those problems that properly propel the machinery of justice and who perhaps also determines the optimal rate of ingestion of cases into the system. Where this internal official differentiation takes place, the participation of a "promoter" of state interests may be so highly regarded that policy-implementing proceedings conducted in his absence are treated as an inferior form, acceptable only in simple cases. There is nothing in the nature of the policy-implementing process to prevent the specialized state attorney from sharing his power to initiate and terminate proceedings with other state officials, including the decision maker.[12] Even if the state attorney has the final say on this matter, no deviation from proper policy-implementing form occurs. Imagine, for example, that an inquiry launched on the initiative of the state attorney shows that the problem involved is of a different order than originally supposed, and that the latter class of problem does not warrant state intervention. If the attorney is indeed a specialist on these matters, he is also the natural candidate ultimately to determine that the official inquiry should now come to an end.

It must be emphasized that this view of the policy-implementing process diverges sharply from conventional portrayals of the "ideal" inquisitorial process. According to conventional understanding, the process is purely inquisitorial only when all aspects of procedural control are concentrated in the person (or persons) who decide on the merits; the participation of state attorneys (or prosecutors) is thought to signal the introduction of adversarial arrangements in the administration of justice. The state attorney is seen as a party engaged in a dispute with the person implicated in proceedings (e.g., a criminal defendant). I disagree with this analysis because it introduces reactive assumptions into the ambience of activist government: while it cannot be denied that the development of a special promoting function can usher conflict-solving forms into the admin-

---

11. It is a frequently encountered exaggeration that the English "popular" accuser was a private *dominus litis*. Consider only that magistrates could abort such "private" prosecutions by refusing to bind over suspects for trial.

12. In the French procedure of the ancien régime, judges were entitled to institute criminal prosecution on their own, independently of the royal prosecutor. See R. Garraud, *Traité théorique et pratique d' instruction criminelle*, vol. 1, 53 (Paris, 1907). In some instances this is also possible in the contemporary Soviet criminal process. See *RSFSR Code of Crim. Proc.* arts. 255, 266. There is also some precedent in America for "inherent" judicial powers to appoint a special prosecutor if the one assigned refuses "to exercise his duty" either to initiate or (more plausibly) to continue initiated proceedings. See "Note, The Special Prosecutor in the Federal System," 11 *Am. Crim. L. Rev.* 577, 579 (1973).

istration of justice,[13] this is not likely to occur in a truly activist state. In such a state there is no equality and no mutuality of rights between the individual implicated in proceedings and the state attorney: individual and state interests are not on the same plane. The state official maintains a superior, perhaps even an exalted position; he can even be on a par with the adjudicator and can exercise coercive powers over the individual (the other "party").[14] Moreover, the proceedings are independent of an actual controversy; even a simulated disputation finds no firm supporting ground. In short, rather than facing a roughly equal adverse party with whom he contends before the court, the private individual is confronted by a powerful watchdog of state policy who is distinguishable from the adjudicator only because of his special function. That official promoters participated in the historical process *per inquisitionem* may pose problems to conventional theory, but not to the views advanced here.[15]

Another variant of the policy-implementing form can be imagined, where private control over proceedings is allowed, but only provisionally, so that official "correction" of private action is always possible. A citizen who complained that an advantage accorded him by the state has been negatively affected may be entitled to file suit and even to withdraw the case from the forum, but the same matter can later be made the object of officially initiated and controlled proceedings. Observe that this arrangement recognizes "rights" and private control only to make them largely illusory: free to exit from the forum by one door, the private individual can still be forced back in through another. Such cumbersome forms are a matter of historical experience; they are encountered in some spheres of judicial administration in periods of transition from reactive to activist positions. One example is the transition in the twelfth and thirteenth centuries from the view that crime is a narrow affair between the victim and the offender to the view that crime calls for the enforcement of governmental penal policy. In thirteenth-century England, after the victim desisted from prosecution, the judge was authorized to "arraign at the suit of the king,"[16] and on the Continent, criminal proceedings instituted by the private accuser could be converted into officially controlled inquisitorial proceedings.[17] As will be discussed in chapter 6,

13. In the last chapter I shall show that the nineteenth-century reforms of Continental criminal prosecutions actually introduced several adversarial forms by separating prosecutorial and adjudicative responsibilities.

14. The Soviet criminal process suggests a telling example. The procurator or state attorney (referred to as "guardian of legality") is the final authority in the all-important preliminary investigation, which includes such sensitive matters as preliminary detention. The defendant cannot address his complaints against the police or other investigators to the court; the procurator has the exclusive reviewing authority. See *RSFSR Code of Crim. Proc.* §2, ch. 18, art. 211–17. Appointed by the Supreme Soviet, the procurators are often viewed as a fourth branch of government. In some Western systems (in their Continental variant), public prosecutors belong to the judicial branch (*la magistrature*), and (as in Italy) may even be irremovable: their parity with the judges is frequently expressed in symbolic fashion by seating them on the same level as the court.

15. See *supra*, ch. 1, n. 25.

16. See W. Holdsworth, *A History of English Law*, 5th ed., vol. 3, 609 (London, 1945).

17. See A. L. Homberk zu Vack, "De diversa indole processus inquisitorii et accusatorii," in J. F. Plitt, ed., *Analecta Juris Criminalis*, 369–72 (Frankfort and Leipzig, 1791).

this duality of enforcement characterizes the contemporary American civil litigation in the public interest.[18] But this arrangement contains admixtures of conflict-solving forms and is not in the pure policy-implementing style.

Content of the Cause

As has been repeatedly pointed out, the policy-implementing process can be initiated independently, without any controversy or existing interpersonal dispute. Indeed, proceedings need not be targeted against any definite person: inquests may be directed toward a general problem, such as the possibility of corruption in an institution. Nor does the disappearance of a dispute which may have initiated the process necessarily signal the end of proceedings: state policy may require that a conflict be provoked or prolonged. The subject matter of the process is thus a recognized state problem that requires official attention and response.

That this state problem should be defined by state officials rather than private citizens is clear, but this is not to deny private individuals a role in shaping the procedural subject matter. Where, as is often the case, an individual grievance gives rise to proceedings, as a rule the aggrieved individual is required to set forth the nature of his complaint. But the purpose of this requirement is only to provide a starting point or preliminary focus for official action; at bottom, an interpersonal dispute is only a symptom of a larger issue whose bounds may well exceed those of the precipitating controversy. An individual's claim for damages for chemical discharge may be indicative of a broader pollution problem involving a great many people; a complaint of theft from a school can lead to an inquiry into problems of lax security or poor discipline in the educational institution. The greater the state's appetite for social transformation, the more tenuous and merely provisional becomes the initial contour of the cause, as silhouetted by private parties. In the limiting case of an extremely activist state, the definition of an optimal agenda for the official inquiry is completely divorced from the definition of the problem as originally suggested by the private party's complaint. In a technocratic setting, the controlling consideration will be notions of forming optimal processing units.[19]

If the determination of procedural parameters should be in official hands, who precisely is to exercise control? Variations of authority structure will be explored in Chapter 6, but there is a question that deserves immediate attention: does the pure policy-implementing process require that ultimate control over the subject matter of the case be vested in the decision maker, as opposed to some other official?

Part of the question answers itself if one considers the effect of binding the

18. Antitrust and securities laws and laws against employment discrimination can be enforced both privately and officially. Such "redundancies" may be saluted by those who value wide dispersion of authority. See R. N. Cover, "The Uses of Jurisdictional Redundancy; Interest, Ideology and Innovation," 22 *William and Mary L. Rev.* 639 (1981).

19. Actual systems that come close to this limit case will be discussed in the last chapter.

decision maker to only those aspects of the underlying problem put to him by some other participating official. Where the problem is defined by somebody else, the decision maker may be forced to reach a decision against his better judgment. For example, if he cannot extend the inquiry into the question of whether a miscreant is a recidivist, the decision maker may be unable to determine the optimal response to the crime in the light of state correctional policy. The decision maker is therefore authorized to examine all aspects of the event or the transaction brought before him. As the "activist" Frederickian legislation formulated it, the adjudicator must consider *das ganze Factum* (the entire fact) rather than aspects of it selected by someone else.[20]

Can the decision maker's control over the content of the cause be reconciled with the participation of a specialized "promoter" charged with selecting the matters that are properly to be brought before the court? The short answer is that, while the decision maker can *examine* all aspects of a problem brought before him, he need not be permitted to extend his examination to a different or additional matter. Where a specialized promoter exists, it is not the decision maker's task to determine either the classes of cases properly subject to disposition or the degree to which cases falling into such classes should be processed. The promoter's determination that a given inquiry should not be extended from one event to another does not compel the decision maker to make a wrong decision on the merits; rather, it prevents him from making *any* decision in what is viewed as a *new matter*. In the end, then, allocation of control over the content of the cause between the adjudicator and an official promoter turns on the elusive distinction between modification of an old and introduction of a new matter—a distinction with which legal systems have to cope in a variety of contexts.[21]

The foregoing discussion of the decision maker's prerogatives assumes that he is more than a figurehead who announces, with appropriate ceremony, a decision made sub rosa by some other official. An activist state, for educational or other purposes, may wish to anchor decision making in a solemn ceremonial event, at which the result of a decision actually made elsewhere is announced by an individual or collective body. Plainly, such ceremonial decision makers have no authority to deviate from what has already been decided.

Measures of Intervention

Suppose that a matter comes up for official disposition in the form of a dispute between two citizens, a plaintiff and a defendant. The "prayer for relief," like the factual allegations, is merely suggestive rather than peremptory or controlling; the appropriate measure to be taken originates in the official perspective, not in the narrow or "partial" points of view of self-interested individuals.

20. *Corpus Juris Fredericianum, Preamble, Point VI: Erstes Buch von Prozessordnung* (Berlin, 1791).

21. Examples of such contexts are the problem of determining whether an occurrence constitutes a single offense or several crimes, or the problem of limiting the preclusive effect of an already decided case.

Thus, for example, because citizens do not necessarily know what is best for them, the court can go beyond what the plaintiff demands, or a proceeding originally cast in the nonpunitive mode may be transformed into a punitive register.[22] It is true that such shifts into the penal mode are likely to be rare, but the primary constraint is the concern of state officials that plaintiffs might be discouraged from voicing their complaints in state courts for fear of ending up as criminal defendants, with the undesirable result that important sources of information might dry up. The open possibility of converting civil proceedings into the penal mode should not be understood to mean that the policy-implementing form of justice displays a preference for punishment as a mode of intervention: the desire of radically activist government to educate and mold its citizens may lead to the embrace of rehabilitation as the preferred goal of intervention in a variety of areas. As in Mao's China, citizens may have to be "rusticated" and transformed by toiling in the fields. The urge to punish is more characteristic of absolutist government, primarily concerned to maintain external order and to combat challenge to its authority.

Because one can never predict in advance how long the intervention will take before it succeeds, the correctional process often consists of a succession of measures amenable to change over a long period of time. Inevitably, the line between rendering and enforcing the decision becomes fluid, illustrating the convergence of adjudication (in the narrow sense) and general administration in the activist state.

Fact-Finding

The discussion of legal process in the reactive state has shown how its objective reduces the importance of ascertaining the real state of the world. Through the eyes of laissez-faire ideologists, truth seems elusive and reality, like the muses, seems always to have another veil. In contrast, getting the facts right is normally one of the preconditions to realizing the goal of the legal process in the activist state. Proper law enforcement requires accurate determination of past events and reliable prediction of future developments. Here, seeking the true facts does not seem an unrealistic, often Sisyphean enterprise: activist ideologies are housed in optimistic epistemology, and the activist administration of justice deals with the routine and easy as well as with difficult matters; it is not concentrated—as is reactive justice—on the residue of hard cases that cannot be settled out of court.

Nevertheless, it would still be an exaggeration to claim—as is often done concerning procedures patterned on the notion of inquest—that the policy-implementing process strives to attain the truth in each and every case, or that it

22. In Eastern European countries that follow the Soviet pattern, judges are free to disregard and exceed the party's prayer for relief in civil cases; the venerable adage, *ne eat judex ultra et extra petita partium*, respected even in the "activist" Frederickian civil process, has been discarded. Conversion from the civil into the penal mode of proceeding was readily possible in imperial China. See M. Shapiro, *Courts*, 181–82 (1981).

is an untrammeled pursuit of accurate information.[23] Even were an activist state to embrace no values that constrain the search for the truth,[24] the attempt to attain the highest possible standard of proof would impose unacceptable costs in terms of delay and various other vexations. Not only must decisions often be rendered on the basis of quite uncertain knowledge, but state policy may dictate that one factual hypothesis be accepted although another is somewhat more likely to be valid. Where the potential for a policy error under competing hypotheses is not equally grave, reliance upon the less probable but also less dangerous hypothesis is a rational response to the need for action under conditions of uncertainty. Thus, rather than saying that the policy-implementing process strives to maximize the chances of discovering the truth, one might prefer to say that it tries to attain optimal levels of fact-finding accuracy, given the various constraints imposed on its operation.[25]

In view of this orientation, it seems clear that private control over fact-finding is not an element of the pure model now under consideration. Whatever can be urged in favor of such private control rests on the assumption that private parties are interested in eliciting the truth and capable of devising satisfactory research strategies; but such an assumption is drained of plausibility in the setting of a truly activist government. Facts needed to determine the propriety of state intervention may be damaging to the self-interest of private individuals, giving them ample reason to hinder rather than facilitate the discovery of such facts. In addition, optimal investigative strategies require a viewpoint independent of narrow partisan perspectives: giving private individuals freedom to determine facts in the activist context resembles letting two lobbyists devise a regulatory scheme in the public interest. The rejection of private control over fact-finding does not imply that private individuals are excluded from participating in the collection of information and examination of evidence. Where low-level officials who perform preparatory investigative activities are absent, the role of

23. For example, Soviet commentators claim that the objective of their process is to ascertain "objective truth"; tolerance of any lesser standard for fact-finding is branded as bourgeois. See T. N. Dobrovolskaia, Printsipi sovetskogo ugolovnogo protsessa, 121–25 (Moscow, 1971). In fact, not even Continental criminal proceedings in the period when judicial torture was legal permitted the untrammeled pursuit of information demanded by the authorities; no matter how coarse and brutal these proceedings seem to us, sensitivity to human suffering, even notions of human dignity, were not totally absent. See M. Damaška, "The Death of Legal Torture," 87 Yale L.J. 860, 879 (1978).

24. To suppose that an extreme activist government disregards human compassion or other human costs entailed by information gathering is neither analytically justified nor historically accurate. It would be equally wrong to associate reactive government with the cultivation of human compassion: as an example, recall that the judge in the reactive process must resist the temptation to assist the weak, for the sake of treating all litigants equally.

25. As the paradigmatic civil case in contemporary America becomes one of "public interest," the value of truth discovery is increasingly emphasized. See A. Chayes, "The Role of the Judge in Public Law Litigation," 89 Harv. L. Rev. 1281, 1296–98 (1976). Similarly, as the inquisitorial law enforcement mode began to make inroads on the older Continental adversarial forms of process, it became customary to stress the greater capacity of the inquisitorial style for "the ventilation of the truth." See B. Carpzov, supra, n. 5.

private parties in fact-finding may even be large and prominent. However, officials in charge of proceedings will refuse to rely exclusively, or even principally, upon informational channels carved by persons whose interests are affected by the prospective decision. Ultimately, control over the fact-finding process must be in the hands of state officials.

This state control can be organized in several ways. One arrangement, usually thought to be mandated by the pure "inquisitorial" form, is for fact-finding to be structured and dominated by the person or persons in charge of rendering the decision on the merits. It is the trier of fact, not some other official, who is primarily responsible for eliciting testimony; he generates the bulk of questions asked of witnesses, decides on the sequence in which they will be interrogated, and the like. This first arrangement fits the ideal policy-implementing style only under a limited set of conditions. It becomes objectionable where it can be shown that the direct involvement of the trier of fact in the production of proof will reduce his chances of reaching an accurate result. Psychological insight suggests that, indeed, this may typically be the case: in order to be an effective interrogator, the trier of fact must occasionally challenge witnesses, and as he does, the calm and dispassionate weighing of evidence may be adversely affected. Furthermore, in order to conduct a focused interrogation, the examiner must form some tentative hypothesis about the facts he is called upon to establish, and as he does, the danger arises that he will be more receptive to information consistent with his tentative theories than to that which is not. In short, good reasons exist to scale down the decision maker's participation in the gathering and production of proof. His greater engagement appears appropriate only in easy cases, where the adverse consequences of psychological "overburdening" are relatively harmless.[26]

Another method, preferable in most cases, is to entrust the gathering of information and the examination of evidence before the decision maker to a specialized official. Alternatively, an official "trial manager" can be appointed who has not conducted a preliminary investigation and whose sole function is to interrogate witnesses and present other proof to the trier of facts.[27] Under both arrangements, the decision maker, initially uninformed, only gradually involves himself in the production of proof and then only to the extent to which his cognitive needs require. The art of suspended judgment can be practiced for a longer time, and evidence can be weighed more dispassionately.

26. In several Continental countries, arguments of this nature were actually used in advocating separation of investigative, prosecutorial and adjudicative functions, formerly united in the person of some judicial officials of the ancien régime. These arguments were reinforced by demands for the separation of powers. See A. Esmain, *Histoire de la procédure criminelle en France*, 502 (Paris, 1882). In Soviet theory, where the separation of powers is treated as a myth, the division of adjudication from prosecutorial investigative powers is supported solely by arguments praising the virtues of functional specialization. See, e.g., T. N. Dobrovolskaia, *supra*, n. 23, 164. For a more general argument, see Y. A. Tikhomirov, *Razdelenie vlastei ili razdelenie truda, Sovetskoe Gosudarstvo i Pravo*, no. 1 (1971): 14.

27. This method of proof taking has recently been recommended for criminal trials in West Germany. See H. Lüttger, *Probleme der Starfprozessreform*, 59 (Berlin and New York, 1975).

Still another possibility is to have two state officials, each predicating his activity on a different factual hypothesis, independently gather information and then develop evidence before the trier of fact through rival use of evidentiary sources. But is this "adversarial" style reconcilable with a pure policy-implementing process? The question is of special interest to Anglo-American lawyers and deserves to be pursued in some detail. It is plain that this style of examining evidence can be considered an option only where the subject matter of proceedings is reducible to two contradictory factual scenarios—as is the case, for example, with the issue of criminal liability. The hypothesis of guilt can be explored by a state prosecutor and the hypothesis of innocence by a state defender. But where the search for the best policy response to a problem requires the scanning of a broad diapason of possibilities or, to borrow a phrase from Polanyi, where the issues involved in the case are "polycentric,"[28] it appears inappropriate to structure the search for truth as a clash of two contradictory positions. In a criminal prosecution, consider an inquiry into the optimal sanction after a finding of criminal liability: rather than continuing with an adversarial clash of officials, it makes more sense to have the two put their heads together in a collaborative effort with the decision maker or to insist on some form of unilateral research into facts required for the optimal sentencing disposition.

Yet even when the problems involved in a lawsuit are reducible to two contradictory positions, the confrontational style of examining evidence must be toned down or weakened. Officials of a truly activist state are regarded more appropriately as promoters of the same ultimate state objective rather than as representatives of two conflicting partial interests. They may be appointed by the same common superior, and they may even agree about the expected outcome. Just as in the canonization proceedings of the Church of Rome, one official may merely play the devil's advocate, opposing the promoter of the faith as a matter of pure form. A further reason for the softening of confrontation relates to the position of the trier of fact in activist proceedings: he cannot be expected to remain aloof from the examination of evidence and must be permitted to intercede whenever he finds a need for information. Where he joins actively in the quest for optimal solutions, the contest between two officials recedes into the background; indeed, it is not inconceivable that now the two official opponents form a coalition against him. Not only are confrontational relations weakened, they are also unstable: adversarial fact-finding only uneasily accommodates activist concepts of the factual bases desirable for adjudication. In a process devoted to implementation of state policy—as in conventional science—a sustained clash of views is perceived as an indication that the matter at issue eludes

---

28. See M. Polanyi, *The Logic of Liberty*, 171 (1951). Lon Fuller has used the distinction between "monocentric" and "polycentric" issues to establish a line between matters that should come before the courts and those that should not; only "monocentric" issues appeared to him justiciable. See L. Fuller, "Adjudication and the Rule of Law," *Proceedings of the American Society of International Law* 54, no. 1 (1960): 1–8. It is sobering to note that commentators of more activist persuasion make similar distinctions and yet regard "polycentric" issues as eminently justiciable. See M. Taruffo, *Il processo civile ,"adversary" nell'esperienza americana*, 154, 251 (Padova, 1979).

conclusive resolution. The more an inquiry progresses, the more it becomes desirable that the ground contested by official investigators be narrowed; far from being an ideal form, a persistent clash over evidence becomes an irritant. A decision made by choosing the view that prevails in the official contest over alternative versions of the facts is acceptable only for lack of a better alternative. It seems much more preferable to decide after both officials have reached agreement that one of the two versions must flow from their research. In activist proceedings, therefore, a point arises where officials discontinue playing their roles and drop their adversarial masks: to insist on the contest scenario for its own sake makes no sense to activist government.

It is now possible to draw a conclusion: because controversy is not the grist of the judicial mill, the fact-finding process can only occasionally be organized in the form of a contest between two officials. This form is diluted and shades into a collaborative effort of state officialdom seeking the optimal solution to the legal problem involved. Whereas in a reactive state all judicial inquiry is readily convertible into an agonistic contest,[29] in the setting of a government that fulfills its activist potential all contest is ultimately but a form of collaborative or parallel inquiry. Clearly, the limiting case of a pure activist model should not be confused with more moderate activist procedures in which there can be much more room for evidentiary contest among officials. There are activist states where no comprehensive view of social life has developed, and no Briarius-like state policy has emerged with a hundred hands to draw officials together. Possessed by activist impulses and yet divided in its view on the governmental interest, officialdom is more like those cacti whose fruit lasts only a day and whose thorns are forever. Standing controversies over which version of the common interest is to be incorporated into the decision leave the adjudicator no choice but to select one of the clashing hypotheses as a basis for his judgment.

Parties as Suppliers of Information

Because the activist state expects all to participate in common endeavors, it also requires citizens to cooperate with authorities in the administration of justice. This duty extends to procedural parties as well; where the supremacy of state interests is both recognized and celebrated, refusal of the parties to cooperate with authorities by reason of the contrary pull of self-interest, or competing

29. Some voices have been raised in America advocating application of contest forms for resolution of scientific problems as well. See Levine, "Scientific Method and the Adversary Model," 29 *Am. Psych.* 661 (1974). Nor is this surprising in a country characterized by the absence of orthodoxy and the lack of fixed intellectual systems in so many fields: where the problem is not so much to find a solution to a problem within an accepted scientific paradigm as to resolve a clash between competing paradigms, stereoscopic vision and an adversarial method of debate naturally appear attractive. On the distinction between solving problems within an accepted framework of "normal science" and the choice of competing disciplinary matrixes, see T. S. Kuhn, *The Structure of Scientific Revolutions*, 2d ed., 120 (1970).

loyalties to family, friends, and the like, finds no strong justification and little sympathy.[30]

The duty to cooperate encompasses, of course, the duty to disclose documents and other material evidence to officials in charge of proceedings.[31] Spurred by the state's desire to superintend social life, those in charge can penetrate the private world with relative ease in their search for such evidence. But more important in this connection is the parties' duty to submit to the interrogation process and to produce testimonial evidence. Absent from the policy-implementing process are not only ideologically mandated compunctions against transforming the party into a witness (namely, strong conceptions of personal autonomy) but also the various structural impediments to such conversion generated by proceedings devoted to dispute resolution. Never accorded full control over procedural action, never a sovereign *subject* in charge of his procedural interest, the party can readily be converted into an *object* of procedural action—that is, into an informational source. Accordingly, a pure policy-implementing process incorporates as one of its defining characteristics the duty of procedural parties to answer truthfully questions addressed to them by procedural officials. This duty is not hedged by various privileges, not even by the privilege against self-incrimination.

If one were to construct a model of the policy-implementing process without these features, many known, historical procedural systems organized on the model of official inquiry would appear to be too "inquisitive" and would be deprived of a categorical niche. For example, well into the twentieth century some Western European countries expressly provided that the criminal defendant had a duty to answer, and it is by no means clear that many systems presently in force do not still tacitly assume such a duty.[32] Unless one believes that the state is an evil force, the existence of such a duty per se need not necessarily symbolize a morally inferior plane.[33]

While the duty to testify and to speak the truth can thus easily be justified in an activist state, its practical implementation may cause difficulties. It is hard to devise an effective and otherwise acceptable method for sanctioning a party's failure to provide accurate information to procedural authorities. Where a party

---

30. This attitude is reflected in the law related to ordinary witnesses. Thus, both refusal to testify or evasion by a witness become serious offenses against justice. See, e.g., *RSFSR Criminal Code*, art. 182. Furthermore, many testimonial privileges dictated by purposes independent of the desire to discover the true facts of the case (e.g., doctor-patient, priest-penitent, news reporter-source) may be either rejected or very narrowly drawn.

31. In "coordinate" policy-implementing systems that tolerate "civil investigations" (and private litigation for law enforcement purposes), the duty to disclose may be in favor of a "semiprivate" investigator rather than the court.

32. See, e.g., the comments to the 1957 Project for a Code of Criminal Procedure for the Swiss Canton Geneve: *Projet de Code de Procédure Pénale, Chancellerie de l'Etat*, 133 (Génève, 1975). More generally, see F. Walder, "Das Verhör," in *Strafprozess und Rechtsstaat, Festschrift Pfenninger*, 184 (Zürich, 1956).

33. On this problem, see G. Del Vecchio, *Studi sul Diritto*, vol. 2, 211 (Milano, 1958); J. Goldschmidt, *Der Prozess als Rechtslage*, 127 (Berlin, 1925); Thomas Aquinas, *supra*, ch. 4, n. 59, id.

has a strong interest not to disclose a fact (e.g., fear of serious punishment), only the prospect of draconian sanctions will induce him to testify and tell the truth. But these draconian sanctions suggest a further problem with the sanctioning mechanism—that is, its human cost. Effective measures to induce a party to respond to questions can be offensive to human compassion and to prevailing ideas about the proper treatment of citizens by the state. Even the ill-famed authorities of the ancien régime, which legalized physical compulsion to extract answers from criminal defendants, were not totally insensitive to this problem and imposed some limits on the use of coercive measures.[34]

However, the problem of answers is only part of the difficulty. Even if effective sanctions are in place to induce a party to respond to the questions, he will be tempted to lie; by testifying falsely, he may try to avoid both the harm to self-interest at risk in truthful replies and the evil of the sanction if he refuses to talk. And as the falsity of his testimony can seldom be reliably established in the ongoing proceeding, the justice system is in danger of being engulfed by inaccurate information.[35] In the end, then, policy-implementing systems must yield to the fact that the party's duty to cooperate with authorities will often lack any effective sanction—turning the threat into a blunt sword.

Most contemporary procedures devoted to policy implementation seem to have departed from this extreme arrangement. Take, for example, criminal prosecutions in continental Europe: the legislation of many Western and some communist systems now provides that criminal defendants—albeit still required to submit to interrogations—have a right to refuse to reply: the right to silence. Moreover, if they choose to testify, their detected lies are not punishable as perjury: the right to lie. Of course, physical compulsion to obtain testimony is now generally outlawed. At the level of legal rhetoric, these are indeed dramatic departures from the pure policy-implementing form, with its emphasis on the

---

34. Not surprisingly, these limits depended to a large degree on the defendant's station in life. See the primary sources collected in M. Damaška, supra, n. 23, 878–79. Coercive measures were permitted not only at an advanced stage of the process to obtain confessions (after sufficient evidence required for the application of such measures had been assembled) but also from the inception of the prosecution to make recalcitrant defendants talk. See I. Clarus, Opera Omnia, Liber 5, quest. 45, no. 6, 550 (London, 1672). But these measures were relatively benign compared to torments permitted in order to extract confessions; Beccaria, the famous opponent of judicial torture, recommended them as a useful antidote to the obstinate taciturnity of some defendants. See C. Beccaria, An Essay on Crimes and Punishments, 150 (London, 1801). Under the name poenae inobedientiae (penalties for disobedience), these measures survived the abolition of judicial torture in France for more than a century.

35. Nor does this end the predicament of the enforcement scheme. In criminal prosecutions, reliable determination that the defendant has lied presupposes (in most cases) that his guilt had already been ascertained, so that measures for punishing false denials (i.e., enforcing the duty to speak the truth) have no place prior to the final verdict—that is, so long as such measures can be effective in promoting discovery of the truth. Judicial torture to extract a confession made sense only because evidence required for its legitimate use was thought to be sufficient to convince the judge of the defendant's guilt. Why then torture at all? One of the most important supporting grounds was related to religious belief: it was believed that a confession repeated after torture indicated repentance and could thus save the defendant from eternal torment for the mortal sin of his crime. Immersing him in the absolving sea of pain prior to the announcement and execution of sentence thus seemed rational.

duty of the party to cooperate with authorities. The actual administration of justice, however, has been affected by these rhetorical achievements to only a limited degree, so that the living law in this area deserves a fresh look.

First, it should be recognized that even as a matter of legal doctrine the rights to refuse cooperation seldom attach in the earliest stages of policy inquiry when decisive information is often obtained through intensive questioning of suspects. Accorded only at a later stage, these rights can thus often be likened to a comb given to a person only after he has lost his hair. When applicable, the right to silence is sui generis because officials retain their right to interrogate: the very fact that the defendant can be produced by force and subjected to questioning by a powerful official is in itself sufficient to create an atmosphere imposing pressure to respond. This pressure is increased in those systems that require no warning about the right to silence. The pressure is further augmented because interrogating officials typically exercise important powers over the defendant. Thus investigators may interpret the defendant's refusal to help in clearing up the facts as an indication that he may interfere with investigative efforts; they may order him detained pending trial without the possibility of release on bail.[36] Trial judges, who carry the main burden of interrogation, are also the sentencing judges, so that the defendant's fear of antagonizing them by failing to respond properly acts as a powerful incentive to speak, quite apart from the fact that, because the trial judge decides on guilt and sentence at the same time, the defendant who wraps himself in silence deprives himself as well of an opportunity to say something in mitigation of punishment. Judges can legitimately draw unfavorable inferences from the defendant's refusal to answer questions, and it is easy to see reasons why Continental defendants who choose to exercise their right to silence are few and far between.[37] Nor is their right to lie any less Pickwickian: inconsistencies detected in their statements will lessen or even destroy their general credibility; in practice, stubborn refusals to confess are as readily treated as aggravating circumstances as confession is conversely regarded as a mitigating ground for sentencing purposes.[38]

36. The danger that the defendant may impede investigative efforts (*Verdunklungsgefahr*) is a ground routinely invoked for ordering preliminary detention in almost all Continental systems of criminal procedure. But there are also various apocryphal grounds, one of which is the investigator's desire to facilitate the interrogation process. On such apocryphal grounds in West Germany see W. Hassemer, "Die Voraussetzungen der Untersuchungshaft," *Anwaltsblatt*, no. 2 (1984): 65. Until quite recently, the defendant's failure to cooperate with investigators could constitute a ground for refusal to credit him for time spent in preliminary detention. See P. Thorman and A. Overbeck, *Das schweizerische Strafgesetzbuch*, vol. 1, 226 (Zürich, 1940).

37. Compare *supra*, ch. 4, n. 58. Recall the ease with which a defendant's statements prior to trial can be introduced in court if he opts for taciturnity.

38. Academic commentators and higher courts usually oppose "automatic" use of confessions in mitigation and denials in aggravation of punishment: what is required is that the two somehow indicate that the defendant is either less or more culpable and dangerous. In the practice of trial courts, however, confessions at least tend to go in mitigation without any additional determination. For West German practice, see H. Bruns, *Strafzummesungsrecht*, 526 (1967). For a more general argument, see still G. Foschini, *Confessione dell'imputato e misura della pena*, *Archivio Penale* (1945), 1, p. 29. Detected lies of the defendant can in some circumstances be punishable as criminal offenses against the administration of justice. See *supra*, ch. 4, n. 60.

Faced with this cornucopia of devices used to induce defendants to talk and tell the truth, an outside observer may easily conclude that such devices are actually mild and roundabout sanctions for the lingering duty of criminal defendants to cooperate with procedural authorities. Unfamiliar with broad legislative schemes that provide commentators with arguments to construct a right to silence and a right to lie, the observer would be more inclined to interpret the situation as one in which the defendant's silence and lies are merely tolerated by the system—no direct sanctions are provided as penalties for them—rather than to erect the defendant's silence and privileged lies into procedural rights personal to him.[39] The ideal of the defendant who cooperates with authorities remains close to the surface of the law, if law is understood as a living enterprise.

iv. POSITION OF THE DECISION MAKER

The centrality of the image of an impartial decision maker in the reactive style of conflict resolution has been shown, and I have discussed how this image requires that he be disinterested and essentially passive. The goal of policy implementation calls for a different key image: what is primarily expected of the decision maker is that he reach the accurate result or that he find the most appropriate solution to a problem as it crystallizes in proceedings. That he may have to spring into action goes without saying. It is equally clear that the issue of his neutrality as between two sides need not even arise, in that there need not always be two parties to the legal process. But even where proceedings are not free from bipolar tensions, the activist decision maker is not bound to treat both sides equally; under some circumstances he may be expected to side with the party who urges what seems to be the correct view and to assist him if he fails to make the right "case" effectively. Hence, in considering the best position and most desirable attributes of the activist decision maker, the paramount issue is to identify those postures and attributes most likely to promote a substantively right disposition of the case. In brief, then, the image of a *righteous* rather than an impartial decision maker expresses the adjudicative ideal in proceedings devoted to the implementation of state policy.

Involvement in Proceedings

In considering various aspects of the activist process, I have repeatedly remarked that the adjudicator remains obliged to expand the argument and to go beyond the material presented by procedural participants whenever such action appears to be necessary to attain the right result. The adjudicator cannot remain aloof and

---

39. The discrepant roles of Continental commentators and outside observers should be noted: while the former seek to participate in the system of justice, to shape it in desired ways, an outside observer is interested in understanding what actually goes on in the system, to make sense of it. This is not to say that Continental commentators never assume the interpretive role and assess the actual position of the criminal defendant as a source of information. Not surprisingly, this usually occurs when they are driven to adopt a comparative perspective. See V. Bayer, "La signification de l'aveu de l'inculpé dans le droit de procédure pénale de certains états occidentaux européens," *Rivista Italiana di Diritto e Procedura Penale*, n.s. 2 (1959): 724.

uninvolved. However, it is obviously difficult to give a general answer to the question of the precise degree of his involvement: that will largely depend on the participation of other state officials in the proceedings. Of course, where he is the only authoritative participant, his involvement reaches the maximum: as decision maker, he assumes personal control over proceedings. But as more and more action is preempted by other officials, a point may come at which the decision maker appears to turn into a passive observer, limited to making a decision on the basis of material assembled by other officials. In those cases where two officials press for contrary solutions to a case, it may even seem that the decision maker becomes an umpire or a conflict resolver, limited to ruling in favor of the more persuasively argued official alternative.

This is a superficial view, however: not only is total abdication of the decision maker's procedural control alien to the pure activist style, but so too is the model of decision making as a choice between competing views, or a mediation among such views. Remember that the procedural mode now being canvassed accompanies a state where a single comprehensive view of social life has been adopted by the government to replace the babel of differing or contrary conceptions of the good. In this latter context, where the government has made no single social theory its own, inquiry into the best policy response to a problem may well require the choice of one of the clashing views on desirable policies to be controlling; the desired outcome of the case may well be the application of the view that prevailed in an agonistic debate of officials advocating competing policy schemes. But in the limiting case of a state fulfilling its activist potential, this is not the likely situation: in this unitary context, the inquiry into the best policy response to a problem appears to be an endeavor requiring accurate analysis within the framework of a single policy scheme; the correct solution within this scheme is the desired outcome of the case. Equally inappropriate in this unitary environment would be a decision embracing compromise, or middle-of-the-road solutions between conflicting positions. In a pure activist process, to decide by means of compromise is like settling the dispute between heliocentric and geocentric theories by holding that both sun and earth revolve around an equidistant axis. Analysis, not choice, is the essence of activist decision making.

I have already pointed out that the activist decision maker becomes uneasy when an official controversy over factual hypotheses persists as the time for decision approaches. The same is true for controversies over applicable policies and standards. Continuing disagreement suggests that the problem in the case is not ripe for disposition, at least not for a definitive one. But what is the activist decision maker to do in this situation? Assuming that he does not launch his own investigation at this point, one possibility is for him to demand further research by other officials so that the products of parallel official inquiries can be made more harmonious. Many existing activist procedures incorporate this arrangement.[40] Alternatively, the decision maker may postpone a definitive decision

40. For example, the Soviet trial court may order a case to be turned to the investigative phase for additional research. See *RSFSR Code of Crim. Proc.* arts. 226, 308. This possibility also existed in some classical Continental systems of criminal procedure.

until such time as he is "more amply informed," ordering only the necessary provisional measures. The much criticized "third way" between conviction and acquittal in the criminal process of the ancien régime (*absolutio ab instantia, plus amplement informé*, etc.) illustrates this second possibility.[41] Of course, circumstances will arise where an irrevocable decision cannot be delayed although official controversies continue. Faced with such a pressing need to decide, the activist decision maker does not follow the path suggested by the procedural logic of party contest: he does not have to rule in favor of the better argued view. Rather, the preferable way for him is to be guided by second-order policies of the state concerning the best solution under conditions of uncertainty; ideas on the best allocation of the costs of error may lead him to decide *against* the better argued alternative, provided that this decision will reduce the negative consequences of being mistaken. Thus, factual doubts in the criminal process can be resolved—depending on the circumstances—either in favor of or against the defendant. The choice of the better argued alternative can be an acceptable strategy for the decision maker only in the absence of an applicable second-order policy—that is, in situations that are far from ideal, indeed, that are deplorably *faute de mieux*.

In sum, the activist decision maker must join in procedural action whenever necessary to attain the right solution.[42] Even where he appears superficially to play umpire of a contest over the better course of action, he remains dutybound to seek the correct result entirely apart from the argument that prevails in the forensic contest or the wishes of procedural protagonists.

The Problem of Extraneous Knowledge

It is apparent that the reactive mode of proceeding creates a bipolar energy field in which all information acquired by the adjudicator outside the courtroom will lead to suspicion of prejudice and bias—be it that his knowledge was privately acquired or that it stems from familiarity with official documentation. In either case, it seems fair to disqualify the reactive adjudicator who is in possession of extraneous information. In contrast, because impartiality is not the central attribute of the activist decision maker, his external knowledge is not so readily assumed to be a disqualifying defect; such knowledge becomes objectionable only if it can cloud substantive vision and endanger the correct disposition of the case. Imagine that millions have observed a homicide on live television, and that the

41. This "intermediate" decision even appealed to some revolutionary spirits in the late eighteenth century. Marat argued that where criminal guilt is not clear but suspicion lingers, the defendant should remain in detention until such time as one can "illuminate the facts." J. P. Marat, *Plan de la Legislation Criminelle*, 172 (Paris, 1794). For similar ideas in German lands, see A. Bauer, *supra*, ch. 4, n. 86, 299. Russian czarist legislation preserved this possibility well into the second half of the nineteenth century.

42. Demand for additional investigation is but a form of such activist involvement, with *ultimate* procedural control in the decision maker.

killer is as widely known as the killer of Lee Harvey Oswald: at the subsequent trial, if the killer chooses to dispute the act of killing, he is not entitled to insist that the adjudicators be only citizens who have not watched this telecast. The adjudicators' familiarity with facts widely accepted as true does not automatically disqualify them and may even be desirable. The trial is not a contest or a game in which the defendant has the right "to put the state to its proof" even with respect to notorious events. The situation is different where the extraprocedurally obtained knowledge is thought not reliable. It may then be feared that the decision maker in possession of such knowledge may uncritically accept his own sensory perceptions—or his own secondary cognitive elaboration of these perceptions—even when his own clash with those of witnesses or with some other means of proof. Decisional rectitude could be adversely affected were he permitted to sit in judgment. Thus because adjudicators are as a rule fungible, whereas witnesses are not, the potential adjudicator must be converted into a witness, and someone else charged with fact-finding.

Divergent settings of authority give rise to different qualms about the adjudicator's "private" knowledge. This can clearly be seen in the example of those activist systems that failed to perceive the hazards of mingling adjudicative and testimonial functions, as was the case with the English criminal jury well into the sixteenth century. The juror's private knowledge was not only *not* frowned upon but was valued and praised. Other settings generate other attitudes. I have noted the importance to the bureaucratic spirit of the separation of the official from the private sphere. It follows that what bureaucratic decision makers observe "officially" in the course of official proceedings is kept rigidly apart from what they observe, for example, in driving home for dinner. Fact-finding should be an official and not a private activity, so that privately obtained information is disqualifying. Such misgivings about external knowledge are inspired by perceived dangers to the integrity of the outcome on the merits, not by desire to assure the decision maker's "impartiality" or to satisfy notions of procedural fairness.

What has been said so far about knowledge of facts also applies to extraprocedural knowledge of applicable decisional standards. At least in hierarchical bureaucratic environments, it may seem preferable that prior to being called to sit on the case the decision maker have a clear view as to the applicable law; where he must be tutored about legal standards as the case progresses, at the outset he is unable to determine precisely what information he will need to decide the case. The usefulness of a particular question or line of inquiry may appear only later, so that procedural steps have to be retraced and resources wasted. Another contrast vis-à-vis the conflict-solving mode of proceedings may be observed where an activist judge, prior to coming to the case, makes known his views on a particular point of law at issue in the suit. If his legal opinion is accurate, it makes little sense in policy-implementing proceedings to doubt his suitability as decision maker, even if there is sharp disagreement between procedural participants concerning the applicable law.

Attachment to the State

It has been shown that citizens of a truly activist state, like notes in a giant fugue, must contribute to the development of a common theme and must share the government's outlook on social life. It follows that state adjudicators must also be committed to the state: an umpire's indifference toward governmental policies is out of place, even reprehensible. The adjudicator's identification with the state becomes undesirable only if it is so intense that, like any consuming passion, it obscures vision concerning the correct demands of state policy. It is mainly in the sense of avoidance of excessive zeal in promoting the state's goals that the activist adjudicator should properly remain "objective."[43]

Do these demands leave any room for the decision maker's independence? When he fully meets the demands placed on him, is he not more enlisted than engagé? If independence is meant to imply neutrality toward and detachment from the policies of the state, the answer must be resolutely negative. Under some circumstances it may even appear désirable for decision makers to seek instruction from appropriate state authority as to how to dispose of a case. If an organization is responsible for defining the policy line, is it not natural for decision makers to consult this organization about the proper policy response to the legal problem at hand? For adjudicators to be selected from among members of an elite political organization is not improper and may even be preferable, even if the elite corps demands strict discipline from its members in following policies and possesses an effective command structure.[44]

Where this occurs, one wonders whether decision makers can be insulated from undue interference by external state authority or from the hurly-burly of day-to-day politics. The best guarantee of such insulation appears where decision makers are treated as specialists or as experts in relating policy goals to contingent events. As decisional standards become more complex, accurate outcomes begin to diverge from solutions attractive in terms of ordinary political intuitions, so that intervention from the outside can be seen as poaching into a specialized field. In this situation, as in the Talmudic story of Achnai's oven,[45] decision makers may be able to assert a degree of autonomy or independence even from the supreme state authority. Powerful political impulses to interfere in the disposition of particular cases can be weakened, just as a mighty river can be disciplined in the outspread web of an irrigation system.

This dynamic has been at work in activist states of communist persuasion.

43. Of course, the adjudicator's objectivity can also be jeopardized by astigmatism of another kind: a personal stake in the outcome of the case might tempt him to sacrifice the right result. Obviously, *nemo judex in causa sua* is an accoutrement of the ideal policy implementer.

44. It is not thought disqualifying in communist countries for judges to be party members, even where the party line suggests the particular outcome of a case quite clearly. For references to similar problems in Western systems, see M. Damaška, in W. J. Habsheid, ed., *Effektiver Rechtsschutz und Verfassungsmassige Ordnung*, 461, n. 66 (Bielefeld, 1983).

45. According to this tale, a dissenting rabbi summoned the divine voice to intervene on his side in a rabbinical dispute. However, even the voice from heaven failed to persuade his colleagues to change their views because they all were experts in the Torah. The story can be found in the Jerusalem Talmud, *Moed Katan*, III, 1. See 4 *Le Talmud de Jerusalem*, trans., M. Schwab 322 (Paris, 1960).

When both the Russian and the Chinese revolutions were still young, authorities unabashedly acknowledged that the ruling party is entitled to intervene strongly in the administration of justice—not only in the sense of setting general policies or demanding that judges inspire loyalty to state causes but also in the sense of giving specific instructions as to how particular cases ought to be decided. Courts were expected to seek guidance from party officials in specific matters.[46] But the view has since evolved that judges are dependent on state authorities only in the sense that they should follow general policy lines drawn by the party. Instructions by party or any other extrajudicial authority specifying how concrete cases should be handled are now declared inappropriate—an undue interference in the course of justice. This freedom from specific instruction is then proclaimed as the essence of judicial independence: broader and more demanding concepts of such judicial independence are criticized as bourgeois myths or "fetishizations" of the judiciary.[47] Obviously, judicial independence arises from the distinction between general and specific instructions—easier to draw in theory than in practice. Of course, to one embued with pluralistic values, this conception of independence seems impoverished. But one should not import into the political landscape of intensely activist states concerns about the independence of the judiciary which prevail in systems of limited government. In the activist landscape, the state appears as a benign force and the center of political legitimacy: judges must be shielded, but only against interference by state officials that is either corrupt (self-serving) or seeks "incorrect" substantive results.

v. THE STATUS OF LEGAL COUNSEL

Compatibility with the Model

In the activist legal process, there are officials who promote a thesis beneficial to a private citizen as part of their official duties and can therefore be regarded by him as a temporary ally. But such officials are not "representatives" of individuals implicated in proceedings: with larger interests in mind, they can act at any stage of the process in ways harmful to private individuals' perceived self-interest. I have already pointed out that a state defender may be appointed in order to examine the hypothesis of innocence and oppose the hypothesis of guilt advanced by the state prosecutor. Yet it would be serious misconduct for a state defender to

46. On early Soviet views, see N. S. Alekseev and V. Z. Lukashevich, *Leninskie Idei v Sovetskom Ugolovnon Sudoproizvodstve*, 62 (Leningrad, 1970). See also A. Solzhenitsyn, *The Gulag Archipelago*, 307 (1973), documenting the opinion of Prosecutor General Krylenko. In Mao's China, courts were required to follow party instructions. See A. E. S. Tay, "Smash Permanent Rules; China as a Model for the Future," 7 *Sidney L. Rev.* 400, 415, 419 (1976). Even in post-Maoist China, some important cases, such as the sentence in the case of Madame Mao, are quite openly considered by party leadership prior to the announcement of the judgment.

47. For a typical formulation of dominant views, see T. N. Dobrovolskaia, *supra*, n. 23, 165. It is interesting to note that while rejecting the division of *powers* in the state, the official Soviet doctrine is ready to extend an accolade to the division of *labor* among state officials, leading to a degree of functional autonomy. See Vydria, "Rassledovanie Ugolovnogo Dela," *Sovetskoe Gosudarstvo i Pravo*, no. 9 (1980): 78. See also Y. A. Tikhomirov, *supra*, n. 26.

argue in favor of innocence against his better judgment or to advocate a particular punishment just because the defendant finds it less onerous.[48] Should a conscientious state defender promote the defendant's interests when those do not coincide with larger state interests, it is by reason of mistaken identification: as with seashells, he has mistaken the pulse for the beat of the sea.

Is it compatible with the policy-implementing process to allow private counsel to assist the party in confronting the officials in charge of proceedings? The general answer turns on whether state authorities regard such assistance as useful to the attainment of the goals of justice. It can be argued that, in the absence of private legal counsel, some legitimate interests of a person implicated in proceedings might be overlooked by busy officials or that his interests may be pursued ineffectively by an inexperienced and anxiety-ridden party. It may also be urged that counsel provide a check on the conduct of officials in charge: by keeping them alert, counsel help reduce slackness; by monitoring excesses of zeal, they help reduce irregular official behavior. To the extent that such arguments seem persuasive to state authority, a space opens up for the participation of counsel in the administration of justice: lawyers' participation now is thought to advance the likelihood of reaching the correct procedural outcome. Arguments pro and con may be weighed differently for different types of proceedings or for different procedural stages. Counsel may thus be excluded from certain cases, or from certain phases of the legal process, but not from the administration of justice generally.[49] If counsel's role is assessed as useful, it may be made mandatory, so that a party who refuses to retain a lawyer will have one appointed to represent him anyway; where individuals are not sovereign in pursuing their forensic fortunes, there can be no right to stand alone and act *pro se*.[50]

Proper Role

So long as the interests of a private party do not clash with the desire of the state to attain the correct disposition of the case, defining the role of counsel is not problematic; the lawyer should be the party's vigorous advocate. But what is his proper course of action when the substantively correct outcome appears likely to

48. It would also be wrong for an official to hide information he has obtained from his colleague who is assigned a contrary role: state officials are not supposed to perform their procedural tasks to the detriment of their common goal—the attainment of an accurate result.

49. At the height of French royal absolutism, defense counsel were permitted to appear before the appellate courts in criminal cases. German criminal procedure of the same period was even more open to lawyers: they were permitted to inspect the dossier of the case and file a brief for the defendant as soon as the official investigation was completed. See B. Carpzov, *supra*, n. 5, quest. 115, nos. 90–101. In civil cases, the ancien régime placed few restrictions on the work of lawyers. It was only in 1781, as part of the reforms of Frederick the Great in Prussia, that members of the bar were prohibited from acting before courts in civil litigation. A special branch of judicial salariat was substituted, charged with both helping litigants and supervising the work of judges. See A. Weissler, *Geschichte der Rechtsanwaltschaft*, 357 (Frankfurt, 1967). This experiment in the spirit of welfare absolutism failed and was soon discarded. Total exclusion of private lawyers from the administration of justice can be encountered in non-Western legal systems.

50. Contemporary systems of justice on the continent of Europe, both East and West, provide for mandatory defense in prosecutions for offenses sanctioned by most serious penalties.

damage his client? In a legal system characterized by the tendency to favor smooth implementation of state policy, there is no place for lawyers who serve the self-interest of clients and create obstacles to the realization of state programs. Is the lawyer then expected to disregard the wishes of his client and to assist state officials in reaching the desirable outcome? This solution naturally occurs in a state that abhors narrow loyalties and demands the sacrifice of lesser on the altar of greater interests; here, counsel's loyalty to his client has no substantial intrinsic merit. On the other hand, this loyalty may be useful to the state in the long run: counsel's failure to turn against his client may advance the overall accuracy of outcomes, even as it may obstruct the correct disposition of a particular case. In other words, counsel's loyalty to his client can be grounded on the discord between immediate and more remote state objectives and adjusted in favor of the latter, rather than based on conflict between individual and state interest and resolved in favor of the former.[51] As suggested earlier, an argument of this nature deserves a serious hearing in an activist state.

For example, consider the venerable question of protecting the secrecy of communication between client and attorney. The effective performance of counsel's tasks requires that he obtain reliable information from various sources, especially from his client. If he is now obliged fully to transmit what he has learned to authorities, his client and his other informants may be reluctant to disclose damaging or sensitive data. A useful informational pool can thus be drained and the larger interests of justice negatively affected. Because such a sequence of events is usually regarded as not too remote a possibility, even strongly activist governments hesitate to require counsel to turn against their client and some form of attorney-client privilege tends to be recognized.[52] But it also seems prudent to provide a safety valve for those instances in which compelling governmental interest in accurate adjudication of a particular case clearly outweighs the more remote, speculative damage to the general accuracy of outcomes.[53]

51. This reasoning may underlie the statement frequently encountered in Soviet legal literature, that interests of Soviet justice and those of the criminal defendant are like "two sides of the same coin." See I. Stetkovskii, *Advokat v Ugolovnom Sudoproizvodstve*, 5, 415 (Moscow, 1972). If the rights accorded the defendant are designed to maximize the attainment of truth in the total number of cases (albeit they may hamper it in some), then this statement begins to make sense. However, if the rights of the defendant are expected to advance truth in each and every case, a conflict of interest between guilty defendants and the government clearly arises: the assertion of at least some defense rights could make the discovery of truth more difficult, so that conflict surfaces between the parochial interest of a guilty defendant to avoid punishment and the state interest in reaching the accurate outcome.

52. Contrary to what is sometimes thought, the prevailing doctrinal view in communist systems is that lawyers should not actively engage in action that reflects unfavorably upon their clients: rather, they should remain inactive. For early views, see N. N. Polianskii, *Pravda i lozh v ugolovnom zashcite*, 49 (Moscow, 1927). On contemporary regulation, see C. Osakwe, "Modern Soviet Criminal Procedure," 57 *Tulane L. Rev.* 439, 523–24 (1983). This is not to say that some lawyers have not occasionally turned against their clients, especially in Stalin's days. See A. Solzhenitsyn, *The Gulag Archipelago (1918–1956)*, 347, 378 (1973).

53. For an example of this view in Soviet legal scholarship, see I. Motovilovker, *Nekotorie Voprosi Teorii Sovetskogo Ugolovnogo Protesessa*, 105 (Moscow, 1964).

If the lawyer is supposed not to harm his client's self-interest, is he then licensed to participate in some cases in bringing about an inaccurate verdict? A system of justice dedicated to the supremacy of state interests must refuse to go so far; a less extreme position seems more attractive. In situations where the interest of the state and the client's self-interest require divergent courses of action, counsel should remain passive, neither actively promoting the right verdict nor assisting his client. For example, knowing or suspecting that a witness has falsely testified in favor of his client, counsel should neither expose the perjury nor contribute to the success of the falsehood by developing the witness's testimony. Under certain circumstances, counsel may even be permitted to withdraw from the case. In evaluating the practicality of this arrangement, it would be wrong to extrapolate exclusively from experiences in those procedural systems where officials are essentially passive and dependent on the parties' lawyers for procedural action. Counsel's selective inactivity may be as damaging to the client as outright disclosure of damaging information to the court. But where "activist" officials inject themselves energetically in interrogations and other courtroom action, the selective inactivity of counsel may pass unnoticed and is, in any event, an unreliable basis for drawing inferences damaging to the client.[54]

Relation to the State

Because a fully activist government dislikes associations independent of the state, it may abolish the organized bar so that counsel are selected from lawyers who are not institutionally organized. Another possibility is to retain bar associations, but to see to it that they turn into quasi-official agencies in the service of the justice system. To prevent their excessive amalgamation with the client's interests, members of the bar may be put on a straight salary or compensated according to some remunerative scheme compatible with various branches of the state's legal salariat. History offers a wealth of illustrations of various possibilities that open up to the activist government intent on regulating the status of legal counsel.[55]

It seems normal to expect that mechanisms for matching counsel with cases will be developed by an activist justice system. The annals of ancien régime policy-implementing justice, as yet unconcerned about public opinion at home and abroad, are replete with frank acknowledgement—even praise—of the practice of excluding certain counsel from certain types of proceedings or certain important cases. In the words of the greatest seventeeth-century authority on the Continental criminal process, Benedict Carpzov, not just any lawyer should be admitted as defense counsel in criminal matters: "only honest, upright and

---

54. Counsel's passivity is thus easier to accept in hierarchical than in coordinate policy-implementing systems. Compare *supra*, ch. 4, n. 78.

55. Among the earliest examples are regulations of the Byzantine emperor Justinian. Particularly illuminating, however, is the checkered history of Soviet policies toward lawyers, admirably recounted by J. N. Hazard, *supra*, n. 3, 34–51.

learned men [should be admitted], not those who inject confusion, who are verbose but not eloquent, or those whose activity procrastinates rather than speeds up the progress of the cause."[56] In our time, the matching of counsel with cases is viewed as a very sensitive matter, so that in those justice systems where this matching goes on, the screening devices used are not likely to be openly regulated. Yet the theory of excluding some lawyers from certain lawsuits makes good sense to a government that finds legal assistance to the party permissible only if it will advance the chance of obtaining accurate results.

Limited Importance

In the activist legal process, where the primary responsibility for reaching the right outcome is vested in state officials, it is not considered desirable that private counsel's talent should play a crucial role. Thus, in contrast to the administration of justice in the reactive state, there is relatively little scope for deployment of counsel's skill and ingenuity. Several aspects of counsel's reduced importance deserve notice.

Independent investigations by counsel are dramatically curtailed, at least in those activist systems that employ an investigative bureaucracy. Lawyers are limited to collecting only such information as is readily available to everyone.[57] Incisive early inquiries by private lawyers come close to tampering with informational sources prior to their use by the officials responsible for finding facts. As I have pointed out, counsel may be excluded from certain stages of the process, especially from the initial phases of criminal prosecution. The costs of this exclusion are not overlooked (early intervention can speed up elimination of groundless charges), but it is feared that early contact between a suspect and his lawyer can help the criminal create plausible but false stories and thus escape altogether his deserved conviction. The balancing of these costs leads to the policy of postponing admission of counsel until such time as the state investigators believe that they have concluded the bulk of their detective work.[58] Even within the limited scope of activity left to him, counsel is not nearly as free to intervene vigorously on his client's behalf as he is in the conflict-solving process of the reactive state. Activist government does not tolerate criticism of its programs from positions contrary to its official philosophy. Thus it would be inappropri-

---

56. See B. Carpzov, *supra*, n. 5, qu. 115, no. 93. Special lists of acceptable counsel in Soviet political trials are discussed in W. E. Butler, *Soviet Law*, 82 (1983).

57. For Soviet views on this point, see C. Osakwe, *supra*, n. 52, 553.

58. This was the solution of the seventeenth-century German criminal process, where defense counsel acquired the right to inspect the file after the conclusion of the investigator's work. See *supra*, n. 49. Essentially similar restrictions on counsel's participation survived in Soviet law until 1972. Soviet counsel can now be admitted even while the investigation is still in progress if the official in charge finds this advisable. Of course, if he thinks the defense counsel will make his task more difficult, he will refuse or seriously limit his activity. But once he has completed his work, the defendant acquires complete "discovery rights" and can request supplemental investigations. See *RSFSR Code of Crim. Proc.*, arts. 47, 120.

ate—even slanderous—for counsel to advocate loyalty to nongovernmental associations to the state's detriment or to praise the virtues of individual autonomy.[59] Another important constraint on powerful and zealous advocacy is related to the structure of policy-implementing proceedings: the thrust of counsel's activity is not directed against a private adversary with the state adjudicator looking on, as in the conflict-solving process, but rather against an official of the state who is actively involved in the investigation. In this context, a lawyer who fiercely challenges material damaging to his client can easily appear to be trying to obstruct the realization of state policies—a serious charge in the eyes of activist government.

When all this is said, an observer from a reactive polity is likely to conclude that counsel's contribution to the policy-implementing process is negligible and readily dispensable. From within, however, matters appear in a different light: even where counsel can do little to change the outcome, as is often the case, there is room for his useful activity. At the very least, he can offer psychological support to parties, blunting the thorns of their anxiety. Even if counsel's advocacy must often be transformed into supplication, this is a contribution that private parties implicated in legal proceedings greatly value. The very presence of counsel is also important as a deterrent to officials' tendency to take procedural tasks too lightly. It would be an unpardonable exaggeration to say that counsel's role in the policy-implementing process is merely cosmetic: within the range of officially approved views, the lawyer can locate aspects of the case both favorable to his client and acceptable from the state's point ov view, so that the outcome of the case can be materially affected by his efforts.[60]

vi. ALTERABILITY OF DECISIONS

In a legal process designed for implementation of governmental policy and in a state devoted to social transformation, the stability of judgments is obviously a matter of low priority. Both the desire to put an end to disputes and the deference to social expectations are weak, in comparison to the legal process of a state committed to maintaining social equilibrium. In principle, all decisions are rendered *rebus sic stantibus*, that is to say, provisionally. If it turns out that a judgment is wrong on the merits, it is difficult to justify any obstacle to reversal and reconsideration. Whether the error in the judgment concerns facts or misapplication of the law, whether reconsideration is favorable or detrimental to the affected parties, whether civil or criminal judgments are involved—all such questions are immaterial. Nor is the finding of the decision maker's mistake a necessary predicate to reconsideration: a judgment correct at the time it was rendered should be reevaluated and altered if newly emerging circumstances

59. See C. Osakwe, *supra*, n. 52, 552–53.

60. Even in the darkest days of medieval inquisition the role of counsel was not superfluous. There is a fascinating little book by a seventeenth-century defense counsel, Bouritsius, showing how lawyers could (especially through appeals to higher courts) render valuable assistance to their clients. Occasionally, efforts of counsel could save defendants from torment in proceedings in which judicial torture was permitted. See J. Bouritsius, *Captivus seu Euchiridion Defensionum* (Lipsiae, 1685).

make a different disposition now more desirable. Still, even the most energetic activist governments discover at some point that some stability and repose is needed. Impatient dreams about incessant adaptation and constant change must be disciplined to cover the ground of the possible. Grudgingly, limited concessions to stability are made, and in their wake, some degree of decisional rigidity— a form of res judicata—emerges.

The history of Soviet justice is a good illustration. For a long period after the revolution, both civil and criminal judgments were amenable to revision without fixed time limits, not only if their factual basis was faulty, but also if they were based on an incorrect application of the law. To set obstacles to the correction of court decisions—even after they have taken "legal effect"—implied bourgeois formalism.[61] Why should a dangerous criminal, for example, profit from an unjustified acquittal only because his liability to punishment was not established at a particular moment? The power to demand revision of judgments that were "final" only in a very weak sense[62] was vested in powerful officials, whom ordinary citizens could only supplicate to launch "supervisory" proceedings.[63] Starting in the 1960s, however, several constraints on the easy revision of "final" decisions were introduced, most notably in the very sensitive area of changing criminal judgments to the detriment of former defendants.[64] Yet the stress on flexible correction of decisions remains clearly visible to the present day; compared to "classical" Continental jurisdictions, such as France, Italy or West Germany, the Soviet move toward stability is modest and even somewhat ethereal.[65]

61. See *Juridicheskii Slovar*, 2d ed., vol. 1, 605 (Moscow, 1956). Hostility to legal formalism, so characteristic of revolutionary periods, was given special pungency in the Soviet Union by reason of the official embrace of Marxism as the regnant theory of society. Insofar as it concerned the law, Marxism contained mainly critical reflections about the legal system, with special barbs reserved for the "formal equality" of bourgeois justice. As Soviet authorities turned to the task of thinking constructively in their own legal system, Marxist critical reflections, while regularly invoked, proved actually to be of little use, perhaps even somewhat distracting.

62. Judgments were "final" only in the sense that private individuals (as opposed to officials) could no longer attack them with available legal remedies and these judgments could now take legal effect.

63. Actual revision was entrusted to high judicial authority that could also initiate "supervisory" review on its own. In fact, high Soviet courts frequently hunt for mistakes in lower courts' decisions on their own initiative. See W. E. Butler, *Soviet Law* 320 (1983), as well as authorities cited therein.

64. The revision of criminal judgments to the detriment of defendants (including those acquitted) is still possible without any time limit on the ground of newly discovered evidence or of *factual* error committed in favor of the defendant. However, correction of *legal* mistakes committed in favor of former defendants is now possible only within a short time limit following the exhaustion of ordinary legal remedies—that is, those remedies that postpone the execution of judgments. See *RSFSR Code of Crim. Proc.* arts. 379, 383.

65. See *infra*, ch. 6, n. 24. Communist China is also comparatively unconcerned about the stability of decisions. During Mao's epoch, the penal process became completely open-ended. See W. C. Jones, "A Possible Model for the Criminal Trial in the P.R. China," 24 *Am. J. Comp. L.* 229, 240 (1976). Not surprisingly, the criminal process of Continental absolutist states also permitted correction of judgments in all matters important to the government, without fixed time limits. See A. Bauer, *supra*, n. 41, 355.

The readiness of an activist state to correct substantively faulty judgments is coupled with a great reluctance to disturb substantively accurate decisions, even if obtained through violation of procedural regulation. In describing the activist government's preference for flexible procedural instructions, I have already touched on this feature of the policy-implementing process. In technical legal jargon, the tendency prevails in activist justice to treat procedural error as "prejudicial" only insofar as such error casts doubt on the propriety of the decision on the merits; procedural error requiring automatic reversal is extremely limited, and the legitimacy of the concept itself hangs by a slender thread.[66] If official misconduct can be discouraged without reversing the right decision, this is the course of action that seems appropriate to activist government. It is immediately obvious, however, that a hierarchically organized machinery of justice can generate more mechanisms that permit deterrence without reversal than can coordinate officialdom. Consider only denials of promotion and similar disciplinary punishments, all readily available to a hierarchical organization. A coordinate activist official is thus somewhat more likely to deny recognition to a substantively accurate decision by parallel authority if the decision is rooted in a violation of procedural standards. Rendering useless the product of one's peer's efforts may be the only effective means to assure regularity of official action in the coordinate apparatus of justice.

66. This attitude bears on the problem of evidence obtained in violation of procedural law: such evidence should be rejected only if it appears unreliable. The idea that evidence improperly obtained should never be used (even if it is cogent) carries little weight in the policy-implementing process. Characteristically, Soviet commentators tend to justify rejection of illegally obtained evidence only by claims that it is unreliable; the problem of *reliable* but illegally obtained evidence receives scarcely any attention. A typical example of the failure to come to grips with this sensitive problem is J. N. Smirnov, ed., *Nauchnoprakticheskii Komentarii Ugolovnogo-Protssessualnogo Kodeksa RSFSR* 100, 107 (Moscow, 1970). Small wonder: the justice system is more easily persuaded to reject evidence secured in violation of standards of official decency if this evidence can also be made to appear necessarily unreliable.

VI   Authority and Types of Justice

Now that two distinct types of proceedings have been derived from the objectives of justice in the reactive and the activist state, I shall reintroduce into this discussion themes developed in the first two chapters, where I examined some marks that hierarchical and coordinate authority leave on the legal process. Hierarchical officialdom has been associated with such procedural features as the succession of methodical stages, reliance on documentation, the tendency toward official exclusivity, and many other characteristics. Coordinate officialdom has been related to features such as temporal compression of proceedings, preference for oral testimony, readiness to delegate procedural action to nonauthoritative persons, and the like. In portraying the conflict-solving and the policy-implementing processes, I have alluded to transformations that these processes are likely to undergo in the differing settings of authority. The time has come to address this subject in systematic fashion. In short, the time has come to examine the ways in which procedural features attributable to different goals of justice interact with features rooted in the character of officialdom.

When the two types of procedure are conjoined with the two types of authority, the resulting combinations fall into the four boxes of the following two-by-two table:

	Policy-implementing	*Conflict-solving*
Hierarchical authority		
Coordinate authority		

This table provides a framework within which to examine the legal process as it is implicated in political ideology and as it is influenced by attitudes toward authority. In each box I shall first explore in an abstract way the interaction of features related to authority and features related to purposes of justice, and then

181

turn to examples of actual proceedings that fall into that particular taxonomic niche. But before this inquiry begins, two reservations are in order.

It is easily foreseen that the same procedural arrangement may sometimes be related both to an ideal of officialdom and to a particular conception of the objectives of justice. For example, in chapter 4 the dominant role of the parties in proof taking was found to suit the position of litigants in the conflict-solving process. But earlier, in chapter 2, it was observed that such dominance naturally follows from coordinate officials' propensity to delegate trial preparation to interested outsiders. Where such double attribution is possible, it will suffice to have offered two mutually reinforcing explanations for a particular procedural form, and I shall refrain from speculating as to which is the more fundamental, and therefore arguably independent, variable. I shall equally resist the temptation to conjecture whether the double attribution denotes an ideal match between the objectives of justice and the organization of the official apparatus.

Conversely, it must also be foreseen that, when combined, the two sets of models will sometimes lead to procedural arrangements with an inherent potential for strife and tension. For example, some arrangements typical of coordinate structures, where officials can block implementation of one another's decisions, can clearly be at odds with forms favored by the policy-implementing process in which deadlocks are undesirable. Confronted with this mix of arrangements, it will suffice that the double perspective has revealed a tension that arises when the justice machinery of a particular structure is used for particular purposes. However, the existence of such internal tensions is not necessarily perceived as undesirable; enemies of bureaucratic centralization can argue, for example, that where coordinate features of a judicial apparatus impede the efficiency of policy implementation, they also impede easy victories of a hurried government.[1] To talk seriously about mismatches of the structure of authority and function of justice is to enter into an ancient and controversial arena of political theory, whose complexity leads far beyond the limits of this book.

i. THE POLICY-IMPLEMENTING PROCESS OF HIERARCHICAL OFFICIALDOM

As defined in chapter 5, at its core the policy-implementing process is an officially controlled inquiry. How is this mode of proceeding adapted to the structure and work habits of hierarchical authority? The most obvious impact on the form of proceedings of this type of authority is that the "activist" inquiry is divided into stages according to the different ranks of officials in charge, and where officials of the same rank are functionally specialized, proceedings are also subdivided into stages according to specialized subtasks.

Observe that in this type of process there is no day-in-court trial as a culminating procedural event—at least not in the sense that the material for the decision is fully presented to the adjudicator as a whole, in one continuous block

---

1. See *infra*, Introduction, n. 19 and accompanying text.

of time and in a form unmediated by prior official action. Rather, the initial decision is made on the basis of material officially assembled over time and then regularly reviewed by higher authority, so that the initial decision is denied the significance it would possess if it were presumptively final. As befits the policy-implementing process, even decisions by the highest authority can be altered in light of subsequent knowledge; but pressures toward orderliness and certainty, treasured by bureaucratic hierarchies, limit the easy reopening of cases in which the highest echelon has spoken. Each discrete procedural stage and episode is integrated into a meaningful whole by documentation in the file of the case. The file thus serves as the repository of information gradually assembled and decisions made en route; it is the spinal cord of the entire proceeding.

When the policy-implementing process is related to the hierarchical apparatus of authority, several variants can be distinguished. The simplest variant knows no specialization in the lowest echelon of authority; officials promiscuously perform analytically separable functions—they investigate, and they render decisions. But in contrast to coordinate all-purpose officials, they are not "autocrats" with broad discretionary powers: locked in chains of subordination, they exercise delegated authority. Ideally, their action is narrowly circumscribed by unconditional standards, and their decisions are subject to regular superior checks.

A historical example of this simple variant is the proceedings before the "investigating judge" in less serious criminal cases during the ancien régime on the Continent. While this judge-investigator was empowered both to gather evidence of crime and to make the original decision, he was expected to be guided by rules even in evaluating the evidence, and he was obliged to facilitate review by superior judicial authority; to prevent the defendant from taking an appeal was in certain cases a serious offense. Nor were appeals the only constraint on such generalist first-instance officials. A further constraint came from the propensity of bureaucratic organizations, especially those composed in tall pyramids, to create official units—panels of low-level officials—in order to permit mutual supervision in implementing centrally imposed policy. *Juge unique juge inique* is an old French adage expressing this idea, a view quite alien to coordinate structures. That some Continental constitutions still enshrine the "guarantee" of collective decision making at the *trial* level remains surprising to many a common lawyer.

As was pointed out in chapter 5, the fusion of functions in the person of the investigating judge is conventionally viewed as a distinguishing feature of the "pure" inquisitorial process. In the present analytical scheme, however, this fusion of functions is less than an ideal or full-fledged form of hierarchical policy implementation. A *division* of labor among officials on the first rung of the hierarchical ladder is closer to the ideal. One possibility for dividing the labor is to charge one official (or panel) with collecting information and another official (or panel) with rendering decisions. Again, the Continental criminal procedure of the ancien régime provides a good illustration: in serious cases the investigating judge was limited to conducting a documented inquiry. Once the inquiry was completed, the file containing all the documents was then transmitted to the primary decision maker.[2]

Another possibility, already mentioned, is to introduce into the proceedings an official who specializes in bringing cases before the decision maker and moving them through the successive stages of the legal process. As observed before, in an activist state this official is regarded as a watchdog of state policy, engaged in the collaborative effort of state officialdom to discover and to implement the correct decision; he does not appear as a party on the same plane parallel with a citizen implicated in the legal process.[3] This "activist" reading of the situation is reinforced when hierarchical authority directs the policy-implementing process. Consider the example of a state prosecutor who is part of a hierarchical organization. Where he is incorporated into a pyramid of state authority, he clearly cannot be fitted with shoes of approximately the same size as those worn by the defendant: even the lowest prosecutor is linked to the center of state power. To place him, as a party, in a position parallel to that occupied by the criminal defendant would violate the hierarchical sense of proper order. It is equally obvious that notions of negotiation and bargaining between the state prosecutor and the defendant are out of place. Where an official close to the center of government begins to negotiate state interests with a private individual, in the perspective of hierarchical authority this practice approximates an abdication of state sovereignty. Indeed, as was claimed by Jean Bodin, one of the sixteenth-century founders of this concept, it is of the very essence of sovereign government that it has no equals with whom to negotiate.[4] *Justice n'est pas ployable.* Even if the state prosecutor were somehow imagined to be a party, the adjudicator's impartiality would not be credible in a hierarchical system of justice; his legitimacy as neutral resolver of the dispute between the parties is undercut by his association—as a professional civil servant—with the same authority that prosecutes the case: two against one. In conclusion, then, the division of labor between the court and a specialized official promoter introduces no conflict-solving forms into the hierarchical activist legal process. On the contrary, hierarchical authority, with its penchant for specialization, regards the division of tasks as a policy-implementing arrangement superior to the generalist version, which concentrates procedural control in the hands of officials who take charge of the case in the first instance.

Still another division of labor can be envisaged; as in the case of the promoter of the faith and the devil's advocate in the canonization proceedings of the Catholic church, two officials can be appointed to argue contrary points to the decision maker. But as was shown in chapter 5, the official contest is a mere surface ritual. That this ritual detracts from an ideal arrangement is again more

---

2. There were minor technical differences in implementing this idea, especially as between German lands and France. See M. Damaška, *supra*, ch. 2, n. 10.

3. See *supra*, ch. 5, n. 14.

4. On Bodin's views concerning the "true marks of sovereignty," see J. Bodin, *De Republica Libri Sex*, Liber I, Caput 10 (London, 1586). The relevant passages are translated in J. Bodin, *The Six Books of a Commonwealth*, Book 1, ch. 10 (London, 1606).

clearly visible with hierarchically organized procedural authority. Here, institutional controversy is treated as disruptive and aspirations strongly tend toward objective nonpartisan attitudes. Just as the Continental prosecutor must file an appeal *in favor* of the defendant if he thinks the attainment of the right result so requires,[5] so players of contrary official roles readily abandon the superficial ritual and jointly seek optimal solutions.

The interweaving of hierarchical authority and policy-implementing justice leads to great reluctance to delegate *autonomous* procedural action to private individuals. While bureaucracies tend to monopolize procedural control, radically activist states are reluctant to let voices competing with the government speak. The result of this synergetic effect of state function and state structure is that private enforcement of state policy is far from an ideal arrangement in the classificatory box now under consideration. I shall soon show how different the situation is in the ambience of activist coordinate officialdom, particularly in the early phases of the transition from an uninvolved to an interventionist government.

The combining of hierarchical organization with policy-implementing justice is in many other respects quite successful. Where the activist state strives toward utilitarian goals, this is scarcely surprising: hierarchical resolve and bureaucratic efficiency offer formidable instruments for the realization of state programs. Once higher authority has formulated a policy, the consistent application of that policy is relatively sure; impasses can be resolved relatively quickly and cleanly. But just as no marriages are truly made in heaven, this one is also not without its share of strife. As a prelude to the study of existing systems, two areas of potential tension and stress deserve particular attention.

It will be remembered that a hierarchical organization can espouse two different kinds of standards for making decisions: one possibility is posited goals, by which officials assess the consequences of alternative decisions; the other is normative standards for the guidance of officials. Because of the historical importance of the second variant, I have focused attention here on legalistic hierarchies. But let us now see what happens to this legalistic orientation in a state that begins to fulfill its activist potential: the tension increases between activist government's preference for instrumental decision making on the one hand and the judicial apparatus's attachment to unconditional standards on the other. It is true that these two dispositions can be balanced and somehow accommodated, so long as the propulsive programs of the state are not pressed with utmost seriousness. But as extremes of truly managerial government are approached, a gradual transformation of the hierarchical apparatus from its legalistic to its technocratic variant should be expected. A state that proposes to turn society into a giant corporation—at once to promote social welfare, cultural enrichment, environmental protection, and much else—must value efficient managers more highly than manipulators of normative programs.

5. For the prosecutor's "nonpartisan" right to take an appeal in favor of the defendant, see, e.g., *West German Code of Criminal Procedure*, §296, II. The tendencies of classic bureaucracies to avoid controversy are discussed in H. Jacoby, *The Bureaucratization of the World*, 154 (1973).

The other kind of friction arises from divergent attitudes to the participation of citizens in legal proceedings. It has been seen that a pronounced activist state dislikes autonomous associations and spontaneous social action, but nevertheless strives to involve citizens in its programs and align them with its policies. As a result, an activist process favors citizen participation in various accessory rituals—mainly as a chorus favorably inclined to and reinforcing governmental policy. But what about the attitude of hierarchically organized bureaucrats toward this citizen participation? They are likely to look askance even at such ceremonial and innocuous roles, regarding them as dilettante meddling, disruptive of orderly and efficient performance of technical tasks. In short, while activist orientation would draw the public in, hierarchical structures would keep them out. The resulting tension can surface even with issues of minor importance.

At this point, it is worth pausing for a moment to consider the relation of hierarchical policy-implementing arrangements to categories of conventional theory. In discussing the policy-implementing process apart from any particular structure of authority, I have repeatedly stated that in some of its aspects it resembles prevailing portrayals of inquisitorial procedure. This resemblance to traditional inquisitorial form has now been increased by the introduction of features associated with hierarchical authority, such as the role of the dossier or the impact of regular appellate review. Among the prominent differences between traditional inquisitorial process and the policy-implementing process before hierarchical officialdom are the greater stress, in our model, on broader aspects of the case, the open-endedness of state intervention, as well as on the educational role of the legal process. Both the proximity to conventional thinking and departures from it will be explicated as I take a fresh look at real-world systems that arguably fit into my first classificatory unit. In doing so, I shall first survey systems that are more removed from ideal forms and conclude by examining those that approximate such forms more closely. I shall begin with Continental criminal procedure of the ancien régime—a procedure long believed to epitomize the "pure" inquisitorial type of legal process.

Systems of Criminal Justice

ANCIEN RÉGIME.   It is instructive to examine the genesis of what is regarded as the characteristically Continental style of processing criminal cases. As in the case of my synopsis of the rebirth of bureaucracy, I must again begin in the twilight of the Middle Ages. The function of the weak central government was, in the main, the prevention of clan warfare. Barely differentiated from civil wrong, crime was primarily treated as a matter between the miscreant and the victim, or between their respective clans. The legal process was aimed at absorbing conflicts by substituting forensic simulation for actual fighting. A form of adversarial proceedings prevailed in what would nowadays be classified as both civil and criminal matters. As the Continental hierarchical bureaucratic apparatus of justice began to develop—pioneered in the late eleventh century by the Church of Rome—the image of the legal process as a contest of two adversaries before the court (a triadic relation) thus appeared quite normal. This disposition was reinforced by some texts of Roman antiquity, then venerated as part of the "rediscovered" codification of the Byzantine emperor Justinian.

The relentlessly expanding and more powerful central authorities, especially those of the church, soon began to covet powers much wider than those of conflict resolution: the ambit of governmental action expanded. In this new environment, crime ceased to be regarded as primarily a matter of concern to the victim and the miscreant; it was now seen as involved in what Aquinas was later to call *communitas politica*. To use a contemporary phrase, criminal "excesses" were now expected to be "corrected" even in the absence of a complaining victim or of a dispute to engage the forum. As a result of these changing ideas on both the agenda of government and the nature of crime, a spin-off occurred from the essentially conflict-absorbing justice of early medieval times; an officially controlled and propelled procedure of inquiry (*processus per inquisitionem*) emerged. Even if nobody came forward as an accuser, the judge was now obliged to begin a unilateral search for the truth about the possible incidence of a crime. Toward this end he was empowered to examine witnesses and to gather other types of evidence, either personally or through officials appointed by him. The suspect's interrogation became the centerpiece of this new procedural form ("he knows best whether he did it, and if he did, what were his intentions"), and the suspect's confession the most precious mode of proof (*regina probationum*). This orientation was almost natural in the innovative legal process of the church, where ordinary judges (bishops) were at the same time father-confessors, accustomed to interrogations and confessions in the "tribunal of conscience." But because the new procedure of inquiry was independent of a dispute between an accuser and a defendant, the confession was treated merely as a precious datum—not as a "dispositive" declaration of one contestant resolving the dispute and thus also dispensing with the reason for continuing the criminal case. The prominence of files on officially performed activities and pervasive appellate review make this new form easily classifiable as a policy-implementing process before hierarchical authority.

The new type of proceeding could consist of a "bipolar" relation between the judge and the defendant, but it could also be an engagement of three persons—the judge, the defendant, and an official promoting the larger interest in suppression of crime before the court.[6] It would be anachronistic to imagine that contemporaries viewed the official promoter and the defendant as adverse parties battling each other before a passive umpire of their disputation: the promoter was instead seen as an official assistant to the judge.

This ecclesiastical procedure was soon taken up with enthusiasm by secular Continental rulers, so that it continually gained ground at the expense of the old adversarial form of criminal prosecution. The office of promoter, variously la-

---

6. See *supra*, ch. 1, n. 17 and accompanying text.

beled in different countries, was also received into secular systems and organized into a hierarchical institution whose responsibility frequently exceeded the bounds of criminal law enforcement. French royal *procureurs* and *avocats*, for example, acquired important powers in civil cases affected by larger interests, and in absolutist Prussia, the royal *Fiskalat* was expected to be a general "guardian" of the ruler's regulations—his *Auge und Ohr* (eye and ear). Because the latter institution, by way of Sweden, came to czarist Russia and was later adapted to the needs of the Soviet government, it is a historian's *bonne bouche* that the mighty Soviet *Prokurator* has a relatively embarrassing pedigree going back to the *promotor fidei* of the Roman Catholic church.[7]

It is important to emphasize, however, that even in its most extreme variants—such as the special proceedings of the Holy Inquisition—the historical inquisitorial process always retained some features and much terminology of the conflict-solving mode of proceeding. Thus, for example, some issues were termed "defensive," although there was often no other party with whom the criminal defendant could share the raising of issues or the burden of proving them; the official investigator was actually duty-bound to build a single "case" by probing on his own, irrespective of the defendant's allegations.[8] More interestingly, the inquisitorial process, although in practice dominant, was regarded as an anomaly or an aberration from regular forms. In its infancy, it required protection by extensive justification, even apologies: as a departure from revered tradition, it was to be used only exceptionally—a necessary evil if the war against crime were to be successfully fought (*ne crimina maneat impunita*).[9] Even later, and until the downfall of the old order, the ancient "accusatorial" process remained to many the theoretical ideal of criminal justice. Scholarly discussion of the inquisitorial procedure was regularly interspersed with ceremonial genuflection before an alternative design of criminal prosecution that always required a complainant, and readily evoked the idea of a dispute.[10] As the apparatus of justice grew increasingly bureaucratic, medieval popular participation was swept away, so that only sporadically were some of its vestiges in evidence. Although educational impulses would surface in the ecclesiastical administration of justice, at-

---

7. For details on how the *promotor* of canon law procedure was adopted in France and elsewhere, see Lefebre, *supra*, ch. 1, n. 17. The Prussian *Fiskalat* is discussed in E. Schmidt, *Einführung in die Geschichte der deutschen Strafrechtspflege*, 3d ed., 180 (Göttingen, 1965). On the circuitous transplantation route of Prussian "guardians of legality" to Sweden, czarist Russia, and eventually the Soviet Union, see M. Kovalevsky, *Russian Political Institutions* (1902); J. Hazard, *Settling Disputes in Soviet Society*, 217–43 (1960).

8. For vestiges of "accusatorial" forms, see B. Carpzov, *Practica nova Imperialis Saxonica rerum criminalium*, Pars III, Quest. 115 (Frankfurt, 1678).

9. Primary sources on initial apologies for the new process of inquiry are collected in F. A. Biener, *Beitrage zur Geschichte des Inquisitionsprozesses*, 45–46 (Leipzig, 1827). Initially, capital punishment could not be pronounced in the new procedural form.

10. In the seventeenth century, Carpzov still treated the *processus per accusationem* as superior to the inquisitorial form. See Carpzov, *supra*, n. 8, Qu. 106. Echoes of this position can be detected even in the eighteenth century, as evidenced by sources cited in Homberk zu Vack, *supra*, ch. 5, n. 17.

tempts to use the secular legal process for the purpose of transforming people were few and far between.[11]

If it takes a radically interventionist government to generate pure policy-implementing forms, then such deviations of historical inquisitorial systems from the model of hierarchical policy-implementing process can readily be understood. In the period of the dominance of the *processus per inquisitionem*, the character of Continental government was far from managerial excess. Well into the sixteenth century, European rulers were imagined primarily as judges or conflict resolvers: that the sovereign power is regulatory or legislative is a comparatively modern idea.[12] So too is the notion of a government whose mission is to manage people. It is true that some popes early made claims to all-encompassing powers of governance, but they were never able to unite *spiritualia* and *temporalia* under their singular authority.[13] Their successors, the absolutist secular rulers, would sometimes display tutorial and managerial urges, but even the most radical among them never attempted a comprehensive transformation of society. To find a political landscape capable of supporting a decisive break with justice conceived of as conflict-resolution, one must seek much more activist government than that of European absolutist princes. It is not surprising that theorists who have tried to construct a type of proceeding by abstraction from the actual criminal law enforcement systems of the old order have always been unable to describe an extreme or "pure" inquisitorial procedure.

Before examining forms of justice in truly interventionist states, I shall review developments in Continental criminal process after the upheavals caused in large part by the widening ripples of the French Revolution.

THE POSTREVOLUTIONARY AMALGAM. I have already touched on postrevolutionary reforms of the Continental administration of justice, focusing upon attempts—more successful in proclamation than actual practice—to relax the inherited bureaucratic centralization of judicial institutions. I shall focus now on postrevolutionary efforts to inject more conflict-solving forms into the inherited Continental procedure of inquiry. Therefore I shall say little here about those characteristics of reformed procedure traceable to the continuing dominance of hierarchical authority: the methodical succession of stages culminating in appeals, the crucial role of the file, weak forms of lay participation in decision making, and many similar features remain on the periphery of the present discussion.

---

11. The secular arm was unfavorably inclined toward *poenae medicinales* (medical penalties) of ecclesiastical criminal law. Yet, traces of an educational and tutorial conception of criminal justice radiating from the church were not altogether absent, even from prosecutions for witchcraft (*crimen magiae*). For an interesting fourteenth-century example, see Bartolus de Sassoferrato, in J. Hansen, *Quellen und Untersuchungen zur Geschichte des Hexenwahns*, 64–66 (Bonn, 1901).

12. See Q. Skinner, *The Foundations of Modern Political Thought*, vol. 2, 289 (1978).

13. For a cursory review of papal aspirations to *plenitudo potestatis*, see M. Oakeshott, *On Human Conduct*, 220–22 (1975). See also *supra*, ch. 5, n. 9. Harold Berman has recently shown how crucial was the late eleventh-century split between ecclesiastical and secular orders for both the specifically Western polity and the law as a whole. This split is the permeating theme of Berman's *Law and Revolution* (1983).

Efforts to weave more conflict-solving patterns into the fabric of Continental criminal procedure were inspired by the tenets of liberal ideology. I have noted that this ideology developed the image of the criminal process as a contest between the accused and the state held before adjudicators independent of the executive branch of government. In an environment accustomed to centralized judicial and prosecutorial bureaucracies dominating the administration of criminal justice, the applicability of this image seemed too limited to be taken literally. Not even liberal reformers thought that any stage of the criminal process should be linked to the existence of an actual disagreement between the prosecution and the defense. That the purpose of criminal prosecution is to apply state policy toward crime independent of the defendant's attitude toward the charges was a deeply ingrained intellectual habit.[14] What seemed attractive to liberal reformers, however, was to structure criminal proceedings, whenever feasible, *as if* there were a clash of opinions between the state prosecutor and the defendant. Contest forms, or *simulation* of a dispute, seemed to indicate at least some recognition that the interest of an individual can legitimately be opposed to the interest of the state: no small achievement in the liberal view. The offshoot of this train of thought was to advocate an amalgam of policy-implementing and conflict-solving forms in criminal cases: the strength of one's liberalism was measured by the degree to which conflict-solving arrangements were thought capable of expansion at the expense of those related to the policy-implementing purpose of proceedings.

Sooner or later, liberal reforms were inaugurated in all Continental countries. In assessing the flavor of the resulting amalgam, however, it is crucial to distinguish between the aspirations of reform legislation and the reality—by no means an easy task. It is bedeviled by the natural inclination of many Continental commentators—committed agents of change in their domestic systems—to exaggerate the extent to which their liberal aspirations have become reality. Perhaps they hope that an Heisenbergian effect will occur, so that the observer will induce a desired change in the observed. Fortunately, the broader comparative perspective helps identify such exaggerated claims.

First, then, what of aspirations? The amalgam of contest and inquest forms was conceived as follows. The old investigation, preceding the decision-making stage, was to be retained because a basically unilateral gathering of evidence was thought necessary to elucidate the truth. But the importance of this initial stage was to be downplayed, and at least some contest forms were to be introduced into it. The role of the investigation was to be reduced by no longer insisting that the investigator gather all the material needed for the decision: his inquiry was to be recast as a mere vehicle for orientation, on the basis of which the state prosecutor would decide whether formally to accuse a citizen of crime. Thereafter, the full

14. This habit continues to prevail, although in a few countries, under the influence of American sociology, a small number of academics now argue that conflict solving is the objective of *all* adjudication. For more recent thinking on the goals of criminal process in the influential German literature, see P. Riess, "Gesamtreform des Strafverfahrensrechts," in *Festschrift für Karl Schafer,* 168–72 (Berlin and New York, 1980).

factual basis for the decision would be ascertained in stages more richly laced with contest forms. Which forms should be allowed in the initial phases? For example, the investigator could decide to examine a witness in the presence of both the defendant and the state prosecutor, provided that a more secretive examination were not mandated by the interest in finding out the truth. Defense counsel was to be admitted from the early stages of the investigation and familiarized, whenever feasible, with the progress of fact-finding; investigative findings could then be challenged and counterarguments presented.

With the investigation complete, the documented file would be transmitted to the state prosecutor for decision as to whether or not the process should continue. If in the affirmative, the prosecutor would file a formal charge with the criminal court, just as a civil plaintiff would lodge a complaint. The factual parameters of the charge would present a limit on subsequent fact-finding. Although proceedings were to culminate in a public trial patterned upon the image of contest, a rigorous contest structure was never even contemplated. For example, although the accused could be asked at the very outset to state his "attitude" toward prosecutorial allegations, even if he failed to contest them and fully confessed—so that there was no contest between him and the state—the judge still would be required to go on with guilt determination. Moreover, issues at trial were not to be separated into a "case" for the prosecution and a "case" for the defense. Instead, the court was to build a single integrated case through unilateral action, limited only by the parameters of the charge. While it was never lost on the reformers that the division of issues into two cases—even if rigorously implemented—permits the state prosecutor to represent larger interests, the reformers regarded it as unacceptable to accord the accused a parallel position and thus a corresponding control over "defensive" issues. Whether all necessary preconditions existed for the criminal sanction was thought to be a decision for the court, not the defendant.

Accordingly, the trial was only meekly to simulate a contest: there were to be opening and closing statements by the prosecution and the defense, and after the presiding judge completed the interrogation of witnesses, prosecution and defense could address questions to them in turn. To mute the significance of the pretrial stages, the reach of the documentary file was shortened: the original decisions were to be based solely on evidence examined directly in court. In contrast to prior law, the court could no longer refuse to decide the case until it was "more amply informed." If the judgment favored the defendant, its reconsideration was to be limited by comparison with the prerevolutionary process.[15] This, in a nutshell, was the prevailing theory of the amalgam.

In reality, however, and although now ideologically in a sort of demi-

15. Nevertheless, in all Continental systems the prosecutor can appeal the judgment of acquittal rendered by the trial court; the original "jeopardy" simply continues. Moreover, in most countries even a *final* judgment can be reversed if the finally acquitted defendant subsequently confesses the crime. It would thus be unwise for a criminal to publish a book depicting the crime of which he was acquitted or to promise the acquitting court that he will not do it again—all practices far from unknown in Anglo-American systems.

monde, inquest forms fared better than liberal reformers contemplated. To begin with, pretrial investigation remained exhaustive, at least in cases of serious crime, and investigators typically found the defendant's presence at witness interrogations or other evidentiary activity potentially dangerous to the elucidation of truth, so that this presence was usually denied. Beyond this, if occasional legislation made the defendant's presence during some investigative activities mandatory, crucial detective work tended to be shifted from traditional investigative judges to police officers, to whose inquiry the defendant's right to participate did not apply. Readers of Simenon's or, more recently, of San Antonio's detective stories are familiar with the ensuing dilatory games, in a low visibility area of police inquiries, between the *inspecteur* and the judge in charge of "formal" investigation. To put an end to these wasteful games, some Continental countries—West Germany, for example—have now abolished the office of the investigating judge.

At trial, information from the investigation continued to exert a strong influence on decision making, notwithstanding protests of academic commentators. There were many reasons for this, but the most widespread was the requirement that the presiding judge prepare himself for proof taking by meticulously studying the file. In the end, preliminary investigation remained the crucial procedural phase of the entire process. To a great extent, the trial became a review of work already done with its original inquiry limited to search for the most appropriate sentence.[16]

To emphasize the gap between aspiration and reality is not to deny that the postrevolutionary reforms moved Continental criminal justice much further away from pure policy-implementing forms than was the case with the criminal process of the ancien régime. Nor could it have been different, in view of changing conceptions of the relation between the individual and the state in light of liberal tenets. Yet if the final flavor of the Continental amalgam is to be evaluated properly, the discrepancy between aspiration and reality assumes a decisive significance.

Continental commentators often claim that the postrevolutionary "mixture" should be located somewhere midway between inquest and contest forms, or at a midpoint between policy-implementing and conflict-solving justice. If this claim were justified, the Continental amalgam would pose serious taxonomic problems; its inclusion into the first classificatory box would be questionable. But regardless of how matters appear in the parochial Continental perspective— to the eye examining itself—a broader comparative vision reveals a different picture. Especially revealing is the vantage of Anglo-American observers, in whose system trials are more genuinely independent of earlier proceedings and more rigorously patterned on the contest idea. Symptomatically, these observers find Continental trials similar to procedures for reviewing results of work done at predominantly inquisitorial stages of criminal prosecution. From their stand-

16. For a rare realistic appraisal of actual practice, see J. Stepan, "Possible Lessons from Continental Criminal Procedure," in S. Hottenberg, ed., *The Economics of Crime and Punishment*, 181, 187 (Washington, 1973).

point, then, even those Continental systems incorporating the largest number of contest forms fit squarely within the "nonadversarial" or policy-implementing engagements.

There is some disagreement among comparativists on whether Continental countries use devices that can meaningfully be associated with bargaining between procedural parties, the process so intimately linked to the conflict-solving style. Much of this disagreement is due to the conflation of unilateral official concessions to the cooperating defendant with explicit bargaining between the prosecution and the defense concerning the exchange of benefits. The first practice is as ubiquitous as the ordinary impulse to accept the norms of reciprocity or to return a favor. Such practices are not offensive to the policy-implementing process, or violative of the hierarchical sense of propriety. They are widespread in all Continental systems of criminal justice. A prominent illustration is sentencing concessions, often routinely accorded to confessing defendants. In contrast, explicit negotiations between the prosecution and the defense leading to deals or bargains are alien to Continental legal sensibilities. There is, of course, no room for charging and sentencing concessions in exchange for the defendant's waiver of trial, because all offenses of some gravity must be processed at trial, regardless of the will of the procedural parties. More important, to grant the defendant a standing to negotiate with state officials over charges or the sentence to be imposed, as well as to allow the court to sanction such deals, is truly offensive to Continental ideas on the proper administration of criminal justice. Only for minor crimes, and in response to the overcrowding of dockets, have some Western European countries recently developed summary procedures that resemble bargained guilty pleas. Most of these procedures, however, involve nonnegotiable prosecutorial offers that the defendant pay a determined fine or face the possibility of a more serious sentence if he chooses to go to trial. The very nonnegotiability of the offer bespeaks the uneasiness with which Continentals approach consensual party transactions in criminal prosecutions: if, for the sake of saving resources, the prosecuting official is sometimes forced to offer bargains to the defendant, the image of a store with fixed prices is much less repugnant than the haggling reminiscent of an Oriental bazaar. In the sphere of petty offenses, a few Continental jurisdictions go even further and allow devices which necessitate negotiations between the prosecution and the defense: if the defendant promises to take certain actions, the prosecution is permitted to drop charges. [17] A few countries that have adopted such procedural devices to cope with the mass of petty crime (predominantly traffic offenses) have taken a significant

17. For a legislative example of such conditional dismissals of charges, see *West German Code of Criminal Procedure*, § 153(a). One must not project onto Europe American expectations that such powers of dismissal lead to a great deal of wheeling and dealing, in which the defendant holds chips of great significance to the authorities. It is sobering to note in this connection that conditional dismissal of charges is known even in the Soviet Union, limited, of course, to minor offenses involving offenders who display contrition. See *RSFSR Code of Crim. Proc.*, art. 51. On the West German example, an American scholar has shown how Continental systems can get along without extensive plea bargaining (J. Langbein, "Land without Plea Bargaining: How the Germans Do It," 78 *Mich. L. Rev.* 204 [1979]).

step away from conventional forms of Continental criminal justice: procedural forms may have gained a foothold on the Continent that are truly in the conflict-solving mode.

THE SOVIET MODEL. Because czarist Russia had adopted a variant of the hybrid procedure just described, it was normal for the architects of the Soviet criminal process to build upon Continental foundations. Elements of the contest style in the mixture lost their ideological support, however, and came under a cloud. The image of criminal process as a dispute between the state and the individual lay beyond any recognizable Marxian contours and contradicted the intensely activist nature of Soviet rule. The criminal process was to be made an effective instrument for the government to repress conduct dangerous to the state and to educate the masses.[18]

This orientation contributed to the strengthening of policy-implementing forms. Relatively meager testimonial privileges inherited from prerevolutionary days were not expanded but were instead curtailed. Family members, doctors, and priests could not refuse to testify against the defendant, as they can in most liberal Continental systems;[19] refusal or evasion of a duty to testify was viewed as a criminal offense rather than a minor infraction.[20] Because admission of counsel at an early stage was thought to increase unduly the opportunity for guilty defendants to obfuscate the truth, lawyers were excluded from preliminary investigations until after the investigator had completed his work and the cat was, presumably, out of the bag.[21] This exclusion was in sharp contrast with regulations supported by liberal Continental reformers to provide for counsel's contacts with the defendant as early as possible in the process. In consequence, the attenuation of the unilaterally probing character of prosecutions—an attenuation that accompanies counsel's participation in procedural activities—was postponed. In addition, the impact of such a streamlined inquiry was significantly enhanced by insistence that it be as thorough and exhaustive as possible. Investigators were required to explore every facet of the case and to persuade themselves of the defendant's guilt before concluding that a case deserved to go to trial.[22]

18. The image of criminal process as a contest with the state was diagnosed as originating *ex partibus infidelium*, from "bourgeois" ideology. See, e.g., T. Szabo, *The Unification and Differentiation in Socialist Criminal Justice*, 13 (Budapest, 1978). Nor was distrust of government—a potent source of procedural form in liberal thought—a consideration in devising Soviet forms of criminal justice: if the state is to transform society, it must be powerful and it must be trusted. Where a benevolent government is in power, it was felt, social ills may be less the consequence of oppressive governmental control than of oppressive lack of control; the party and citizenry should exercise whatever supervision against abuse is necessary. See M. A. Chelzov, ed., *Ugolovnyi Protsess*, 428–29 (Moscow, 1969).

19. However, as noted before, counsel was exempt from testifying against his client.

20. See *RSFSR Criminal Code*, art. 182.

21. See *RSFSR Code of Crim. Proc.*, arts. 199–207. Compare also *supra*, ch. 5, n. 58.

22. As previously noted, Continental systems are more reluctant than many common-law jurisdictions to take the defendant to trial on the basis of merely "orientative" investigations. Yet, on this point, Soviet process is much more demanding than traditional Continental mixed procedures: taking the defendant to trial on the mere "probable cause" that he committed a crime is branded by Soviet commentators as a "bourgeois" attitude. See, e.g., N. S. Alekseev and V. Z. Lukashevics, *Leninskie Idei v Sovetskom Ugolovnom Sudoproizvodstve*, 72 (Leningrad, 1970).

The strongest reason for the weakening of the contest admixtures in the design of Soviet pretrial stages was the increased stature and prestige of the office of state prosecutor (the Procuracy). No longer may the defendant's complaints against investigative action reach the court, as they can in non-Soviet Continental systems. Instead, these complaints must now be addressed to the procurator in his capacity as "guardian of legality."[23] He was made undisputed master of the pretrial process, supervising the work of investigators (his employees), and he, not the court, independently decided on such sensitive matters as the preliminary detention of the defendant. To view this towering official, linked to the very center of governmental power, as a mere "party" in dispute with the defendant made no sense at all. Rules devised by Continental liberal reformers to preclude the substantive use at trial of information obtained at earlier stages of the process—including police inquiries—were rejected as formalistic. As a result, the audit character of trials was strengthened, even in comparison with the conventional Continental amalgam. In harmony with the policy-implementing mode, even those judgments accorded legal effect could be revised if they were wrong on the merits; indeed, the grounds on which a "finally" decided case could be reopened became identical with grounds on which judgments not yet "final" could be appealed.[24] With relative ease, the stability of decisions could thus be traded off for accurate results mirroring the "objective truth."

It is instructive to look at these features of Soviet criminal prosecution through conventional Continental lenses: the investigative phases of the process seem orphaned of contest forms and too relentless in their probing; trials appear overly influenced by work done beforehand, too much of a foregone conclusion; the format seems too limited for effective action by defense counsel; stability of judgments seems too shaky and decisions too easily modified to the detriment of the defendant. In their totality, the features of the Soviet system outlined so far appear to Western European lawyers as a partial throwback to Continental inquisitorial procedure after the abolition of judicial torture but before liberals began to leaven it with elements of the contest style. Observe the subtle irony, however: such assessments reproduce almost exactly the impressions which common lawyers regularly express about the conventional Continental amalgam—impressions dismissed as caricatures by classical Continental lawyers, much as the similar impressions just registered are dismissed by officials in the Soviet judicial apparatus.

23. See *RSFSR Code of Crim. Proc.*, ch. 10. It must be realized that there is nothing sacrosanct to Soviets about court (as opposed to the Procuracy's) protection of the criminal defendant: the idea of the judiciary as an independent branch of government is rejected as a mystification of actual power relationships.

24. See *supra*, ch. 5, n. 64. Compare also *RSFSR Code of Crim. Proc.*, arts. 342, 379. It is true that in noncommunist Continental systems *ordinary* appellate remedies can be directed both against legal and factual errors, and that they operate both in favor and to the detriment of the defendant. But, after these remedies are exhausted, the stability of decisions is quite rigid: final judgments can never be reversed or altered on the ground of *legal* error favorable to the former defendant (such as a mistaken interpretation of a criminal statute beneficial to him); on factual grounds, final judgment can be changed to the detriment of a former defendant only in a very restrictive class of cases. See, e.g., *West German Code of Crim. Proc.* §362.

According to their desire to use justice to transform society, architects of the Soviet criminal procedure also broke new ground and produced features without precedent in the historical inquisitorial process. This it became the duty of the Soviet judge to attend to issues larger than a single instance of criminality. Where appropriate, the judge was expected to issue a special ruling, independent of the judgment as such and directed to the social situation giving rise to the crime. The ruling was to be dispatched to the group or institution believed responsible for the situation, with a request that it report back on the "corrective" measures taken.[25] The judge could also decide to hold court in the locale linked to the crime involved—the defendant's place of residence, for example— and use this occasion to try to influence both the defendant and the locality, setting them both on the path of righteousness. Another mechanism unknown to Continental inquisitorial systems was to accord individuals or groups various ancillary roles in criminal law enforcement with the purposes of aligning them with state policy and (where relevant) pressuring criminals to change their ways. At trial, so-called social accusers and defenders could be admitted to voice their opinions on the crime and the criminal.[26] It was assumed, of course, that such citizen participation was to be guided by "activists" loyal to the government; spontaneous action, possibly challenging to the government, was not welcomed.

These and similar arrangements elude legal categories developed by Continental procedural scholarship. Most particularly, they elude the categorization as "inquisitorial." They also seem to merge the criminal process much too easily into larger systems of administration and social control; defendants seem in *statu pupilari*, to excess, treated more like juvenile delinquents than fully grown persons. Expressed in terms of the categories I propose, these "novel" features are but exemplars of a policy-implementing style suited to a truly managerial government.

Not only is the mission of Soviet government more managerial, but the structure of its authority is in many respects more hierarchical than is the case with traditional Continental judicial organizations. Soviet high courts are authorized to exercise a more powerful leadership than their older counterparts in Western Europe—at least since the reforms instituted in the wake of the French Revolution. For example, these courts can issue binding instructions on how inferior courts should apply the law.[27] They review decisions of courts below

25. For example, an incidence of theft from a plant could lead to demands that supervision of workers leaving the factory be increased. See *RSFSR Code of Crim. Proc.*, art. 321.

26. On such accusers and defenders, see H. Berman, *Soviet Criminal Law and Procedure: The RSFSR Codes*, 95 (1966). Some mechanisms to mobilize the citizenry are extrajudicial; for example, the defendant can be released to the custody of various groups. Alternatively, if it involves a minor offense, his case can be transferred for disposition to so-called comrade's courts, which pressure miscreants to mend their ways. *RSFSR Code of Crim. Proc.*, art. 209. On such extrajudicial mechanisms, see L. Lipson, "Law: The Function of Extra-Judicial Mechanisms," in D. W. Treadgold, ed., *Soviet and Chinese Communism: Similarities and Differences*, 144–67 (1967).

27. See H. Berman, *supra*, n. 26, 104–05. The highest judicial body of czarist Russia exercised similar powers. Cf. I. J. Foinitskii, *Kurs Ugolovnago Sudoproizvodstva*, vol. 1, 181 (St. Petersburg, 1899). Current Soviet legal doctrine denies that these instructions, although binding, represent an

without appeal, on their own motion, and can take any case from subordinate courts and decide it themselves (the right of "devolution"). As a result, Soviet courts are more streamlined and integrated, a more efficient tool for the attainment of state policies than classical Continental courts. More than the latter, they resemble units of a bureaucratic institution. Of course, the greater unity of the Soviet machinery of justice is also related to the unifying role of the ever-present party as a monolithic instrument, the sole voice and executor of state programs. Even if invisible on formal organizational charts, this unifying influence is strong and should not be overlooked.[28]

In comparison with traditional Continental judicial organizations, what has been weakened in the Soviet apparatus of justice is the legalism of its officials, clashing with the instrumental approach to law demanded by its activist ideology. This clash was particularly prominent and intense in the early period of Soviet rule when inherited Continental logical legalism was repudiated as a hypocritically apolitical method. It was thought that procedural rules can be replaced by mere instructions, always to be disregarded if such deviation would advance the interests of the Soviet state or if "revolutionary consciousness" so required. Lately, however, legalism has been treated by Soviet authorities with less hostility and sometimes with a measure of ambivalence. In view of pronounced bureaucratic centralization, this change is easy to understand: hierarchical authority values consistency, and one way of achieving it is to insist on "strict observance of rules"—especially by officials in the lower echelons of authority. In the absence of scientific techniques to guide a search for optimal solutions through consequentialist schemes, it seems desirable to insist on punctilious observance of the normative programs adopted by higher authority.[29]

It may be that the apparatus so organized could conflict with the desire of the Soviet state to involve citizens in the administration of justice. As I have pointed out, while activist ideology wishes to draw citizens into the legal process,

---

instance of judicial norm creation: instructions, it is proclaimed, create no new law, but only direct how existing law should be applied. However, studying instances of such binding instructions, an outside observer has little difficulty finding that more often than not they contain matters that would be considered clear examples of interstitial legislation by the judiciary in other systems.

28. It is the party that also coordinates and integrates the judicial and various extrajudicial mechanisms of criminal law enforcement into a coherent whole. This is part of the "overall policy leadership" of the party over the administration of justice. See T. N. Dobrovolskaia, *Printsipi Sovetskogo Ugolovnogo Protsesa*, 87, 164–65, (Moscow, 1971). It is not widely known that the Soviets abolished a relatively independent form of lay participation in the administration of justice— the czarist criminal jury. Jurors were replaced by lay assessors who decide together with professional judges and are thus more easily controllable. Because these assessors are dominated by professionals, much too much is made of the fact that—in contrast to classical Continental jurisdictions—lay assessors also sit in the trial of civil cases.

29. In the text, I use the term *legalism* in its meaning as defined in ch. 1. In their own rhetorical framework, Soviet official commentators tend to paper over the tension between demands for "strict observance of rules" and the (instrumental) desire to reach an accurate outcome. One technique is to make exaggerated claims about the virtues of Soviet procedural law: it is supposed to be so finely adapted to the realization of substantive goals, and so artfully drawn, that strict adherence to procedural rules by itself guarantees the achievement of wished-for results.

hierarchically organized bureaucrats do not regard citizen involvement with unmixed enthusiasm. Of course, they do not object to transferring cases to activist groups, such as comradely courts: the transfer can even be welcomed as a way to reduce the pressures of heavy caseloads. It is another matter to let outsiders participate in officially directed proceedings; eager amateurs may inject irrelevant matter, delay proceedings, or negatively affect the atmosphere that surrounds serious bureaucratic pursuits. The Soviet judge may thus feel obliged to conduct a "circuit session" (*vyezdnya sessia*) in the park of an industrial plant. But while this locale may be didactically suitable and may appeal to the public as a sort of judicial *fête champêtre*, the judge may find it a less than fully serious setting for procedural action.[30]

MAO'S CHINA. While Soviet criminal process easily qualifies as both a pronouncedly activist and hierarchical system, it does not reach the potential extreme. For a glimpse of such a limiting case, one must turn to China in the period of Mao's managerial socialism. Hierarchically organized officialdom has deep roots in this country, and here also one finds a long history of managerial government, unparalleled by the absolutist governments in the West.[31] The soil was thus prepared for rapid growth of bureaucratic and activist forms of criminal justice when in 1948 the Chinese government embraced an ideology demanding at once radical transformation of society and the emergence of a new socialist man.

Consider first some striking features of the official apparatus involved in the criminal process. All officials were supposed to be "separate persons in one body," a unified bureaucracy to be run by a single ministry.[32] While the police—administrators par excellence—were made by far the most important part of the single organization, the courts and the Procuracy (copied from the Soviets) were not much more than decorative, ultimately superfluous appendages.[33] Control over the propriety of procedural activity was to be ensured mainly by supervision of hierarchical superiors, rather than by questioning and challenge by individuals implicated in the criminal process. Appeals and other attacks on decisions were interpreted as acts of defiance of authority, and thus discouraged. In this authoritative setting, the criminal process turned into a purely administrative enterprise to repress crime and convert miscreants. Attempts to mold and reform defendants could begin prior to any announcement of their guilt. Lawyers were barred from participation so that even the minimal sounds of contention associated with their activity could not be heard. At no point in the process was all the

---

30. For perceptive remarks on internal tensions in the Soviet legal system, see L. Lipson, in Kassoff, ed., *Prospects for Soviet Society*, 106–08 (1968).

31. The mandarin bureaucracy differed from its counterpart on the continent of Europe, however, in that it was not "logically legalistic." See the excellent account of the administrative flavor of old Chinese law in P. Heng-Chao-Ch'en, *Chinese Legal Tradition under the Mongols* (1979).

32. See A. Barnett, *Cadres, Bureaucracy and Political Power in Communist China*, 6–9 (1967); W. C. Jones, "A Possible Model for the Criminal Trial in the P.R. of China," 24 *Am. J. Comp. Law*, 229, 238 (1976).

33. W. C. Jones, *supra*, n. 32, 241.

assembled evidence adduced in the presence of the defendant. Even trial, in the form of an audit of earlier work or simply a ceremonial occasion, became optional and was reserved for those cases which promised to have a wider educational impact. Where held, trials were reduced to a solemn announcement of the sentence, reminiscent of the "final law day" at which results of official inquisitions were proclaimed in the old criminal procedure of some German lands. Notions of res judicata were virtually unknown or were criticized as formalistic and "bourgeois." In fact, the handling and possible conversion of criminals were conceived as ongoing, possibly lifelong engagements.[34] Criminal justice and administration merged: dealing with offenders became part of the broader effort to manage and transform society.

The Chinese have since returned to more conventional forms of justice, resembling the Soviet model quite closely. But it is instructive to imagine the reaction of Soviet lawyers to the state of affairs that existed for a while under Mao's leadership. To Soviet eyes, Chinese investigations would appear defective in that they ignored the possible contribution of the defense after investigators had concluded their detective work. Chinese defendants would seem to have been deprived of many rights accorded their counterparts by the Soviet system and turned into objects of didactic manipulation prior to any guilt determination. If conducted at all, the trial would appear devoid of any substantive significance, a mere morality play and a fait accompli. The instability of decisions would also seem excessive. At least to the modern Soviet eye, the blatancy with which the Chinese Communist party interfered in pending cases or justice officials consulted with the party would be repugnant. In short, Soviet lawyers would likely express the same criticisms that are directed against their own criminal procedure by Continental lawyers, accustomed to the conventional pastiche of contest and inquest forms.[35] On the other hand, as seen from Mao's Beijing, Soviet criminal process would reveal a family resemblance with conventional Continental systems, albeit pruned of overt allusions to contest and similar formalisms. Obviously, to confront a Maoist system thus comes close to an end point of the polarity depicted in chapter 5: the policy-implementing model is not so extreme or theoretical as never to be approximated in reality.

It might be observed that the Chinese style of criminal law enforcement just described no longer qualifies as a *legal* procedure. While the process remained subject to numerous internal regulations even during the turbulent years of the Cultural Revolution,[36] regulation per se—even if consummate—does not suffice for a process according to "law." No doubt, one can refuse to recognize state regulations as central to the law; one can also associate adjudication with conflict-resolution. But this mode of categorization is clearly too narrow for those groping toward a legal language common to mankind in the late twentieth century: it smacks of the dogmatism of the untraveled.

34. See J. Cohen, *The Criminal Process of the P.R. of China*, 44–46 (1968).
35. Observe also that some of these negative impressions also correspond to those registered by Anglo-American lawyers confronted with the conventional Continental criminal procedure.
36. W. C. Jones, *supra*, n. 32, 242.

A POSTSCRIPT ON THE ROLE OF THE VICTIM. One distinctive feature of Continental systems, in both their classic and Soviet variants, is that they accord more than a mere testimonial role to the victim of crime. Does this feature diminish the hierarchical activist character of Continental proceedings? The answer to this question depends on the specific nature of the victim's participation in criminal prosecutions.

It seems clear that a pure hierarchical activist system of justice does not permit the victim to control such important matters as the initiation and termination of prosecutions. Activist disposition requires that the state retain sole power to select suitable vehicles for articulating the values and realizing the goals of government. The victim cannot force the state to communicate wrong or trivial lessons to society through its process, nor can the victim preclude communication that the state regards as important and desirable. Victim control over proceedings does not accord well with hierarchically constituted authority: where legal proceedings imply enforcement of state policy, as do criminal prosecutions, they also fall within the jealously guarded province of official expertise. In short, private prosecutions are anomalous in a hierarchical activist process. If retained by force of tradition or some other reason, they are apt to undergo important transformations. These transformations will be considered later against the background of enclaves of private prosecution for minor offenses in Continental systems.[37]

The most common forms of victim participation are more modest in both Soviet and Continental criminal proceedings. Some of a victim's rights stem from the joinder to the prosecution of his claim for damages arising from the crime. Leaving to one side this parasitical civil suit, what are the victim's typical rights? During the investigation, he may make submissions or suggest that certain evidence be adduced. If the authorities decide to discontinue proceedings at this stage, the victim is usually empowered to ask higher officials to overrule their subordinates.[38] At trial, he can put questions, appear by counsel, and propose a particular judgment to the court. Sometimes he also has limited rights of appeal, but seldom concerning the decision on the merits.

The victim's minor role does not imply private party control over procedural action and is therefore compatible with proceedings devoted to the implementation of state policy. It may even appeal to activist ideology: the participation of those harmed by criminals can supply the human dimension that sensitizes the public to state goals, enhancing the official power to implement policy through the spectacle of the trial. But what is the likely attitude of hierarchical

---

37. In discussing hierarchical conflict resolution *infra*, I shall try to show how prosecution by the victim actually turns into a vehicle for seeking private satisfaction hardly distinguishable from certain tort actions.

38. The West German system of "mandamusing" the state prosecutor to press charges is described in J. Langbein, *Comparative Criminal Procedure: Germany*, 102–04 (1977). Perhaps more interesting is the Austrian system of "subsidiary prosecution": see *Austrian Code of Criminal Procedure*, §48. This system, developed during the last decades of the Austro-Hungarian monarchy, was disseminated to several central and eastern European countries and is still in force in some of them.

authority toward such a victim's input into the criminal process? Because bureaucrats need no lay outsiders in nontestimonial roles, even the modest part played by the victim of crime is greeted with minimal enthusiasm. Higher echelons of hierarchical authority may deem it useful only as a device to keep lower echelons on their toes, limiting the free play of subordinates and supplementing hierarchical monitoring. But given the generally inhospitable climate generated by a bureaucratic environment, one should not expect a vigorous use of victim's rights in Continental proceedings—a use capable of weakening the secure hold of officials over procedural events.[39] Wholly apart from this, observe that to find nontestimonial parts for the victim is much easier in Continental than in Anglo-American criminal procedure. There, the victim has few ancillary rights because important stages of common-law prosecution are structured as a contest of two sides, so that introduction of a third actor into bipolar litigation can adversely affect the incentives required to sustain it.[40] If Continental officialdom were to preside over such criminal proceedings, even such modest victim participation would cause serious friction. It is thus precisely because Continental criminal procedure is *not* a bipolar contest, although it likes to make allusions to it, that the voice of the victim can easily be accommodated. His action does not obstruct the smooth progression of criminal prosecution, and hierarchical authority can tolerate outside interference in its sphere of expertise.

Other Types of Proceedings

Until now I have drawn illustrations of hierarchical activist procedure from the area where these forms of legal process first appeared: the sphere of criminal prosecution. As the agenda of government expands, such configurations begin to penetrate other segments of justice; the more the state undertakes to direct social life, the more the resolution of civil disputes no longer limits the locus of state concern, and civil proceedings acquire broader objectives. It is natural in this situation for pressures to mount to shape proceedings so as to permit the attainment of larger state objectives. One small step in this direction is to leave initiation of lawsuits in private hands but accord to state officials the power to influence the outcome of litigation. The move is modest because it is party initiation that gives the necessary weight to activate the legal process to what is— in substance—a recognized state interest.

ABSOLUTIST PRUSSIA. The latter move was made by the rulers of eighteenth-century Prussia, who, more than absolutist princes elsewhere, displayed some eudaemonistic concerns for the welfare of the classes on which the regime fed.

---

39. Even when the victim has an eye on his claim for damages, either appended to the criminal case or litigated independently, it would be wrong to expect the forceful action that equivalent rights would probably provoke in an American courtroom.

40. It is easy to design various forms of victim participation in presentencing hearings, but it is much more difficult to find a place for the victim at the contested trial. On these problems, see A. Goldstein, "Defining the Role of the Victim in Criminal Prosecutions," 52 *Miss. L.J.* 515, 557–58 (1982).

These concerns led to extensive regulation of various spheres of social life; the amount of beer one might legitimately consume over a period of time, the number of guests one might lodge, and similar matters were all treated as subjects fit for state regulation.[41] Not surprisingly, in view of such *parens patriae* concerns, civil justice came to be regarded by political authority as saturated with strong "public interest" and in need of reform.

The procedural innovations inaugurated by Frederick the Great have already been noted in various contexts. I have commented that while private parties retained a monopoly over the initiation of civil actions, Frederickian legislation permitted the judge to disregard the factual allegations of the litigants whenever the interest of justice so required. Furthermore, the doors of civil justice were closed to members of the private bar, and a special class of civil servants (*Assistänzrate*) was established to better adjust lawsuits to the tenor of state values.[42] Yet the litigants' private control over the lawsuit was retained in most relevant aspects, including the remedial process. In any event, going against the grain of powerful traditions, Frederickian reforms were short-lived and exerted—even when in force—only a limited impact on actual practice. In the West bolder departures from a model of lawsuit that accords validity and range to private concerns lay in the distant future. They had to wait for the Bolshevik Revolution—that is to say, for the victory of a political ideology that would readily underwrite the demise of privately dominated civil action.

THE SOVIET MODEL. The basic outline of Soviet civil process shows the unmistakable imprint of the conventional Continental style of adjudicating private disputes. Since I have not yet discussed this style, however, I shall temporarily leave the basic outline undefined. Within this outline only arrangements that can be traced to the influence of pronouncedly activist ideology, and are characteristically Soviet, are of interest for the moment.

From the inception of Soviet rule, the separation of any sphere of justice from the interests of the state was resolutely repudiated. What was then to be the goal of civil proceedings? The satisfaction of the plaintiff came to be viewed only as a part of larger objectives: the transgressor of civil law was to be taught a lesson, and society at large was to be educated to habits of compliance with the law. The aims of civil and criminal justice thus converged.[43] No longer a mere conflict resolver, the Soviet civil judge was expected to take vigorous control over the case. It became his duty to get to the bottom of things, even if that implied disregarding the factual allegations of the litigants. His thorough preparation of the case for trial, including, when necessary, the examination of the parties, was expected to lead to an uninterrupted trial similar to that contemplated in criminal matters. The judge was also authorized to disregard the prayer for relief—if

---

41. See Boehmer, *Grundlagen der buergerlichen Rechtsordnung*, vol. 1, 174 (Tübingen, 1970). On welfare tendencies present in Prussian absolutism, see H. Jacoby, *supra*, n. 5, 33–35.

42. See *supra*, ch. 5, n. 49.

43. After the revolution it was seriously debated whether a distinctive civil procedure was needed at all. See J. Hazard, *Settling Disputes in Soviet Society*, 401–05 (1966). For a discussion of objectives of the Soviet civil process, see Shargorodskiv, "O roli i sootnosheniyi prinuzhdeniya i ubezhdeniya v prave," *Sovetskaiya Justicia*, no. 14 (1961): 3.

mandated by the correct policy approach—and to order a remedy different from that sought by the plaintiff. Independently of his narrow disposition of the dispute, he could issue a special ruling intended to produce larger "corrective" consequences in society, much as in a criminal case. Alternatively, he could send a copy of the civil judgement to a local group or association with demand that it be read and debated at meetings. Supervision of measures so ordered could be entrusted to lay members of the civil court. In another parallel to criminal cases, civil trials could be held in circuit at the litigants' residence, place of work, or similar location. A family dispute, say over alimony, could be used by the judge to inculcate desired attitudes into the group.[44] In a major departure from tradition, private individuals were denied monopoly over the initiation and termination of lawsuits. A special role in breaking this monopoly fell to the watchdog of larger interests—the Procuracy: members of this rigidly hierarchical organization could institute a civil case on behalf of unwilling citizens, provided important rights were involved. They could also move the court to prevent the parties from withdrawing from the forum. In the course of proceedings they were empowered to obtain copies of relevant documents, to seek extension of proof, to make a variety of motions, and to appeal ("protest") the judgment even if actual litigants had failed to do so. As in criminal matters, "finally" decided cases could at any point be reopened at their insistence; they were charged with the continuous supervision of the consequences of official action.[45]

Associations of citizens were also authorized to intervene in civil proceedings and, under certain circumstances, to initiate them.[46] It would be a serious mistake, however, to compare the procedural action of such Soviet groups with the ability of public interest groups in pluralist polities to obstruct or delay the realization of governmental projects. Spontaneous social action is at odds with the preeminence of the party which dominates the government and embodies the will of society as a "monistic" instrument. From a comparative point of view, it is therefore reasonable to suggest that such civic groups may be considered as para- or crypto-agencies of the Soviet government. Their intervention in or occasional invocation of the civil process hardly disrupts the working of the hierarchical activist judicial apparatus.

It follows from this brief sketch that the Soviets have fleshed out the skeleton of the Continental lawsuit with novel forms: where the Procuracy, civic activists, or the judge choose to employ their comprehensive power to expand the bounds of narrow disputes, the ensuing civil proceedings are no longer in the conflict-solving mode. Instead, they become vehicles of policy implementation. But it is easy thus to overstate the disparity between conventional and Soviet civil justice. Uniquely, Soviet forms draw their inspiration from and are sustained by

44. For various forms of enlisting participation of citizens in civil proceedings, see Kitchatov, "Formi privlecheniya obschestvennosti," *Sovetskoe Gosudarstvo i Pravo*, no. 12 (1961): 76–85.

45. The origin of the Procuracy's role in the civil process is recounted in J. Hazard, *supra*, n. 43, 217–46.

46. Forms of this participation are discussed in Kitchatov, *supra*, n. 44. See also D. M. O'Connor, "Soviet Procedure in Civil Decisions," in W. La Fave, ed., *Law in the Soviet Society*, 77–78 (1965).

an ideology whose ambitions exceed its effective reach. While governmental ideologues insist that any dispute absorbed into the justice system provides an opportunity to implement some conflict-transcending policy, or at least to exert an educational influence on participants, the larger implications of cases are in practice often difficult to divine and their didactic potential may be dubious. Igor and Olga bring cases of such disappointing nature to Soviet courts every day that, confronted with them, the Soviet judge necessarily assumes the posture of a conflict resolver while other guardians of larger interests remain on the sidelines. The civil process now unfolds in ways that a common lawyer would hardly distinguish from civil actions in some Western Continental countries.[47]

This is not to say that the Soviet system fails to offer striking and original examples of the displacement of judicial conflict solving by administrative and managerial procedures. Where the economy is organized by an encompassing plan and the firms are owned by the state, disputes among economic agents cannot be considered in isolation from the overall functioning of the state economy. If problems arise in the preparation and execution of contracts among state firms, an administrative perspective on these problems necessarily prevails. Clearly, conflicts generated by the interaction of these firms are not the stuff conventional litigation is made of: they fall within the jurisdiction of a special tribunal, the Arbitrazh, obligated to institute a case on its own initiative if the firms involved have no wish to sue and the state interest calls for action.[48] In essence, Arbitrazh is an administrative agency and proceedings before it are at bottom administrative in nature.

Another area in which Soviet administrative processes swallow up conflict-solving forms is that encompassing reaction to complaints of illegal action taken by ubiquitous state officialdom. Citizens cannot sue the administration or other agencies of the state in court; the aggrieved or concerned citizen must try to enlist the help of the mighty Procuracy. In the exercise of its general powers of supervision, the Procuracy can investigate state agencies; it possesses broad "discovery" powers and can force officials to surrender documents or otherwise provide necessary information. But if in such circumstances an instance of "illegality" or a pattern of such behavior is detected, no court proceedings ensue: instead, the matter is brought to the attention of the appropriate hierarchical superior and is framed as a problem for internal resolution.[49]

47. This is especially the case with relatively informal civil proceedings patterned on the Austrian model. For a good sketch of this model, see A. A. Ehrenzweig, *Psychoanalytic Jurisprudence*, 266–69 (1971). Observe that the Soviet government officially disapproves of many market transactions that actually take place in Soviet society: if such transactions lead to disputes, they are settled in ways that avoid official scrutiny. In consequence, many matters never reach the civil court that would immediately raise larger policy issues. For conjectures on this point, see D. M. O'Connor, *supra*, n. 46, 60.

48. On the peculiar nature of proceedings before the Arbitrazh, see O. S. Ioffe, and P. B. Maggs, *Soviet Law in Theory and Practice*, 201–03, 306 (1983); R. F. Kallistratova, *Razresheniye sporov v gosudarstvennom arbitrazhe*, 12–20 (Moscow, 1961).

49. See *1955 Statute on Prokuratorial Supervision*, art. 23, ch. 2. Compare also G. Morgan, *Soviet Administrative Legality* (1962).

ii. THE CONFLICT-SOLVING PROCESS BEFORE HIERARCHICAL OFFICIALDOM

There are many ways in which proceedings structured as a two-party contest are affected by a multilayered judicial apparatus staffed with civil service bureaucrats. But it will suffice for comparativist purposes to examine the impact of this type of authority on the confrontational aspects of proceedings and on the requisite passive stance of the decision maker.

Several factors associated with hierarchical authority combine to reduce the lawsuit's potential for turning into a fierce disputation. Litigation chopped up in discrete installments and unfolding before several echelons of authority lacks a focal point for the unleashing of the partisan agon; the loser of one round may prevail in the next; and "punches can be pulled." Another factor relates to the ubiquitous reliance on documentation of activity performed at earlier procedural episodes: in preparation for a subsequent session, officials are expected to draw on the file of the case so that at least part of what they learn is no longer the direct product of party contest. The further the litigation progresses, the greater the concentration of such mediated information in the total pool. Remember also the tendency toward official exclusivity of hierarchical structures: at least some activities which an ideal conflict-solving process would entrust to the litigants become the monopoly of officials in charge of proceedings. But the greater the official share of procedural action, the more reduced is the scope for direct, unmediated interaction of the parties in dispute. Of course, no phase of the proceedings can be performed by the litigants alone in the total absence of the moderating effect of official presence. Quite naturally, then, the parties' contest before hierarchically organized bureaucrats tends to be low-keyed: confrontational aspects of the lawsuit are thus reduced or diluted.

How does the environment of hierarchical authority affect the passive role of the decision maker required by the conflict-solving mode of proceeding? As I have observed, notions of bureaucratic prerogative demand that he personally take charge of some procedural steps which authority of a different type would delegate or share with litigants and their counsel. In this sense, the hierarchical official as a conflict resolver may appear as a relatively active protagonist of the legal process. But in striking contrast to his stance in policy-implementing proceedings, he is not self-propelling: because initiation and termination of lawsuits, as well as the definition of issues, are all matters in which conflict resolution implies party sovereignty, he must be moved by the litigants. Once moved, he is far from a relentlessly probing investigator with the concièrge curiosity he evinces in the policy-implementing mode. Nor should he be expected to probe zealously on his own if his efforts can at any moment be rendered useless by the inviolable admissions and stipulations of the parties. Thus, springing from notions of bureaucratic prerogative, his primary responsibility for some procedural steps (e.g., interrogation of witnesses) tends to be treated loosely—he lacks drive and tends to be inert. In this deeper sense he is actually passive, in a reactive stance, and in need of prodding by the parties. But the absence of his investigative zeal cannot be replaced by vigorous action of the litigants, given that the hierarchical apparatus of authority frowns upon private procedural enterprise.

Yet hierarchical authority does not necessarily stifle the litigants' control over the lawsuit. It has been noted that rationalist bureaucracies shape proceedings to their animating purposes, so that at least those aspects of party control that seem implicit in the conflict-solving purpose become more sacrosanct and untouchable than in a setting of procedural authority less committed to placing procedural forms into a consistent purposive scheme. Important reasons can no doubt be imagined that tempt the adjudicator to encroach on party control for the sake of larger interests. However, much better than their counterparts in a coordinate organization, hierarchical officials are prepared to live by the rigidities of a narrow conflict-solving role mandated by laissez-faire ideology: they are case-hardened professionals. Nor can they escape their narrow role—when this seems desirable to them—by exercising "inherent" discretionary powers. What they can and cannot do in the hierarchical apparatus is determined by relatively unyielding rules. In brief, where the perceived purpose of a proceeding requires that parties be masters of the lawsuit, hierarchical bureaucracies can preserve this private control with great rigidity.

It follows from what has been said so far that the conflict-solving process before hierarchical authority tends to be deprived of potent instruments of truth discovery. Parties themselves are not permitted to "privatize" fact-finding, and officials lack their usual drive in searching for the truth. But one should not fail to realize that in a reactive polity intensive and probing factual inquiries are much less acceptable with a hierarchical than with a coordinate judicial apparatus. In the former, factual inquiries are part of official prerogative, and even if initiated and their contours defined by private parties, the probing still comes from civil servants who bring the powers of government to bear on the administration of justice. Beyond this, the results of fact-finding are recorded in official documents of evidentiary significance, documents which travel as part of the dossier to the very center of the state government. In coordinate organizations, in contrast, fact-finding is readily delegated to private litigants, so that one member of civil society investigates another, and the products of the litigants' efforts are not readily available to ultimate power holders. All other things remaining equal, then, the independent inquisitiveness of hierarchically organized officials is more threatening to the vision of self-governing society than is the search for the truth in the legal process before coordinate officials. The former must be kept on a shorter leash.

Having thus outlined those characteristics of the hierarchical reactive process that are most important for comparative purposes, I shall leave abstract discussion to one side and now examine some real-world procedures that qualify as examples of the hierarchical reactive style.

Continental Forms of Civil Procedure

THE ROMAN-CANONICAL PROCESS. This prototype of Continental civil procedure was primarily the product of purposive efforts, dating from the twelfth century, to adapt the dispute-settling mechanisms of the Middle Ages to the evolving structure of the Roman Catholic judicial authority. Where this authority was not faced with instances of "infamy" or "excesses", as in criminal matters, the initiation of lawsuits naturally remained an exclusive prerogative of the parties. After some initial hesitation, the definition of facts in dispute was also thought to lie in the hands of the litigants. But developing notions of bureaucratic propriety and order were deemed to require that the judge or some other court official personally take charge of a variety of procedural activities. To administer justice came to be regarded as an eminently technical, professional pursuit. Most important for comparative purposes was the demand that professional officials, *ex officii debito*, take over the examination of evidence offered by the parties. This examination proceeded methodically and could be stretched over several separate sessions. The very presence of the litigants at these sessions was deemed undesirable; it was feared that witnesses could be intimidated and confused, that disorder and disruptions could obstruct the calm and methodical ventilation of the truth. So while the parties were asked to suggest what questions were to be addressed to witnesses, their interrogation became part of exclusive official prerogative. It was regarded inappropriate for litigants directly to exchange documents of evidentiary significance: where a party was obliged to disclose a document, he was to bring it to the judge (*editio*). All procedural steps officially taken had to be recorded, not only for the inspection by the parties, but also to preserve the informational basis for the original decision maker and reviewing authority.[50] Under conditions then prevailing, the voyage of the file through all the levels of the appellate process sometimes took decades.

Yet it must be noted that the Roman-canonical process did not permit total domination of lawsuits by the litigants, even in areas where party control was in principle recognized; only private control over the beginning of a lawsuit was truly sacrosanct. Once proceedings got under way, court officials exercised important powers to intervene in proceedings for the sake of preserving justice (*aequitas*), so weighty in ecclesiastical courts. Issues and facts not presented by the parties themselves would sometimes be elicited. This may be doubted by those familiar with many legal maxims developed by scholars of the period— maxims that seem to assume a passive and inert civil judge. In practice, however, the principles expressed by these widely quoted sayings were laced with exceptions permitting the judge to turn activist.[51] It must also be realized that Roman-canonical authorities insisted—although with less rigor than in criminal mat-

---

50. For an excellent nutshell portrayal of the Roman-canon civil process, see R. C. Van-Caenegem, "History of European Civil Procedure," in *International Encyclopedia of Comparative Law*, vol. 16, 17–19.

51. While tags such as *ne procedet judex ex officio* (i.e., the judge should not act of his own motion) are regularly invoked, it will suffice to consider encompassing obligations of the ecclesiastical judge "moved by equity" to supplement the parties' action as enumerated by one of the greatest fourteenth-century authorities on Roman-canonical process. See Baldus de Ubaldis, *In Decretalium Commentaria X 1.5.3.*, nos. 6–10 (Taurinum, 1578). The latent activism of the judge in secular proceedings has recently been illustrated with the example of German lands by F. Bomsdorf, *Prozessmaximen und Rechtswirklichkeit*, 62–65 (Berlin, 1971).

ters—that the judge be the seeker of truth.[52] Testimonial privileges that emerged early on were based mainly on fear that certain witnesses might lie rather than on the acknowledgment of values that compete with the desire to establish the truth.[53] These departures from what a pure hierarchical reactive style may demand can easily be explained: the ideology of uninvolved government had yet to be born, and even had it been alive, it would have clashed with aspirations of authority, both imperial and sacerdotal. Besides, as was pointed out in chapter 1, the influential ecclesiastical government never fully developed characteristics associated with the hierarchical ideal—characteristics that support rigidity in preserving party autonomy, where this autonomy is recognized.

Only slightly modified, this process of ecclesiastical origin was adopted by secular courts, and its forms prevailed on the continent of Europe throughout the ancien régime. The habit thus became deeply ingrained to view the civil judge as responsible for proof taking. Equally ingrained became the habit of associating litigation with a series of discrete sessions without a clear focal point. Documentation, hierarchical appeals, and similar features also came to be associated with the forensic resolution of disputes.

THE CIVIL PROCESS OF LAISSEZ-FAIRE. Somewhat miraculously, old forms of civil procedure survived the upheavals of the French Revolution with fewer changes than the administration of criminal justice. While revolutionary reforms introduced the lay jury into segments of the criminal process, decision making in civil cases remained—even in the postrevolutionary period—the exclusive province of professional judges. Until the more recent advent of mass litigation, few pressures were felt to induce the temporal compression of civil litigation.

Yet within this ancient framework important changes began to take place at the turn of the nineteenth century. It was then that Continental scholars constructed a rigorous model of the lawsuit as a dispute of two autonomous parties before a passive court. Self-consciously derived from the conflict-solving objective of justice, this model was recommended as an ideal in the sphere of "mine and thine,"—property—where rights were regarded as waivable and social relationships were treated as amenable to independent ordering by civil society. The civil process, now imagined as a mere continuation of private transactions by other means, was to be governed by very broad notions of party autonomy.[54]

52. See W. Ulmann, "Medieval Principles of Evidence," 62 Law Quarterly Review, 77 (1946).

53. Concerns about perjury also led to the testimonial incapacity of the parties. To be sure, the litigants could be interrogated by the judge, but only for the purpose of formulating issues in dispute, not for the purpose of proving them. Because different officials often presided over pleadings and over proof taking, the separation of testimonial and nontestimonial roles of the parties was a technical refinement not without practical significance.

54. For references, see K. W. Nörr, Naturrecht und Zivilprozess, 25, 48 (Tübingen, 1976). The model in question was mainly the work of German scholars, following the seminal efforts of Nikolaus Gönner in the beginning of the nineteenth century. For the original version of the model, see N. T. von Gönner, Handbuch des deutschen gemeinen Prozesses, vol. 1, 268 ff. (Erlangen, 1801). A refined version of Gönnerian theory comprises two organizing principles for civil process: one postulates mastery of the parties over the rights in dispute (Dispositionsmaxime), the other, party

The scholarly model affected the administration of justice and deserves to be briefly outlined.

In some respects, party dominance over lawsuits was now indisputable and more rigorously maintained than in the old Roman-canonical practice. For example, not only were parties to be sovereign in determining the facts to be ascertained, but they were also to supply the legal theories applicable to the controversy. The earlier emphasis of Roman-canonical authorities on the discovery of truth was greatly weakened. The judge was resolutely denied any power to call witnesses on his own. The old maxim, "no one is expected to supply weapons to his adversary," now found strict applications: only minimal obligations were to be imposed on litigants to surrender to the court documents of evidentiary significance. Testimonial privileges, heretofore based on cognitive considerations, were now to be anchored in values independent of or in conflict with the search for the truth—privacy, family loyalty, even fear of financial ruin.[55] While the old rule that parties are incompetent to testify was rejected, so too was the idea that they could be compelled to offer testimony: a duty to make declarations against self-interest seemed inhumane. As I have remarked in chapter 4, if allowed to take the stand at all, the party was to have a sweeping right to refuse to answer questions. Some extremists even advocated the position that no prosecution for perjury should lie if a party decided to testify (to avoid harmful inferences from refusal to speak) and was caught lying.[56]

Although impelled by desire to allocate as much procedural control as possible to the parties, the architects of the new civil process were still constrained by deeply ingrained notions of judicial prerogatives. Self-executing party action, akin to American pretrial discovery, was not even contemplated; traditional judicial powers of interrogation appeared natural and were retained. Of course, judicial questioning did not appear overly disturbing, since Continentals were accustomed to the practice of the civil judge asking only questions suggested by the litigants.[57]

Upon examination, this model of civil procedure will be seen to reflect many features of the pure conflict-solving procedure defined in chapter 4, adapt-

---

initiative for procedural action (*Verhandlungsmaxime*). The implications of these organizing principles were widely followed in the legislation of Continental countries. For a comparative survey, see M. Cappelletti, *La Testimonianza della Parte nel Sistema dell' Oralita*, vol. 1, 353, 375 (Milano, 1962). This distinction was domesticated for American use in the 1930s. See R. W. Millar, "The Formative Principles of Civil Procedure," 18 *Ill. L. Rev.* 1–36 (1923). French lawyers followed their own paths, but reached essentially similar results as those following German theory. See E. Glason and A. Tissier, *Traité theorique et pratique de procédure civile*, 656–61 (Paris, 1926).

55. See *supra*, ch. 4, n. 53. For illustrations of the (to common lawyers amazing) right of Continental witnesses to refuse to answer if "faced with an immediate financial loss," see *Code of Civil Proc. of the Swiss Canton Zürich*, §159. Suprisingly, a similar provision appears in *Yugoslav Federal Law on Civil Procedure*, art. 227.

56. This view was sporadically reflected in legislation. For example, under Austrian influence, it found its way into the law of the Kingdom of Yugoslavia and was for a while retained by the communist government. See S. Triva, *Gradjansko Procesno Pravo*, vol. 1, 439–43 (Zagreb, 1965).

57. See *supra*, ch. 4, n. 50 and accompanying text.

ed to an environment of hierarchical bureaucratic judiciary. This model was adopted by legislation in several Continental Countries during the course of the nineteenth century, and in several others, it was viewed as a desirable blueprint for reform. As a result, the prevailing Continental forms of civil procedure were in important aspects then more rigorously attuned to narrow conflict resolution than coeval forms of civil justice in Anglo-American lands. Classical civil proceedings in common-law countries were a much more potent vehicle for the discovery of truth, and adjudicators were much less litigant-dependent or "reactive," than their counterparts on the Continent. This springs clearly into focus even if one's vision does not include—as it should—the equity side of Anglo-American civil process. Mainly because common-law observers of the European scene tended to be overly impressed by the highly visible judicial powers of interrogation, penetrating in criminal but harmless in civil cases, it became customary for common lawyers to label the Continental civil process as "inquisitorial."[58] At the same time, to Continental observers imbued with liberal ideology, many aspects of Anglo-American civil justice appeared insufficiently respectful of individual self-interest and overly probing—too committed to ascertaining the real state of the world.[59]

CIVIL JUSTICE IN THE WELFARE STATE. The apotheosis of party autonomy was to be of short duration. Before the nineteenth century was out, many Continental countries passed legislation curbing party control and "activating" the judge. If it were necessary for the "right" solution, he was now supposed to intervene in the framing of issues; he could demand from the litigants clarification as to what they allege and what they want to be proved; he could even correct some consequences of litigants' faulty advocacy. To the extent that he actually chose to inject himself into proceedings, he would introduce—to a degree—new factual and legal issues.[60] Moreover, broader duties were imposed on the parties to surrender evidence in their possession or to cooperate with the court in other ways so that "the truth may prevail."[61] From their inception, these legislative reforms were justified by rejection of the individualism associated with the tenets of classical liberalism.[62] But—especially in more recent times—some reforms can also be attributed to the crowding of dockets in industrial states. To be efficient, case-flow management necessitates the weakening of litigants' control over the progress of cases.

Yet, after all is said and done, the resulting departures from classical forms

58. For examples, see C. T. McCormack, *Handbook of the Law of Evidence*, 12, 503 (1954); E. M. Morgan, *Basic Problems of Evidence*, vol. 1, 60 (1957).

59. See the perceptive observations of M. Cappelletti, *Processo e Ideologie*, 332–33 (Bologna, 1969).

60. See R. Schlesinger, *Comparative Law*, 4th ed., 393 (1980). Practice varied from country to country regarding the extent to which judges actually abandoned their posture of noninvolvement.

61. In most countries these reforms were linked to the rise of consumer protection and similar phenomena of the welfare state. While Continental codes of civil procedure seldom provide broader discovery, new duties are usually imposed by special legislation. See *supra*, ch. 4, n. 66.

62. See F. Klein, *Der Zivilprozess Oesterreichs*, 186–87 (Mannheim, Leipzig, and Berlin, 1927).

of hierarchical conflict resolution are not as significant as might be expected. The characteristic piecemeal style continues to the present day, notwithstanding legislatively expressed preference for "concentrated" trials in the name of greater efficiency;[63] the file remains the backbone of proceedings, even as virtues of the viva voce are often extolled; judges still depend on the parties in important ways. Judges are denied powers to call witnesses freely or to exceed the contours of the controversy; to disregard the prayer for relief or to accord the plaintiff more than he has asked for is still forbidden. Generally speaking, the truth-finding potential of civil proceedings is rather limited, especially when compared to Continental criminal justice. The use of the party as a source of information is modest, even where mechanisms exist for extensive interrogation. Broad testimonial privileges remain largely intact.[64] In the still prevailing view, civil justice—as opposed to criminal—should be relatively unconcerned with accurate fact-finding.[65]

It will not have escaped the reader's attention that I have focused on suits brought in the litigant's self-interest. In welfare states, however, civil litigation is increasingly used for the protection, and sometimes also for the definition, of larger or "public" interests. The protectors of these interests can be either governmental officials or individuals and nongovernmental associations.[66] For comparative purposes it is important to emphasize the special difficulties facing nonofficial enforcement of public interests in traditional Continental systems. Predictably, the mainspring of the opposition originates in the hierarchical bureaucratic apparatus of authority: the fusion of public and self-interested action is viewed here with greater suspicion than in a setting of authority accustomed to rely on outsiders. Proper incentives for vigorous private enforcement of the public interest may easily appear corruptive. Hierarchical officialdom values a consistent, uniform approach and systematic action that citizens' suits in the public interest are not likely to supply. Some fear that the administration of justice itself might become unduly politicized.[67] It therefore appears preferable to entrust enforcement of regulatory policies and the protection of larger in-

---

63. See *supra,* ch. 2, n. 9.

64. Specialists in transnational litigation know that it is much easier to obtain information from witnesses in common law than in Continental civil proceedings. Thus, where financially acceptable, they use mechanisms of international judicial assistance to obtain testimony from common-law courts for use in Continental civil litigation or arbitration proceedings.

65. More effective fact-finding devices in civil than in criminal cases would be a "mismatch" of the two branches of justice. Compare H. Baade, "Illegally Obtained Evidence in Civil and Criminal Cases: A Comparative Study of a Classic Mismatch," 51 *Tex. L. Rev.* 1325–62 (1973).

66. A comprehensive survey of possible enforcers of the public interest can be found in M. Cappelletti, "Governmental and Private Advocates for the Public Interest in Civil Litigation," 73 *Mich. L. Rev.* 794–881 (1975). In pluralist countries, citizens' associations can and often do invoke the judicial process in opposition to the government.

67. See N. Luhmann, *Legitimation durch Verfahren,* 2d ed., 122 (Darmstadt, 1975). For special problems of "popular" actions in West Germany, see I. Markovits, "Socialist vs. Bourgeois Rights," 45 *U. Chi. L. Rev.* 612, 618 (1978). Compare also insightful remarks by H. Kötz, "Public Interest Litigation: A Comparative Survey," in M. Cappelletti, ed., *Access to Justice and the Welfare State,* 112–16 (1981).

terests to traditional official "promoters"; if they lack the requisite specialized knowledge, then new "specialized" officials should be appointed to avoid reliance on the haphazard action of people outside the official apparatus.

Conflict-Solving Forms in Continental Criminal Justice

THE OLD ACCUSATORIAL PROCESS. Earlier in this chapter I noted that a form of prosecution by the victim survived the rise of the inquisitorial process on the Continent and that, for a long time, this form was treated as the ideal design of criminal proceedings. Shorn of its early medieval features, it was adapted to the hierarchical organization of the judiciary and made quite similar to the Roman-canonical civil process from which it was for some time imperfectly distinguished. In this mode of proceedings, the victim of a crime controlled the initiation and termination of prosecution; albeit under pain of forfeiting a sum of money, he could withdraw charges at any time. The criminal defendant retained many attributes of a party, and although he could be subjected to questioning by the judge, coercion to extract answers from him was forbidden.[68]

In terms of practical importance, however, the ancient process *per accusationem* was almost totally eclipsed by the officially controlled inquisitorial procedure. The old form continued to play a part only in the area of minor crime, where authorities found little if any independent interest to enforce criminal law policy. Sporadically, defendants of the noble classes would lay claim to be treated according to this theoretically superior procedure, mainly because—even where contaminated with inquest forms—it was far less ruthless than the dominant process *per inquisitionem*.[69] Only in a small number of jurisdictions were absolutist bureaucracies strong and ambitious enough to wholly displace this form of private prosecution. The victim usually retained only "secondary" or "subsidiary" rights to set the wheels of justice in motion where responsible officials remained inactive; rulers found the mechanism useful as a check on their burgeoning judicial bureaucracy.

MODERN PRIVATE PROSECUTION. Pockets of such prosecution survive in several Continental countries, where a limited number of misdemeanors can be prosecuted only if the victim presses a criminal charge. Typical examples are minor offenses against dignitary interests, some forms of petty larceny, or the infliction of minor bodily injury. Where the public prosecutor is not entitled to take over the prosecution of these misdemeanors without the victim's consent, the private prosecutor retains exclusive control over the continued existence of proceedings and over the scope of factual inquiry.[70] But the resulting criminal case does not

---

68. For the old Italian forms of this process, see H. Kantorowicz, *Albertus Gandinus und das Strafrecht des Skolastik*, vol. 1, 87–120 (Berlin, 1907). For the variant in Carpzov's Saxony, see B. Carpzov, *supra*, n. 8, Quest. 106.

69. See E. Schmidt, *supra*, n. 7, 100. In some countries the importance of the accusatorial process was eroded by permitting the judge, confronted with serious proof difficulties, to "switch" into the inquisitorial mode. Compare Carpzov, *supra*, n. 8, Quest. 107, no. 59.

70. This is the case in Austria. See *Austrian Code of Criminal Procedure*, §46. By contrast, the West German prosecutor can always replace the private party, who recedes into the role of an intervenor with a watching brief. Compare J. Langbein, *supra*, n. 38, 101.

unfold exactly as does a Continental civil lawsuit. For example, the failure of the defendant to contest the charges does not provide a dispensation from judicial guilt determination.[71] Because trials in private prosecution cases are not preceded by extensive official investigations, much of their "audit" character is lost.

Why are such citizen actions included in the category of hierarchical conflict resolution? Are they not engaged in implementation of state policies toward crime and aimed at attaining the usual goals of punishment? The answer emerges from analysis of the motives that impel the victim to press criminal charges. In some cases, he pursues his financial interest in order to obtain a favorable settlement of the damage claim arising from the misdemeanor; private criminal prosecution gives the victim leverage in the ongoing bargaining process with the defendant—the tortfeasor. However, where the privately prosecuted misdemeanor does not give rise to a separate tort claim or can lead only to "symbolic" damages, the victim is driven by desire to obtain vindication: the fines sought in private prosecution (imprisonment is hardly ever imposed) can be regarded by a comparativist as rough substitutes for the nonexistent punitive damages that could otherwise be sought in a tort action. Phrased differently, the fines sought provide an outlet for feelings that could otherwise be satisfied by hefty damage awards.[72] Observe, parenthetically, that most conduct subject to private prosecution on the Continent usually constitutes an intentional tort—but not a criminal offense—in Anglo-American systems.[73] What the state actually tries to achieve in offering its forum to a private prosecutor is to provide a safety valve for private outrage, a valve whose absence could lead to disturbances—possibly to the private exaction of vengeance. It cannot seriously be maintained that what the state tries to achieve is to implement its usual punishment goals—moral suasion, deterrence, rehabilitation, or similar ends. In short, proceedings upon a private charge serve no policy goals independent of the resolution of an interpersonal conflict; the existence of these proceedings is conditioned by the existence of such a private conflict. Hence cases of private prosecution for misdemeanors on the Continent may justifiably be treated as instances of disguised conflict resolution or as a peripheral aberration in the context of policy-implementing justice. It should not be surprising that the Continental apparatus of justice tries to discourage such private action or is most reluctant to convict on private charges.[74]

Outside of the area of minor crime, private control over law enforcement may be found only in a limited number of Continental countries as a check against the inactivity of officials primarily responsible for criminal prosecutions. The French public prosecutor, for example, does not completely monopolize

---

71. However, the defendant can persuade the private prosecutor to withdraw the charges and settle out of court.

72. The difference remains, of course, that whereas punitive damages go to the victim, the fine accrues to the state.

73. This is the case with some injuries to personal reputation and privacy. Only very recently have a few Western European countries made these injuries actionable torts. In this connection see the famous *Soraya* case as reported in R. Schlesinger, *supra*, n. 60, 580–81.

74. For West Germany, see Kunert, in Löwe-Rosenberg, *Strafprozessordnung*, 22d ed., comments to §374, comment no. 1 (1972); H. J. Hirsch, "Gegenwart und Zukunft des Privatklageverfahrens," in *Festschrift für Richard Lange*, 815–17 (Berlin, 1976).

criminal law enforcement; the victim who shows that he is entitled to claim tort damages can request that the investigating judge institute criminal proceedings if the *procureur* has failed to do so.[75] While the prosecutor technically remains responsible for the conduct of such victim-initiated proceedings, he usually leaves the victim to do the prosecuting. Similarly, in Austria, the victim has a right to take over the prosecution from inactive state officials, who nevertheless can take charge at any stage of the criminal process.[76] Undoubtedly, even if only secondary, such private powers detract from rigid hierarchical arrangements as I have defined them. The private individual can overrule the agenda of state officials; his grievance against the accused takes precedence over the official appraisal of the best course of action. But it would be wrong to assume that such secondary prosecutors seriously detract from or threaten the usual tone of Continental proceedings dominated by the civil service judiciary. Once under way, proceedings are firmly under official control, and so is the decision whether punishment should be imposed. Private settlements are not dispositive because, as has been noted, the public prosecutor can decide to continue the prosecution even where the defendant and the subsidiary prosecutor have made an out-of-court settlement and the subsidiary charges have been withdrawn. In short, proceedings still serve the implementation of state policy and the private voice remains muted.[77]

iii. THE CONFLICT-SOLVING PROCESS BEFORE COORDINATE OFFICIALDOM

Now to be canvassed is the realm of judicial apparatus dominated by amateurs who take turns in administering justice, who are free from hierarchical supervision, and who are receptive to considerations of substantive justice. How do such coordinate officials act as conflict resolvers, presumptively imbued by the ideology of laissez-faire? In other words, what imprint does coordinate organization leave on the conflict-solving process?

At the outset, it is important to recall the pressures toward temporal concentration of proceedings generated by the coordinate organization. Because of these pressures, it is unlikely that the parties' dispute will be orchestrated staccato, or as a sequence of discrete installments: the contest of the parties is

75. It is not necessary for the victim actually to file a civil complaint; it suffices to show that damages could be sought *in principe*. See R. Merle and A. Vitu, *Traité de Droit Criminel*, 2d ed., vol. 2, 67–68 (Paris, 1973). For a good overview of the French *partie civile* action, see A. V. Sheehan, *Criminal Prosecution in Scotland and in France*, 21–22 (1975). Recall that the French judiciary has a long tradition of being empowered to investigate independently of the views of state prosecutors: *toute juge procureur général*.

76. See *Austrian Code of Crim. Proc.*, §48. In practice, subsidiary action independent of a parasitic civil suit for damages is of little importance. Observe that in Austria the public prosecutor does not participate in the subsidiary prosecution, but can take it over.

77. Strong movements are underfoot that would curtail the rights of private individuals to interfere in state prosecutions. For France, see A. V. Sheehan, *supra*, n. 75, 23.

preferably waged during a single, continuous forensic episode. Further concentration of the lawsuit derives from the absence of a reprise of the contest before higher levels of authority: proceedings in the first instance are normally final in nature.

Of course, if the single procedural episode—the trial—is to flow continuously, it must be prepared. But because there are no low-level officials to perform necessarily discontinuous detective work, trial preparation is left to the parties in dispute: each assembles evidence in support of his contentions. In an official apparatus whose ranks are fluid, there can be no strong objection against this delegation of activity to outsiders; as I have repeatedly stated, where officials are themselves amateurs, they can assert few compelling reasons for excluding other amateurs. Special devices, unknown to hierarchical authority, appear to enforce compliance with private investigative demands. As parties are driven be self-interest, these private investigations can become powerful vehicles for the discovery of information. Ideally, the preparatory activity of the parties does not involve officials at all; authorities must be brought in only to resolve possible subsidiary disputes regarding the proper reach of private preparatory activity. No longer is a lawsuit identified with action presided over by officials, as in proceedings before hierarchical officials.

The adjudicator characteristically comes to the case unfamiliar with the controversy. He cannot study an official dossier concerning preparatory activities where there is no such document. Inevitably, a great deal of procedural action— and at trial, too—is performed by the litigants. At least initially, they are the only ones who can interrogate witnesses effectively and present other evidence. Accordingly, information is conveyed in an intensely disputational form that permits each litigant to challenge immediately what the other has elicited or presented. Of course, trials may easily become noisy squabbles, but this spectacle can better be tolerated by coordinate officials—used to this sort of thing—than by methodical bureaucrats. Nor is the weak mediating role of officialdom the only source of the fierce confrontational character of proceedings; the intensity of forensic contest is further enhanced by the possible finality of the verdict. Since there is no regular "next stage" before higher authority to which the loser can appeal, the party cannot afford to temporize but must say to himself "my time is now." Briefly, then, coordinate authority reinforces the morphology of contest which is demanded by the conflict-solving process.

Is this also true of the adjudicator's passive posture? In an important sense, the answer is affirmative. With so much trial action conducted by the litigants, the adjudicator easily recedes into passivity: he listens to the arguments and proof advanced by the parties, he monitors their compliance with the ground rules of a fair contest, and at the conclusion of the trial, he reaches a decision, announcing which side has prevailed. His detachment is supported by the belief—generated by the ideology of the reactive state—that the forensic dispute presents no larger issues exceeding the desirability of its resolution, and that letting the parties fight it out is the best means to absorb a conflict.

The conception of legal proceedings as conflict can realistically be extended even to those controversies which involve state officials as disputants. Where state authority is fragmented, clashes among officials are a daily occurrence, and they cannot be avoided by various "hierarchical" devices, such as transfer of the matter in contention to a common superior. Institutional loyalties and esprit de corps among state officials are also lacking. Where there is no fusion of authority at the top, it is easy for feuding officials to find a neutral third to whom the dispute can be taken for impartial resolution. But the conception of legal proceedings as contest can also be maintained in disputes involving a citizen and a state official. Two factors, already mentioned in other contexts, combine to produce this result. Because the decision maker is not a civil servant, he is not immediately suspect as biased in favor of the official side to the controversy. Because the official disputant is not hierarchically linked to the center of state government, his position vis-à-vis the private litigant,—parallel, if somewhat skewed—is still not so imbalanced as to make the idea of a contest between rough equals a transparent parody. In consequence, the coordinate organization of procedural authority expands the zone in which conflict-solving arrangements can be contemplated as a feasible form of legal proceedings.

The synergetic effect of coordinate authority and conflict resolution as the purpose of proceedings can be observed in yet another respect. Remember that in the pure conflict-solving style party control extends to the free adaptation of procedural regulation according to the special circumstances of the parties' situation. Because the parties can stipulate to modification of standard practices, the lawsuit can be finely tuned or linked to the undertow of negotiation that characterizes litigation in a reactive state. But while the exclusivity of hierarchical officialdom and its bureaucratic rigidities erect barriers to such inventive activity by the litigants, coordinate authority readily accepts even this additional element of procedural laissez-faire; the lawsuit's form can be custom-made rather than rigidly prefabricated.

Now let us turn to the area of tensions in the reactive state between coordinate organization and the conflict-solving process. To do so, it is necessary to revert to the position of the coordinate conflict resolver. As I have noted, his inactivity is not a product of clear conceptions of proper adjudicative functions in the coordinate apparatus. Such conceptions, expressed in unyielding rules, characterize hierarchical officialdom. Rather, the passive stance of the coordinate adjudicator is located on pragmatic grounds: unfamiliar with the dispute, he is ill prepared to take charge of procedural action himself. There are no firm barriers to judicial activism: the adjudicator perceives himself as an autonomous agent with inherent power to intervene in the parties' contest if he so chooses. Because the exercise of discretion permeates all aspects of his temporary office, his detachment at trial is essentially an exercise in self-restraint, buttressed by the ideology of noninvolvement. However, like a dormant volcano, he may under certain circumstances erupt into vigorous activity.

As his activism may readily conflict with the parties' control of litigation, the circumstances that can lead to abandonment of judicial self-restraint deserve closer scrutiny. Remember here that coordinate officials are not case-hardened professionals, used to exercising the emotional economies necessary for detachment from the destinies of procedural participants or suitable for narrow concentration on the facts in issue between the litigants. What exacerbates malaise with impersonal postures is that adjudicators are exposed to live testimony in the immediacy of the courtroom drama. They hear and see the parties and other forensic actors directly rather than as reflections in cold files that distant officials silently leaf through in the cloistral calm of hierarchical authority. Thus even if the norms espoused by coordinate officials urge minimal emotional commitment—some sort of Calvinist reserve—these officials still find it difficult to behave like referees in a debating club whose task is to focus solely on better argumentation of narrow issues. Imagine that, because of some peripheral reason, their sympathy is evoked by a party who also is the weaker advocate, bound to lose if the contest logic is to be strictly maintained. It is likely in this situation that a coordinate official may project himself powerfully into trial proceedings: he may insist on subjecting witnesses to searching queries or may demand additional proof on his own. But in so doing, assistance is extended to one litigant, and the impartial posture required by the conflict-solving ideal is abandoned. Moreover, sudden involvement with procedural action can threaten the mastery of the parties over the lawsuit: the limits of freedom and autonomy cannot clearly be discerned in the chiaroscuro of official discretion that permeates the coordinate type of authority. Nor is it inconceivable that private mastery over the lawsuit be endangered in even those limited areas where hierarchical officialdom—if imbued with laissez-faire ideology—regards the autonomy of procedural parties inviolable. Accordingly, even if adjudication is monopolized by an elite that espouses reactive political doctrines, the attitudes of coordinate officials can sometimes weaken or even reject arrangements otherwise ideally suitable for the reactive style of conflict resolution.

The pursuit of a related tension leads to consideration of the position of the parties as evidentiary sources. It has been demonstrated that a pure reactive style of conflict resolution does not permit a party to be converted into a witness against his will: the sovereign master of a lawsuit may not be transformed into an evidentiary source to be examined—unless he freely chooses to undergo this Saul-to-Paul conversion. But the meaningful implementation of this conflict-solving idea presupposes an adjudicator capable of distinguishing the testimonial and managerial components in the position of the party, and who is furthermore willing to abide by the dictates of this distinction. Professionals can be trained both to separate the two aspects of the party role and, when deciding from the dossier, to draw no evidentiary inferences from mere allegations, questions put to witnesses, or similar "managerial" activity of the litigants. In contrast, coordinate authority is clearly inhospitable to observation of this important conflict-solving form: laymen have little understanding of the technical intricacies—sometimes serpentine—involved in separating testimonial and nontestimonial roles. Observing the parties' conduct in the courtroom, they can hardly avoid drawing testimonial conclusions from purportedly managerial acts. In consequence, the conversion of litigants into informational sources easily becomes an element of the coordinate (but not hierarchical) conflict-solving style.

In earlier chapters, I have repeatedly alluded to factors that conspire to make the conflict-solving process consummately lawyered and the reactive state a fertile soil for the activity of attorneys. Now that the interplay of coordinate authority and conflict-solving justice has been examined, a subplot in this conspiracy can be identified: tensions between procedural purpose and the character of officialdom can be reduced by admitting lawyers into the proceedings as professional assistants to the parties in dispute. When the management of the lawsuit is entrusted to lawyers, the parties fade into the background, and their behavior now offers fewer opportunities for the drawing of evidentiary inferences. Their autonomy can be better protected: acting as a distant, inscrutable master of the lawsuit no longer carries the inevitable burden of offering testimony. An additional advantage of drawing lawyers into the process is that the passive position of the adjudicator can thereby be stabilized: professional lawyers can efficiently sift out "emotionally charged" information that provokes neophyte adjudicators to exceed their narrow conflict-solving mission. There is yet another advantage. I have described how the delegation of trial preparation to the litigants in coordinate settings contains the seeds of the parties' trial activity: the division of issues into two cases—one for the claimant, the other for the respondent—is present *in nuce*. In the absence of lawyers, however, the line between the two sequential cases demanded by the conflict-solving style cannot be expected to be clear: rambling arguments obliterate it. It is the activity of lawyers that enables the crisp sequencing of action in favor of one and in favor of the other disputant to occur.[78]

Civil Disputes in Anglo-American Jurisdictions

Although the coordinate style of conflict resolution can be found in a variety of legal cultures, the procedural systems deriving from England contain the most graphic illustrations.

JUSTICES OF THE PEACE AND CIVIL DISPUTES. To the present day, some civil disputes can be adjudicated by laymen in Anglo-American jurisdictions, but indicia of the style now under consideration were shown with particular clarity in proceedings before their forebears—the justices of the peace of eighteenth- and nineteenth-century England. These amateurs—country gentlemen—epitomized almost completely the ideal of coordinate officialdom. Technically acting on royal commission, they were actually free from central supervision; their part-time service in matters of local government embraced administrative, judicial, and even legislative functions in the promiscuous fashion characteristic of nonbureaucratic forms of authority. Their decision making was inspired more by

---

78. Attorneys also prepare the case for a continuous coordinate trial by organizing issues through some sort of pleading mechanism.

common sense and social convention than by outcome-determinative rules. As I have already indicated, to outsiders their judgments appeared "Solomonic."[79]

Although best known for their part in the administration of criminal justice, their diffuse jurisdiction extended to civil matters as well. What were proceedings before them like? We do not know very much: official documentation was not required, as it was on the Continent, nor were civil proceedings so interesting as to give rise to popular literary accounts. But since lawyers seldom appeared in local courts, one can safely assume that proceedings were informal; litigants personally presented their cases unconstrained by technical rules of procedure and evidence. Under these circumstances, one can imagine that trials involved a great deal of noisy exchange among procedural participants as well as a bare minimum of bureaucratic routine. Yet it seems equally obvious that the justice of the peace was capable of displaying detachment and remaining above altercations, *au-dessus de la mêlée*. With his needs securely provided for, this local potentate could even cultivate an attitude of fair gamesmanship in matters of justice: the country gentleman knew what was "cricket."[80] But his conflict-solving posture was unstable; if he felt that a particular dispute revealed a larger need to exercise social control, his vague and flexibly changeable jurisdiction presented few obstacles in his self-paved path away from narrow conflict solving.

CLASSIC CIVIL PROCEDURE. Here I shall concentrate on only those features of classic litigation that appeared strange to Continental visitors. Cross-cultural perplexities which the comparative scheme proposes to explain must now be brought into focus.

The procedural implications of the duality between law and equity have intrigued Continental observers at least since the seventeenth century. It seemed odd to them that the center of English government would tolerate two independent, partially overlapping authorities for the disposition of civil cases—the common law courts and the chancellor. Was the duality not irreconcilable with the emerging idea of a single "legal order"? Besides, how could the jurisdiction of the chancellor be so deeply enmeshed in discretion that equitable relief seemed to be more a matter of grace than of right?[81] This wonderment is easily explained as the reaction of one who takes hierarchical ordering of authority for granted and is contemplating a judicial organization with pronounced coordinate features, such as vague sharing of authority and large doses of official discretion.

Many aspects of trial in common-law courts were also curious to visitors coming to England from across the Channel: a "day in court" in lieu of sequential sessions; emphasis on direct testimony instead of the evidentiary role of the file of the case; fragmentation of the tribunal into judge and jury instead of the unitary office of Roman-canonical *judex*. Truly astonishing in the Continental

---

79. Compare A. Mendelssohn-Bartholdy, *supra*, ch. 2, n. 37.

80. The emphasis on "fairness" and a "sporting" approach is often thought to be rooted in the eighteenth- and nineteenth-century English country squire experience. See J. Ortega y Gasset, *History as a System*, 130–31 (1961).

81. For a good discussion of this judicial "polytheism," see A. H. Pekelis, "Legal Techniques and Political Ideologies; A Comparative Study," 41 *Mich. L. Rev.* 665, 690–91 (1943).

view was the degree to which decisions of the lay jury—the paradigmatic adjudicator—escaped supervision through regular appellate mechanisms,[82] as well as various mechanisms designed to avert the damage of unchallengeable verdicts arising from dubious premises.[83] I have dealt with these contrasts before and shall not retrace familiar ground.

What does deserve a closer look, however, is the role of lawyers in English central courts. After the jury ceased to be a self-informing body, lawyers gradually took over the presentation of evidence and argument in court. Their trial activity produced important changes: where informal altercations heretofore dominated, a formal sequencing of "two cases" with all of the technicalities of introducing evidence began to take shape. Parties faded into the background, and their trial activity no longer permitted ample evidentiary evaluations.[84] The interrogatory action of the judge, never prominent, was further diminished, and the jury sank into passivity, often as inscrutable to the parties as the Sphinx. Increasingly, the outcome of the lawsuit turned on the skills of advocacy: courtroom tactics, evidentiary rules, and legal arguments became more and more recondite. As a result, to litigate a case became a very costly enterprise.

Imagine the architects of the Continental nineteenth-century process observing the progress of a garden-variety civil case in England. It would appear to them that the private legal profession had usurped many functions that properly belonged to the judiciary or some other court official—even in a laissez-faire state. Although otherwise relatively unconcerned in their own systems about the fate of impecunious litigants, Continental lawyers would be driven to wonder how many people could afford the services of the now indispensable lawyers to perform so many actions that were—in their native systems—in the province of the judiciary.[85] In short, they might easily have concluded that the English manner of administering civil justice accorded too much scope for the independent action of members of the legal profession acting on behalf of their clients.[86]

But this belief would be shaken in some situations: on occasion, the judge would intervene in proceedings and vigorously interfere with the management of the case by the litigants' lawyers. The Continental lawyer would be led to inquire into the "legal basis" for such intervention and would be shocked to discover the latent "inherent" powers of the judiciary to overrule the parties—powers that defy articulation in terms of clear and rigid rules. Especially disturbing to the Continental's liberal disposition would be those judicial powers with discretion-

---

82. Some control was vested in the trial judge, who could refuse to accept the verdict or enter a judgment despite a contrary verdict.

83. For example, rules on the sufficiency of evidence.

84. It might be objected that even prior to this, parties could not be turned into evidential sources because they were technically incompetent to testify. But as I have suggested before, in practice the litigants' utterances and demeanor were assessed by decision makers. The distinction between testimonial and nontestimonial aspects of the role of the parties was largely illusory in proceedings before lay adjudicators.

85. See M. Rheinstein, ed., *Max Weber on Law in Economy and Society*, 228 (1967).

86. On possible residual differences between Continental and Anglo-American liberal ideology see *supra*, ch. 3, sec. 3.

ary and sacerdotal resonance that obscure a clear answer to the question of who is in control—the judge or the parties.[87] Ironically, English judges could be found interfering with party management of the lawsuit even in those areas where Continental systems of the laissez-faire period protected the litigants' control over the case with great rigidity and consistency of purpose. For example, if the Continental civil judge attempted to extend the proof beyond that suggested by the litigants or to call a witness on his own, such behavior would immediately provoke sharp reaction and rebuke from higher courts. In England, in contrast, nothing seemed effectively to bar a powerful and independent judge from pressuring the parties to bow to his wishes and proffer additional evidence.[88] As a result of such residual and ill-defined judicial powers, the autonomy of English litigants would suddenly appear to Continental observers as quite unstable—in effect exposed to the trial judge's sufferance. They would be tempted to conclude that the principal guarantee against interference with the *dominus litis* position of the parties was the refusal of the judge to flex his muscles in the sphere of "mine and thine" with which a typical civil lawsuit was concerned. In other words, the self-restraint of the judiciary, rather than legal regulation, would seem to support the laissez-faire of civil litigation.[89]

A further surprise to Continental liberal observers would have been the great probing power of English civil procedure. As I have pointed out, liberal reformers on the Continent soft-pedaled the importance of truth discovery in civil disputes; as a result, in most jurisdictions testimonial privileges were conceived broadly, discovery devices were weak, and parties were exempted from the duty to testify. Confronted with the English system, Continentals marveled: how can this allegedly most liberal administration of justice tolerate the searching discovery of documents, or the requirement that litigants testify against their pecuniary and other self-interests? Part of the answer has already been suggested: to one who desires to keep the government at arm's length, private investigative powers—that is, the search for information by one citizen against another—appear not nearly so threatening as probing for truth by civil servants who are hierarchically connected with centers of state power. Besides, it may well be that a concentrated trial before passive lay fact finders, who must be attuned to

87. At this point, recall the logically legalistic mind that seeks unequivocal (either/or) answers; if it cannot be asserted with certainty to a Continental lawyer that a party arrangement is completely safe from overruling by the judge, he is likely to conclude that control over the party's arrangement is reserved for the judge.

88. It is true that the judge himself could not call a witness or raise an issue not raised in the pleadings, but as he exercised relatively great discretionary authority in so many matters, the mere indication of his wish that some evidence be proffered or some argument be made would typically suffice. It is also true that English judges would seldom interrogate witnesses searchingly, but until the more recent rise of regular appellate procedures, there was little recourse against such aberrational practice. Observe that American appellate courts do not treat seaching judicial interrogations as *reversible* error unless the trial judge acted in an unfair or biased way. See e.g., *People* v. *Rigney* 359 P.2d 23 (Calif. 1961) (opinion of Traynor, J.).

89. This explains the metaphorical remark of Mendelssohn-Bartholdy, quoted *supra*, ch. 2, n. 32, and accompanying text.

evidentiary standards ad hoc, generates significantly greater need for information than installment-type proceedings before professional civil servants.[90]

Conflict-Solving Forms in Anglo-American Criminal Process

Since criminal law enforcement cannot entirely be fitted into the conflict-solving
mode of proceeding, at least in modern states, Anglo-American criminal procedure remains, in the last analysis, a policy-implementing process.[91] As such, it
will be considered immediately hereafter. The issue to be addressed here is the
comparatively striking fact that more contest forms can be identified in Anglo-
American criminal prosecution than in any other contemporary system of criminal justice. I have alluded to this fact several times before and shall now consider
it more closely.

Explanation of this phenomenon may begin with the recognition that
coordinate authority acts to reinforce the conflict-solving style in matters where
state interests are implicated—as they clearly are in criminal prosecution. I have
earlier suggested that where the fact finders are lay jurors rather than career civil
servants, the image of the decision maker as an independent arbiter between the
individual and the government gains in credibility. But the coordinate organization of the state's prosecuting arm also lends credibility to the contest design of
proceedings.

This should be clear in the example of the ancient but still operative English
system of citizen prosecution on behalf of the Crown. Any citizen (although now
almost always the victim) can press charges for any crime, including the most
heinous ones. Commingling self-interest and public-spiritedness, this system
was congenial to the traditional English judicial apparatus; where the number of
officials is small and they are not fully bureaucratized, it is natural to encourage
ordinary citizens to step forward and participate in criminal law enforcement.
While proceedings pressed by the victim were not a pure system of private
prosecution,[92] nevertheless such accusers, arguing with the defendant in court,
brought pronounced disputational features into criminal trials.

What about the public prosecutors in America? It is well known that they
gradually managed to obtain a monopoly of initiative, so that the victim of a
crime was deprived of a voice, at least in decisions not to prosecute.[93] Is it not then
inevitable that prosecution was converted into a nonpartisan vehicle for enforce-

90. See Damaška, *supra*, ch. 2, n. 10, 540–46. Observe also that the traditional civil law jury
was required to reach an unanimous verdict, whereas the decision of Continental courts can be less
than unanimous.

91. Ideal in the conflict-solving mode would be an exclusive system of victim prosecution,
with the victim and the defendant in full control of their respective cases.

92. See *supra*, ch. 5, n. 11, and accompanying text.

93. How the public prosecutor acquired his monopoly is recounted in A. Goldstein, "Prosecution: History of the Public Prosecutor," in S. Kadish, ed., *Encyclopedia of Crime and Justice* (1983).
The victim retains an influence on the decision to prosecute because for many types of offenses,
authorities seldom launch a prosecution unless the victim is willing to swear a complaint and thus
promise testimony at trial.

ment of the criminal policy of the state? A closer look at the organization of the American prosecutorial arm quickly reveals that the imagery of criminal proceedings as a form of contest can still be maintained. American prosecutors are not a hierarchically organized state bureaucracy, as they are in virtually all Continental countries. They work mostly alone, or with a few assistants, free from effective hierarchical supervision.[94] Being locally elected, they depend for their staying power in office on the electorate rather than on institutional superiors. Rather than expecting promotion to a more elevated prosecutorial position as a reward for good service, they view political rewards as a stimulation: good performance can result in election to City Hall, Congress, or some other political office. No matter what initial impressions suggest, even in the federal system the situation is not radically different. Here, fear of a hierarchical Justice Department has led to the virtual autonomy of United States attorneys, who are in addition mainly transient political appointees. In this situation it is clear that American prosecutors should not be perceived as local representatives of a uniform national law enforcement machine, as they are on the Continent; they are not striving to implement government policy toward crime because there is only seldom such policy. In the absence of instructions coming from the government, they may readily associate such policy with their own views and acquire a degree of personal stake in a criminal case, so that they may experience the outcome of criminal prosecutions as instances of personal victory or personal defeat.[95] To presume that they are engaged in a dispute with the accused may even be a beneficial substitute for absent bureaucratic incentives for zealous law enforcement. In short, the American prosecutor can much more easily imagine himself in a partisan role than can a low-level Continental trial prosecutor, who is often quite reluctantly obliged to press a case, pursuant to the mandates of his "impersonal" office. The local American prosecutor also does not bring the prestige and weight of national government to bear on the case. Because the situs of great social power can lie outside of government, the sphere of influence of at least some defendants may equal or exceed that of the local prosecutor. It is thus easier in America than in Europe to imagine the prosecutor as a party in a roughly parallel position with the defendant—a position required by the concept of criminal procedure as a conflict-resolving mechanism. It is *pro tanto* also easier to engraft conflict-solving forms on American than on Continental criminal prosecutions.

A few comparatively striking examples of these forms deserve attention. As is to be expected, the pretrial process is cast mainly in the policy-implementing mode, but even in the earliest stages contest forms are in evidence. For example, if interpreted as a purely partisan pursuit, the police inquiry would surely be distorted; nevertheless it makes frequent allusions to contest forms. In

---

94. See K. Davis, *Discretionary Justice*, 208 (1971). For comparisons with Europe, see M. Damaška, "The Reality of Prosecutorial Discretion," 29 *Am. J. Comp. Law* 119 (1981).

95. In a hierarchical bureaucracy a prosecutor feels that he has done a good job even if the defendant is acquitted: more than in America, his rewards depend on technical and thus relatively neutral evaluations of performance. The imagery of "winning" and "losing" criminal cases is much more congenial to American than to European prosecutors.

fact, a single integrative investigation is conspicuously absent: the police and the defendant prepare their separate "cases," creating familiar problems of mutual discovery and the maintenance of rough equality between the contestants.[96] Much more so than in Europe, preliminary detention can present a serious obstacle for the defendant's preparation of his case. Various forms of negotiation between prosecution and defense constitute the characteristic undertow of the pretrial process, just as do party negotiations in a civil case.

Although the guilty-plea mechanism appeared historically for reasons independent of the vision of criminal justice as conflict resolution, this characteristic feature of Anglo-American criminal procedure perfectly dovetails with conflict-solving forms. As I have repeatedly suggested, if criminal proceedings are indeed devoted to the resolution of a dispute, it makes little sense to insist that proceedings continue if the defendant refuses to oppose the claims and demands of the prosecution. Of course, the mere possibility of the defendant's pleading guilty creates ample room in criminal prosecutions for negotiations and haggling between the parties. Against a concession, the prosecution can try to persuade the defendant to concede guilt so that a contested trial need not take place. It is true that, as a result of bargains struck, the truth-revealing potential of criminal judgments may be severely diminished. If a defendant who in fact committed rape may be convicted of simple assault, one who is innocent of rape charges may feel seriously pressured to plead guilty of assault in order to avoid the risk of far more serious punishment should the case go to trial and end in conviction. But as in a civil dispute, accurate verdicts lose some of their importance if the unspoken assumption is that the criminal process is a means of settling a dispute between the state and an autonomous individual. A comparativist should not overlook the impact of the screening effect of guilty pleas on the confrontational character of common-law trials. Only disputed cases come before the adjudicator, so that there is at trial a firm foundation for contest forms. This is quite unlike the situation on the Continent, where every case must be tried—even if the accused has fully confessed—so that disputational arrangements are often eviscerated. Incidentally, this provides an additional ground for the general impression of Anglo-American observers that Continental trials are mainly an audit of work previously completed. I have observed that the explanation lies partly in the fact that Continental trials are well prepared and that documents containing material of this preparation find their way into the trial. It is apparent that, even were Continental trials not as thoroughly prepared as they are, their staple docket would still be the routine uncontested cases which are weeded out of common-law procedure through the guilty plea on arraignment.

I have dealt in various contexts with contest forms at the common-law trial

---

96. Such is the resilience of the idea of two independent investigations in America that it has easily survived the rise of the "welfare" institution of public defenders. It is now possible for the latter and public prosecutors to conduct parallel investigations, both publicly financed. Writing in the 1930s, Thurman Arnold still thought that such parallel inquiries would constitute an absurdity. See T. Arnold, "Trial by Combat and the New Deal," 47 *Harv. L. Rev.* 913, 922 (1934).

and shall not detain the reader with further repetition. One form does deserve to be reiterated, however, because it is often overlooked by those who compare Continental and Anglo-American trials: matters that Europeans treat as unitary prerequisites of criminal punishment can be separated in Anglo-American systems into distinct issues, as they are in civil litigation, and each party required to raise, argue, and prove his respective issue. It is thus for the prosecutor to prove a robbery, but it is for the defendant to raise the issue that he was acting under duress, threatened by a third person. Although the rigidity of this separation has been greatly relaxed in the past few decades, it has still not entirely disappeared. To the extent that the defense still retains the monopoly of raising some defensive issues, it can still force a substantively erroneous outcome upon the justice system. Thus, if for some reason best known to him the defendant fails to raise the defense of duress, he can be convicted even if he appears to be innocent in terms of the substantive doctrines applicable to the facts of the case.[97] While this situation is clearly undesirable in a policy-implementing system, it can be justified in the conflict-solving process of a laissez-faire state.

In invoking political ideology, I have already touched on the other strong reinforcement of contest forms in Anglo-American criminal prosecutions, quite apart from the traditional coordinate organization of both courts and prosecution. During the period of the eighteenth and nineteenth centuries when conflict-solving forms were being developed and honed in civil proceedings of Anglo-American countries, various currents of liberal ideology then exercised their most powerful hold on the Western legal imagination. As I have pointed out in chapter 3, the idea that to administer criminal justice is to resolve a dispute between the government and an autonomous member of civil society fully crystallized in this epoch, and not before. The notion that state interests should be treated as merely another private interest also appeared in this period. In consequence, conceptual space was created for transferring argumentative styles first used in civil litigation to the administration of criminal law: images such as "balancing the advantages of litigants" or giving litigants "equal weapons" assumed considerable intellectual force in the shaping of procedural arrangements generally.[98] Both facilitated and given greater plausibility by the coordinate organization of authority, these arguments enabled the formal design of the criminal process as a contest to be carried much further in Anglo-American countries than in continental Europe. So it is not altogether strange or unexpected that from the contemporary Continental perspective, Anglo-American

---

97. See *supra*, ch. 4, text accompanying nn. 23–25.

98. Given liberal preoccupation with formal equality, the focus was also on building ever more sophisticated "defensive weapons" for the accused in his contest with the state. What was pushed into the background was the problem of who can afford the use of increasingly costly procedural opportunities, as well as the impact of these developments on the total cost of the justice system if cases were normally to go through the trial stage. Negotiations between prosecution and defense with the end of avoiding the costly trial seemed acceptable to what Dewey would call the "trafficking ethics." See J. Dewey, *German Philosophy and Politics*, 57–58 (1915).

criminal prosecutions appear too deeply embedded in the style of private law-suits, too indifferent to the need of accurate and effective enforcement of substantive criminal law.[99]

iv. THE POLICY-IMPLEMENTING PROCESS OF COORDINATE OFFICIALDOM

Into the last category of my classificatory table fall systems where the legal process is understood to be devoted to the implementation of state policy, but is administered by coordinate officialdom. There is no precise analogue in conventional theory for the resulting coordinate activist style of proceeding. The widely accepted conception of the inquisitorial system comes close, because it too expresses a legal process independent of dispute resolution and geared to law enforcement. But as I have repeatedly said, the inquisitorial process embraces features deeply rooted in the hierarchical organization of authority, and it is constructed against the background of a state insufficiently managerial to permit full deployment of activist forms of justice. In order for coordinate activist arrangements to emerge, the inquisitorial mode must be purged of its hierarchical stylistic elements and fitted with features congenial to a truly managerial government; a procedural topography must be described for which there are no maps.

The concept of inquiry remains: activist justice requires than an investigation be launched into the best policy response to the precipitating event. But in the coordinate judicial apparatus this inquiry is sui generis: the methodical probing by state officials, which can be stretched over time and divided into stages with subtasks for specialized officials, is absent. Absent also is an all-encompassing official dossier—crucial to decision making—which coagulates the results of widely scattered activities into a solid whole. Inquiries carried out by coordinate officials are less structured and temporarily more compressed; as I have observed, the apparatus of justice functions in sporadic bursts of activity, devoting continuous blocks of time to its tasks.

The collection of material for the decision and the taking of other necessary steps are easily entrusted to outsiders, including citizens whose interests are directly implicated in the official inquiry. It should be remembered, however, that the object of legal proceedings requires that such outsiders not be placed in positions where they could frustrate or compromise the goals of the activist

---

99. The Continental observer is shocked, even outraged, to learn that, even if acquitted, American defendants must pay court costs and the hefty fees of their lawyers (unless they qualify for legal aid). Such strong reaction is understandable because of the Continental's assumption that the American criminal process is as devoted to policy implementation as his own, so that acquittals tend to be plausibly related to the defendant's innocence (given the orientation toward truth discovery). As he discovers that acquittals in America often depend more upon the forensic skills of defense counsel than on the actual innocence of the defendant, his negative reaction is greatly alleviated. For an example of Continental indemnity schemes for acquitted defendants, see T. Kleinknecht, *Strafprozessordnung*, 32d ed., commentary to §467(I), 1165 (München, 1975).

government; ultimate control over proceedings therefore remains in official hands. Outside participation in coordinate inquiries tends to comprise a mix of complaints and reports to authorities and so on, and the self-serving interest is thus harnessed to the pursuit of larger objectives. An important contrast with the hierarchical activist style should be noticed at this point: in the diffuse light typical of the coordinate environment, there are no clear discontinuities between official and nonofficial spheres. Where ambiguous hybrids of official and non-official tasks abound and semiofficial action flourishes, the use of private individuals as enforcers of activist programs cannot be so clearly unacceptable as it is in a hierarchical activist administration of justice.

In the activist mode, coordinate officials are self-starting, instituting proceedings on their own, independently of any actual controversy, complaint, or request. At sessions devoted to examination of assembled material, they may initially stand back, letting outsiders bring forward matters needed for the decision; but whenever they feel that the attainment of the right result so requires, officials intervene in the goings-on to probe on their own initiative or demand that outside participants perform or omit certain actions. Unlike their posture in the reactive mode, they are not indifferent to the outcome of proceedings; activist ideology requires that they be committed to the realization of state policy and that they reach the optimal result. While their great powers are seldom exercised in the reactive setting, now they often make use of it, unconstrained by bureaucratic routine, rigid regulation, or hierarchical supervision.

Because the interests and views of participating individuals often clash, heated arguments often flare up in coordinate inquiries, but since proceedings are divorced from bipolar disputes, these arguments can be polycentric. The absence of sharp contours in the relations among participants in coordinate proceedings deserves to be stressed again. Unofficial altercations can easily shade into semi-official disputes over alternative conceptions of desirable action. But there is more: the decentralization of authority opens up the possibility for genuine *official* disputes over state policy. Yet it is misleading to estimate the volume of such official controversies by extrapolation from the experience of essentially reactive states with only a few activist programs. In this "mixed" setting, different views on the social good can be embraced freely, not only by members of civil society, but also by various fragmented centers of power, including the judiciary.

In a truly managerial state, however, officialdom has its all-encompassing philosophy, and the dictates of the ruling elite greatly decrease the chance of official clashes arising over policy matters. The unity of coordinated officials can often be ensured independently of organizational hierarchical charts. Yet official altercations over the best policy response to a problem do occur and accord disputational features to coordinate inquiries. Moreover, where an office and its holder are imperfectly distinguished, as is the case in coordinate organizations, to complain against an office is essentially similar to complaining against an individual. Once again, it may be seen how a coordinate apparatus of authority provides an environment in which contest forms—albeit modified—seem applicable, even in proceedings devoted to the implementation of state policy rather than only to narrow interpersonal disputes.

The desire for stability that provides the distinctive imprint of justice in the reactive state should not be projected into the setting now under consideration. Where matters involving the state are concerned, a coordinate official is always ready to reconsider his decision if he finds that it was wrong or that it requires modification in light of new circumstances. If he feels that a decision by a parallel official is erroneous, he is ready to block its execution or to contemplate some other constraining action. Because the apparatus of justice is replete with jurisdictional redundancies and vaguely shared authority, the opportunities for such "collateral" action are legion, even when one allows for shared values and the ideological unity of coordinate officials. Of course, because economic, educational and other state policies often require prompt and decisive action, this feature of the activist coordinate process can be a source of considerable frustration. It is only a symptom of a wider tension between the activist function and the coordinate structure of government—a tension to which I have alluded several times before. The more activist the government, the greater this tension, and the more the coordinate apparatus of justice begins to resemble an octopus whose tentacles lack proper neural interconnections. But one should not attribute the efficiency expert's concern about "dysfunctions" to the part-time draftees, generalist judges, and semiofficial procedural protagonists who compose the coordinate apparatus of justice. In their scheme of things, such dysfunctions, even if clearly perceived, may be an acceptable price for an otherwise desirable state of affairs.[100]

But in identifying these tensions, I have come to a good starting point for a survey of actual justice systems that approximate the procedural morphology sketched thus far in abstract terms. I shall locate them in Anglo-American jurisdictions usually viewed through lenses that focus on often superficial conflict-solving features and leave the policy-implementing underside of the administration of justice somewhat blurred.

Historical Forms in Anglo-American Justice

THE SELF-INFORMING JURY. Although the pristine English jury has by now become a faded and unrestorable fresco, it is reasonably certain that members of this jury, convened by royal judges to express the voice of the countryside, were permitted to conduct their own "detective work." At least in part, the operation of this jury system consisted of informal inquiries carried out by temporary lay officials—a clear instance of coordinate activist form.

INVESTIGATIONS AND ADJUDICATION BY JUSTICES OF THE PEACE. Less hidden in the recesses of history is the jurisdiction of justices of the peace, whose all-purpose office encompassed important criminal law enforcement authority.[101]

---

100. See *supra*, Introduction, n. 19 and accompanying text.
101. See S. Webb and B. Webb, *English Local Government: The Parish and the County*, vol. 1, 294–304, 319–446 (1906).

They were empowered to conduct investigations of serious crime individually, and composed in panels, they could adjudicate minor offenses. Their decisions eluded regular control by central authority, and their activity was both scantily regulated and quite informal; traces of their action were not preserved in dossiers. Comparatively speaking, they were clearly more "autocratic" and more powerful than low-level investigators in the coeval inquisitorial process on the Continent. In sum, proceedings before them reveal characteristics of a "coordinate" inquest style.

THE GRAND JURY. As it functioned during certain periods of its history, the grand jury furnishes another illustration of inquest form adapted to the setting of ad hoc lay officials. In contrast to current American practice, there was no public prosecutor to act before the jurors, so that grand jury proceedings must be imagined as informal amateur inquiries. Unlike conflict-solving proceedings, the grand jury's action was not necessarily based on complaints against a designated person or even targeted at a particular crime. Widely ranging inquiries into issues facing the community were possible, broader in scope than the *inquisitio generalis* of the old Continental criminal process. [102]If grand jury proceedings resulted in an indictment and the accused pleaded guilty, sentences would be imposed on the basis of informal inquiry by local amateurs. But indictments could have been accompanied by reports addressed to wider problems than the particular instance of criminal conduct before the jury. Such reports can be viewed as rough analogues of "the special ruling" a Soviet judge may issue in the hierarchical activist context.

THE CRIMINAL PROCESS AT ASSIZES. In the preceding section, I have dwelt on the incorporation of contest forms into the English criminal process, a development that began in the course of the eighteenth century. But the reader may wonder how this process was structured in the course of the sixteenth and seventeenth centuries, when criminal justice emerged from medieval circumstances and jurors were no longer self-informing. The roughest outlines of the process are known with reasonable certainty and should be included here.

Justices of the peace would cursorily collect and sift the evidence brought to their attention by informants and, if warranted, would bind the defendant over for trial. The ensuing trial might be thought to have been predicated on conflict-solving ideas: the defendant was asked how he pleaded, and the trial would take place only if he contested the charge. But it is plain enough by this point that to import into that early period notions of disputation between members of civil society and the state would be anachronistic. Historically viewed, pleadings were a product of the thirteenth-century rejection of trial by ordeal by the Church of Rome; the substitution of the jurors' fallible human judgment for the judgment of the deity required the defendant's consent. [103] In later times, the linkage of the trial to contestation ("no contest, no trial") was characteristic of unmethodical

---

102. On the history of the grand jury, see G. Dession and I. Cohen, "The Inquisitorial Functions of Grand Juries," 41 *Yale L.J.* 687 (1932). On the *inquisitio generalis*, see B. Carpzov, *supra*, n. 8, quest. 107, nos. 5–10.

103. See R. Van Caenagem, *The Birth of the English Law*, 146, n. 193 (1973).

and nonsystematic administration of justice. Following a skimpy, unprofessional inquiry into the facts of crime, the system was prepared to impose—without trial—even the most serious punishments tolerated by the temper of the times, unless by contesting charges, the defendant insisted on explaining away the allegedly mistaken accusation.[104] Trials were in the main unstructured or informal "altercations" among the accused, the witnesses, and the complaining victim. While "two cases" were present *in nuce*, they were as yet undifferentiated. Both judge and jurors freely interceded in the arguments, a practice that would sometimes lead to mutual exchanges between the two component parts of the tribunal. While the defendant was technically not a witness and could thus not be examined under oath he was readily used as a testimonial resource and subjected to extensive judicial interrogation. Given the conversational informality of proceedings and the lay character of the jury, one could not expect the adjudicator to abide by fine technical distinctions between testimonial and nontestimonial uses of the defendant's statements. Besides, trials were also assessments of the defendant's character, revealed independently of any testimony. Lawyers seldom appeared to support the charges, and until the mid-eighteenth century, defense counsel were barred from participating in felony trials.[105] The early trial was essentially an occasion for the adjudicator to establish whether the charges were or were not correct—or to put it differently, whether the prerequisites existed to justify imposition of punishment.

Despite the later liberal infusion of contest arrangements into the Anglo-American criminal process, it would be naive to take ideological slogans at face value and to view the entire "adversarial" criminal process of the liberal epoch as a vehicle for the settlement of disputes between government and the citizen accused of crime. To try to demonstrate here that this image fails to account for the initial stages of the criminal process would be more tiresome than instructive. It is more important to dispel the notion that the guilt-determinative stages of the trial process turned into a dispute-resolving mechanism. True, in most instances this appeared superficially to be the case: a plea of not guilty was the precondition for the trial to commence. But it should not be overlooked that the judge could refuse to accept a guilty plea, so that trial could take place in the absence of a genuine controversy between the prosecution and the defense. Even if rarely, the epiphenomenal nature of the disputation would come to the surface.[106] At least in some American states, the judge was also authorized to create artificially the absent dispute between the "regular" prosecutor and an individual by appointing

---

104. Perceptive remarks on the purpose of the "preadversarial" common-law trial are found in J. Langbein, "Shaping the Eighteenth-Century Criminal Trial: A View from the Ryder Sources," 50 *U. Chi. L. Rev.* 1, 123, 133 (1983).

105. These trials without lawyers have recently been explored by J. Langbein, "The Criminal Trial before the Lawyers," 45 *U. Chi. L. Rev.* 263–306 (1978). See also Langbein, *supra*, n. 104.

106. Where the defendant's guilty plea was based on a deal with the prosecution, the judge's failure to accept it did not necessarily abort the controversy: now the prosecution would normally press more serious charges, and the defendant would oppose them.

a special prosecutor and directing him to initiate prosecution.[107] Nor should it be imagined that the trial judge maintained the passive role of an umpire under all circumstances. There was as yet no welfare state right to free legal assistance, so that where an impecunious defendant pleaded not guilty, the judge would often assume an "activist" posture and try to elucidate facts favorable to the defense on his own.

The postconviction process was entirely free from allusions to conflict-solving forms and, with appellate review of sentences virtually nonexistent, was also a graphic example of one-level, discretionary decision making.[108] Sentences could be imposed without trial upon the plea of guilty, so that the disposition of the case rested directly upon the result of inquests conducted by various amateur officials—constables, justices of the peace, and so on. In sum, then, though richly adorned with contest elements, Anglo-American criminal justice was—even in the heyday of laissez-faire—in the policy-implementing mode on balance, and thus falls into the classificatory box now under consideration.

Contemporary Activist Justice in America

The worldwide trend toward an enlarged role for government—so dramatically evident in Britain—can also be observed in America. Since the New Deal, and in an atmosphere of managerial social engineering, numerous governmental programs have been instituted, administrative regulations have begun to proliferate, and the agenda of government has greatly expanded. For some time, it has been fashionable to discuss the rise of an interventionist "activist" state. Yet, needless to say, the American government has not embraced an overall program of social transformation or taken over management of the economy by displacing the market as the organizer of production and exchange. Large spheres of social life remain exempt from governmental control, left to be guided by the forces of the market. Playing a curious counterpoint to the ideology of activism, the old political belief that the state is an evil force to be contained has survived the increased demand for governmental intervention and dependence on its programs.

Thus, from the vantage point our comparative concerns confer, these internal perceptions of activism require correction: in comparison with a truly managerial government—I have called it activist—American activism is quite limited and progressing unevenly: the polity is an unstable mixture of activist and

---

107. These powers still survive; sometimes they are spelled out in a statute. See *In re Ringwood Fact. Find. Comm.*, 324 A.2d 1, 4 (N.J. 1974). More often, however, they are regarded as part of the judiciary's "inherent" powers. See, e.g., *Forsythe v. Coate*, 546 P.2d 1060 (Mont. 1976). Observe that in Connecticut, prosecutors are appointed by judges. *State v. Moynahan*, 325 A.2d 199 (Conn. 1973). The resultant blending of powers is a source of bewilderment to Continental observers.

108. Another facet of coordinate authority was the discretionary flexibility with which the judge could postpone the execution of the criminal sanction (a power denied to Continental judges of the epoch), thus paving the way for modern "rehabilitative" devices such as probation.

reactive impulses in which the latter still predominate. In fact, many aspects of governmental intervention are impelled by the desire to maintain a society guided by the invisible hand of the market mechanism rather than the visible hand of self-conscious governmental plans. Yet no matter where the present form of the American polity is placed on the activist-reactive continuum, and in spite of more recent attempts to contain the spread of governmental interventionism, the fact remains that important regulatory policies exist and governmental programs are now in place. They exert pressure on the inherited justice system and induce transformations that I shall briefly trace.[109]

My concern here is with *coordinate* activism. But is the American apparatus of government still characterized by amateurism, decentralization, hostility toward legalism, and similar features that I have associated with the coordinate type of authority? In internal perspective, the activist American state is inseparable from bureaucratic centralization. To an external observer, however, it is one of the most striking facets of the American brand of state activism that the state apparatus continues to be permeated by features attributable to coordinate authority. These surviving features—especially in the machinery of justice—are more pronounced than in any other modern industrial state. Although I touched on this theme in the first chapter, this robust contention requires more substantiation, and the subject must be taken up again.

Foreign observers will not deny the mid-century American bureaucratization of government, but they are likely to assess it as comparatively modest and sporadic. Where in other countries decisions are reserved for senior career officials, they are often made in America by political appointees. More readily than elsewhere, official positions are entered ad hoc and laterally, with careers alternating between the more lucrative private sector and less remunerative public employment. This was observed in the case of prosecutors, but it is also true of the police and the judiciary in many states. Also comparatively striking is the absence of bureaucratic exclusivity: functions are easily shared or even completely delegated to outsiders, even amateurs or nongovernmental specialists. Of course, juries continue to be called upon to participate in adjudication—although the matters they now have to decide often require instant expertise in complicated regulations. The enforcement of some important programs is entrusted to individuals or private groups, even if such delegation leads to haphazard implementation or redundancy with official enforcement. Private attorneys' general are quite prebureaucratic actors, in light of bureaucratic tendencies toward systematic action and toward the separation of private from official spheres. In a typical "coordinate" style, official functions are often fused, distinctions are blurred, and bailiwicks overlap. Thus the Congress, experiencing a difficulty in writing a budget, may engage in the micromanagement of some matters that seem to belong to the core prerogatives of the executive. But nowhere is this better illustrated than in the example of those federal judges who in "structural"

---

109. Important changes have also occurred in ideas on what constitutes the paradigmatic form of law. See J. Mashaw, "Law in the Activist State," 92 *Yale L.J.* 1129–73 (1983).

injunction cases go far beyond specific commands or prohibitions to themselves direct and manage the transformation of prisons, schools, or other institutions. While not even Montesquieu, theorizing in his Gascon vineyards, ever contemplated an absolute functional separation, such *freins et contrepoids*, such conjoining of administrative, legislative, and judicial functions, would drive him to despair.[110]

Most astonishing to a foreign eye is the continuing fragmentation and decentralization of authority. Thus while a regulatory or social welfare statute may create a central office, such as the Environmental Protection Agency, this office need not have nationwide branches entrusted with uniform enforcement of the activist policy. Instead, enforcement can be delegated to the states and from there even to localities. A state may pass a criminal statute, but because there are few statewide prosecutorial organizations, the enforcement of such statutes continues to be entrusted to county attorneys. Or a welfare activity may be federally funded, such as legal services for the poor, but the local grantees of these funds are left much to their own devices as to how to carry out their tasks.

Not all administrative agencies are part of an unified executive, as are ministries in other welfare countries, so that the law enforcement officials in such independent agencies cannot be removed by the chief executive. In many places where a foreigner would expect to find unity at the top, he finds instead loose associations of feuding power centers.[111] Even within a single "hierarchy"—a system of state courts, for example—one seeks in vain for rigid relationships of super- and subordination. The tendency of low-level judges to take independent action is unchecked by any significant emphasis on mechanisms such as internal promotion; the lower one goes in some state court hierarchies, the more judges depend on their constituencies rather than on superiors.[112] Where judges are composed into panels, they continue to exercise power in a vigorously personal style reminiscent of Max Weber's prebureaucratic modes of dominion. Thus, for example, individual members of federal courts of appeal show reluctance to apply standards adopted by the whole court (en banc decisions) if such standards lead to

110. Montesquieu, *De l'esprit des lois*, Livre XI, ch. 6. A telling recent example of the blending of administration, regulation, and adjudication in the activity of the lower federal judiciary is the reform of the Arkansas prison system. See O. Fiss, and D. Rendleman. *Injunctions*, 2d ed., 528–752 (1984). The famous case of *Miranda* v. *Arizona*, 384 U.S. 436 (1966) illustrates the "incidental" but openly legislative activity of the United States Supreme Court.

111. This is true even of the armed forces, with their loosely integrated Joint Chiefs of Staff. Closer to the center of our interest, at the United States Supreme Court, it is common for the justices to refuse to accept as dispositive a holding with which they disagree. For example, in *Rook* v. *North Carolina*, 102 S.Ct. 1741 (1982), Justices Brennan and Marshall refused to accept the majority's holding on the death penalty as expressed previously in *Gregg* v. *Georgia*, 428 U.S. 153 (1976).

112. See H. R. Glick and K. N. Vines, *State Court System* (1973); P. S. Atiyah, *supra*, ch. 1, n. 63. Also comparatively striking is the fact that American trial judges exercise powers so important that a more hierarchically structured system would confide them only to the highest echelon of judicial authority or to a prestigious nonjudicial body. The most telling example here is the power of the American trial judge to strike down legislative enactments as unconstitutional. In Europe such power is vested in a highly placed constitutional court, a sort of superlegislature, or delegated to special "constitutional councils." See *supra*, ch. 2, n. 39.

what they deem to be unjust results. Should their independence be more restricted than if they were members of a court that had no divisional hearings and never decided en banc? Quite naturally, such assertions of independence can negatively affect the clarity and uniformity of the case law emanating from the federal courts.[113] There are no indirect mechanisms to foster unity of outlook, such as common training in some analogue of French national administrative schools. That rigid legalistic attitudes hardly fit into this institutional ambience is clear: discretionary departures from normative standards are easily accepted and often celebrated; multifactor balancing tests, leaving a great deal of latitude to decision makers, are preferred to outcome-determinative rules.[114]

In summary, features I have associated with coordinate authority have survived the changes inaugurated in the aftermath of the New Deal. Thus, much as the *functions* of the contemporary American state are a mixture of activist and reactive impulses, so the actual *structure* of the state apparatus—especially the administration of justice—is a hybrid of bureaucratic and prebureaucratic forms. Activist policies are often implemented by an apparatus whose chief characteristics are its lingering coordinate attributes. This situation partially explains why "public" issues in America are not so readily associated with "state" issues as is the case in so many welfare states. The focus of American political life is not so closely linked to the "government," and continues to be located in "society" at large. What forms of justice appear in this environment? That they should be amorphous and unstable should be expected.

FROM LAISSEZ-FAIRE TO A WELFARE STATE MODEL OF THE CRIMINAL PROCESS. Although increased concern is exhibited about the public interest in criminal procedure, even a cursory look at this "activist" concern reveals that it is actually a mixture of activist and reactive impulses. Just as the American welfare state has intervened in the economy to correct failures of competitive markets rather than to replace them, so its intervention in criminal proceedings was aimed at redressing the competition of the parties rather than to eliminate it. The merely formal equality of the prosecution and defense, or the rough symmetry of their procedural rights, ceased to be the central preoccupation of the legal mind. Rather, "substantive equality" was seen to require that the state equalize the opportunity of the parties to use their procedural weapons. The indigent defendant was guaranteed free legal aid, and the view evolved that convictions should be reversed if assigned counsel was ineffective. As a further

---

113. A notorious example from the 1960s was the irreconcilable variations of the *Mallory* rule regulating the admissibility of confessions, a rule adopted by the District of Columbia Court of Appeals en banc. See A. L. Alexander, "En Banc Hearings in the Federal Courts of Appeals," 40 *N.Y.U.L. Rev.* 563, 582–85 (1965). Continental court systems are governed by more regular and much more rigorously enforced mechanisms for removing intramural conflict. Of course, uncertainty can also stem from Supreme Court decisions where, owing to numerous concurring and dissenting opinions, it may sometimes be virtually impossible to ascertain the "institutional" view.

114. Because American high courts have vast discretionary powers to control their own dockets, they can indulge their political instincts and select for disposition those matters that address politically important issues. The resulting judicial potential to make politically "creative" rather than "narrowly" legalistic decisions inevitably increases.

step away from strong laissez-faire positions, free legal aid was no longer left to the charitable instincts of the private bar; public defender offices were set up across the land. In consequence, two publicly funded offices can now be locked in adversarial clashes—one expected to advance the public interest, the other specialized in safeguarding the private interest of the individual client. Party autonomy has not ceased to command respect, however: the indigent defendant retains the right to reject legal assistance and act as his own counsel.[115] Nor should one imagine that the move beyond a formal balancing of advantages has progressed evenly, with respect to all the crucial aspects of the criminal process. Plea bargaining continues to be encouraged and is legitimated by the courts even in situations where little has been done to equalize the "bargaining power" of the prosecution and the defense.

I do not mean to suggest that a potential does not exist for developments that *curtail* rather than *support* the free management of criminal cases by the parties. There were many indications in the 1960s and 1970s that this potential for restriction will be put to use, provided that activist dispositions continue to gain in strength. Of particular interest in this context is the significant, albeit uneven, decline in importance of rigid division of issues into one set for the prosecution and the other for the defense. It has been seen that reactive justice requires each party to be accorded a monopoly over the introduction of matter forming part of its respective issues. Judges should not interfere with the "tactical choices" of the parties, although these choices inevitably affect the accuracy of the outcome. Of course, the discretionary powers of the American judge always permitted interference with this party monopoly, but "reactive" judges would seldom find it in the "public interest" to exercise their prerogatives. As activist attitudes gain in strength, this passivity is no longer warranted: issues in a criminal case appear more and more as preconditions for the proper enforcement of penal policy—preconditions that should be determined in the interest of justice. As a result, the effective division of issues into two sequential cases has been greatly weakened and now tends to be mainly evidentiary. Thus, although a matter is "for the defense," it can still be raised by the court—sometimes even by the prosecution—but the defense continues to have the burden of producing some evidence on the matter and in some cases must also bear the risk of failure to persuade the fact finder as to the existence of defensive matter.[116]

The 1960s offered many examples of alternative means by which the independent conduct of the defense can be curtailed. Sensitized to larger issues, activist judges became willing to scrutinize and sometimes to disallow the waiver

---

115. See *Faretta* v. *California*, 422 U.S. 806 (1975).

116. See *supra*, ch. 4, nn. 23, 24, and accompanying text. It is true that the defendant's "burden of production" can sometimes be sustained if there is some evidence of defensive matter in the proof offered by *either* party. Comparativists should note another residual evidentiary effect of the division of issues: a defensive issue can be reached at trial only after full consideration of the prosecution's case. More recently, *Faretta* (*supra*, n. 115) and its progeny have dampened the readiness of judges to introduce affirmative defenses. See S. Kadish, S. Schulhofer, and M. Paulsen, *Criminal Law and Its Processes*, 4th ed., 839–40 (1983).

of rights, so crucial to the criminal process of the reactive state.[117] They were also willing to invoke more readily their power to refuse to accept guilty pleas.[118] Of course, activist impulses could also lead to challenge of prosecutorial pre-rogatives; the state's withdrawal of charges can be questioned, and if a judge feels strongly about a matter, prosecutions can be ordered.[119] One should scarcely be surprised that the limits of judicial interference with the conduct of the prosecu-tion and the defense are veiled by uncertainties. The still strongly coordinate authority tolerates vague blending and overlaps of power.

Where activist attitudes prevail, the trial judge is no longer sovereign in his decision to remain a mere arbiter of incidental party conflict. Now, appellate courts will be found increasingly willing to find so-called "plain error" in trial court proceedings—that is, error that requires judicial intervention in the ab-sence of any objection raised by the litigants.[120] Observe also the proliferation since the 1930s of statutes and rules of procedure which explicitly empower the trial judge to call witnesses *sua sponte*. Granted, this power is seldom exercised in practice and, if exercised, is typically used to obtain opinion, not fact, witnesses. But where the judge perceives a strong public interest in a case, he may assume a vigorously probing role. What prevents him from projecting himself even more into trial proceedings is, to a considerable extent, traceable to features I have linked to coordinate authority. He has no dossier of the case, and in his ignorance, he is driven to allow the parties to keep the courtroom initiative.[121]

Demands for more uniform penal policy and more professionalism strain the existing coordinate structures. Until the mid-seventies, there was in America no independent right of appeal of the sentence, so that attempts were made to reduce disparity in sentences by typically coordinate and inefficient instruments, such as sentencing councils and conferences where judges tried to establish com-

117. See *supra*, ch. 4, n. 6, and accompanying text. While this scrutiny increased through the 1960s, the more recent trend seems to have been toward *less* scrutiny. Compare *McCarthy* v. *United States*, 394 U.S. 459 (1969) with *Marshall* v. *Lonberger*, 459 U.S. 422 (1983) and *Comm.* v. *Anthony*, 475 A.2d 1303 (Pa. 1984).

118. For the denial of the right to plead guilty, see *Lynch* v. *Overholser*, 369 U.S. 705 (1962); *People* v. *Chadd*, 28 Cal. 3d 739 (1981). This is not to say that judicial interference with pleading autonomy is not still an extraordinary event, especially in regard to nolo contendere pleas.

119. See A. Goldstein, *The Passive Judiciary*, 54 (1981). Such judicial power to order initia-tion of a criminal case or to appoint a prosecutor is alien ("too inquisitorial") to modern Continental criminal justice systems. Note the paradox.

120. The readiness of appellate courts to invoke the plain error rule should not be exagge-rated, however, especially in the most recent case law. See *U.S.* v. *Frady*, 456 U.S. 152 (1982); *Engle* v. *Isaac* 456 U.S. 107 (1982).

121. The situation changes where, as at the sentencing stage, the judge has at his disposal the presentencing report and vast powers to seek additional information. Here, as instanced by some white-collar crime cases, judges can be so "activist" as to inject themselves into corporate decision-making processes in order to remedy "dysfunctions" related to corporate criminal behavior. A strengthening of activist ideology also tends to intensify the tension between the criminal process as a battle of counsel and the larger interest in truth discovery. It has occasioned extreme proposals that counsel be obliged to report to the judge some facts they learned from their clients. See M. Frankel, "The Search for the Truth: An Umpireal View," 123 *U. Pa. L. Rev.* 1 (1979).

mon policies to be applied on a voluntary basis. Where in other systems certain policies would preferably be imposed through internal hierarchical methods, they are in America often still pressed in a typical coordinate fashion—by the refusal of one power center to recognize the work of another. The judicial exclusion of evidence illegally obtained by the police is a telling example; local police forces elude hierarchically imposed internal standards.

The picture that finally emerges is one of dynamic syncretism. There arise intricate and unstable combinations, which mix new forms inspired by shifting activist concerns with more traditional forms inspired by conflict-solving notions. These combined forms interact with the perduring, although weakening, traditional pattern of widely distributed authority, creating unique pastiches that defy analytical categories, but remain within the mode of coordinate activism.

PUBLIC INTEREST LITIGATION. The most perplexing examples of coordinate policy implementation are found in the more recent American practice of using civil procedure in the "public interest." These cases take many forms, but the variant of greatest interest here is a lawsuit brought by a plaintiff acting on behalf of a large interest group against the miniofficialdom of a school, hospital, prison, or independent governmental agency. The relief sought exceeds mere damages for past action or the limits of conventional injunctions against immediately impending breaches of the law. The plaintiff's principal aim is to change the future conduct of the defendant or to bring about "structural reform" of an institution. Such litigation is likely to involve the court in administrative (supervisory) activity and even in an exercise of "minilegislation." The court's activity is crowned by the issuance of a document spelling out new rules of behavior to be observed by officers of the institution to be reformed. In sum, the court is engaged in a combination of adjudicative, administrative, and legislative actions, and the adjudicative component in the mix may be quite modest.[122]

It is true that even in such cases the traditional conflict-solving forms are not discarded. A complaint, or a controversy, is required to set the wheels of justice in motion, and sequential adversarial steps (such as the exchange of briefs, direct and cross-examination, etc.) are meticulously observed. But the traditional arrangements of civil procedure became an increasingly transparent cover for what is essentially a policy-implementing process. No longer used as a vehicle for conflict resolution, litigation is now actively encouraged, and financial incentives are devised to stimulate interest groups to sue and invoke the legal process. If the litigant in the public interest "wins," he obtains his attorney's fees from the

---

122. For discussion of public interest litigation, see A. Chayes, "The Role of the Judge in Public Interest Litigation," 89 *Harv. L. Rev.* 1281 (1976); O. Fiss, "The Supreme Court 1978 Term; Foreword: The Forms of Justice," 93 *Harv. L. Rev.* 1 (1979). Increasing judicial control over civil lawsuits can easily be observed outside the realm of "structural injunctions." Activist concern with securities regulation, antitrust, the bargaining power of product consumers, and similar matters have given rise to extremely complex litigation involving great numbers of litigants. If each plaintiff and defendant were required to conduct his case independently, duplication of effort and great confusion would ensue. No wonder, then, that the tendency has increased, mainly in federal courts, to involve the judge in the conduct of such multiparty cases. See *Manual for Complex Litigation*, 5th ed. (1982).

vanquished opponent, but if he "loses," he need not compensate the winner for its legal costs. Widely ranging factual inquiries, deemed unacceptable as "fishing expeditions" in the old mode, may now be launched to establish whether the need for reform exists, even if this leads to new disputes or exacerbates the old.[123] The parties' control over the boundaries of the lawsuit is eroded by reason of the injection of public interest into the case; ambiguous standing requirements permit the judge to draw additional parties into the suit—parties better prepared or situated to move the process in the direction favored by the court. Trials are less the climactic centerpiece of a lawsuit than the occasion for bringing issues of public policy into focus: these issues can be "tried" even if not pleaded in the complaint[124] and can readily be pursued in the course of the ongoing remedial process, on appeal, or in collateral proceedings. Judicial power freely to fashion the best policy response to a problem is not rigidly limited by the form and scope of the prayer for relief and cannot easily be reconciled with the idea of the lawsuit as a device for conflict resolution.[125] In brief, public interest litigation more and more resembles the marsupial wolf that only looks like a wolf, but is actually a sort of opossum.

In spite of such pronounced policy-implementing characteristics, public interest litigation retains overtones of "reactive" justice. Plaintiffs—often private groups—pursue partial interests, which blend with their self-interest, rather than common goals of the state. In contrast to the vision of truly managerial states, the vision of society underlying public interest litigation is one that presupposes conflict—female and male, black and white, consumer and producer, rich and poor—a vision that fosters aggressive assertion of rights rather than one that seeks the definition of tasks, duties, or obligations. Nor is there often any discernible state interest; what is the nature of the public good is a matter of intense controversy. Judges often have no strong policy views of their own and are thus more often umpires than ideological actors. Their decrees incorporate compromises and settlements[126] rather than results of a comprehensive social theory with whose implementation they are entrusted.

The rise into prominence of American public interest litigation is not only a product of moderate activist impulses; it is also intimately linked to a governmental structure in which authority is widely distributed. Where there are so many checks and balances, the realization of activist ideas is a difficult enterprise: vehement controversy over policy alternatives produces more animated standstills than discernible movement. What remains to an activist group, frustrated

123. On reforms of discovery laws in the 1930s, permitting such broad inquiries, see *supra*, ch. 4, nn. 57, 67, and 68.

124. *F.R.Civ.P.* 15(b). Note that amendments of pleadings can now be made even *after* judgment. Even if not amended, but actually "tried" by implied consent, certain issues can be resolved by the judge.

125. See *F.R.Civ.P.* 54(c); *Bail* v. *Cunningham Brothers, Inc.*, 452 F.2d 182 (7th Cir. 1971).

126. Decrees in public interest litigation are often substantially negotiated and agreed upon documents. See A. Chayes, *supra*, n. 123, 1309. For examples, see O. Fiss and D. Rendleman, *supra*, n. 111, 774–78.

by stalemates in other branches of government, is to find a "coordinate" judge who agrees with its notion of desirable change and is willing to take public interest litigation in hand. Thus a program that can, in differently structured activist states, be formulated in the legislature and implemented by vigorous executive action has its last chance in American courts: an independent and powerful judge, with the legacy of his ill-defined powers still strongly present, can be at once a minilegislature, an administrator, and a player of the more specific judicial role.

It is undeniable that where an imperfectly hierarchical judiciary is involved in making and implementing policy, considerable uncertainty and instability are introduced into the legal system, quite independent of the ambiguities resulting from absence of a single comprehensive theory of the social good. Different judges can each set off on a different voyage of discovering best solutions. The appellate process, engrafted upon a traditionally one-level procedure, is not designed to be a regularly employed mechanism; higher courts can be quite selective in deciding when and in which cases to announce public policy and thus contribute to greater unity. But even the apex of the judicial system seldom issues a single institutional opinion; where each justice retains his independent view—quite in harmony with the coordinate ideal—the legal voices emanating from the most august judicial body are seldom in unison. It may well be that a society conditioned to hierarchically constituted authority might find the resulting levels of dissonance, uncertainty, and instability intolerable. Americans can live with it, however. Ideas on the desirable degree of order and unity should not be projected from an environment that produced formal geometrical gardening styles into a milieu whose topiary art consists of loose groupings of plants, rocks, and water left to their own devices.

Afterword

With these remarks I have concluded tracing the fortunes of activist and reactive justice in hierarchical and coordinate judicial organizations. At the same time, the task set in this volume is largely complete: a framework has been created within which to examine the legal process as it is rooted in attitudes toward state authority and influenced by the changing role of government. Many connections between justice and polity that were incorporated into this framework have been previously suggested by social and political theorists, but I have attempted to give more coherence to their insights and to trace connections they discovered to more detailed aspects of the legal process.

In separating procedural forms related to the organization of authority from those related to the functions of government, I have suggested an approach more discriminating than conventional theory. This scheme therefore promised a somewhat better orientation in the midst of so many faces and moods of justice: the sense of similarities and differences can be sharpened, and new relationships can be detected where none were perceived before. Moreover, many procedural arrangements that appear strange to an outsider become more comprehensible if their affinity to certain types of state authority can be demonstrated. Misunderstandings that arise among those conditioned to different political organizations can be traced to their sources. In short, the capacity to move between procedural cultures in this troubled world can be somewhat improved. The contrary dispositions of government and the divergent patterns of its organization presented here can also advance the understanding of our own administration of justice. Even within a single country, attitudes toward state authority can be deeply ambivalent. To paraphrase a poet, two roads to justice often diverge in our own midst: we wish to travel both and to be one traveler. While we like to lament the bureaucratization of justice, we also hold values dear that are inseparable from it; while we want our judges to display impartiality, we also want them to exhibit "activist" involvement.

But there are limitations built into this approach—limitations that must clearly be identified in these closing pages. Throughout this volume I have analyzed the legal process as informed by factors from the political dimension of social life. This I have done in the belief, acknowledged at the outset, that political factors play a central role in accounting for the grand contours of procedural systems. These factors are not, however, the sole determinants of procedural form. Even a lawgiver with carte blanche to mold the forms of justice to his own political convictions would soon discover the limitations of political ideology as a source of inspiration. He would often be unable to establish which procedure is preferable in light of his political persuasion, and thus he would be compelled to make choices by drawing on existing inventories of moral and cultural experience, the fabric of inherited beliefs, and similar considerations. The history of Soviet and Chinese experiments with the administration of justice testifies to this difficulty in translating the poetry of ideology into the prose of procedural form. Clearly, then, even under most propitious conditions, determinants from the political sphere account for only a limited number of procedural phenomena. This scheme should be used with such qualifications in mind.

The policy-implementing and the conflict-solving processes were constructed around two distinctive objectives of justice and premised on the assumption that the legal process is structured to suit them. But it is plain that hierarchical and coordinate authority are not equally preoccupied with distinguishing these two aspects of the legal process or with insisting on a sharp dividing line between adjudication (norm application) and legislation (norm creation). Where hierarchical bureaucracies specialize and differentiate functions, coordinate authority tends to fuse them. The two types of authority are also not equally prepared to adapt procedural form to its recognized objective: while bureaucracies are sensitive to this problem and are prepared to remedy it, coordinate authority dislikes rationalist overhauls of existing procedures, preferring an accretive and prudential approach of gradual modification. How this asymmetry affects my scheme is clear: the conflict-solving and the policy-implementing models, because organized around discretely defined objectives, are "biased" in favor of a more rationalist type of authority. Inevitably, proceedings before coordinate officialdom present more complex mixtures of activist and reactive forms—mixtures that require qualification of the terms in which, for the purpose of analysis, I have pigeonholed them.

This leads me to the last caveat. This book sought to discern and to define distinctive styles in the tangled mass of procedures through which justice is variously administered around the world. The reason for this effort was the belief that, without a suitable typology, comparative studies of procedural form cannot even begin. But as my scheme was applied to existing systems, most of them were found to be pastiches of the pure styles I have identified. If the real world is one of mixtures, the reader must have wondered, what is the point in developing pure styles? To reuse an earlier analogy, have we not fixated most of the time on the coffee and the milk, forgetting that cappuccino will be the norm? The answer to this query, to which I have alluded before, is similar to the one a student of chemical elements would give to a critic pointing to the ubiquity of compounds: it is hoped that a kind of analytical chemistry can be performed on existing procedures and that, in the process, some of their mysteries can be brought to the surface and observed. Of course, one should not expect more from this type of analysis than it can deliver: that a building may be classified as an exemplar of a particular style, or as a mixture thereof, tells us very little about the individuality of the building. But one must realize that explorations of individuality become possible only after one has first obtained conceptual instruments with which to see and discuss individuality in terms of generic notions. If my scheme contributes to the storehouse of concepts with which the variation of procedural form can be identified and analyzed, and if it suggests new and fruitful lines of inquiry, we can live with the scheme's imperfections.

Index